D1590277

Christian Materiality

Christian Materiality

An Essay on Religion in Late Medieval Europe

Caroline Walker Bynum

ZONE BOOKS · NEW YORK

2011

ZONE BOOKS
1226 Prospect Avenue
Brooklyn, NY 11218

Printed in the United States of America.

Distributed by The MIT Press,
Cambridge, Massachusetts, and London, England

Library of Congress Cataloging-in-Publication Data

Bynum, Caroline Walker.
Christian materiality : an essay on religion in late medieval Europe / Caroline Walker Bynum.
p. cm.
Includes bibliographical references (p.) and index.
ISBN 978-1-935408-10-9 (alk. paper)
1. Church history—Middle Ages, 600–1500. 2. Matter—Religious aspects—Christianity—History of doctrines—Middle Ages, 600–1500. 3. Religious articles—Europe—History of doctrines—Middle Ages, 600–1500. 4. Miracles—Europe—History of doctrines—Middle Ages, 600–1500. 5. Europe—Religious life and customs. I. Title.

BR270.B96 2011
231.7'309409024–dc22

2010039309

For Ramona Naddaff

Contents

Here is a moving insistence on touching and being touched; what is god is "only" an intensified mode of this sensate givenness. God is physical, not metaphysical.

—David Shulman, *Spring, Heat, Rains: A South Indian Diary*

Talkative things instantiate novelty, previously unthinkable combinations. Their thingness lends vivacity and reality to new constellations of experience that break old molds.... [T]he new thing becomes a magnet for intense interest, a paradox incarnate. It is richly evocative; it is eloquent. Only when the paradox becomes prosaic do things that talk subside into speechlessness.

—Lorraine Daston, "Speechless," *Things That Talk: Object Lessons from Art and Science*

Preface

This book began as three lectures given in May 2007 at the Hebrew University in Jerusalem. I am grateful to my hosts for their warm hospitality and to the audience that assembled despite the logistical difficulties and frustrations of a university strike throughout Israel. The invitation to give these lectures came after almost a decade in which I have traveled to Israel annually to participate in the selection of postdoctoral fellows, to conduct workshops with graduate students in medieval European history, and to lecture at several of the country's universities. I am grateful to my Israeli students, colleagues, and friends for the challenge and rewards of the energetic intellectual life I have never failed to find there.

I have kept not only the original title of the lecture series but also the topics included under it, although I have expanded the second lecture into two chapters. I have increased the number of examples adduced and in some cases spelled out the argument more fully, but I have resisted the temptation to write a different book. Although I have defined unfamiliar attitudes and objects, keeping to the original intention of addressing an audience with no special interest or expertise in Christianity, I have not simplified the intricate and contradictory assumptions and practices I explore. Paradox remains paradox, complexity remains complex. Above all, I have tried to keep things short. I have, however, added to the original lectures both an introduction and a conclusion that suggest the implications of the argument for the comparative study of religion and for the sweep of European history.

Once again, as I have had occasion to do in the past, I thank the staff at Zone Books for their technical assistance, their expertise, their patience, and their love of books. Beyond the Zone offices, there are many people to whom I owe gratitude for stimulating, augmenting, and clarifying the ideas that appear here. I will not append a list; I have acknowledged all of them in other prefaces. But I am no less grateful, though I leave my debts on this occasion anonymous. I must, however, mention the five readers of the manuscript, each of whom brought a special expertise: Peter Brown, Lorraine Daston, Jeffrey F. Hamburger, Joel Kaye, and Dorothea von Mücke. Each has saved me from errors and infelicities of presentation, and I am grateful to each. I also thank Colum Hourihane and Adelaide Bennett Hagens of the Index of Christian Art, Meighan Gale, Hubert Treiber, Erik Thunø, Alexandra Suda, Nino Zchomelidse, Jiří Fajt, and Jeffrey F. Hamburger for assistance with the plates. Belle Tuten, Maria Tuya, Terrie Bramley, and Guenther Roth helped with proofreading and with editing. Above all, I thank my editor, Ramona Naddaff, in whom I have found the spheres of publishing excellence, scholarship, and friendship joined. I dedicate this book to her.

Introduction

Nicholas of Cusa and the Hosts of Andechs

In 1451, the papal legate Nicholas of Cusa, sent to Germany to preach church reform, issued a decree at Halberstadt. That decree categorically rejected the supposedly miraculous objects that had proliferated in Germany over the previous seventy-five years. Cusanus stated:

> We have heard from many reliable men and also have ourselves seen how the faithful stream to many places in the area of our legation to adore the precious blood of Christ our God that they believe is present in several transformed red hosts [*quem in nonnullis transformatis hostijs speciem rubedinis habere arbitrantur*]. And it is clearly attested by their words, with which they name this colored thing [*talem rubedinem*] the blood of Christ, that they thus believe and adore it, and the clergy in their greed for money not only permit this but even encourage it through the publicizing of miracles.... [But] it is pernicious...and we cannot permit it without damage to God, for our catholic faith teaches us that the glorified body of Christ has glorified blood completely unseeable in glorified veins [*sanguinem glorificatum in venis glorificatis penitus inuisibilem*]. In order to remove every opportunity for the deception of simple folk, we therefore order that...the clergy...should no longer display or promulgate such miracles or allow pilgrim badges [*signa plumbea*] to be made of them.[1]

The decree was reissued in somewhat different versions at Mainz and Cologne. At Mainz, a reference to the veneration of bloody cloths was included. Although specific sites were not mentioned, Cusanus probably had in mind the famous hosts of Wilsnack, which were visited by the English holy woman Margery Kempe on her continental pilgrimage, the popular bleeding-host site at Gottsbüren, and the miraculous altar linen at Walldürn, on which the face of Christ had allegedly appeared in drops of spilled Eucharistic wine.[2]

It is no surprise to specialists in the fifteenth century to find Nicholas of Cusa rejecting such holy objects as transformed wafers and blood-stained altar furnishings. A committed man of action who evolved from supporting councils to championing the papacy, always with the goal of effecting reform, Nicholas of Cusa devoted much of his life to efforts to improve the morals of both clergy and laity by stamping out venality, superstition, and mechanical religious practices. Yet he also produced a series of spiritual and contemplative writings, the earliest and best-known of which, *On Learned Ignorance*, argued that God is beyond the reach of human reason and that there is no proportion between finite and infinite. Christ's undestroyability, like God's unknowability, was increasingly a central theme of his Christology.[3] Although Nicholas, like all orthodox theologians, had to stress that Christ truly died in the Crucifixion, spilling salvific blood for humankind, he developed, in a series of complicated arguments, the claim that Christ's humanity was never divided or corrupted, even in the short period between the death on Calvary and the resurrection of Easter Sunday. Indeed that humanity served as a *manductio*, a leading back of all creation to God.[4] As our link to the God who lies beyond all categories and divisions, the human Christ was, to Cusanus, beyond any real dissolution. Never fragmented, he could not leave holy particles behind or appear again in even miraculous stuff on wafers, altar cloths, or wood.

In his reforming efforts against what were suspected to be fraudulent pilgrimages fueled by popular credulity and clerical greed, as in his negative theology, which strained sometimes toward light, sometimes toward darkness, but always toward a God beyond human categories, Cusanus is sometimes taken as a paradigmatic fifteenth-century figure. Looked at from the perspectives I just elaborated, it is not unexpected to find that he fulminated against pilgrimages to holy stuff. Yet Cusanus was himself forced into contradiction. Called upon to pronounce on the supposed miracle hosts of Andechs, which some claimed to have been consecrated by the sixth-century pope Gregory the Great, Cusanus approved the pilgrimage.[5] Avoiding any reference to blood spots on the consecrated wafers (that is, to their metamorphosis), he based his approval on their incorruptibility (that is, their changelessness). Ever the politician, Cusanus perhaps acted to avoid offending the duke in whose region the pilgrimage took place. The duke was favorable to the reform agenda; both Cusanus and the pope he served needed ducal support.

But this somewhat curious and perhaps compromising incident is significant for two reasons quite different from the political situation it reveals. First, it shows that it was almost impossible for church leaders and theologians to avoid the issue of holy matter. The transformed statues, chalices, wafers, cloths, relics, and even mounds of earth to which the faithful made pilgrimage in the fourteenth and fifteenth centuries presented a challenge that was theoretical as well as practical for a religion that held that the entire material world was created by and could therefore manifest God. Second—and ironically—Cusanus's approval of supposedly transformed objects rested on the claim to miraculous changelessness: the hosts' supposed resistance to the natural processes of decay and fragmentation. Issues of how matter behaved, both ordinarily and miraculously, when in contact with an infinitely powerful and ultimately unknowable God were key to devotion and theology. The God who lay beyond the world in unimaginable and unanalyzable darkness or light was also a God to whom human beings were led back by a human Christ—a Christ whose substance (in the Eucharist) and even whose particles (in blood relics) might be present on earth.

The chapters that follow are not an effort to smooth over the inconsistencies we see in Cusanus's actions and ideas or in those of his contemporaries. They are rather an exploration of one of the central contradictions of the later Middle Ages: the increasing prominence of holy matter in a religion also characterized by a need for human agency on the part of the faithful, a turn to interiority on the part of spiritual writers and reform-minded church leaders, and an upsurge of voluntarism, negative theology, and mysticism. In this extended essay on the period from circa 1100 to circa 1550, I stress one pole of this contradiction—a pole that, where noticed, has been misunderstood. I call this pole "Christian materiality."

I do not mean, by this phrase, to return our understanding of the later Middle Ages to old interpretations of the period as one of literalizing and mechanistic piety, a morbid fixation on death and hell, or a fascination with intimate and slightly embarrassing details of the holy family's domestic life. Nor do I adopt another conventional interpretation—one that sees reaction against such things as reform before the Reformation. I mean rather to take cult objects such as the Andechs hosts as only one type of holy matter in a piety characterized by intense awareness of the power of the material and to understand the theology, devotional writing, and natural philosophy such objects stimulated as a locus of some of the period's most profound religious exploration. In the paradox—we might even say the crisis—of holy matter lodged at the heart of late medieval religion, we may see seeds and foreshadowings of the coming reformations (Catholic and Protestant), but my point is not to interpret the period, as is so often done, with a view to what comes after. This book is intended to understand the period's own character by taking seriously aspects usually treated cursorily or with incomprehension and condescension.

It seems wise to begin by setting out explicitly two aspects of this study that may appear problematic to other scholars: the periodization I argue for and the understanding of "materiality" I employ.

The Periodization of Holy Matter

The early Middle Ages is frequently described by historians as a period in which people inhabited an animistic and insecure world.[6] Philosophical exploration of the laws of nature supposedly disappeared before what was at best encyclopedic collecting of bits of past learning. Chroniclers recounted rains of blood from the sky; extraordinary events such as comets and ordinary objects such as buckets and cabbages were taken to be messages from God or manipulations by demons; tales of miraculous vengeance by Christ and the saints proliferated.[7] Such descriptions have sometimes led to a view of early medieval piety as credulous, mechanistic, and materialistic, dominated in practice by the use of apotropaic objects and in theology by a confusion of the physical and the spiritual. In comparison with this, the later Middle Ages has been characterized in recent scholarship as moving toward inner piety and visuality.[8] A number of phenomena have been adduced in support of this interpretation. By the thirteenth century, for example, pilgrims tended to visit cult sites to offer thanksgiving after receiving visions rather than traveling to holy graves to make petitions.[9] Viewing the elevated Eucharist came, also in the thirteenth century, to substitute for physical reception of consecrated bread and wine.[10] By the fourteenth century, images sometimes replaced relics as conveyers of healing power.[11] A visionary and visual culture flourished, one in which revelations to women played a crucial role.[12]

Although there are elements of truth in this interpretation, one might argue that it puts things backwards. Matter was a more insistent and problematic locus of the sacred in the twelfth to sixteenth centuries than in the early medieval period. (The operative words here are "insistent" and "problematic.") Indeed the great popularity of enduring Eucharistic miracles such as the hosts of Andechs or the corporal at Walldürn—objects unheard of in early medieval culture—suggests that the piety of the later period might be characterized as a turn to, rather than away from, the object. To argue this is not to deny the complex ways in which holy matter pointed its viewers and users to something beyond.[13] It was exactly the materialization of piety that created theological and disciplinary problems for the church, stimulating not only resistance from dissident groups but also intellectual creativity on their part and the part of their opponents. The striving for inwardness and for encounter beyond all word, thought, and representation that characterized such fifteenth-century theologians as Nicholas of Cusa was, in part, a response to the increasing prominence of holy objects. Holy matter was, as I will elaborate in the chapters that follow, both radical threat and radical opportunity in the later Middle Ages.

Of course, no historian would deny that physical objects were already central in the religion of late antiquity. As Peter Brown, Patrick Geary, Arnold Angenendt, Victor Saxer, Cynthia Hahn, and many other students of the early Middle Ages have stressed, saints' bodies and body parts and all sorts of materials that had touched them (water, cloth, earth, and so forth) were understood to contain and transport a power to heal or protect;[14] objects such as candles and herbs blessed by clergy or holy people were understood to convey power as well. Devotion to the cross, as to the crucified God-man, was central to early medieval spirituality; and cross relics, followed by other relics of the Crucifixion and of the saints, spread across Europe from the fourth century on. Recent scholarship, relying on dendrochronology, tends to give earlier dates than were assigned previously to beautiful and expressive visual objects such as those monumental German and Italian crucifixes of which the famous Gero crucifix from tenth-century Cologne used to be thought the earliest.[15] Already by the tenth century, craftsmen were creating vibrant three-dimensional sculptures, such as the Golden Madonna of Essen (see fig. 7, p. 55) or the St. Foy reliquary in Conques, that announced their power through the precious metals and jewels with which they were adorned (although such objects were still very expensive and very rare).

But living holy matter (animated statues; bleeding hosts, walls, and images; holy dust or cloth that itself mediated further transformation) is mostly a later medieval phenomenon. It was the decades around 1100 that saw not only a new enthusiasm for some of the older forms of holy matter—an enthusiasm triggered partly by access to relics from the Holy Land made possible by the crusades—but also the appearance of new kinds of animated materiality. Although stories from the Byzantine church of bleeding images were told earlier, a vision received by Peter Damian in circa 1060 is usually considered the first case of a claim literally to drink blood from the crucifix.[16] As Giles Constable has shown, assertions that bodies were literally and miraculously branded with the cross appear in accounts of the first two crusades, although there are hints of such claims in the eleventh century.[17] The earliest cases of stigmata (the wounds of Christ appearing on the bodies of adherents, sometimes miraculous, sometimes self-induced) are late twelfth century and are often described and depicted as carvings or inscribings into the bodies of the devout, not by Christ but by the crucifix. Such claims proliferated in the thirteenth to sixteenth centuries.[18] Eucharistic visions are reported earlier, but references to transformed Eucharistic objects that endure (called by German scholars *Dauerwunder*) appear first in the late eleventh or twelfth century (and then only very occasionally), and documented pilgrimages to them are found mostly after the widely publicized Parisian miracle of 1290.[19]

It is in the later Middle Ages, moreover, that stories proliferate of relics animating or themselves undergoing metamorphosis. In Naples, the blood of St. Januarius (a supposed martyr of the early fourth century) has, since the later fourteenth century, been claimed to liquefy in early May and on the saint's feast day in mid-September; on one occasion it supposedly stopped an eruption of Mount Vesuvius.[20] Although stories of bread, herbs, water, and other material things that cure or convey power are found in early saints' lives, and some (for example, the oats blessed on Christmas Eve and thought to protect animals during the coming year) may have roots in folklore or pagan practices,[21] widespread references to such things, and the rituals for blessing them, come mostly from the fourteenth to sixteenth centuries.[22] Most instances of animated images and paintings (at least in the West) come from the fourteenth to seventeenth centuries, and are often accounts of older objects (twelfth- or thirteenth-century) that change color, weep, bleed, or walk in order to rekindle devotion or protest neglect.[23] Despite the fact that images sometimes replaced relics in healing miracles, these images functioned in a way that suggests that they conveyed power as physical objects.[24] Hence, they are more analogous to the relics they replaced than to the visions they sometimes depicted. Even when it was a vision that provided the occasion for a new cult, the apparition tended to be materialized almost immediately into an object. Small physical reproductions of the miraculous event—prayer cards, badges, little silks, and so forth—became important, in part because they could be taken away and referred to in prayer long after pilgrimage to the site of the ephemeral revelation had been completed, but in part because they were felt to incorporate the event itself.[25] To take a well-known early modern example: the Virgin of Guadalupe in the New World *became* to many adherents the supposedly miraculous picture of her that appeared on the cloak of the peasant who received the apparition in 1531.[26]

In the period after 1100, new forms of devotional art—especially panel paintings and the devotional statues German historians call *Andachtsbilder*—burst onto the religious scene. Some of the most expressive and monumental devotional images, such as winged altarpieces, were creations of the fourteenth century, and it was in the fourteenth and fifteenth centuries that devotional figures with articulated arms and legs came to be featured as part of the liturgy. For example, a wooden figure of Christ was sometimes lifted by ropes into the rafters at the feast of the Ascension or laid in a sepulcher on Good Friday (fig. 1). Although gold and precious gems were employed earlier to adorn three-dimensional sculptures, new techniques and new materials made possible the proliferation of devotional objects,[27] and those who crafted

Figure 1. Painted wood sculpture of Christ in the sepulcher from the Cistercian convent of Lichtenthal, made in the middle of the fourteenth century. Such sculptures were often used to act out the events of Good Friday and Easter Sunday. The fact that the feet and toes of the Christ figure are badly worn makes it likely that they were kissed in the liturgy. A host was perhaps placed in the figure's chest and buried with him in the grave on Good Friday. Badisches Landesmuseum Karlsruhe, Inv.-Nr. V 12456 a-g. (Photo: Badisches Landesmuseum, Karlsruhe.)

them used the powerful and multivalent physical stuff of which they were made (vermilion paint, parchment, gold leaf, jewels, brocade, leather) to underline doctrinal points or induce spiritual reactions. The way in which such objects were constructed came to call attention to their materiality by means both obvious and subtle. Some images included *tituli* (texts inserted, often on banderols) that enjoined the worshiper to kiss them; others deployed their layers of presentation in such a way that the inner part of the object was three-dimensional, whereas the outer panels were flat, thus impelling viewers to experience greater tactility as they penetrated to deeper soteriological significance.[28] (See fig. 30, p. 96 for an example of such *tituli*, figs. 38, 13, and 14, pp. 133 and 68–69, for examples of three-dimensionality in the inner, feast-day opening of a winged altar.) Moreover, devotional objects themselves both inspired and reflected a proliferation of inner visions in which physical things were crucial. Hence visions, like iconography, became more "material" in their content.[29] Visionaries *saw* grace as a golden tube, Christ's veins as woven cloth; artists depicted the Eucharist as a winepress or grain mill. (See figs. 24 and 25, pp. 84–85.) Even the enigmatic Trinitarian God beyond knowing was evoked by the illuminator of the Rothschild Canticles as a bundle of textile or a starry wheel (fig. 2).[30]

At the same time, of course, image hating—and image bashing—increased. And it is significant that the visual objects attacked (usually three-dimensional statues and stained glass) were those that were most tactile, friable, and materially insistent. Spirited rejection of relics, sacramentals, and *Dauerwunder* also increased. Moreover, as we will see, thirteenth- and fourteenth-century scholastics tended to naturalize the miraculous, employing various theories to rein in material and physiological transformations without denying them entirely. The very theologians and ecclesiastical authorities who castigated as heresy the denial of images or divinely transformed matter endeavored with equal fervor to theorize such objects as only triggers of devotional response, not visible instantiations of the divine. In praxis and theory (both philosophical and theological), material transformation was affirmed and denied—the subject of fascinated ambivalence.

Throughout the Middle Ages, matter was defined—and explored—as the locus of change. Spontaneous generation fascinated, as did various sorts of action at a distance, such as the lunar pull on tides, and these phenomena tended to be theorized as the action of bodies on bodies. By the fifteenth and sixteenth centuries, even in learned circles, there was a growing sense that material objects were not merely labile but also alive. Even phenomena such as magnetism came to be conceptualized as animation. Skepticism concerning alchemy and astrology gave way to their enthusiastic embrace. Stories of werewolves and the metamorphoses caused by witchcraft came to be understood by some as literal rather than illusionary transformations. But, needless to say, these discussions carried with them increasing anxiety, disagreement, even an impulse to persecute. Behind both the enthusiasm for material change and the hostility to it lay a keen sense that matter is powerful, hence dangerous, because transformative and transformed.

Materiality

It should by now be clear that what I mean by "holy matter" is complicated. I include relics (bones and body parts that generated and focused pilgrimage), contact and effluvial relics (material stuff such as cloth or dust that supposedly became holy through contact with Christ and the saints or their burial places or that erupted or oozed from holy bodies), sacramentals (objects such as bread or herbs that absorbed power through ritual blessing or through contact with other sacral objects), the material of the Eucharist and other sacraments (the bread and wine of the mass, the oil of anointing, the water of baptism), and *Dauerwunder* (miraculous transformations that not only appear but also endure, thus becoming themselves foci of devotion). I also include the devotional images—statues, winged altarpieces, prayer cards,

Figure 2. Folios 84r, 104r and 106r of the Rothschild Canticles, New Haven, Yale University, Beinecke Rare Book and Manuscript Library, MS 404. Although the texts in this Trinitarian section of the prayer book emphasize the difficulty of seeing God, the Trinity is evoked in homey images of knotted cloth, fire, and wheels. On folio 84r, the three figures of the Godhead are caught up into a knotted cloth or veil, which signifies a hiding that nonetheless reveals. In the miniature on folio 104r, Father, Son, and Holy Spirit disappear into the circle of their Unity, yet toes, hands, and wing tips remain visible. In folio 106r, the Trinity as Unity whirls in a starry circle, and the veil is drawn back so that the soul of the worshiper can itself disappear into the glory. (Photo: Beinecke Rare Book and Manuscript Library, Yale University Library.)

stained glass, and so forth—that proliferated in the later Middle Ages. It is in this context that I emphasize the widespread appearance of animated statues and wall paintings. And in Chapter 1, I relate such animation to their formal qualities of plasticity and tactility—aspects of medieval art that Michael Baxandall and Herbert Kessler, among others, have emphasized.[31]

The goal for the crafters of such things as pietàs, Books of Hours, and winged altarpieces was, I argue, not so much conjuring up or gesturing toward the unseen as manifesting power in the matter of the object. Medieval art was neither naturalistic nor illusionist. Unlike the painting of a Renaissance Madonna, for example, in which the artist concentrates on making the viewer see paint on canvas as fabric or skin and hence (among other things) admire his or her skill at creating illusion, a medieval image induces the viewer to notice that it is made from paint and wood or vellum and ink. But the stuff of which medieval images were made was not incidental to their form or simply functional, nor indeed was it only an iconography to be decoded. The viewer cannot avoid observing the particular materials employed (see fig. 6, p. 54), and these materials have multiple meanings, again both obvious and subtle. Some are, as current slang puts it, "in your face"; others need to be decoded. For example, the crystal on a reliquary was a window to look through, but it mattered that the window was crystal; it encased the bone within in the nondecayable quintessence of heaven. Thereby it not only made a statement about the status of its contents as already glorified, it also raised them to glory. (See fig. 19, p. 76.) Moreover, late medieval devotional images call attention to themselves not just as materials but also as specific physical objects. Depictions of Christ's body as a charter on which nails or a flail write in blood ink *are* what they depict when the charter is drawn on real skin—that is, parchment. (See fig. 28, p. 92.) This argument will become clearer in Chapters 1 and 3 when I discuss the visual rhetoric of parts and wholes. Here I point out simply that I am not so much making a general statement about how all objects "mean" or "perform" as claiming that late medieval devotional objects speak or act their physicality in particularly intense ways that call attention to their per se "stuffness" and "thingness."[32]

Holy objects did not fall simply and easily into the categories I just listed: relic, contact relic, image, and so forth. Rather, they tended to be conflated.[33] Panel paintings and three-dimensional sculptures occasionally had relics inserted in them, or in the case of panel paintings, in their frames.[34] Hence, what modern art historians would call "iconography" or "image of" could become the thing itself. For example, in the Holy Cross chapel of Karlštejn Castle in Bohemia, rebuilt by Charles IV in the 1360s, the painting of Christ on Calvary between Mary and John has bits of the true cross, even of the thorns, lance, and sponge of the Crucifixion, embedded directly in it.[35] (See fig. 37, pp. 118–19.) Conversely, images and wafers that bled and oozed, changed colors, spoke, and moved by themselves—especially in cases where they produced stuff that could be preserved—became relics, asserting their transcendence (their more than ordinariness) exactly by asserting their materiality. Indeed, we often do not know whether late medieval monstrances contained relics, the Eucharist, or *Dauerwunder*, so similar was the treatment of these objects devotionally and liturgically. (See figs. 21 and 42, pp. 78 and 146.)

Despite the conflation of holy objects to which I have just pointed, it may appear that the term "materiality," as I employ it, is only a homonym. Neoplatonic theories of the soul of the universe or scientific understandings of the magnet may appear to have little to do with theological discussions of Eucharistic miracles or pilgrimage patterns. To relate, much less assimilate, a sophisticated playing with the stuff of depictions to a popular belief in living statues or bleeding wafers of the sort anthropologists and historians often call "animism" may appear simply a category confusion.[36] Such interpretations may even seem to return the culture of the later Middle Ages to the kind of literal freezing of symbol into object that Johan Huizinga is sometimes thought to have attributed to the period.[37] But despite my admiration for

Huizinga and my conviction that his arguments have been undervalued and often misunderstood, I am not returning to them. Nor am I arguing that all these "materialities" are the same thing or had the same trajectory or chronology. I am connecting, not equating, the tactility of art, the pervasive stress on all sorts of religious objects, a shift in natural-philosophical formulations, and the increase of miracles of material transformation. Nonetheless, I will suggest, by the end of this book, that there was a basic understanding of matter that underlay both medieval practices and the complicated, learned arguments that concerned relics, images, sacramentals, and *Dauerwunder*. In contrast to the modern tendency to draw sharp distinctions between animal, vegetable, and mineral or between animate and inanimate, the natural philosophers of the Middle Ages understood matter as the locus of generation and corruption. Although questions of the difference between living and nonliving and worries about decay and dissolution were common, the basic way of describing matter—the default language, so to speak, into which theorists tended to slip—was to see it as organic, fertile, and in some sense alive.

It therefore turns out to be significant that theorists employed parallel intellectual strategies to rein in very different sorts of holy things, arguing that—whether image or relic, bleeding host or bits of wax—such objects merely referred beyond themselves or triggered a power other than their own. Yet people, even dissidents who objected increasingly violently to relics, *Dauerwunder*, and images, did not behave as if such materiality merely gestured beyond itself. The forcefulness with which they fought it reflected fear of it. Moreover, the same theologians who theorized relics and images as pointing beyond themselves vehemently condemned those who denied their veneration. It was iconoclasm, not credulity or enthusiasm, that was characterized as "heresy." And the philosophers whose arguments in some cases naturalized transformation miracles displayed an understanding of physical change that made more probable exactly the sort of miraculous events they wished to rein in or deny. Medieval ideas of the material and the sacred both restrict and unleash the power of matter. By the time I come to the theories of the intellectual elite in Chapter 4, I will argue that their conception of matter ties together attitudes toward physical objects as diverse as fear of their animation, on the one hand, and the sophistication of their deployment of materials, on the other.

Beyond "the Body"

Because my use of the term "materiality" may mislead, a brief cautionary note is necessary. Much recent work in Cultural Studies has focused on "the body," on "materiality and agency," and on "material culture."[38] But what I mean by "materiality" is not quite what these terms mean in any of their current denotations or theoretical implications. I am interested here not so much in what we can learn from archaeology or from chemical and dendrochronological analyses of medieval objects as in how they functioned and what they meant religiously. Moreover, I have not attempted to engage with technical work on the physical stuff of medieval art. Lying in the background of my argument are, of course, facts about late medieval society that made increased spending on church furnishings and private devotion possible; I am not unaware of how new pigments and woods made statues vivid in depiction and altarpieces easier to acquire.[39] But my study is not an exploration of the material conditions of production.

Nor am I addressing general questions of materiality in culture. Although my sense of the "agency" of objects does parallel, in certain ways, the insights of Bruno Latour, Alfred Gell, Daniel Miller, and other social scientists,[40] I do not intend to contribute to universalizing theories about the power of things. Moreover, I do not here engage directly with art-historical scholars, such as Hans Belting and David Freedberg, who are interested in theorizing response.[41] Questions of how we talk about visual objects in the era before art,[42] theories about the agency of ordinary objects (from domestic aids to scientific equipment),[43] and the somewhat reductive investigations into the physiology of seeing currently popular with some art historians have, of course, shaped the way I have pursued my topic.[44] But my argument is a historical one; it explores the cultural background to the emphasis on material objects found at a particular moment in Western Christianity. Despite my use of quotations from David Shulman and Lorraine Daston as epigraphs to evoke the sense of objects I am exploring in this book, my focus is not on cross-cultural comparison. Indeed, as my conclusion below will make clear, I intend the specificity of the late medieval situation to cast some doubt on generalizing that has been done by others.[45]

I am also not explicitly engaging recent work on the history of the body. I in fact find some of it problematic insofar as it has tended to substitute the term "body" for "human individual" or "person."[46] In this study, I am interested in bodily metamorphoses (for example, stigmata), especially where they parallel transformations in other sorts of matter—in bleeding hands that are analogous to bleeding wood and bleeding bread. But as I have made clear in earlier work, I do not equate person with body.[47] What I wish to do here is not so much to explore body as a crucial part of psychosomatic self or person—a topic about which I have written before—as to move beyond study of "the body" to study of matter itself.

In what follows, I explore medieval understandings of cult and praxis by resituating understandings of body (*corpus*) where medieval theorists themselves located such understandings—in conceptions of matter (*materia*). As we will see in Chapter 4, medieval theorists, following Aristotle, Isidore, and the entire natural-philosophical tradition, understood "body" to mean "changeable thing": gem, tree, log, or cadaver, as well as living human being. Understood in medieval terms, to explore "the body" was to explore stars and statues, blood and resin, as well as pain, perception, and survival. The materiality I study here includes human bodies, but body is in no way the equivalent of—although it is integral to—what we call "self."[48] Resituating body in matter, however, helps us to a far more complex understanding of how medieval persons responded to other persons and the world of which they were a part.

A second point is related to this. Much sensitive recent work on medieval images and objects—on devotional art, on relics, on miracles—locates the physicality so central to medieval Christianity in the doctrine of the Incarnation: the teaching that God came into a human person (that is, an entity whose individuality and identity is constituted by soul and body) with the birth of Christ.[49] This is not wrong. The Byzantine defense of icons at the time of the iconoclastic controversy (725–842) was related to defenses of Christ as fully human—as incarnate God. Later Western defenses of Eucharistic visions and wonders, like defenses of relics of the Crucifixion (above all blood relics), were statements of the full humanity of Christ and of the accessibility of that humanity. But more was at stake than the doctrine of the Incarnation. As we will see throughout the chapters that follow, the support for and criticism of such accessibility through the physical stuff of panel paintings, bones, and consecrated bread was an exploration of the nature of matter—a question, that is, of ontology as well as of Christology. Jean-Claude Schmitt and André Vauchez are right that the presence of so many physical objects in late medieval religion was a "logical working out" of the doctrine of the Incarnation, just as Euan Cameron is right that late medieval religion can be considered an overbalancing of devotion onto objects and saintly presences and hence onto the humanity rather than the transcendence of Christ.[50] But in the later Middle Ages, the expression of and reaction to Christ's humanity, even his bodiliness, were part of a larger religious discourse about the material itself and how it might manifest or embody God. If Christ took all his bodily particles into heaven—so some theologians argued—we ordinary humans can hope for similar reassemblage in resurrection. If he left particles behind—others argued—we might gain grace through those particles.[51] Exactly how God acts through matter was a disputed question long after the belief that Christ was both God and man (man being understood as a psychosomatic unity) was established as dogma.

Matter as Paradox

My argument proceeds in steps. After establishing in Chapter 1 the materiality of late medieval devotional objects and placing this in contrast to theological discussions that seemed to reduce them to merely gesturing toward the divine, I move in Chapter 2 to consider other forms of holy matter and suggest that much contemporary theory tended to reduce their role also to pointing beyond or deriving from the material (usually via clerical consecration, which implied clerical control). According to such theorists, sacramentals were only signs of God's grace or expressions of pious hopes for blessing; relics were mementos of the saints; bleeding hosts were special effects created to reward faith or banish doubt. Yet there was a contradiction. Formulae for blessing objects such as water and bread suggest that power lies *in* them. People behaved as if relics were the saints. The Eucharist itself *was* Christ. And many understood *Dauerwunder* to be the body and blood of Christ in a more immediate sense even than the Eucharist. In Chapter 3, I then move to demonstrate the complicated understanding of holy matter such a contradiction involved by considering medieval attitudes toward part and whole, both in praxis and in theology.

In Chapter 4, I consider theoretical (natural-philosophical as well as theological) discussions of matter itself. In a world where alchemical change, the possibility of human/animal metamorphosis, spontaneous generation, and manipulation of matter by magic and witchcraft were increasingly topics of fierce debate among intellectuals, matter itself was under interrogation. I argue here that understandings of matter themselves focused on both controlling and unleashing its power.

In the Conclusion, I turn to a larger context for my argument, especially its implications for comparative study. I also consider paradox as a basic interpretive principle. Here, I argue that paradox lies at the heart of late medieval Christianity. And paradox, I suggest, is not dialectical. Paradox is the simultaneous assertion (not the reconciliation) of opposites.[52] Because of the paradox not just of Christ's Incarnation (God in the human) but also of divine creation (God's presence in all that is infinitely distant from him), matter was that which both threatened and offered salvation. It threatened salvation because it was that which changed. But it was also the place of salvation, and it manifested this exactly through the capacity for change implanted in it. When wood or wafer bled, matter showed itself as transcending, exactly by expressing, its own materiality. It manifested enduring life (continuity, existence) in death (discontinuity, rupture, change). Miraculous matter was simultaneously—hence paradoxically—the changeable stuff of not-God and the locus of a God revealed.

The materiality of art with which I begin thus brings us full circle. Images encapsulate the paradox I try, in these chapters, to explore. When they insistently display—and even comment on—their own materiality, they show that they are matter. In other words, they show that they are not God. But matter is God's creation—that through and in which he acts. Matter is powerful. In their insistent materiality, images thus do more than comment on, refer to, provide signs of, or gesture toward the divine. They lift matter toward God and reveal God through matter. Hence, it is hardly surprising that they call attention to the material through which they achieve their effects rather than merely using it to create the illusion of something else. Nor is it surprising that they frighten, empower, or console, sometimes even speaking, bleeding, or weeping—in other words, that they disclose, not merely signify, a power that lies beyond.

My purpose in this book is not to minimize the central importance of Christ's Incarnation in Christian theology. Indeed, insofar as creation is, to some medieval theologians and mystics, summed up in Christ, my interpretation should enhance our understanding of medieval theories of the Incarnation.[53] Nor is it my purpose to deny aspects of the later Middle Ages other than materiality or to relate the significance of holy objects only to ideas of matter. Rather, I hope to redress the balance of recent scholarship by calling attention to a characteristic of the period that is often reductively understood as superstition or exteriorized devotion and to embed that aspect in a broader context than is usually recognized.[54] Doing so may tell us something about the place of materiality in the *longue durée* of Western history and perhaps even stimulate us to think more deeply about the problematic nature of matter—the stuff and condition of human existence medieval theorists struggled with such sophistication to understand.

CHAPTER ONE

Visual Matter

Recent historical and art-historical work has emphasized seeing and visuality.[1] The trend is obvious when we notice how references to "the gaze" have proliferated in the titles of articles and books. In much of this work, theories of seeing, textual descriptions of visions, literary strategies and metaphors, and what modern critics call "works of art" (panel paintings, sculptures, manuscript illuminations, and so forth) have been conflated, partly because the term "image" itself is so multivalent.[2] In this chapter, I wish to turn all of this around and focus not on the topic often recently discussed apropos late medieval religious art—vision or visuality—but on the problem images presented as *material*.[3] I do this as one step in my treatment of medieval uses of and attitudes toward matter, and I choose to begin with what we today call "art" because the visual may provide, particularly for nonspecialists, a more immediately graspable introduction to late medieval religiosity and sensibility than do the rather abstruse discussions of matter and physicality we find in theologians, natural philosophers, or even preachers. But this chapter can also stand alone as a consideration of the problem posed for late medieval Christians by the fact that the objects they used for worship and meditation—for the exciting and displaying of devotion—were made from matter: sheepskin, wood, pigment, silk, linen, stone.

I will devote most of this first chapter simply to demonstrating the ways in which late medieval art was "material." And I mean by "material" several quite different things—each of them complex and broad. My analysis will emphasize, first, the proliferation of devotional objects (what German historians call *Andachtsbilder*) in late medieval religious praxis. Figures of Christ on a donkey to be pulled into the church on Palm Sunday, jointed wooden Christ figures buried in a sarcophagus on Good Friday or lifted into the ceilings of churches to depict the Ascension, Christ dolls to be laid in cradles at Christmas—such things were all new in the high Middle Ages.[4] (See figs. 1, 3, 4, and 11, p. 63.) Winged altarpieces that open to display three-dimensional scenes of the Nativity, Crucifixion, or the crowning of Mary have usually been considered a creation of fourteenth-century northern Europe.[5] (See figs. 13 and 14, pp. 68–69.) By the fifteenth century, the devout not only meditated on pictures of the physical instruments that had crucified Christ, the prayer cards they used in meditation sometimes had on them raised figures (rather like Braille), so that meditating was as much tactile as visual.[6]

Second, I argue that the crafters of such art unabashedly used their materials in a way that calls attention to them, rather as certain modern artists call attention to the media of art—paint, canvas, stone, steel, and so forth—although the purposes of medieval and modern artists in doing so are not the same.[7] Some medieval images are simply images of artistic materials; we find in manuscripts and on walls, for example, completely nonrepresentational panels of color, swirls of shaped stone, and so forth. (See fig. 6, p. 54.) Even where representational, medieval depictions are sometimes more tactile than visual. The gorgeous hunger cloths embroidered by medieval nuns for liturgical celebrations, for example, often present their elaborate iconography in white thread on white linen so that the figures are barely visible from a distance. They ask to be touched, more than seen.[8] Indeed, it is a characteristic of medieval images that their crafters tended to employ materials explicitly as themselves rather than creating an illusion, or a naturalistic depiction, of them through other media. For example, when medieval craftsmen dressed the Madonna, they were apt to paste brocade or leather on her statue rather

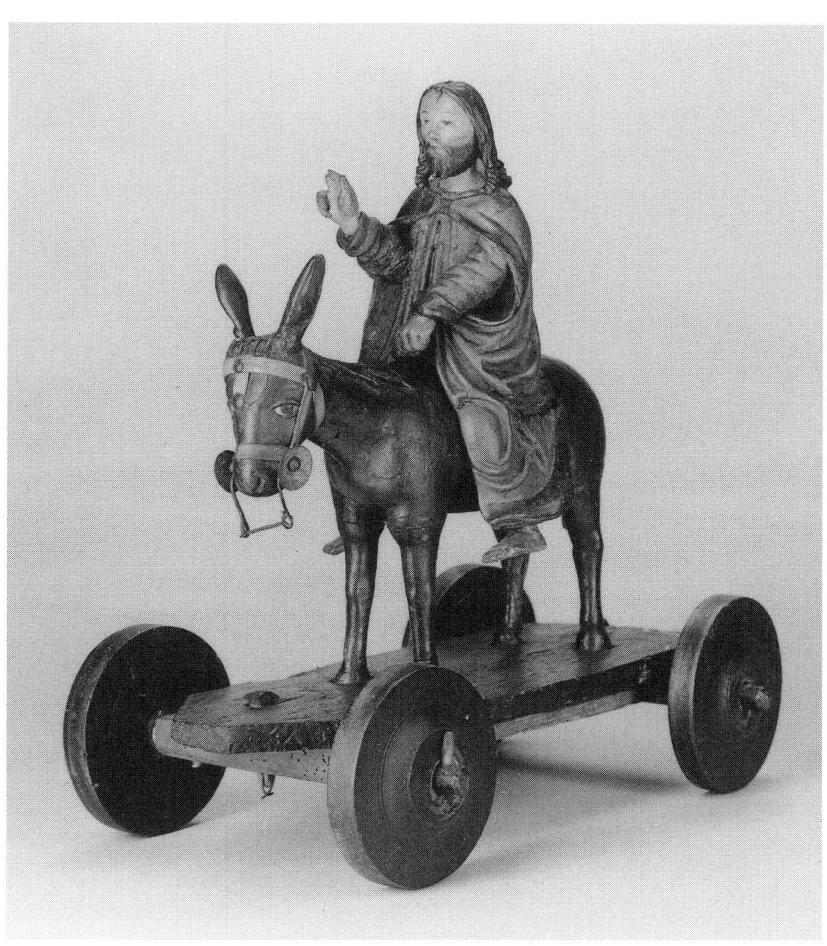

Figure 3. Limewood sculpture of Christ on a donkey (45 cm high), made in the sixteenth century for the Dominican Cloister of St. Katherine in Wil. The nuns probably pulled this figure through their cloister on Palm Sunday, imitating the entry of Christ into Jerusalem told in the Gospels. We know that in the Middle Ages, nearly life-size versions of such figures were drawn through churches, and the people took part in the procession by throwing branches. Schweizerisches Landesmuseum Zürich, Inv.-Nr. LM 6778. (Photo: © Swiss National Museums, Zurich.)

Figure 4. Painted wooden Christ doll (36 cm high) from Cologne, about 1500. Such dolls were produced in large numbers from the mid-fourteenth century on. Sometimes lavishly dressed (as in Figure 8) to indicate Christ's royalty, sometimes naked to stress his humanity, they were displayed for veneration in convents, parish churches, and private homes. Nuremberg, Germanisches Nationalmuseum, Inv.-Nr. Pl. O. 320. (Photo: Germanisches Nationalmuseum, Nuremberg.)

than creating the illusion of cloth through paint (fig. 5). Such deliberate and sophisticated use of materials makes a theological and devotional point and compels a reaction: the gorgeously robed lady is queen of heaven. The physicality we encounter in devotional objects (often in their combination of colors, depth of relief, textures, and materials) reflects and results from the fact that they are not so much naturalistic (that is, mimetic) depictions as disclosures of the sacred through material substance.[9]

Third, I will treat the motifs of art, arguing that it was characteristic of late medieval iconography to emphasize physical objects—not only bodies but also inanimate objects. Indeed, artists often chose to represent as inorganic or mechanical what we moderns would think of as bodily or organic—or vice versa—or they played with the idea that the sacred might be manifest in both. This is far more than simply a matter of art illustrating allegories or typologies, although many of the objects in medieval works—coral necklaces, mousetraps, lilies, fire screens, winepresses, and so forth—need iconographical decoding.[10] A woodcut of the bleeding hand of Christ may, for example, depict that hand as blazoned on a shield or as itself a woodcut; the woodcut of Christ's wound is then also a woodcut of a woodcut. (See figs. 32 and 33, p. 100.) The image depicts itself as a physical image as well as depicting what it reveals.

Fourth, I will extend my argument for the importance of materiality to a different sort of visual: written descriptions of visions. Here, too, for all the presence in contemplative theory of a strong sense of the apophatic—that is, of negative theology, of achieving a glimpse of the divine through passing beyond into wordless, imageless "unknowing"—descriptions of visions are filled with concrete objects. Especially in the accounts of visionary women, the holy and the other is not only understood and imaged but also mediated through what we moderns would call inanimate things.[11] Thus, these visions, so often used by recent critics as evidence or examples of medieval theories of seeing (in the sense of optics) or of the visual, are in fact textual in form and material in content.[12]

Figure 5a–b. Painted wooden pietà, probably from before 1350, now in the Museum des Sankt-Petri-Domes, Fritzlar. The body of the obviously dead Christ figure nonetheless erupts in fresh red blood. The medieval figure seems to have had papier-mâché drops pasted on. The two holes in the chest wound indicate that the Christ held a monstrance there, which would have contained a consecrated host or possibly a relic. The Virgin's garment had real leather trim. Figure 5a shows the figure before restoration; Figure 5b is of the statue as restored. (Photos: Foto Marburg/Art Resource, NY, and Landesamt für Denkmalpflege Hessen, Restaurierungswerkstatt, Rest. Weller-Figure.)

Finally, I will be treating cases in which objects we moderns think of as "art"—panel paintings, statues, sometimes even the walls of buildings—supposedly came alive, so that matter in a quite literal sense conveyed the holy. This argument is related to a more universalistic one about the "power of images" made recently by David Freedberg, among others—the argument, that is, that many cultures fear images (especially three-dimensional images) as alive. Such "deep structures," both of culture and of psychology, may in some sense underlie the outburst of animated images in fourteenth- and fifteenth-century western Europe. But I am considering here a historically situated phenomenon, not a universal one.[13] I think we can understand both the enthusiasm for and the fear of images in the period of northern European iconoclasm only against the background of other outbursts of holy matter—and of theories defending and condemning them—in the same period and as a result of the insistent materiality that is a characteristic of late medieval art.[14] Some images came alive, were feared to be alive, or were thought to be misunderstood as alive because many material objects were not only analogies to, but also disclosures of, the divine.

Image Theory

Before I turn to images, I must discuss a textual tradition. I do this in order to underline the astonishing ambivalence concerning the matter of images that we find in that tradition. Understanding the extent of this ambivalence is crucial for two reasons. First, it is only after we explore the ambiguity of materiality that we see how remarkable is the fact—and how in need of explanation—that material images of all sorts (brightly painted, three-dimensional sculpture; stained glass; altarpieces that combine panels and carving; and so on) erupted onto the religious scene in the Latin West. Second, the standard account of the image ambivalence or image hating we call "iconoclasm" has focused too much on the question of representation of the divine—as if the problem were only the impossibility of picturing God—and too little on the problem of matter itself. Yet the Western discourse about images never completely lost an awareness that their physicality is a problem, that manifesting the divine in the material is at best a paradox, at worst an invitation to idolatry. Only by recognizing that medieval worshippers thought of images as matter will we understand the way in which images themselves insist on that of which they are made as both the opposite to and the disclosure of God.[15] Returning our attention to exactly what the texts say about the danger and power of matter per se helps to explain both the resurgence of iconoclasm in sixteenth- and seventeenth-century Europe and its defeat in the course of Western history, which was, in the long run, anything but image-hating. Thus, I begin with a discussion of theological texts.

Awareness of the problem presented by the materiality of images—its dangerous link to and possible inducement of idolatry—was nothing new in the Christian Middle Ages. It went back to the Second Commandment (Exod. 20:4–5: "Thou shalt not make to thyself a graven thing...") and to the book of Wisdom, which condemns idols as "brittle vessels" that have not "the use of eyes to see, nor noses to draw breath, nor ears to hear." "Man made them.... For, being mortal himself, he formeth a dead thing with his wicked hands. For he is better than they whom he worshippeth, because he indeed hath lived, though he were mortal, but they never" (Wisd. 15:13–17).[16] To the Hebrew preachers, prophets, and lawgivers, graven images were dead matter, the opposite of the living God.

Repeatedly in the Christian tradition, Christians used this charge against images. In the eighth and ninth centuries, iconoclasts in the Byzantine Empire argued, as an inscription placed in the stead of a Christ image put it: "The Lord does not allow a portrait of Christ to be drawn without voice, deprived of breath, made of earthly matter, which is despised by Scripture." At the same period, some in the West (for example, Claudius of Turin) who also rejected images explained: to adore an object such as the cross is not only to adore an instrument of torture; it is also to adore the stuff of creation.[17] If one tries to justify this by arguing that Christ, who was divine, hung on the cross and made it holy by his touch, one might as well adore everything he touched: Mary's womb, his cradle, his diapers, the lance that pierced him, and so forth. And one could then adore all cradles, lances, even the entire earth, because Christ walked on the earth. But this is undignified and counter to the glory and transcendence of God.

Even those who defended images as material tended to find the fact of their materiality deeply ambiguous. The great Eastern iconophile, John of Damascus, who argued that matter lies at the heart of Christian worship, was careful also to emphasize, as did his iconoclast opponents, the incorporeality and uncircumscribability of God. John wrote:

> It cannot be denied that flesh is material and is created. Is it not matter therefore, through which I receive salvation, that I venerate and adore?... Is not the wood of the cross most blessed and happy? Is the sacred and venerable mount, the place of Calvary, not material?.... Are not the ink and paper of the Gospels material? Are not the body and blood of our Lord material? Either remove all worship... of these things, or allow... the veneration of images.[18]

But John also insisted: "I do not worship matter, but the creator of matter." And he was, as we will see, a major source of the Western understanding that images "declare and make manifest that which is hidden."[19] Although acknowledged as the gift of the creator, matter was understood to point beyond itself. Whether defended or denied, the materiality of devotional objects—and not merely their function as representation—was at issue in the debate over icons.

In Western discussions, too, the problematic nature of matter was explicitly addressed. The *Libri Carolini*, penned in 790–92 by Theodulf of Orleans not to oppose images altogether but to reject what Theodulf thought to be the Eastern theological justification for them, argued for the superiority of Eucharist to icon by seeing images as crafted of inferior stuff and by inferior persons. Disagreeing with the Damascene's conflation of types of devotional matter, Theodulf assumed a hierarchy of the stuff of creation:

> Because the Lord said in the Gospel, "the true adorers are those who adore the Father in spirit and truth [John 4:23]," we are astonished at the folly of those who are roused to adore images and... dare to place them at the same level as the body and blood of the Lord, saying "as the body and blood of the Savior passes [*transit*] from the fruits of the earth and becomes a mystery, so images made by the work of artisans and constructed to resemble persons [*conpaginatae ad earum personarum*] become things of veneration [*transeant venerationem*]." But the sacrament of the body and blood of the Lord was given to us by himself, mediator between God and man [1 Tim. 2:5], in commemoration of his Passion and our salvation, and is made [*conficiatur*] by the hand of the priest and invocation of the divine name, whereas images, which do not receive the imposition of hands of the mystery of consecration, are formed and composed by those who know the art of painting and are skilled at making colors. And when the priest consecrates... he asks that the species be carried by angels to the altar of God... but the painter... seeks above all beauty and by the arrangement of colors to add something to his work....
>
> There is indeed a very great difference... between the sacrament... and images executed by painters.... The former is consecrated by the priest invoking the divine name, the latter painted by a painter with the erudition of a human technique; the former is carried by angels aloft to the altar of God, the latter is placed by human hands through their skill on walls to startle the eyes of those looking at them.[20]

Although Theodulf here invokes several reasons for suspicion of images, one of his concerns is that icons are made of paint through purely human skill. In other words, a depiction in matter that aspires to be like a person is misleading insofar as it aims at illusion, lowly stuff masquerading as the saint it evokes; only

God in consecration can lift matter (bread and wine, treated in Theodulf's source as simple fruits of the earth) to glory. The materiality of the image is not the only problem, but it is clearly a problem.

Even after the defeat of iconoclasm in Byzantium (842), doubts about images continued in the West, and they continued to be doubts not just about representation but also about the matter of images. In the eleventh century, a group of dissidents at Arras and, in the twelfth century, the followers of Peter of Bruys opposed the veneration of objects, particularly the cross.[21] And whatever debate there may be among scholars about whether the Cathars of southern France were a separate religion from Christianity or mostly a construction by their Christian opponents, they clearly represented to those opponents resistance to any presence of the holy in matter—that is, to the veneration of images and relics, to the conviction that the Eucharist is Christ's body, to belief in bodily resurrection at the end of time, and so forth.[22]

Orthodox preachers in the fifteenth century urged (as an anonymous treatise of 1470 put it): "If you believe that the image has some divine power, virtue, or ability to succor contained in it . . . this is quite against the Commandment and is idolatry."[23] Or as the tract *The Road to Heaven*, printed in 1484, exhorted: "It is against the Commandment to worship carved, engraved, painted or other images, either for their own sake or for them to give one assistance, since they cannot give more help than any other piece of wood or pigment can [*denn als ein ander holcz oder ein andere varb*]."[24] Lollards (followers of John Wycliffe) in fifteenth-century England and the followers of Jan Hus in Bohemia in exactly the same decades went further, opposing not only the worship of images but any recourse to them whatsoever, except simple crosses and the Eucharist.[25] The Lollard William Whyte said no honor could be given to images because they are dead, even if carved in the likeness of men; it would be better to worship trees, he said, because they are at least alive. To this, his opponent Thomas Netter replied that if living trees are better than dead wood, why should one not venerate live sheep rather than dead sheepskin—that is, parchment? (He meant, of course, the Scripture written on it.)[26] Protestants such as Karlstadt and Zwingli argued that religious art was the graven images forbidden in the Second Commandment, and some sixteenth- and seventeenth-century reformers progressed beyond distrust to image smashing, an activity sometimes carried out with real hatred toward the statues decapitated and crushed to bits.

Lurking behind these charges was the repeated assertion that matter is dead, the lowest stuff in nature; hence, artificial objects made from it are further away from the living God than anything else in creation. Such a way of articulating distrust of images may have roots in the ancient Greco-Roman idea that manual labor (which includes making things) is a servile and despised activity—a notion reflected in the passage of the *Libri Carolini* quoted above.[27] It may also reflect, if distantly, Hebrew ideas of the dead body as polluting[28] and Platonic (or Neoplatonic) notions that the material is in some sense unreal, or even evil. But as expressed in the Christian Middle Ages, the idea takes an odd turn, as the quotations from William Whyte and Thomas Netter suggest. It almost seems to imply that living matter might image God.

Repeatedly, those who oppose images (and some who support them) admit that, according to Genesis 1:27, man is "made in the image and likeness of God" and argue that—if anything earthly can be revered in God's place—it should be the living rather than the dead. Some iconoclasts in the ninth century said only the Eucharist (bread in which the living Christ is present) or a living man can be an image of God.[29] And in 1489, a commission that examined the theses of the humanist Pico della Mirandola understood Pico's objection to venerating objects to entail the idea that man should be most adored of all things in creation because he is closest to the living God.[30] Moreover, the Neoplatonism that permeated medieval mystical writing and even some scholastic theology could be understood to suggest that all matter—because it emanated from God—was in some way linked ontologically to him, even as it fell away, morally as well as ontologically, toward nonbeing. Hence images (including verbal images or metaphors, artistic creations, and indeed, all earthly things) might in some sense participate in the eternal, transcendent One.[31] And "participate" could carry overtones of more than simple reflection or mirroring; it could mean to share being with—although at a very great distance. Some contemplative and visionary writers, such as Bonaventure and Hildegard of Bingen, saw God's footprints everywhere in creation; Mechtild of Hackeborn even conflated Christ's humanity with twigs, grass, and earth.[32]

Nonetheless, adoration of living stuff was rejected by both orthodox and dissident theologians, along with adoration of "rotten sticks and dead stones." The struggle to retain a gap between God and creation led to a tendency to lump together all that was not God. What was understood to be Pico's notion that humanity might be venerated because living horrified those who examined him for heresy. The Lollard taunt that trees are more alive than panel paintings was not intended to advocate tree worship. What the heated debate over images makes abundantly clear is that, for more than a millennium, the discussion about Christian religious art frequently focused on the stuff of which it was made, and that stuff—however understood—was problematic. The charge of opponents was not merely that images were dead matter; it was also that people who revered them mistakenly thought they were alive.[33]

The anxiety and stridency of image deniers—that is, their paradoxical sense that images are threatening both because they are dead and because they are not—may seem odd. Recent work by art historians on the history of image theory gives a different sense of the basic narrative. We are usually told that, whatever changes were rung on the theory, the Christian answer to the challenge of the Second Commandment was clear: images were not venerated for themselves but for that to which they pointed. Only God was worshiped or adored.

The usual scholarly story sees this standard, orthodox answer developing fairly consistently.[34] Gregory the Great, the pope who died in 604, gave (we are told) the first version of Western image theory: images teach, aid memory, and excite devotion.[35] Carolingian theologians, who by and large misunderstood the nuanced and Neoplatonic idea of symbol employed by Byzantine defenders of images, consolidated a Gregorian sense of image as that which gestures toward but does not literally contain the divine. Following John of Damascus, Thomas Aquinas in the thirteenth century distinguished *dulia*, veneration given to images because they point to something beyond, from *latria*, adoration offered to God (although in a complicated contradiction, he defended *latria* to the cross).[36] Statues cannot be alive, argued Thomas, because inanimate things cannot move themselves.[37] We must, as any good Aristotelian understands, acquire knowledge through the things of this world, but the very lowliness of figures, metaphors, and images is useful. This lowliness keeps us from confusing them with God.[38] Even in the early sixteenth century, Martin Luther, worried by the excesses of the Peasant's War, asserted that God's word alone saves but that no one really confuses painted or carved images with God.[39]

Christian anti-Judaism came into the discussion. In an odd twist of supersessionist logic, many Christian theologians argued both that Jews had religious art authorized by God (the cherubim of the Ark of the Covenant [Exod. 25:18–20], Moses's bronze serpent [Num. 21:8–9]) and that Jews were forbidden to make graven images because they, being literalists, inevitably slipped into idolatry. Hence the fate of the bronze serpent, destroyed along with other idols by Hezekiah (4 Kings 18:4). Christians, however (so the argument went), were permitted images because they, being able to understand at a spiritual level, saw beyond them.[40] Western theorists insisted (although not without some debate in the eighth and ninth centuries) that Christ could be depicted in images because, in the Incarnation, the godhead had become a visible, touchable, material body.[41] But because Christ was also divine, Christians could—indeed would—see beyond earthly matter, not only to glorified flesh but also to a transcendent God beyond all images.

Why, then, the anxiety? If images only point beyond, what was so threatening to orthodox Christians in the fifteenth century about heretics castigating them as dead matter? And, on the other hand, what was so disturbing to sixteenth-century critics that they not only insisted on images as inanimate but also progressed in some cases to cutting off their heads as if they were anything but? If Gregory the Great's theory of images as aids that gesture toward the beyond was really the accepted ideology, where lay the threat—either in objects themselves or in attacks on them?

The simple answer is that for all the emphasis of late medieval theorists on seeing beyond, people in the fourteenth and fifteenth centuries were surrounded by material images as never before.[42] And matter was problematic. It was not static and inert; it was by definition potent and changeable—both that which decayed in death and that which teemed with new life. However much some recent scholars may have insisted that late medieval practice focused on vision more than object,[43] objects were what the faithful revered, traveled to, and made offerings for. However much medieval intellectuals may have insisted on an ontological gap between image (or sign) and exemplar (or signified), what images displayed was their materiality. And as critics and supporters of images both feared and upheld, matter was not mere dead stuff. In later chapters, I will locate attitudes toward images (both their content and their material) in the wider context of "scientific" (that is, natural-philosophical) theories of matter. But in the remainder of this chapter, I turn simply to demonstrating the materiality of late medieval images in the several senses of "material" I outlined earlier. For until we understand medieval art in a new way—until we see how it plays with, uses, and interrogates materiality—we will not understand what it is that we need to explain. And we will see late medieval objects in this new way only by considering a variety of examples.

The Materiality of Images: Two Theoretical Considerations

As Herbert Kessler has pointed out in his brilliant and original book *Seeing Medieval Art*, medieval images announce their "overt materiality."[44] The materials of manuscript illuminations, panel paintings, and three-dimensional sculpture do not vanish by mimicking other things: Parchment shows through wash (as in the Darmstadt Gospel Book); the robe of the Virgin Mary displays real jewels (as in the Essen Golden Madonna); her cloak has strips of leather or brocade glued on (as in the Fritzlar pietà).[45] (See figs. 5, 6, and 7.) We are often misled by what we see in museums today, where colors have faded or been cleaned, gems or faux gems have been prized free from statues. Medieval art was highly colored. Statues were often dressed and festooned with jeweled necklaces (fig. 8). Indeed, in Catholic Spain, where such practices continue to this day, some statues of the Virgin lost their inside bodies almost entirely and became simply frames from which a gorgeous wardrobe was hung.[46] (See fig. 9 for an early modern example.)

This emphasis on the materials of which art is made has nothing to do with realism. We see this clearly in the example I just gave. The Virgin in Spanish processions was obviously not intended to represent a historical figure. She was not supposed to "look like" the Jewish girl who gave birth to a baby named Jesus. Indeed, the statue does not present her as a physical body at all. The emphasis is neither on identification of her physiognomy nor on realism or naturalism, on making her look like a woman. It is clear she is a kind of coat hanger with a head and torso. (In some cases, such statues appear to have only heads and hands.) The emphasis is on the glory and complexity of her attire—on her garb as regal, suiting the queen of heaven.

Two points are important here. First, medieval devotional art is at the opposite pole from the art of the southern or northern renaissances that followed it. Renaissance artists aimed for mimetic, illusionistic modes of representation that deliberately try to trick the senses (as in the well-known story from Pliny the

Figure 6. Frontispiece to St. Luke's Gospel, folio 126v of an eleventh-century Gospel Book; Hessisches Landesmuseum Darmstadt, Cod. AE, 679. The illuminator is clearly interested in the blue and green washes themselves and in the parchment that shows through them, carefully framed in an acanthus leaf border. (Photo: Hessisches Landesmuseum, Darmstadt.)

Figure 7. The famous Golden Madonna from Essen, 980/990; Treasure of Essen Cathedral, Inv.-Nr. 2. The limewood core is entirely covered with gold leaf, affixed to the statue with golden nails. The medieval figure had more jewels and filigree than we find on the sculpture today. (Photo: Anne Gold © Domschatz, Essen.)

Figure 8. Christ Child with its medieval costume, from the convent of Heilig Kreuz in Rostock, about 1500. Although the clothing survives relatively infrequently, Christ dolls were often elaborately dressed and were used in liturgical performances, especially by nuns and beguines. The belt on this figure states that the statue contains a relic of the true cross. It thus illustrates the conflation of relic and image that was common in medieval devotion. (Photo: Hugo Maertens, Staatliches Museum, Schwerin.)

Figure 9. Spanish processional figure of a type used from medieval to modern times. The statue is not a body at all, but simply a frame from which an elaborate wardrobe is hung. (Collection of Susan V. Webster, Photo: Hernán L. Navarrete.)

Elder's *Natural History* of Parrhasius's painting of the curtain, of which Renaissance readers were fond).[47] In contrast, medieval artists expected viewers to notice and admire the stuff they employed *as stuff*. Although they sometimes used imitation gems in place of precious ones or cheaper pigments to simulate more expensive, the gold or crystal or faux ruby is to be encountered as such, not as a painterly illusion. A medieval image is an object in a way that a Renaissance or modern painting is not. The gorgeous textile behind a medieval Madonna (whether it is painted or pasted on) is a frame for, a declaration of, her sacrality. The painted Renaissance curtain or dress, exactly because it is so precisely like a curtain or dress, makes it clear, finally, that it is not what it depicts. The self-consciousness of the Renaissance playing with illusion—its very success as illusion—calls attention both to the naturalism and to the "nonobjectness" of art. In contrast, the self-consciousness of medieval art calls attention to its objectness.

The materials of medieval art were, of course, pregnant with significance. They often (although not always) called attention to themselves not as mere stuff but as significant stuff, and the significance lay in the specificity of that stuff. Like was supposed to signal like—red to signal blood, gold heavenly light.[48] And new varnishes and pigments made this more possible from the twelfth century on, when more vibrant reds and yellow washes over silver, for example, made the blood of sacrifice and the crowns of heavenly glory more vermilion and golden than ever before. If the point to be made was the royalty of the queen of heaven, the gold had to look like gold. If Christ poured out ever-living sacrificial blood, that blood had to be bright, living red, not opaque or brown.[49] Indeed, medieval theorists had a far more complex sense than our modern one of what virtues and powers were represented by various gems and colors.[50] But the point of the objects that furnished medieval churches was not what we would call "realistic" depiction of bodies, figures, or events. The point was the power of the materials to evoke, to conjure up—to represent not so much in the sense of "looking like" as in the sense of "manifesting the significance of." If even expressionist depictions of the Crucifixion show the bodies of the two thieves as excruciatingly twisted while Christ hangs serene, this is not because a historic scene of three executions is realistically presented (a scene in which one of the victims suffered less) but because the central figure is human and divine, both sufferer and redeemer (because transcender) of suffering (fig. 10).

A second point must also be underlined. As is clear from my reference to the significance of various metals and gems, medieval art did rely on what we tend to call "representation" or "similitude" (if not on mimesis). To be effective devotionally, an image of Christ or the Virgin or St. Barbara must be "like" or "of" Christ or the Virgin or St. Barbara, at least in the sense of being recognizable as such, just as red must be recognizable as blood. But to be accepted as an image "of" a saint, the figure must not so much look like the saint (who knew what the Magdalen had looked like?) as have the attributes (palm branch, tower, chalice, etc.) conventionally associated with that saint or combine elements known from earlier depictions. Hence, being "an image of" or "representing" is not a matter of mimesis, although it can be a matter of reproduction (in Walter Benjamin's sense) or recombination.[51]

In other words, a figure can represent or be "like" a saint—that is, carry his or her power or presence—in the sense in which a person (for example, an ambassador or a friend) can represent another person—that is, not by looking like but by standing in for (either as delegated or not).[52] In this sense, a painted or sculpted image of a saint represents the saint in a manner parallel more to a relic than to a portrait, although a relic has a physical connection to its origin that a panel painting does not. A painted or carved image can also represent by reproducing or recombining iconographic elements. Regardless of what the "real" Madonna looked like, one statue of the Virgin may be recognizable as such because it closely reproduces another statue; such reproduction conveys and enhances, not diminishes, power. Indeed, there will usually

Figure 10. The so-called Kaufmann Crucifixion, Bohemia, ca. 1340. Gemäldegalerie, Staatliche Museen zu Berlin. Of a type known as the "Crowded Crucifixion," the scene telescopes into one eternal moment many of the events surrounding Christ's death and shows his body suffering yet serene, dead yet pouring forth living blood. (Photo: Bildarchiv Preussischer Kulturbesitz/Art Resource, NY.)

be some elements of similitude or recombination (although not of mimesis) in devotional images. A figure of St. Barbara will usually be a female figure. But St. Mark can be represented by a lion as much as by a man, the Virgin by a lily or a garden. What makes the image recognizable is not similitude *stricto sensu*, but some other identifiable indicator.

It is also worth noting here (although the point relates more to iconography, which I treat below) that the attribute that allows us to recognize the saint is occasionally a body part (Agatha's severed breasts or Lucy's eyes) but more often an instrument of torture (Catherine's wheel, Lawrence's griddle, Margaret's dragon, or Barbara's tower). Such attributes are yet another example of the significance of materiality in this sort of representation. The instrument that inflicted suffering is not only a sign that enables us to identify the saint, it also conveys the experience of martyrdom and the fact of triumph over it.[53] The power of such a painting lies not in any realistic depiction. (Even where gruesome torture is shown, the martyred saint is depicted not as suffering but as in contact with heaven.) The power lies in its representation of (in the sense of standing for and conveying) the holy person. And such representation is signaled by an object. Even in paint, Catherine is identified by a combination of the torture wheel and the female figure holding it. It is the wheel and Catherine's triumph over it that gives Catherine's devotee access to her experience and her power.

The Materiality of Images: Examples

In what follows, I wish to argue that late medieval devotional images not only announce rather than obscure what they are made of but also make sophisticated and sometimes self-conscious use of this materiality. The matter (e.g. parchment) of an object (e.g. a manuscript drawing) not only frequently calls attention to how it is constructed (lines are clearly ink scratches on skin, whose grain is not obscured), it often makes an explicit devotional or theological comment thereby. The point of the flesh on a painted medieval Madonna was not to be fleshlike, nor was it to obscure the wood or stone underneath; the point was for the thick, polished surface to gleam, denying the change flesh is heir to.[54] On the pietà from Fritzlar (see fig. 5, pp. 42–43), for example, we see not only a thick, smooth, white face on Mary but also insistent, shiny, high-relief blood drops on Christ.[55] The blood is alive, red, barely coagulated, although Christ is obviously dead. Such devices call attention as much to the stuff of which they are made as to the moment of grieving and suffering lifted by the art into eternity. Or to put it better, we can say that by calling attention to how they achieve their effects, they underline the paradox of life and death, grief and triumph, they manifest.

If we consider another example, the so-called "beguine cradle," made for a Christ doll owned by a group of medieval religious women and now in the Metropolitan Museum in New York, we see first that the cradle is, of course, a bed, complete with embroidered coverlet and bells (fig. 11). As such, it underlines the ordinary babyness of the Christ child. But it is not only a cradle. It is also shaped to echo a cathedral. Hence, the very architecture of its wood announces that it is in several senses a place for the God-man, complicating what "presence" means in a way it would take paragraphs of words to explain.[56] That an object can simultaneously *be* (not merely signify) two objects—both bed and church—calls attention to the simultaneity of Christ's life stages. Because of the foreshadowing built into biblical narrative, with which ordinary people were familiar from preaching and liturgy, the baby (in the crib) was always already redeemer (on the altar in the church). Human (vulnerable in the cradle) and divine (glorious in the cathedral) were simultaneous in the story of salvation. The way in which the object *is* both crib and cathedral is not here a matter of symbolism; we are not confronted with a cradle that symbolizes something else. Rather, we are confronted with a cradle that is also a church. Depending on how we look at it, it is one or the other or both. We see it as two objects, serially or simultaneously, not as a process of transformation or as one object

Figure 11. Liturgical cradle from the Grand Beguinage in Louvain, fifteenth century. The little crib, into which a Christ doll was laid in liturgical performance, is carved to look like a church with windows. It is thus the place where God appears, as baby in a cradle and redeemer on the altar. (The Metropolitan Museum of Art, gift of Ruth Blumka, in memory of Leopold Blumka, 1974 [1974.121a-d] Image © The Metropolitan Museum of Art.)

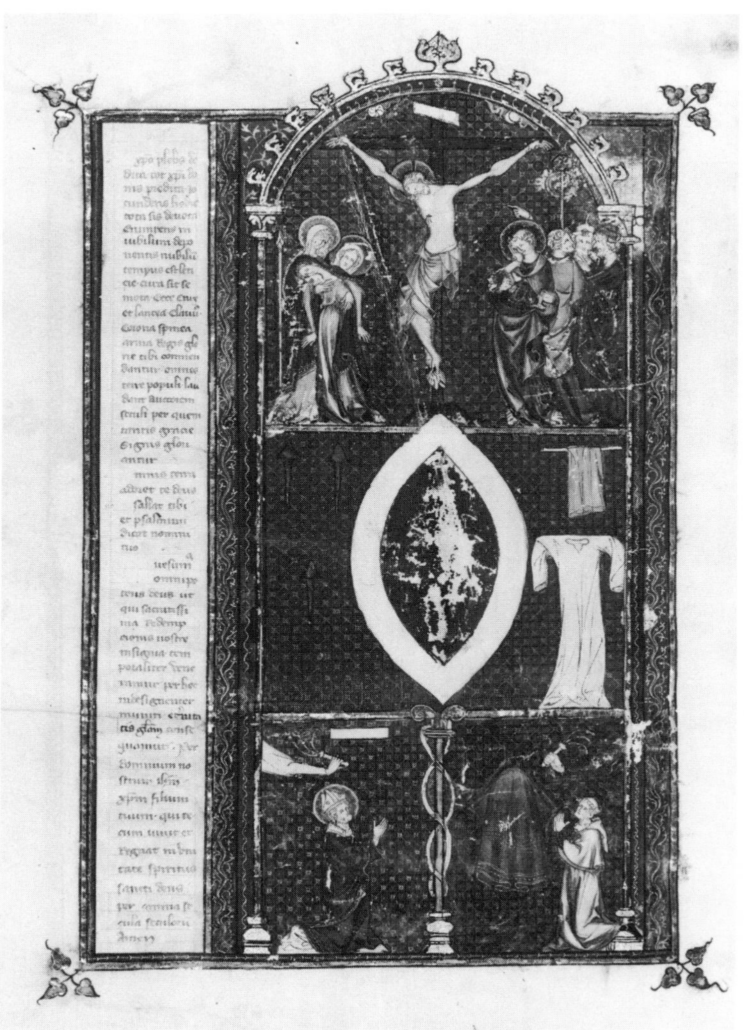

Figure 12. Folio 140v, Paris BN MS Fr. 574, from 1320. Below the Crucifixion, Christ's side wound is displayed with some of the *arma Christi* (the instruments of Christ's Passion, which were understood both as his insignia and as weapons aimed against him and deployed by him). The mandorla-shaped image of the side wound has been kissed or stroked by the devout to the point of effacement. (Photo: Bibliothèque nationale de France, Paris.)

pointing to something else beyond it. The objects are things that each echo and reinforce the significance of the other. And both are three-dimensional, tactile, handleable. Although their significance is not reached fully unless one has knowledge of the religious context, one can see the simultaneity of bed and church simply by looking at the object. It calls attention to what it is at least as much as to the something else (the Savior) it announces.

Viewer Response

Influenced too much by the Gregorian theory of images accepted by most medieval theologians, modern scholars have sometimes overemphasized the elements of "seeing through" or "pointing beyond" in such objects and images. They have understood the flagrant tactility of the handling of materials as a sort of "come-on" to draw viewers toward the unseen. And they have taken such objects as the beguine cradle more as symbols of something else than as artifacts. But there is a problem with this interpretation, unless we want to argue that most medieval viewers were stuck at a lower level and responded incorrectly to what they saw. For we know that medieval devotees responded to the overtly tactile appeal of such objects. They kissed and fondled them—actions still apparent to us centuries later in the many cases where a key part of a manuscript illumination or statue has been rubbed smooth by the contact of devout lips and fingers.[57] (See fig. 1, p. 23, and fig. 12.) Robert Suckale, for example, has described statuettes with grooves where strings of pearls or rosaries were applied and later torn off and worn patches so deep that the owners must have handled them "day and night."[58] Rather than passing beyond in quiet meditation, the medieval devout frequently treated such images as a locus of the divine. Indeed, the images themselves sometimes instructed the devout to venerate them with mouths and fingers, as we see in a little woodcut of Christ's wounds from circa 1490 that offers protection and indulgences to those who kiss it.[59] (See fig. 30, p. 96.)

Materiality as Self-Referential

What I want to stress here, however, is not merely viewer response. I want to go further and argue that this art both sublimates and emphasizes what it is made of; in so doing, it comments on the nature of matter and materiality. If we consider, for example, a winged altar from the Cistercian cloister of Ihlow, now in St. Lambert's Church in Aurich, in Frisia—a quite typical workshop piece of the years around 1500—we see that it plays in complicated ways with "looking at" and "looking through."[60] But the tactility, the stuffness, the carved woodness, so to speak, of the work is, I suggest, our final impression.

When closed, the altarpiece depicts the so-called Mass of St. Gregory, an iconographical motif very common in fifteenth-century Europe, especially in the North.[61] (See figs. 13 and 14.) It represents a legend according to which Pope Gregory the Great saw a vision of Christ appear on the altar while he was saying mass. The motif is often said to derive from a tale in the ninth-century Life by Paul the Deacon about a woman who doubted the Eucharist during one of Gregory's celebrations. But that version of the story is very seldom depicted.[62] The focus of the standard, late medieval iconography was rather the pope's vision of the crucified Christ, usually—but not always—at the precise moment of consecration and often in the company of an impressive ecclesiastical retinue, the members of which do not see the Christ figure. Thus, the iconography seems to be about seeing an unseen that is, although hidden, really there—in other words, it seems to be about demonstrating the doctrine of the real presence of Christ in the bread and wine of the Eucharist and about affirming the phenomenon of visionary experience.

But for an image about seeing, the depiction on the outer wings of the Ihlower/Aurich altar is very curious. The vision of Christ as the Man of Sorrows is far up to the right, clearly unseen by anyone in the two divided central panels that depict the vision scene. Moreover these panels are split in such a way that the Christ hanging on the altarpiece behind the pope (which is itself a painted panel) is cut away. Hence, no one, not even in this case the pope, seems to see the vision, and the central crucifix is erased, inviting us to go beyond, as if the real is there, undepicted and undepictable.

What we see in figure 13 is, however, the ordinary, weekday presentation of the altar. On feast days, it would have been opened, all that complicated playing around with motifs of seeing and not seeing folded back (fig. 14). Inside was a carved and gilded Crucifixion, a much more tactile, material scene—because three-dimensional—than the outer wings; it represents a scene of death in the round yet lifts that death to eternity by glorifying it in the most immortal of substances, gold. As Günter Bandmann has commented about such winged altars, the center—more plastic as well as more gilded—is not the highest point iconographically; God the Father or some other representation of triumph is usually at the pinnacle. In this altarpiece, the highest place, spatially and perhaps theologically, is occupied by the two flat and painted panels that depict manifestation and are located above and to either side of the Crucifixion. But the central carving is the place where viewers intersect with the divine.[63]

Thus, the Ihlower/Aurich altar both transcends and affirms (but never eclipses) its physicality. The viewer may be invited to penetrate *through* the outer image, but what he or she reaches is, in this case, another (even more plastic and tactile) image. However much the uniform goldness of the inner scene may remove it from suffering and death, the carved, in-the-round quality moves viewers into it, inviting their presence. There is space (at least imaginative space) for the viewer not only in front of but also between the figures. Indeed, the viewer's awareness that the altarpiece moves, the doors opening to reveal a deeper content on particularly important days, suggests a straining forward toward participation. Yet the ambiguity of matter is complicated further by the fact that the inner carving is flanked above by those two images of visual manifestation: the *Ecce Homo* (which invites seeing) and the *Noli me tangere* (which warns against touch).

Figure 13. Passion altar from Cloister Ihlow; Flemish, from Antwerp, ca. 1510–15; now in St. Lambert's Church, Aurich. In its closed state, the altar depicts the motif of the Mass of St. Gregory, popular from ca. 1400, especially in the north of Europe. In this particular version, the suffering Christ, who allegedly appeared to the pope, hovers in a small panel above and is not seen by any figure in the central image, which is itself split so as to obscure even the crucifix. (Photo: Niedersächsisches Landesmuseum, Landesgalerie, Hannover.)

Figure 14. Passion altar from Cloister Ihlow, now in Aurich. In its open state, the Ihlower altar displays the Crucifixion in glorious, heavily gilded, three dimensionality. (Photo: Niedersächsisches Landesmuseum, Landesgalerie, Hannover.)

The same transcending, yet affirming of matter that we find in the central shrine of the Ihlower altarpiece can be seen in reliquaries. (See figs. 15, 16, 17, 18, 19, 20, 21, 38, 39, and 43.) By the later Middle Ages, they call attention not only to the materials of which they are made (crystal, gold, gems) but also to the materials (bones, cloth, wood) they contain. A number of reliquary triptychs for pieces of the true cross, for example, show the same move toward plasticity and tactility in the inner panel that we find in the Ihlower/Aurich altar. Not only does the materiality of the cross thrust itself insistently forward by the way it is centrally framed, but the figures who present it to us are also often in full or half relief and gilded, while the flanking side panels (both open and closed) are flat.[64]

From the twelfth century on in the West, we find many examples of what German historians somewhat inappropriately label "speaking reliquaries"—that is, containers whose shape mimics body parts (arms, fingers, ribs, etc.) We also increasingly find reliquary-monstrances—receptacles that reveal through crystal windows or disks the cloth or body fragment within.[65] Although, as historians Cynthia Hahn and Anton Legner have recently demonstrated, arm and foot reliquaries do not necessarily contain arm and foot bones, they do underline the bodily stuff they hold. But this bodily stuff is hard, decay-resistant body stuff (bones and ashes, not flesh); moreover, its nature is glorified as well as revealed. Hence, reliquaries—especially those of the later Middle Ages—explore and expose materiality in complicated ways. Denying the corruption of flesh by displaying body as hard, apparently dead bone, they simultaneously sublimate partition and deadness by sheathing such stuff in the gold and gems explicitly associated in Scripture and sermon with the life of the heavenly Jerusalem.[66] For example, in the reliquary of Thomas Becket's blood (fig. 15), the blood itself (which is presumably a few rusty, dried flakes) is hidden in a casket, not displayed, but a large jewel has been constructed on the top by backing rock crystal with red foil to evoke the redness of blood. The stuff of the jewel is palpable and shouts out living redness, but it plays visually with its own physicality; it is neither the blood in the container nor the ruby it appears to be.

In contrast to reliquaries, which both sublimate and reveal the object within, unveiling its decay-resistance as bone or wood yet lifting it to immortal life through gold and crystal, other medieval sculpture is obsessed with displaying not just death but also the decay that reliquaries resist. The quite common motif of the *transi* tomb (a sculpture in which a decaying, worm-eaten corpse lies beneath a gorgeously clothed member of the elite, represented more as sleeping than as dead) uses the stone from which it is carved to image slimy, percolating flesh (fig. 22). And the rarer motif known as "Frau Welt" (fig. 23) or, in its male version, the "Prince of the World" shows behind an elegant, aristocratic figure who faces us, the back and buttocks of a body eaten by worms and toads.[67]

Perhaps it does not go too far to suggest that the process operating here is in some ways the opposite from that which we find in the Ihlower/Aurich altar or the reliquaries I just discussed. The Frisian altarpiece and the Becket reliquary lift physical vulnerability into glory by gilding either a depiction of dying and death or an actual body fragment; the changeable (friable, partible) is revealed as such, but it is exactly its character as changeable that is cancelled, even denied, by gilding it or encrusting it with gems. Part it may be, but not a putrefying part. And even its partialness is denied by the permanence of gilding, by presenting it in a container that purports to show a far larger body segment than resides within, or sometimes even by accompanying it with a text or iconography that refers to resurrection.[68] In contrast, Frau Welt and the lower part of the *transi* tomb are almost always naked stone; it is as if the transformation works the other way. Putrefaction is not just imaged; it is not just emphasized; it is made permanent. In the *transi* tomb, it is the clothes above (elegant and ordered) that deny decay, but below, the body seems (oxymoronically) frozen in its character as decayable and decaying. In figures such as Frau Welt, this-worldly greed, pride, and

Figure 15. Reliquary of Thomas Becket's blood, from between 1173 and 1180, made by a Rhenish goldsmith in England. In traditional casket form with a lid like a gabled roof, the reliquary suggests that the fragments housed inside are gathered into a whole, yet the simulated ruby on the lid, constructed of clear glass and red foil, signals the bright red blood supposedly contained within. (The Metropolitan Museum of Art, gift of J. Pierpont Morgan, 1917 [17.190.520] Image © The Metropolitan Museum of Art.)

Figure 16. French reliquary chasse from ca. 1175–80; Widener Collection, National Gallery of Art, Washington, D.C. In the twelfth century, relic containers shaped like churches became popular. Both their form and the decoration of gold, brilliant enamel, and precious gems suggest that the bodily fragments and dust within are lifted to heavenly glory and gathered into a whole, just as believers are incorporated into the body of Christ, the church. (Photo: Board of Trustees, National Gallery of Art, Washington, D.C.)

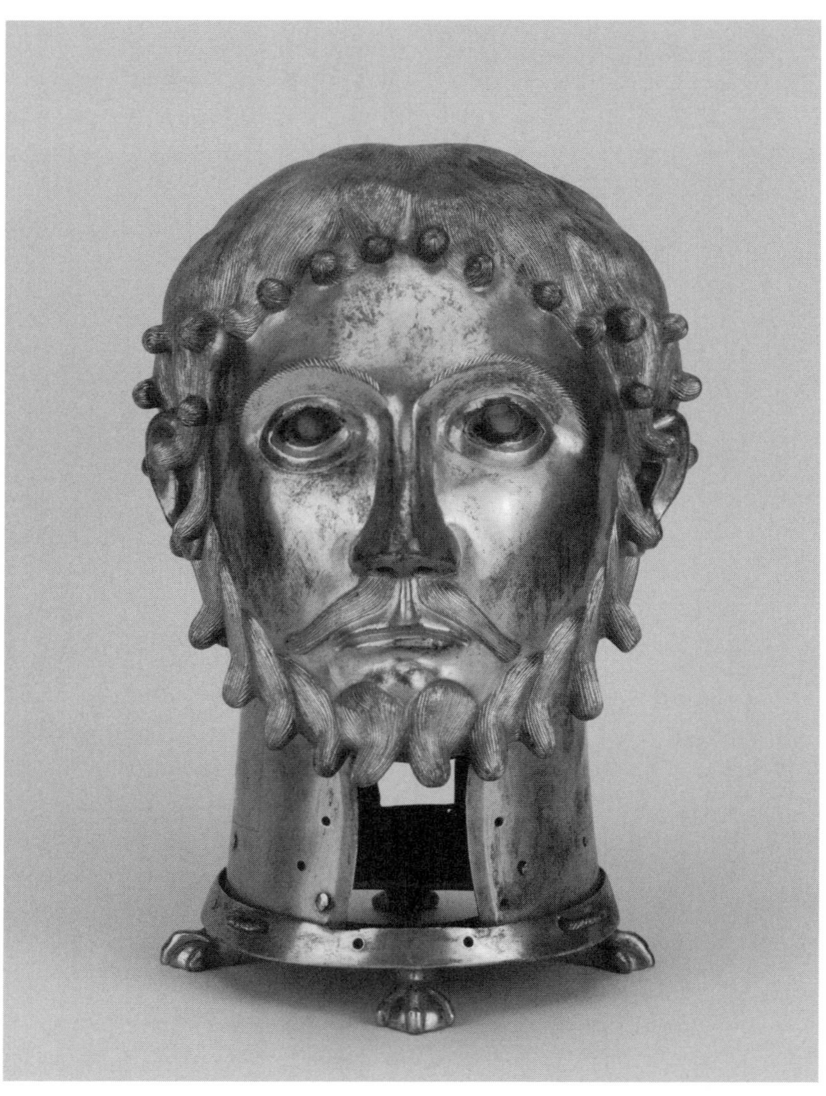

Figure 17. Head reliquary of John the Baptist, twentieth-century copy of stolen original, from the first quarter of the twelfth century, made in Lower Saxony. Kunstgewerbemuseum, Staatliche Museen zu Berlin, Inv.-Nr. 1903,37. The reliquary probably contained relics of the Baptist, perhaps a tooth. (Photo: Bildarchiv Preussischer Kulturbesitz/ Art Resource, NY.)

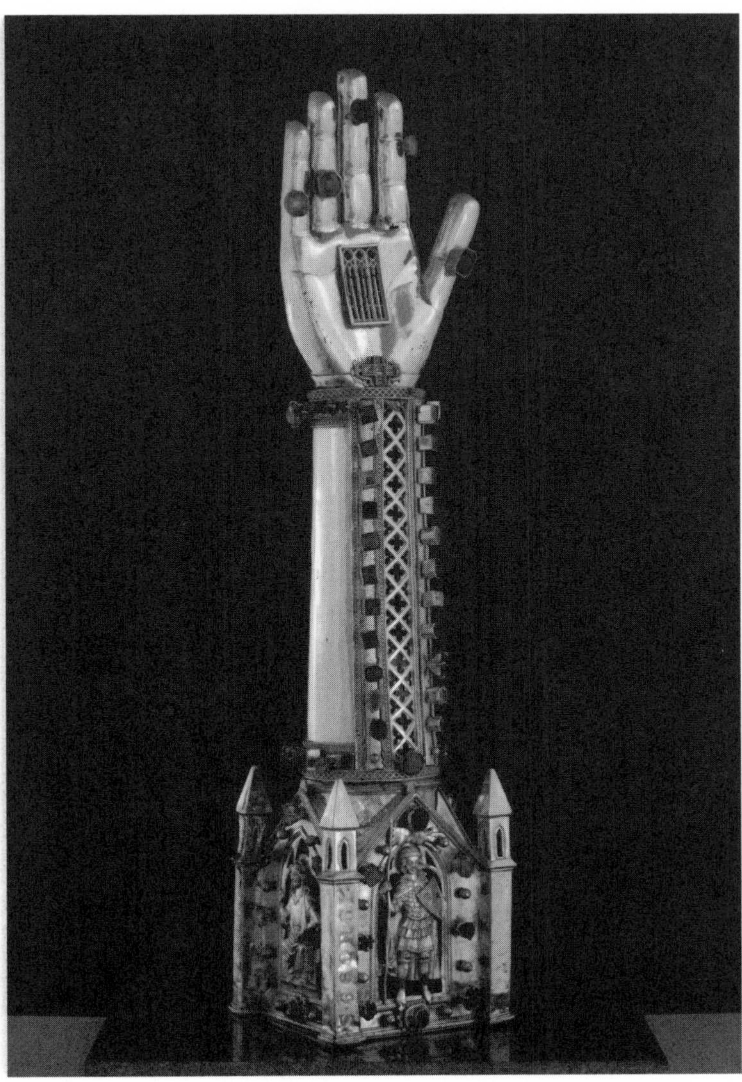

Figure 18. Arm reliquary from the Benedictine Convent of St. George, Prague, first quarter of the fourteenth century. The wrapped relic—part of a right humerus—is sheathed in armor, whose lacing is simulated by an openwork trellis through which the relic is visible. A seventeenth-century inscription on the back says "arm of St. George martyr." (The Treasury of the St. Vitus Cathedral in Prague, © The Prague Castle Administration. Photo: Jam Gloc.)

Figure 19. Arm reliquary of St. Nicholas of Myra, showing a mummified finger within, from Halberstadt Cathedral, made shortly after 1225. Exactly how the relic relates to the acquisition of holy booty by German crusaders after the sack of Constantinople in 1204 is unclear. The display of the finger naked but behind crystal and decorated with gems is an example of the growing interest in making the stuff of relics visible, but sheathing it in incorruptible material reflecting the heavenly Jerusalem. (Photo: Domschatzverwaltung, Halberstadt.)

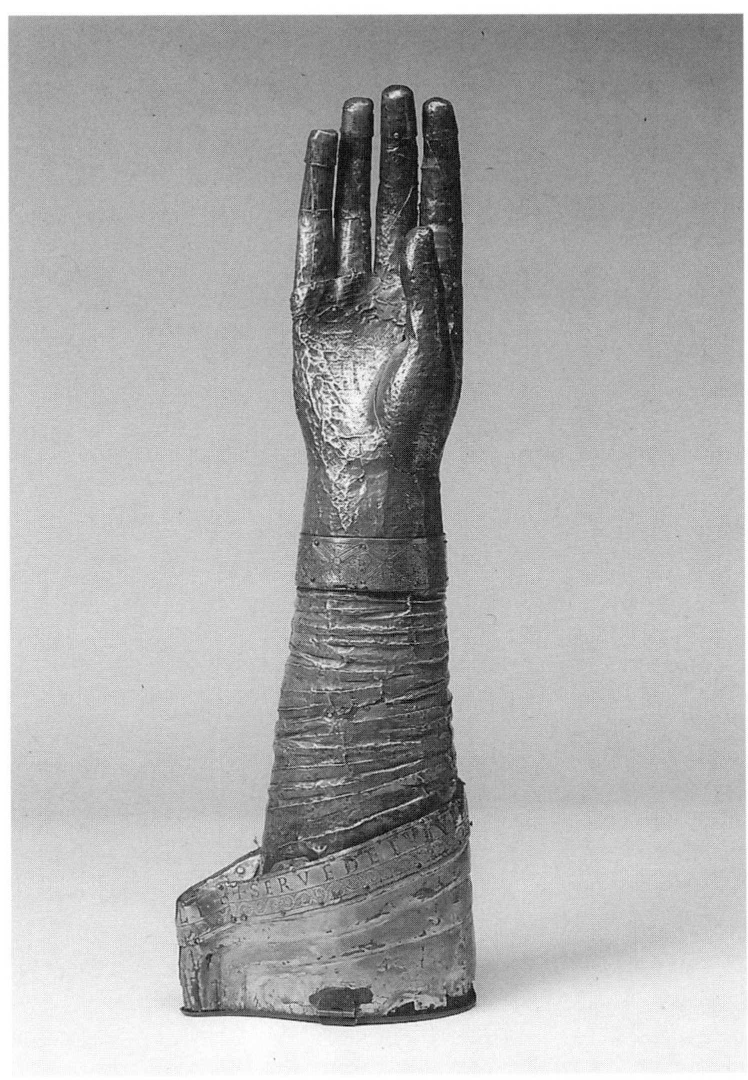

Figure 20. Arm reliquary of St. Basil from the treasury of Essen Cathedral, second half of the eleventh century. This is one of the earliest reliquaries made in body-part form. Supposedly containing within a relic of Basil of Caesarea (d. 379), the hand is covered with a liturgical glove indicating the saint's episcopal rank. (Photo: Jens Nober, © Domschatz, Essen.)

Figure 21. In the thirteenth century, the practice emerged of displaying relics in monstrances, such as this fourteenth-century example from Cologne. Such containers, used interchangeably for displaying relics and consecrated hosts, sheathed the holy matter in the crystalline permanence of heaven while simultaneously revealing that it is of the stuff of earth. (Photo: Rheinisches Bildarchiv, Cologne.)

luxury erupt in stone behind and under the garments of privilege. The bad body is forever metamorphosing into toads and worms; even its clothes are eaten by and fuse with toads and vipers. Garments slither into fragments, skin itself opens like slits in fabric. No gems or gold here, no rescuing or transcending of physicality through glitter and gleam. Rather, stark, hard, perduring decay. The depiction makes deterioration permanent, rather like those figures in Dante's inferno who undergo fragmentation and reassemblage forever.[69] There is a fear of matter here that underlines its appropriateness as signifier of evil.

Yet, as the reliquaries make clear, changeable matter is also the means—the *only* means—by which the transient can be visually imaged as permanent and transcendent.

Such analysis takes us far from what we are usually told about such objects. Even the great, often misunderstood Johan Huizinga, who had a feel for the complexity of late medieval symbols, saw them as a kind of reduction or rigidifying of an earlier, more labile and perceptive sensibility. *Transi* tombs and *memento mori* have become clichés for the morbidity of the later Middle Ages. And recently, historians have tended simply to see such concerns as induced by living in cycles of war, famine, and plague or to find in them avoidance of—or escape valves for—scapegoating and persecution of "the other." My point here is not to deny either the horror of much medieval experience or its relevance to the content of iconography and the artistic treatment of bodies and of material. Mitchell Merback and Valentin Groebner, for example, are certainly right to relate a late medieval obsession with violence, torture, defacing, and sacrifice to ugly aspects of the social and political world.[70] I wish only to resist a tendency to reduce art to a projection—or a denial—of social structure. I suggest rather that this art grapples with and utilizes what it is made of in a way that underlines and hence interrogates the fact of materiality. Behind it is an understanding of matter as *by definition* that which changes. Hence, first, its appropriateness to image evil (the percolating flesh of Frau Welt), second, an insistent need

Figure 22. Grave monument of the type known as a *transi* tomb, constructed for himself in 1424 by the archbishop of Canterbury, Henry Chichele (d. 1443). The archbishop, depicted with open eyes, reposes above in gorgeous vestments. Below lies his naked, rotting corpse. (Photo: National Monuments Record, Swindon.)

Figure 23. Seen from the front as a beautiful woman with elegant clothing, the figure known as Frau Welt is eaten from behind by toads and worms, a clear example of evil and deception represented as decay. Worms Cathedral, about 1300. (Photo: Foto Marburg/ Art Resource, NY.)

to sublimate or subsume it into glory (the Becket reliquary), and, third, a confidence that it can be a place of metamorphosis, one where humans can break through to the holy or it can be disclosed to them (the Ihlower/Aurich altar's central shrine). I will return in a later chapter to the understanding of matter that lies behind this. It is enough here to signal how different is my approach from some discussions of the death-obsessed, plague-ridden Middle Ages.[71]

Material Iconography

In the above analysis, I have moved almost imperceptibly from the materials of medieval art to its iconography. For the two cannot be separated. One could, of course, argue that material and content can never be separated. Even a completely nonrepresentational modernist work such as a drip painting by Jackson Pollock will conjure in the viewer some reminiscences of and references to objects or events associated with certain colors, shapes, textures, and so forth. But in any case, medieval art objects—representational if not mimetic or realistic—employ a complex play of subject and material. They use rather than deny the associations of materials. The employing of gold to overcome putrefaction comments not only on the nature of putrefaction but also on the nature of gold. What is represented by what is crucial.

As the examples I have already treated suggest, medieval iconography is extravagant in its physicality.[72] Moreover, such iconography was often quite expressionist and bizarre.[73] Hence, late medieval moralists such as Jean Gerson criticized it as "shameless," Protestant reformers attacked it, sometimes physically, in the sixteenth century, and the Council of Trent, held to consolidate Catholicism against the Protestant threat, legislated against what it called "disorderly" (*inordinatum*) images and "unusual things" (*ullam insolitam*).The authorities at Trent clearly referred by such phrases not only to the possibly erotic and prurient but also to the new and peculiar.[74] Twentieth-century scholars, busy cataloguing motifs and finding sources for them in the writings of high theology, have sometimes failed to notice how odd some of this really is.

Consider for a moment two of these bizarre images (figs. 24 and 25).[75] In the theme known as Christ in the Winepress, we see Jesus staggering beneath a cross, which has been made by the artist into a very complex apparatus for crushing grapes. In the so-called "Host Mill," Christ is depicted as a sack of grain poured (sometimes by his mother, sometimes by the four evangelists) into a mill; wafers of bread and/or a baby issue below. We are usually told that such themes illustrate the theology of the real presence or, in technical language still debated in the fourteenth and fifteenth centuries, transubstantiation.[76] But it is important to note how bold—almost religiously perverse—such iconography is. For all the complicated explanations of theologians that bread and wine become body and blood, what we seem to see here is the opposite: a sort of reverse transubstantiation. We see Christ squeezed under a very material machine; the red stuff in the basin evokes wine as well as blood and underlines their visual similarity. It is as if Christ's blood becomes wine. Indeed in the late fifteenth-century Middle Rhenish panel shown in figure 24, bunches of grapes float in the blood as if the bodily fluid Christ spills is congealing into fruit. In the Host Mill, what we see at the top of the image are grain sacks; the miraculous transformation is flour into bread and baby in the mill itself. In at least some versions, the change is first from wheat to wafer, then wafer to Christ (fig. 25). Thus, even where transubstantiation is not visually reversed, such iconography materializes as well as somatizes God.

We see such materializing and somatizing also in free-standing statues of the Virgin, both those found in the early Middle Ages and those from a much later period. Although the materialization is slightly more implicit here, the visual impact is nonetheless startling.

One of the late medieval devotional objects castigated by such orthodox preachers as Gabriel Biel and expressly forbidden after

Figure 24. Depicted on the outer wings of a Crucifixion triptych from the last quarter of the fifteenth century, the Eucharistic motif known as Christ in the Winepress seems here to show a sort of reverse transubstantiation. Bowed under a complex machine for crushing grapes, Christ's body pours forth blood that appears to become wine in the basin where grapes, both purple and red, seem to congeal out of the liquid before it flows on into the chalice. Koblenz, Mittelrhein-Museum Inv.-Nr. 1979/18. (Photo: Stadtverwaltung, Koblenz.)

Figure 25. Host Mill on a Swabian retable of about 1440, open state. Mary, with the assistance of the four evangelists, provides the stuff of salvation by pouring grain into the funnel; saints turn the mill; the prelates assembled below receive wafers that seem to become the baby Christ. The body of Christ is here fragmented and crushed in order to appear as a salvific whole. Ulmer Museum Inv.-Nr. AV 2150. (Photo: Schmidt-Glassner, © Ulmer Museum.)

Figure 26. This devotional object from late thirteenth- or early fourteenth-century Cologne is a small nursing Virgin, which opens to show the Trinity inside. (The crucified body and dove have been broken off.) Such objects depicted for Christians the idea that Mary is the tabernacle that houses God. In a sort of doubling of the idea of the mother of God as container, they were sometimes used to hold the consecrated host. (The Metropolitan Museum of Art, gift of J. Pierpont Morgan, 1917 [17.190.520]. Image © The Metropolitan Museum of Art.)

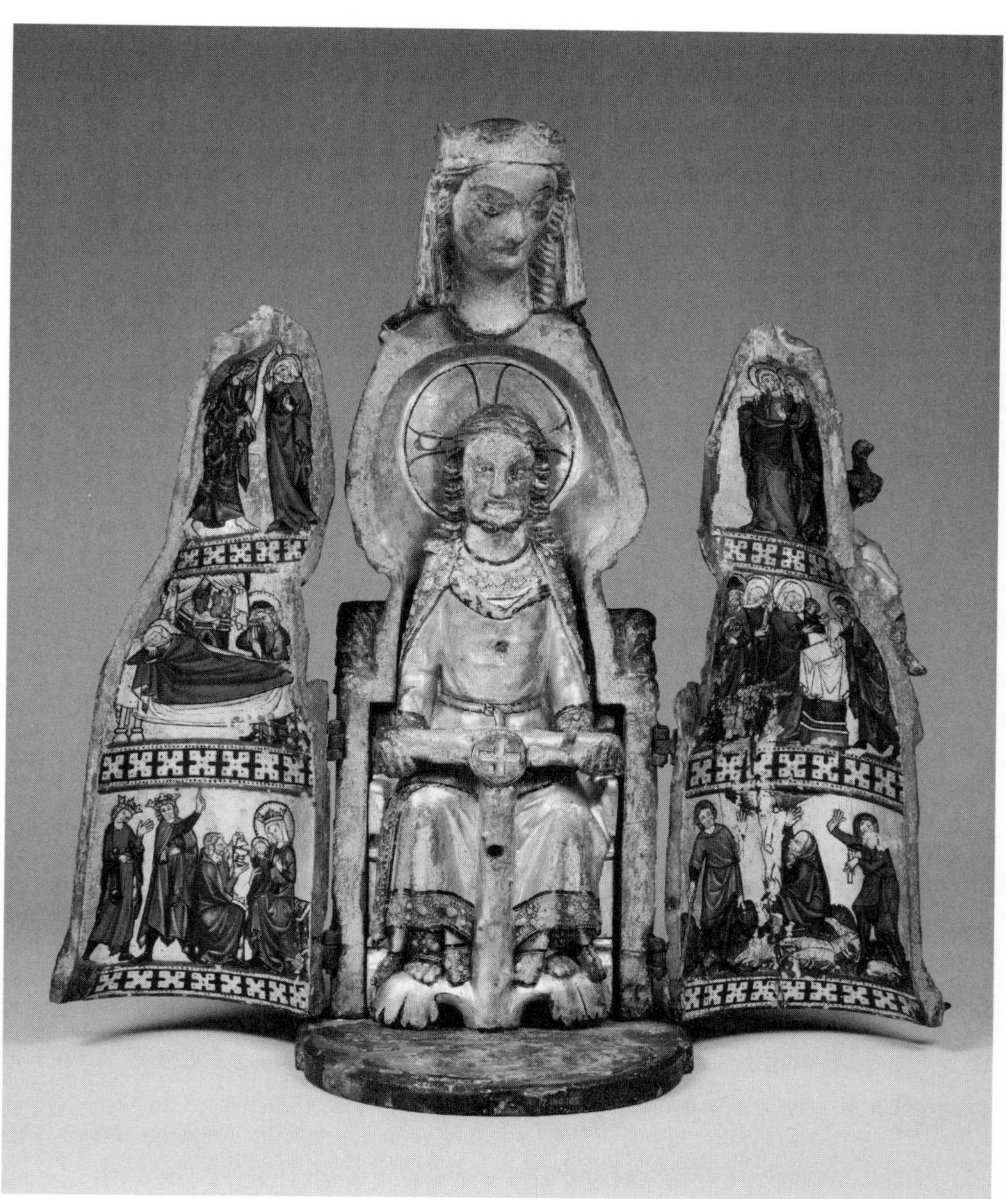

the Council of Trent was the so-called "Opening Virgin" (fig. 26). What bothered critics explicitly about the "Vierge ouvrante"—or at least some versions of it—was the implication that all three persons of the Trinity (God the Father, Christ on a cross, and the Holy Ghost) were inside the Virgin Mary while she was pregnant with Christ. To the theologians, this seemed incorrect Trinitarian theology. But what the devout saw was not just the Trinity inside Mary; they also saw Mary as a box, a physical container that opened and closed like a winged altarpiece. And the figure was in fact a container; some Opening Virgins seem to have served as tabernacles for keeping consecrated hosts.[77] Indeed, Mary statues had been material containers for hundreds of years. The first free-standing sculptures in the West are the so-called "Throne of Wisdom" statues, which were, as we know from the work of Ilene Forsyth, sometimes relic holders or repositories (see fig. 27).[78] Thus, in the early Middle Ages also, the devout encountered Mary as a container or vessel. Moreover, although the container aspect of these early figures is sometimes hidden (occasionally it has taken x-rays to find the relics inside them), their materiality is flaunted in another way. Mary not only sits on a throne, she *is* a throne, her body a seat on which her child perches to rule the world. It is less Mary's body than her materiality—her role as physical support—that is stressed visually. (See fig. 27a.) What we see is at least as much a chair with drapery and arms as a maternal figure. In such devotional objects, body and material thing (the pregnant or lactating Mary and a Eucharistic cabinet; the lap of Christ's mother, a relic container, and a piece of furniture) seem to fuse or become each other. And there is a theology underlying the fusion/confusion, for Mary *is* the container and revealer of the divine. Queen of heaven, she is a throne for one mightier than herself, simultaneously providing and displaying the child who will rule and save the world.

Yet this Mary is also a body—and a body that contains a body. In the case of the "Vierge ouvrante," she contains the body that hung on the cross (a carved crucifix); she sometimes contains as well the literal body of God in the consecrated Eucharist. In the case of the Throne of Wisdom, she often contains bits of the bodies of saints. Moreover, as some scholars have underlined, this body-container was in a sense animated by use and ritual. Throne of Wisdom statues were carried in processions. "Vierges ouvrantes" were opened and closed in private devotion almost as if giving birth. Hence, as body becomes object visually, so object becomes body in ritual and prayer. Paradoxically, to materialize is to animate—something we will fully understand only when we come, in Chapter 4, to medieval understandings of matter itself.[79]

Another example, in which iconography plays even more self-consciously with the stuff it depicts, is the so-called "Charter of Human Redemption," found on fol. 23r of the fifteenth-century Carthusian miscellany in Brit. Lib. Add. MS 37049 (fig. 28). Christ stands on Calvary (indicated by little skulls), yet the leg of the cross descends below him so that he also appears to be suspended on it. Or is it the leg of the cross? It may be a leather strip from which the seal depends, but some further object lies behind the seal, so that it almost seems as if the cross itself pierces the charter, in which case it also pierces Christ. He, in turn, displays a charter that offers salvation to humankind, yet his hands are bored through with nails that make holding anything impossible, and his blood runs onto the text. Moreover, his body, pockmarked with blood spots, blends into the charter below the side wound. Indeed, his body has almost become the charter. The self-referentiality of the image is no accident. The charter depicted is a record on parchment—that is, on skin. Christ's body is skin, too, and (as several scholars have recently noted) a number of twelfth- to fifteenth-century devotional texts use the image of pen as flail or nail, blood as ink, and Christ as manuscript (even sometimes explicitly as charter) when evoking the Flagellation or the Crucifixion. Henry Suso, as is well known, carved the name of Christ in his chest with a stylus, thereby transmuting his own skin into living parchment.[80] In such images and phenomena, the motif of Christ as text—which reflects the complex theological

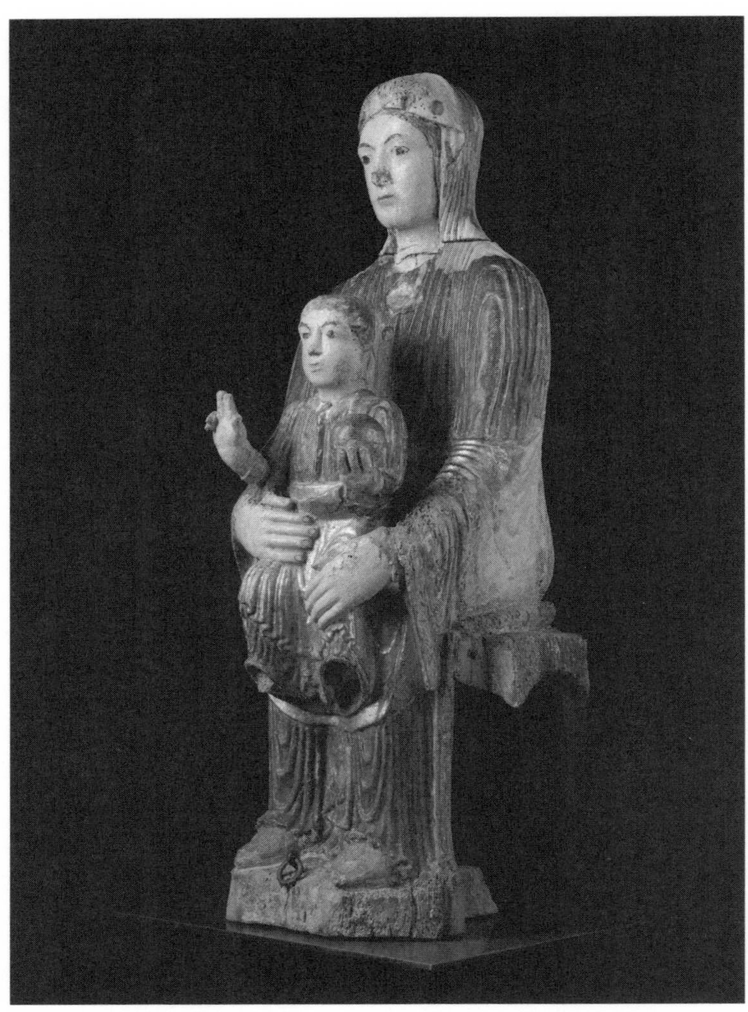

Figure 27a. Virgin and Child, from the last quarter of the twelfth century, found in Clermont-Ferrand in 1874. This type of statue has been called by historians the "Throne of Wisdom" because the Virgin bears on her lap the Christ child, who reigns as God. The first free-standing sculptures of the Middle Ages, these figures were carried in processions. Many contained relics. Thus, Mary is literally as well as figuratively a vessel bearing holy matter. She also herself visually becomes a material object. Sitting on the throne, she herself *is* a throne on which her son sits as lord and savior of the universe. (Photo: Michel Urtado, Réunion des musées nationaux/Art Resource, NY; Musée nationaux du moyen âge-Thermes de Cluny, Paris.)

Figure 27b. Another view of the Virgin and Child from Clermond-Ferrand. The photograph shows the opening for relics in the image's back.

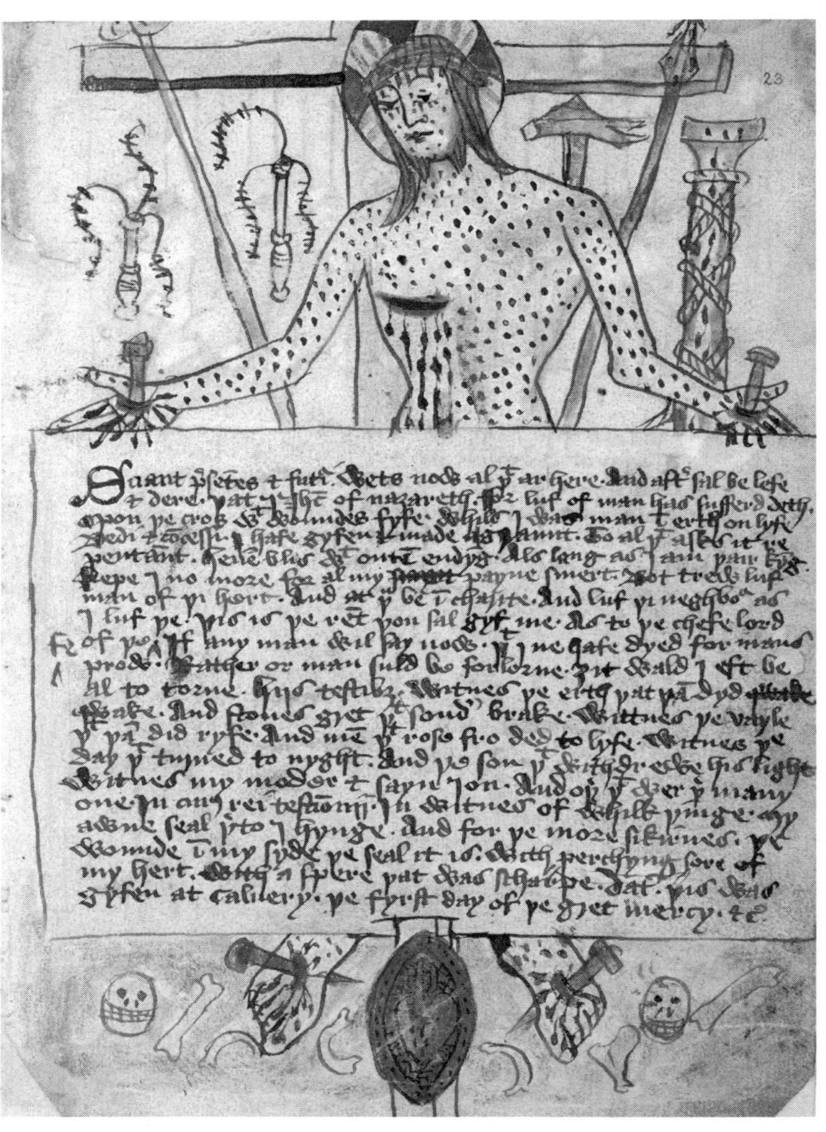

Figure 28. Folio 23r, Brit. Lib. Add. MS 37049, a fifteenth-century Carthusian miscellany. Christ stands on Calvary, surrounded by the *arma Christi* and displaying a document. His blood-spotted body seems to become the charter below the side wound, illustrating the popular devotional theme of Christ as charter of salvation and calling attention to document, page, and body as skin. (Photo: © British Library Board.)

concept of Christ as the Word of God (John 1:1–18)—is literally depicted. But there may also be another level of playing with the motif. Brit. Lib. Add. MS 37049 has only two vellum leaves, and the folio on which this Christ as charter/text/Word appears is in fact paper. Nonetheless, there is also an echo here of the fact that manuscripts, like charters, often *are* skin.[81] However crude the draftsmanship may be, the way in which the image refers to its own materiality is anything but crude. And the more it calls attention to itself as skin—the stuff on which it is inscribed—the more graphic is the body it evokes.

I take a final example in which the iconography comments both on itself and on its material and technique. A very common iconographic motif in the fifteenth century represents the late medieval devotion to the five wounds of Christ (two in the hands, two in the feet and one in the side)—a devotion that underlines the idea of Christ's blood as sacrifice offered to expiate the sins of the world. (See figs. 29, 30, 32, 33, and figs. 44 and 46, pp. 198 and 202–203.) Here, I wish to make four points about this wound iconography. (I will return to some of these aspects in Chapter 3.) First, the Savior's body often disappears entirely, to be replaced by fragments, parallel to the relics I mentioned earlier. (We see this in figure 29, an altar panel from Ulm about 1500.) Visually, the motif seems to contradict the emphasis in late medieval devotion and theology on the wholeness of Christ; it also contradicts the biblical account of Christ's death. John 19:31–36 explicitly emphasizes that the body of Jesus was not broken: "Then the soldiers . . . came; and they broke the legs of the first [thief] and of the other that was crucified with him. But after they were come to Jesus, when they saw that he was already dead, they did not break his legs. . . . And these things were done that the scripture might be fulfilled: you shall not break a bone of him."[82] Even his cloak was not divided (John 19:23–24). Yet in such representations (as in reliquaries), the body is presented as parts.

Second, despite what I asserted above, the visual partition of Christ's body is not entirely parallel to relic division. These images insist on Christ's parts as living and bleeding flesh, whereas the form of reliquaries stresses the hardness of bodily remains. Thus, Christ's body parts are a sort of double paradox. Relics are part and whole, but Christ's parts are not only part and whole, they are also dying and alive, changing and defying change. Five-wound images stress body parts as alive and bleeding, yet they also divide the body and control it. They show it spilling forth or oozing red, liquid, uncoagulated blood, yet they contain both the part and the bleeding. In the Ulm panel (fig. 29), the feet and hands are fenced in with flower petals, the bleeding heart with a barrier of thorns. The fact that the iconography refers to standard devotional objects—the petals to the rosary, the thorns to the crown of thorns—does not negate the way in which the frames work graphically to contain the bleeding inside and to gather the body parts into a whole. These frames make a visual as well as a doctrinal point. We see this even more clearly in the two woodcuts I analyze below (figs. 32 and 33). There, the blood is controlled both by being caught in the Eucharistic chalice and by the border of the shield on which the parts are depicted. The parts, gathered together by the borders of the shield, are the body of Christ that hung on the cross.

This brings me to my third and fourth points. Christ's body is not just divided and reassembled in this iconography, it is also materialized.[83] And this is so in two very different senses. First, the side wound is treated, in some devotional images, not only as the body but also as the measure of Christ. In a woodcut from circa 1490, brilliantly analyzed by David Areford, the wound represents Christ's entire body, connecting face, hands, and feet (fig. 30).[84] In this, it is parallel to other images in which the side wound stands in for the entire Christ. It does so, for example, in the Bohun Book of Hours, where we find, below depictions of the human Christ scourged and crucified, a representation of the Resurrection in which Christ's body has been replaced by a large, mandorla-shaped wound, lifted skyward from his sarcophagus by angels (fig. 31).[85] But what is more interesting for my purposes

Figure 29. *Arma Christi* with the Five Wounds, Buxheim Altar, about 1500. In this depiction of Christ's five wounds, surrounded by the instruments that tortured him, the body disappears entirely, to be replaced by bleeding fragments. Petals, evoking the rosary, and a wreath, representing the crown of thorns, provide a frame, which pulls the bleeding parts together so that they seem to form a whole figure. Thus, visually as well as devotionally, violated part fuses into salvific whole, yet remains forever pierced and bleeding part. (Photo: © Ulmer Museum.)

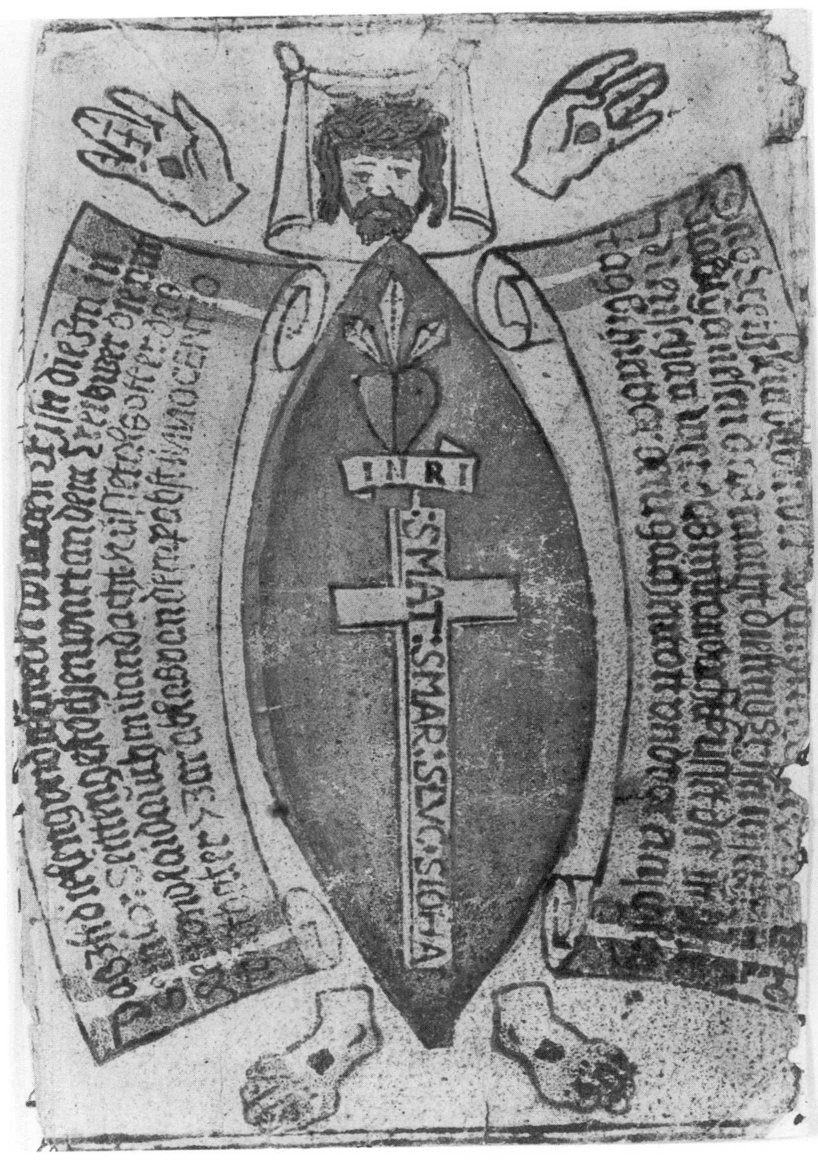

Figure 30. Wounds of Christ with symbols of the Passion, woodcut, about 1490; Rosenwald Collection, National Gallery of Art, Washington, D.C. Tipped vertically, the side wound visually becomes the body of Christ, binding the wounds in the feet and hands into a whole. It is also materialized into a measuring stick and an amulet. The scroll to the right states that the little cross in the wound, multiplied by forty, gives the true length of Christ and, when kissed, protects against disaster; the left-hand scroll promises seven years indulgence for kissing the wound. (Photo: Board of Trustees, National Gallery of Art, Washington, D.C.)

Figure 31. Folio 9v from a Book of Hours made for the Bohun family; Pommersfelden, Graf von Schönborn Schlossbibliothek MS 348 (2934). In this depiction of the events of Holy Week, Christ's body has been replaced in the Resurrection scene by a large mandorla-shaped side wound, lifted skyward by angels. (Photo: Foto Marburg/Art Resource, NY.)

here is the fact that the wound in the 1490 woodcut is treated explicitly as a measuring rod (fig. 30). The scroll to the left of the wound reads: "This is the length and width of Christ's wound which was pierced in his side on the Cross. Whoever kisses this wound with remorse and sorrow, also with devotion, will have as often as he does this, seven years indulgence from Pope Innocent." Clearly, there is something about the fact that it is purported to be an accurate measure that gives the image power. In kissing it, one earns an exactly calculated quantity of remission from the much-feared sufferings of purgatory. The explicit reference to the image as measure suggests its use in quantifying both prayers and the rewards of prayers.

There is also, in this image, the implication that measurability is self. This is even clearer in the scroll to the right, which refers to the cross shown inside the wound and reads: "This little cross standing in Christ's wound measured forty times makes the length of Christ in his humanity. Whoever kisses it with devotion shall be protected from sudden death or misfortune." Here, the length of Christ is apotropaic—a protective amulet against disaster. It is also Christ himself.[86]

The assumption that the multiplier cross is Christ echoes a fairly common medieval idea that a measure of the person is in some literal sense the person; to measure is to absorb something of the power of the measured self by contact with it. Supposed life-sized imprints of the footprints, height, and so forth of Christ and the Virgin were sometimes revered as contact relics. Pilgrims brought back from the Holy Land reproductions of the measure of Christ that were treated as more than reproductions, because they had touched places touched by Christ. According to a widely circulated story, Charlemagne had possessed an exact measure of Christ given him by an angel.[87] In this case, the measure is more than a reproduction or representation, because it comes from heaven itself. Some of the prayers that ask Christ to shield believers through his measurement speak as if Christ's length *is* his person: "Oh Lord Jesus, I beg you, because you have sheltered me with your length . . . protect and shield us poor sinning people. . . . Hide me in your length . . . as your godhead hides itself in your humanity. . . . Hide me in your holy wounds and be my protection against all my enemies."[88] In a different, but related devotional practice, a length of cord or leather was often treated as if it were the devotee. A standard donation to churches in the later Middle Ages was a measure of wick or candle wax calibrated to the height or girth of the person giving it, as if quantity of measure were self.[89]

In the use of the side wound as measure, an image of Christ's body thus becomes a kind of contact relic. The wound is treated as if it is both a physical measuring rod and a way in which the actual body of Christ is made present to believers, who, through the simple act of kissing and multiplying by forty, can participate in his salvific power. The wound is here quite literally an object.

There is, however, another, very different way in which Christ's wounds are materialized. This is what we might call a "visual materialization." In this final, visual twist, the oozing, bleeding body parts are depicted as insignia on banners or painted shields.[90] Such depiction not only materializes Christ's body and body parts but also makes sophisticated comment on its own method of representing the holy.

For example, in two entirely typical fifteenth-century woodcuts (figs. 32 and 33), the five-wound image appears to be affixed almost like a placard to the cross, where, according to the biblical account, Christ hung whole and undivided. Hence, these little woodcuts comment on themselves as depictions, both calling attention to—and denying—their status as representation. The material image on the cross (that is, the shield) becomes what it represents (Christ), and yet at various levels, the image denies this: it is, after all, an image of an image, a woodcut of a shield of painted wood.[91] The depiction of parts both is—and is not—an undivided, salvific, and glorified whole. Here, as in the Ihlower/Aurich altar, the materiality of what is represented is used in a highly sophisticated turn, but, as in the Charter of Human

Figures 32 and 33. In these devotional woodcuts from the late fifteenth century, the five wounds of Christ appear on a shield as his coat of arms. Although the bleeding pieces remain insistent parts, the border of the shield frames them and gathers them into a whole. The shield stands in for the body on the cross, thereby calling attention to the image as image—simultaneously a representation of a representation and a disclosure of the salvific power of Christ. (Photo: Bodleian Library, Oxford University.)

Redemption from Brit. Lib. Add. MS 37049, the materialization goes a step further. In these five-wound images, as in the depiction of Christ's body as the skin of a charter, body becomes object, object becomes body. Indeed, the woodcut of Christ as parts, painted on a shield hanging on the cross, carries self-referentiality even further than does Brit. Lib. Add. MS 37049 folio 23r. The shield is, of course, a coat of arms and must be understood against the background of the so-called "*arma Christi*," with all the complex overtones carried by the word *arma* (among them, chivalric identification, weapons of defense and offense, instruments and effects of execution). As his insignia, the shield stands for Christ. But by the way in which it materializes Christ, it also calls attention to itself as a depiction of a depiction. By hanging the image on the cross itself exactly where Christ hung, it suggests not just that part is whole but also that it *is* in some sense the sacrificed God-man. We begin to see that the materiality of the image itself and the materiality of the iconography reinforce each other and that both involve an understanding of matter that cries for further exploration.

But before I turn to such exploration, I must describe several other aspects of what I am calling "visual materiality."

The Material in the Visionary

As I said at the beginning of this chapter, we are often told that the fourteenth and fifteenth centuries in Christian Europe emphasized the visual. The claim is clearly correct.[92] Visions became more and more common. Women especially, thought to be more bodily than men and more in need of corporeal help, were encouraged to meditate on Scripture in a way that led to intense visualizing of scenes from the lives of Christ, Mary, and the saints.[93] It is little surprise that, after such intense mental and spiritual exercise, they often saw the figures on which they meditated appear before them. If the sisters of the Grand Beguinage in Louvain played with a Christ doll, put it to bed in a cathedral/cradle, or cuddled it against their breasts, it was only a tiny step to seeing Christ appear in the cradle or on the altar in church. Despite theories of contemplation in which the visionary was urged to rise above visualization, despite repeated clerical warnings (especially toward the end of the period) against feigned apparitions, vision accounts were a mainstay of devotional literature. Even those who could not have visions found intense pleasure in reading about them.

What has been less emphasized, however, in recent accounts of visualization and vision is how concrete medieval visions were. Their content is highly somatic and material. Both as received and as described, they are full of physical objects. Consider an example from one of the great religious texts of the later Middle Ages. Gertrude, called "the Great," a nun at the Saxon convent of Helfta in the second half of the thirteenth century, wrote down her own "seeings" or "revelations" and was also the subject of a more lengthy text written by her sister nuns. In book three of this text, known as the *Herald of Divine Love*, one of her sisters recounts a quite typical vision:

> Then, pondering within herself with the greatest wonder and gratitude the gratuitous kindness of God to her, and considering her wretchedness . . . in the greatest dejection she plunged herself, as was her custom, into the lowliest valley of humility. . . . [And] the Lord who, though he inhabits the highest heaven, loves to impart his grace to the humble (Ps. 112:5–6) seemed to send down a sort of golden tube, like a drinking straw [*auream quamdam fistulam*], from his heart which was hanging suspended like a lamp over the soul who was cowering in the valley of humility. Through this tube he caused to flow into her in a wonderful way all that she could desire. . . . If she desired to have some spiritual ornament, or anything which the human heart conceives of as desirable and pleasant, instantly all the sweetest and happiest thoughts and sensations flowed into her through the tube we have mentioned.
>
> After some time . . . she heard as though in her heart a most sweet voice . . . singing . . . "Come to me, my own! . . ." [And] she felt herself

to be drawn in an indescribable way, through the tube we have mentioned, into the heart of God.[94]

Gertrude's biographer makes it clear that the descent of the golden straw was an inner experience—what the Church Father Augustine of Hippo called "spiritual vision"—and warns, with an almost postmodern sensitivity to problems of subject and voice, that "what she there felt, saw, heard, tasted, touched, is known to her alone and to him who deigned to admit her to such a union."[95] Gertrude herself worried about this interiority. She understood that some might question the source of her visions, and she saw that claims to hear God's voice might be merely self-validating.[96] Nonetheless, it is striking how physical and concrete is the mental image (the "phantasm" or "semblance") in which Gertrude's sister nun describes Gertrude's experience of encounter with God. Grace flows to her through a direct pipeline—a golden tube similar to the liturgical straws through which medieval Christians received the communion wine or saw their priests receive it.[97] Glossing the experience, Gertrude's biographer underlines it as more than visual: "saw, heard, tasted, touched." The "vision" is auditory, gustatory, and tactile as well.

In an even more startling set of images, the book of visions from the fourteenth-century convent of Töss describes the nun Adelheid von Frauenberg as desiring that her body "be martyred" for the baby Jesus. Adelheid asks that her kerchief be used for his diaper, her veins woven into a little dress for him, her blood poured out for his bath, and "all her flesh . . . used up for all sinners." Her visual imagination not only turns self into sacrifice, for Christ and the world, it also turns body into physical object. Blood becomes bathwater; veins are woven into fabric for baby clothes. Although the highly somatic and material language remains an image of spiritual yearning at this point in the text, later in the account, such descriptions become full visions.[98] Much about the date and authorship of the sister book of Töss is disputed, but it is clear that we see here a reflection of the actual meditational practice of cloistered women.

In such meditational practice, it was not only intangibles such as mercy or grace that seemed to jell into matter or body—gold, or wood, or fabric; veins or blood. Actual devotional objects also became bodies. A chronicle from the convent of Katharinenthal in Switzerland reported, for example, that a nun who touched the hands and feet of a Christ figure lying in a sarcophagus felt them to be "flesh and blood as if a living person were lying there."[99] A sister at Emmerich thought she felt God himself when she clutched cloth against her breasts.[100] What is striking here is not so much the experience of divine sweetness or comfort found often in meditational literature as the claim that physical material becomes flesh in the encounter with God.

Needless to say, thirteenth-to-fifteenth-century vision accounts such as Adelheid's or Gertrude's were shaped not only by the prescriptions and warnings of confessors but also by genre expectations. Collections of "revelations" or "showings" were supposed to make claims to startling somatic experiences and to employ extravagant material images. But my point here is not to argue that visions such as the golden tube are merely literary tropes, as some German scholars have suggested.[101] Nor is it to take all such accounts literally, as others have proposed we should.[102] I am not arguing that Gertrude saw a golden pipeline descending from God (although she may have) or that Adelheid's veins became a baby dress. Neither Adelheid's prayers nor her visions were intended to be understood literally, although who is to say that some of her spiritual suffering may not have felt to her like a weaving and ripping of veins? My point is that these visions, in their rhetoric and in the sense of the physical such rhetoric reflects, privilege the material and not only the somatic. Indeed, they blur the line between the bodily and the material in such a way as to suggest that all matter is animate and intentional, pregnant with layers of significance.

Living Images

I have argued that medieval images, whether in wood and paint or in prayer and the imagination, were often, in a stunning and quite specific sense, material—tactile, textured, architectural, often colored and/or three-dimensional. They invited touch and taste as well as sight, not so much pointing beyond the stuff of which they are made as reflexively exploring and commenting upon its ways of evoking and representing. In their insistent materiality, they seem to articulate a power not so much beyond as within themselves.

Indeed, as we have seen, it was in exactly this period that human efforts to make art move and speak increased. Devotional statues were built so as to be amenable to being dressed, manipulated, and paraded in liturgical or private religious performances. Wooden Christ figures were fabricated with moveable arms or wheels, with crowns and loincloths that could be exchanged, or with doors in their chests to hold consecrated hosts or relics.[103] (See figs. 1, 3, 4, 8, and 11, pp. 23, 39, 40, 56, and 63.) Iconography itself animated objects in complex ways. The Mass of St. Gregory—a motif I discussed briefly above in analyzing the Ihlower/Aurich altar—seems to have begun around 1400 as the combination of a half figure of Christ appearing in his sarcophagus (based on a prototype from Santa Croce in Gerusalemme in Rome) with a depiction of Pope Gregory at the altar, sometimes celebrating mass. As many scholars have stressed, the image is a complex exploration of inner and outer viewing—that is, of seeing the Eucharistic elements and seeing through them to spiritual presence. But what is important in this connection is to note that, over the course of the fifteenth century, the vision of Christ animates visually. Increasingly, he is depicted as if he is an altar retable that has come to life in a narrative scene or a carved body that has descended from the crucifix onto the communion table. From a static, iconlike half figure, ambiguously both alive and dead, he becomes a full figure, steps forward out of the sepulcher, and pours blood into the chalice in an action seemingly aimed at both pope and viewer. Not of course a literal depiction

Figure 34. Virgin and Child with Sts. Stephen and Leonard, venerated today as "Santa Maria delle Carceri," Prato. More than a century after it was painted, a child saw this fourteenth-century image step down off its wall to clean an abandoned prison. Crowds who gathered claimed to see the figure move and weep. Almost at once, the site was authenticated by the local bishop and a church built. (Photo: Erik Thunø.)

of animated art, this enormously popular motif nonetheless unquestionably depicts, with increasing insistence, the life of a vision, and it depicts that life as the animation of an altar retable or crucifix.[104]

Efforts not just to depict objects as animate but also to bring them to an appearance of life by mechanical means were not limited to religious settings. Secular rulers and aristocrats patronized artisans (and even magicians) who fashioned moveable and indeed automated images. Paralleling Christ dolls that were made to ascend into ceilings or roll into sanctuaries, we find, in princely courts, dragon statues that blew smoke, mechanical singing birds, fog machines, and giant figures that voiced solemn pronouncements via speaking tubes.[105]

There is, however, an even more dramatic sense in which late medieval images were matter—living matter. For despite the insistence of heretics that these images were only "rotten sticks and dead stones," both dissidents and orthodox acted, as I suggested at the beginning of this chapter, as if they were not. In the fourteenth and fifteenth centuries, some images came alive in public and communal ways that went well beyond even the claims of nuns who felt fabric or wood to be flesh.[106] Indeed, statues or frescoes that were thought to alter physically or to animate in response to the needs of Christians for reward, healing, succor, or revenge are especially phenomena of the late fourteenth to seventeenth centuries, although it is important to note that the objects themselves often predate the moment of their animation by several hundred years.[107]

In Prato in 1484, for example, a child supposedly saw the Virgin Mary come down from a wall to clean an abandoned prison. Crowds who flocked to the spot saw the image change color, weep, sweat blood, open and close its eyes; within a few weeks, the bishop authenticated the site, and a church was soon built around it (fig. 34).[108] There are contemporaneous cases in Italy in Todi, Montepulciano, Florence, and Genoa, and in Germany at Altötting, Grimmenthal, and Regensburg—to cite only a few examples.[109] A fourteenth-century Italian Franciscan who visited Damascus reported a similar phenomenon.

> The monastery of St. Mary of Serdinale [Seidenaya] is built on a rock at the end of the city. . . . [B]ehind the high altar there is a grate window, four feet from the ground, and behind there is an image of the Virgin Mary: and this image is fleshlike, and from it much holy oil exudes, which has virtue. . . . [T]his oil in seven years becomes flesh; and I took some with me and it is good against every infirmity and every peril of the sea. . . . [W]e have experienced it and have escaped many storms.[110]

According to other traditions, the part of the icon that turned to flesh perspired and grew breasts, which lactated on some occasions and bled on others.

As William Christian Jr. has astutely pointed out, even in cases where shrines were established at the sites of collective visions, the cults tended to focus not on the place where the saint or Virgin had supposedly appeared but on an image that the apparition revealed. Statues or paintings thus discovered were usually said to have animated (glowing with light; weeping, sweating, or bleeding; resisting relocation or even traveling back to their original sites) as proof of the holy event. Of 137 medieval and early modern shrines in Catalonia listed in a seventeenth-century inventory Christian has studied, 111 commemorate the finding of an image to which the apparition pointed; only 14 are sites of the visions themselves.[111]

Images frequently came to life to protest neglect by the faithful or the emergence of competing shrines. They sometimes defended themselves against iconoclasts who attacked them or denied their power.[112] In the fifteenth century at Neukirchen bei Heiligenblut in Bavaria, for example, a Hussite struck a statue of the Virgin in the head, and it spewed forth blood in protest. The statue, with the sword still embedded, was venerated for centuries. In an earlier story (circa 1200), which clearly has an Eastern prototype, Gervase of Tilbury describes an attack by a Jew on an *acheiropoietic* (that is, heavenly) image of Christ kept in Rome. The image supposedly bled in protest.[113]

In some cases, cures were effected by such animated images at a distance through the simple act of an adherent's prayer to the Virgin, followed by subsequent journey to her shrine to give thanks for the miracle. But sometimes the power of the image was itself transferred by physical object. Robert Maniura has shown that in the case of Mary of the Prison in Prato, pilgrim tokens—either woodcuts or little lead replicas of the fresco—were touched to the mouths or bodies of the sick.[114] The statue of the Schöne Maria in Regensburg, located on the site of a razed Jewish synagogue after the expulsion of 1519, was said to work miracles, and cloths touched to it were used to cure sick cattle.[115] Down into the seventeenth century, engraved images of the Madonna of the Garden near Genoa were said to work miracles by touch.[116] At Erding, just north of Munich, where a miraculous Eucharistic host had supposedly been found, the little models of a Christ figure that adherents took away after pilgrimage were actually made of earth from the host-finding site; in this case, a reproduction of the miracle (a depiction of Christ bleeding in the host) was conflated with physical stuff that had touched it.[117] At Walldürn, the devout took away little silk replicas of a miraculous corporal (a piece of altar linen supposedly stained with Eucharistic blood); these images, which depicted the face of Christ that had allegedly appeared on the altar cloth, had been touched to the original holy cloth and had absorbed some of its power.[118] Pilgrim badges sometimes included a small mirror, which was understood to have captured holy rays issuing from the object to which pilgrimage was made; the rays were understood to cure physical as well as spiritual ills. Cords measuring the length of Christ and of his tomb, of Mary's grave, and of the marble slab on which Christ's body was supposedly prepared for burial were brought home from the Holy Land and were thought to carry the power of the original object with them, shielding the bearer from troubles as different as hailstones, the devil, and the pangs of difficult childbirth.[119]

As Christian has shown in the Spanish cases he analyzes, visions, like images, often left tangible proof behind. A number of sites claimed handprints or footprints produced by apparitions of the Virgin. At Tortosa, a holy belt (apparently a birthing girdle), allegedly given by Mary to an especially holy priest, was revered at least from the mid-fourteenth century on. Francisca la Brava, from Quintanar de la Orden in the province of Toledo, questioned by both town officials and the Inquisition in 1523, claimed, as did several of those who testified on her behalf, that the Virgin Mary had given her a candle wrapped in a piece of silk and a "black stone" or magnet.[120] As I pointed out in the Introduction, the famous New World site of Guadalupe became to adherents almost immediately not the place where the Virgin had appeared but the place where her image could be seen miraculously imprinted on a peasant's cloak; when the devout carried away reproductions of that image, they carried an echo or trace not so much of the vision as of the miraculous garment. Visionary experiences tended to result in a holy matter that itself animated or transformed, both authenticating and reproducing the original eruption of the sacred.

Such cases blur both the line between original and reproduction and the very different boundaries between vision, body, and fabricated object; each souvenir image both depicts and *is* the miracle whose power it conveys. The Erding model pictures the miracle but does more than picture, for it is made of the actual holy earth into which the host supposedly bled. In a slightly (to us) more tenuous connection, the Walldürn silks depict the corporal miracle but also contain, by direct contact, the aura of the original altar cloth. Measures of Christ and Mary, or their handprints and footprints, bear the power to heal not only because they are accurate mathematical representations of an original length but also because they have been touched to the place where a supremely holy body was, but is no longer. Mirrors capture physical rays of light that carry in them the power of the displayed miracle from which they emanate.

Images sometimes engendered or reproduced their own details. André Vauchez has analyzed a report from the canonization process of Peter of Luxembourg (for the year 1388–89) in which a priest is said to have applied an image of Peter to the stomach of Charlotte of Bourbon, who was suffering a difficult labor. Not only was the child born healthy, but it also bore the features of Peter of Luxembourg, as displayed on the image.[121]

Such transfer of similitude or likeness has roots in very ancient notions of imprinting, as seen, for example, in the story from Genesis, chapter 30, of Jacob's flocks conceiving spotted offspring when confronted with spotted rods. But the transfer, not just of color or health but also of mimetic, personal likeness from image to living child by physical touch, is unusual. Vauchez uses the incident to demonstrate the way in which images were replacing relics in healings. Although I do not disagree with this, my point is a somewhat different one. What I underline is the similarity of image and relic in use and effect—and in their materiality. Exactly as a relic of Peter's body might have done, the image of Peter transfers his power to the mother and her unborn child, and the transfer is accomplished by physical contact. Yet there is also a difference from relic healing. Peter's image, because it is an image, transfers something of his likeness as well. Although, as I explained above, to be "of" or "like" in medieval art is more complicated than mimetic similitude,[122] in the case of Peter's image, an almost genetic sense of reproduction creeps in. The material object is able not only to imprint a body but almost to inseminate it.

There is, we should note, nothing mechanical about the healings, or the reverence, or even the imitation that objects such as Peter's image or the Walldürn silks supposedly produce.[123] Simple application of the object guarantees neither miracle, nor vision, nor even increase of devotion. Nor is the sheer materiality of the lead token, earthen image, woodcut, mirror, or bit of silk alone effective. Someone must revere the image and its token. Miracle occurs, as recent scholars put it, in the space between object and believer.[124] To the adherent, the power is *in* the image, but the miracle is an encounter with this power. Nonetheless, what I emphasize in the cases I am discussing here is that the encounter is with a physical figure, often a *transformed* physical figure, and that its presence is frequently carried through further physical objects that participate in its power.[125]

As Pierre-André Sigal and other scholars have shown, late medieval miracle accounts came increasingly to emphasize action at a distance—that is, healings and revelations that occur because visions are seen or vows made.[126] Adherents tended to visit shrines after miracles occurred, rather than seeking them out in order to ask there, in that physical place, for the saint's aid in times of distress. This trend might seem to undercut my argument about materiality. Nonetheless, the same period saw a proliferation of animated images, which were often discovered as a consequence of a collective visionary experience, and an increase as well of objects that conveyed the power of images when taken away from shrines. Even in cases where healing followed vows and preceded visits of thanksgiving to the saint's shrine, objects increased in importance in another sense. The period was one of great growth in the offering of *ex votos*—little images of healed body parts or of terrifying experiences (the horseshoe that dented someone's head, for example)—intended not merely as thanksgiving gifts or symbols of a miraculous event but as something of the healed self offered back to God.

The Cross

Moreover, we must not forget those other cases in which images and objects supposedly came alive and impressed themselves on bodies. I refer above all to the cross. The significance of the cross on which Christ was executed, supposedly discovered by Constantine's mother Helena in circa 326 and distributed in pieces as a relic throughout Christendom over the next millennium, is far too vast to treat here.[127] I mention only two ways in which it comes into my story of late medieval materiality, especially in the form it increasingly took from the eleventh century on, that of the crucifix. The first is that a number of later medieval Christians experienced the figure on the cross as coming to life in order to comfort or accuse them. Peter Damian's vision (from the late eleventh century) of drinking the blood that dripped from the hand of the crucified and Rupert of Deutz's twelfth-century account of embracing the crucifix, which offered its open mouth for a kiss, are two of the earliest, most titillating, and most often discussed examples.[128] My second point is that the cross itself, sometimes its wood and sometimes the body it bore, impressed itself on other bodies. During the first two crusades, as Giles Constable has demonstrated, we not only hear of Christian soldiers who wore the sign of the cross sewed on their garments or even branded it into their flesh with a glowing iron, we also find claims that crosses appeared miraculously on the bodies of crusaders in life or after death.[129]

And then there are the cases of stigmata—the wounds of Christ allegedly appearing in the bodies of adherents, usually women (although the best-known case, Francis of Assisi [d. 1226], is a man).[130] Some stigmata were clearly self-induced, and some were received in fervent, body-altering trances. But some were supposedly received while meditating before the cross. As Chiara Frugoni has brilliantly explicated, iconography represented the most famous example, that of St. Francis, as an impressing of the crucifix into Francis's hands, feet, and side.[131] More and more, depictions of the event utilized black or red lines to indicate the direction of impact, as if, like rays of light focused by a lens, the wounds of Christ actually seared themselves into Francis's flesh (figs. 35 and 36).

The story of the miracle, redacted by St. Bonaventure in the *Legenda Maior* of circa 1263 to serve as the official account, stresses the artistic parallel. As Bonaventure tells it: "on a certain morning about [the time of] the feast of the Exaltation of the Cross," Francis saw a seraph bearing a crucifix. And when he "came down from the mountain," he bore with him "the image

Figure 35. St. Francis receiving the stigmata, late fifteenth or early sixteenth century. Panel from the predella of an altarpiece of the Holy Spirit, Siena, Pinacoteca Nazionale. Although the wooden cross is not depicted, the posture of the Christ figure, with arms outstretched and feet as if nailed together, makes it clear that what imprints itself into Francis's body is a animated crucifix. (Photo: Alinari/Art Resource, NY.)

Figure 36. Hand-colored woodcut made by one Caspar (active in Regensburg about 1470–80) and later pasted into a book from the Franciscan house of Ingolstadt. Munich, Bayerische Staatsbibliothek, Rar. 327. On this little prayer card, red lines show the wounds of the crucifix impressing themselves into Francis's body, not as a mirror image, but as if the devotional object—flipped around so that right side matches right side—were being absorbed into Francis's flesh. (Photo: Bayerische Staatsbibliothek, Munich.)

[*effigiem*] of the Crucified, which was not imprinted [*figuratam*] on tablets of stone or wood by the hands of a craftsman, but marked [*descriptam*] into the members of his body by the finger of the living God" (cf. 2 Cor. 3:3; Exod. 31:18).[132]

Bonaventure's language makes clear the arguments of medieval theologians that only God can craft or enliven flesh, that it is living men (not dead wood and stone) that are image and image potential.[133] But it also suggests that imitation and even assimilation to Christ can come through the contact of ordinary human bodies with a carved figure hanging on a wooden cross; what the seraph bears is a crucifix. Moreover, Bonaventure uses the metaphor of artistic production to describe such contact; the wounds are not "imprinted" (or "incised") but "delineated in" (or "marked into") Francis by the finger of God. The passage from 2 Corinthians 3 has been exteriorized and literalized. Whereas Paul said simply that "our epistle" is written by the Spirit "not in tablets of stone but in the fleshly tablets of the heart," Bonaventure uses the Pauline language to describe the imprinting or stamping of the marks of a crucifix in Francis's exterior flesh.

As figures 35 and 36 suggest, much of the iconography of the stigmatization depicts Francis as marked both by the living Christ and by a devotional object: the crucifix. For example, in figure 35—a panel from the predella of a late-fifteenth-century/early-sixteenth-century altarpiece—the posture of the winged Christ figure, with feet together and arms outstretched as if nailed, makes it clear that it is a figure from a crucifix, although the wooden cross is not depicted. In such depictions, animated image and God himself fuse.[134] And at least in Bonaventure's description, Francis becomes not only the "alter Christus"—an especially vivid and explicit imitation of the bodily as well as the spiritual Christ—but also a devotional image, that is, an incised tablet or woodcut. Hence, in such accounts, Francis almost becomes an object produced by an object. Yet he is a living object, as is the crucifix that carves his flesh and brings forth from him living blood.

In a sense, the cross, as revered in the Middle Ages, is both image and object, both representation and relic, both animate and inanimate stuff (body and wood). Present in reliquaries all over Christendom, it is the material on which Christ hung, its wood impregnated with his blood. And in legends of its origins, which circulated widely, it was understood to have sprung from a branch planted on Adam's grave; thus it is also an Old Testament relic.[135] As the crucifix, a devotional object found on innumerable altars, it is a depiction, a representation of the moment that saved the human race. It thus conflates the categories of relic and image, which medieval theologians (like some modern historians) struggled to keep distinct, and blurs the line between object and reproduction/representation (as do the mementos from Walldürn and Erding).[136]

Indeed, in an even more explicit and obvious blurring, a few late medieval paintings combine (that is, *literally* conflate) cross as image and cross as object. In the Holy Cross chapel of Karlštejn Castle in Bohemia, which I discussed in the Introduction, the painting of the Crucifixion has bits of the cross and of the *arma Christi* embedded in it (fig. 37). The painting makes the Crucifixion present not only by representing it but also by displaying in it supposed fragments of the objects that were used on Golgotha. And there are other medieval objects that conflate relic and image in complex and sometimes secret ways. A number of monumental crucifixes have been found to contain contact relics of Christ in either the head or the chest of the *corpus*: cross relics, stones from the Holy Sepulcher, a bit of the column of the flagellation, and so forth. A few contained consecrated hosts.[137] The little dressed Christ child in figure 8 (p. 56) wears a belt that informs us that a relic of the true cross has been incorporated into the "sweet child."[138] The Norfolk Triptych from the area of the Meuse about 1415 has a cross relic under the layers of paint. A Marian panel by the Master of Froedenberg (about 1410–1420) incorporates what appears to be a bit of an earlier panel of rare wood presumably imported from the Holy Land.[139] In this case,

Figure 37. In the Holy Cross Chapel of Karlštejn Castle in Bohemia, rebuilt by Charles IV in the 1360s, the painting of the Crucifixion has a bit of the true cross in the chest, a thorn in the halo, a bit of nail in the nails, a piece of the lance in the side wound, and a bit of sponge next to the body. The relics were perhaps placed after the painting was completed. A quite graphic Man of Sorrows located on the wall directly under the Crucifixion has a large opening for a relic container. (Photo: Jiří Fajt.)

the relic contained in the image is a relic of an image. Whereas in many of these instances, the relic is hidden in the object, by the late Middle Ages, devotional figures of Christ sometimes contained Eucharistic or reliquary monstrances in the place of the side wound, thus making quite visible their incorporation of Christ's body as consecrated host or of a contact relic saturated with his blood.[140]

The conflation of object and image, body and matter, representation/reproduction and numinous thing, is the point I wish to emphasize here. And it is in the later Middle Ages that it radically intensifies. Indeed, Hans Belting has suggested that images were authorized first by the presence of the holy in them.[141] The first free-standing sculptures in the West—figures of the Virgin and Child known as Thrones of Wisdom—were sometimes, as we have seen, containers for relics (see fig. 27b, p. 91).[142] So were some early monumental crucifixes. Several of the most revered medieval images were alleged to be *acheiropoieta*—that is, made by heavenly, not human hands. For example, the icon of Christ in the *Sancta sanctorum* at St. John Lateran in Rome was, according to a legend that goes back at least to the twelfth century, sketched by St. Luke and completed by an angel.[143] According to Belting, such images managed, after several hundred years, to free themselves into a different sort of significance and authenticity, valued for their per se beauty, realism, and so on. That is, the initial conflation of holy object and representation (in the several senses of the word "representation") made the emergence of mimetic representation alone and by itself possible, although only by radical rejection of earlier understandings. But the Christian materiality I am discussing here seems less a moment in the transition between cult object (image as the focus of worship) and art object (image valued for itself) than a vital characteristic of a distinct period of the European Middle Ages—that from the late eleventh to the sixteenth century. It is this period that produced the plethora of devotional images—statues of the Trinity, pietàs, winged altarpieces, embroideries, and so forth—that are, to many people today, the most familiar and salient characteristics of late medieval culture. Although we do see, in the long run, a transition from object to "art," what characterizes the later Middle Ages as a period in itself is an intensification of materiality in all aspects of the visual (even the textual visual—that is, accounts of visions). And this is not an attenuation of an earlier medieval mentality but something new, as my account above makes clear.

Belting is right: in the long run, image did become "art." Yet it triumphed as art partly because, while in many cases shedding "cult," it retained something of the late medieval understanding of the power of the material as material.[144] It is no accident that the late Middle Ages saw alongside virulent hostility to images not only an increasing awareness of the power of materiality but also a self-conscious understanding in iconography and craftsmanship that the stuff of which objects are made is part of their impact. This understanding involves more than a sense that matter is powerful, hence dangerous. It involves a sense that matter is per se living—a sense that much late medieval philosophical analysis was directed to exploring and controlling, even combating.

Conclusion

My purpose in this chapter has been to underline the sophistication with which late medieval art deploys its materiality. I have wanted thus to provide a corrective to recent accounts of medieval images as primarily a means of seeing beyond, as gesturing toward the unseen. In this sense, the chapter stands by itself as an argument about medieval devotional images as material. But I also intend this chapter as an introduction to medieval attitudes toward matter. For, as I have adumbrated here (and we will see more about it in Chapter 2), Christian materiality was a problem, as well as an opportunity, for late medieval Christians. Certainly it made for difficulties for the clergy, who found it hard to control statues that came alive, such as the Madonna of Prato, or visions that empowered women, such as the account of Gertrude receiving sweetness directly from God through a golden tube. Exactly because paintings and woodcuts, as well as mementos, could convey the power of images over distances, shrine attendants insisted on keeping a monopoly on touching such woodcuts or clay models to the originals. But the threat of matter's potency affected more than clergy and theologians. The attacks of dissidents and reformers, frequent from the eleventh century on and culminating in image smashing in some parts of Europe in the sixteenth century, suggest that ordinary people, too, feared the images they sometimes visited for succor. And they feared them, as they craved them, because the images were in some sense living matter.

With this I return where I began, to the theological tradition. For the one thing that my analysis makes certain is that late medieval images were not really, as the Lollards charged, "dead stones and rotten sticks." Or rather, as the obsession with putrefying flesh in monuments such as *transi* tombs suggests, they were perhaps "rotten," not "dead," precisely because it was so extraordinarily difficult for people in the later Middle Ages to see any matter as truly dead, in the sense of inert, rather than rotten or fertile—that is, percolating with threatening, yet glorious physicality.

When the Protestant John Hooper summed up the rejection of images in 1547, he repeated the argument that had outraged orthodox theologians for almost a thousand years: images are dead. Anything living—the very grass of the fields—is better than paint or scratchings on dead stuff. Yet Hooper described exactly the sort of pictures that had seemed to many fifteenth-century Christians to carry extraordinary power. Indeed, he might have been referring to the images of Christ's wounds hung on the cross that circulated in England scarcely three generations before—the sort of images seen in figures 32 and 33 (p. 100). Hooper said:

> [Christ] hanged not the picture of his body upon the cross to teach the people his death.... The ploughman, be he never so unlearned, shall better be instructed in Christ's death and Passion by the corn that he soweth in the field, and likewise in Christ's resurrection,

> than by all the dead posts that hung in the church.... What resemblance hath the taking of the cross out of the sepulcher, and going a procession with it, with the resurrection? None at all.[145]

The magisterial historian of English piety, Eamon Duffy, has argued that Hooper's words express "incomprehension"; the world in which images came to life and matter conveyed miracles was past. I am not sure. We see hostility in Hooper's words—and dismissal—but we also see a lurking awareness that, for several centuries, Christ's successors *had* hung images of his body on the cross to teach the people. Hooper would not have argued so vociferously against images if he had not still feared their capacity to elicit response. Many of those in the next English generations who decapitated statues to show that their power was dead clearly suspected that it was not.[146]

In Chapter 3, I will come back to the sort of images Hooper describes and consider another problematic aspect they present: the paradoxical dynamic of part and whole. But first I turn, in Chapter 2, to an exploration of the other kinds of holy matter popular in late medieval Europe.

CHAPTER TWO

The Power of Objects

What modern scholars call "religious art" proliferated widely in the late Middle Ages, as we have seen. Baby Jesus dolls lay in cribs close to the altar at Christmastime. Images of the saints were carried in procession through town and countryside to provide healing and protection. These devotional objects were not just decorative embellishments of church and chapel or devices to direct attention to the invisible. People behaved as if images *were* what they represented. To materialize was to animate. The more physical such devotional objects became, the more they were thought sometimes to come alive. A nun at the convent of Katharinenthal touched a wooden Christ figure and felt flesh and blood; a child saw a neglected fresco of the Virgin weep and wink.[1] It was especially wall paintings and three-dimensional sculptures, in all their overt tactility, that in the fourteenth and fifteenth centuries moved, wept, sweated blood—and were later hacked to pieces by those who hated them. The enthusiasm and anxiety such objects produced had everything to do with their materiality.

In Chapter 1, I began my exploration of Christian materiality with such "art objects." I now turn, in this chapter and the next, to the other forms of holy matter prominent in medieval Europe: relics, contact or effluvial relics, sacramentals, and the Eucharist—both the "ordinary" Eucharist, understood literally to have become the body and blood of Christ at consecration, and the miraculous appearances known by modern historians as *Dauerwunder*. In a sense, I proceeded backwards when I began my discussion with images rather than with these other forms of Christian materiality. For these other forms became important well before the period in which images (materialized and animated) proliferated so extravagantly.[2] Moreover, it might be suggested that in these forms, materiality is even more closely tied to spiritual power than it is in images. Bodily relics and Eucharist are less like what they present than are statues and pictures (if "like" is understood to mean mimesis), but they *are* what they present. The bones of the saints are the saints by origin and descent; pictures of them are not. Hence, cloth (or other material) that had touched the bodies of Christ, Mary, or other holy people might seem to have more immediate physical contact with the sacred than did pilgrim tokens touched to statues in order to absorb oil or power.[3] The bread and wine of communion were—so Christians were taught—the actual body of God available for incorporation into the adherent's own body, even if they only rarely appeared as flesh and blood.

I began my discussion with images, however, both because they are the aspect of medieval Christianity most accessible to a modern sensibility and because in the debates about them, anxiety about materiality—about the religious status of "dead stones and rotten sticks," as the Lollards put it—is most easily seen. Furthermore, as I explained in Chapter 1, the distinction between being something and imaging it was far from clear in medieval piety.[4] Some devotional images were thought to be in a special sense what they imaged, either because they contained relics or because legend held them to be *acheiropoieta*—that is, not made by human hands. In other cases, materials that had been touched to holy objects were thought to have become that with which they had made contact. Cords or lines that measured Christ's length or Mary's foot brought devotees into the presence of their departed bodies. Depictions of Christ's side wound that placed measures of his body length inside were both images of that wound and Christ's body itself.[5] (See fig. 30, p. 96.) Although they have been treated by modern scholars as if they were different genres, relics, images, and the Eucharist were revered by the medieval faithful in similar ways—accompanied by incense and candles, displayed in cases of crystal and gems, bowed before, and prayed to. Indeed, they were conflated, with no sense of incongruity. The Fritzlar pietà (see fig. 5, pp. 42–43), for example, probably held a reliquary in the graphically rendered side wound; the devout would thus have responded both to a depiction of flowing blood and to the Eucharist or a physical bit of holy bone, perhaps manifested through and protected under crystal.[6] Winged altarpieces, like the one from Cloister Ihlow, now at Aurich, analyzed in Chapter 1, often contained tabernacles for the Eucharist in the central shrine or displayed reliquaries just in front, so that the tactility and plasticity of the central panel was reinforced by the presence of other holy matter, although the scene was also lifted, by gilding, toward glory. In such objects, likeness and presence merged. Hence, it is easy to understand how relics of the Crucifixion (pieces of the sponge, lance, etc.) fused in people's minds with depictions of them and the depictions were then revered almost as the objects themselves.[7] People stroked and kissed such images as if Christ himself were present in them all; all "represented" him, although some in our modern sense "looked like him" and others did not.

Two Caveats

In moving now to consider forms of holy matter other than devotional images, I must make two prefatory points. First, I underline a chronological argument made in the Introduction. The Christian materiality I am arguing to be characteristic of the later Middle Ages both was and was not new. What I am suggesting in this book is that certain types of material objects, crucial in early medieval Christianity, continued to be central in the later Middle Ages, even as spiritual writers, theologians, philosophers, and dissidents found them more and more problematic. Hence, such objects came to be theorized in increasingly and necessarily complex formulations. I am also arguing that it was in the period after 1100 that holy matter began to manifest its power in new ways.

Enthusiasm for older forms of holy matter did not abate in the twelfth to sixteenth centuries. Relic collections swelled prodigiously.[8] Both the employment and the proliferation of sacramentals increased.[9] As Robert Scribner has perceptively pointed out, the insistence on holy matter is in some ways counterintuitive; it was easier, in fact, for the faithful simply to use conjurations or verbal formulae for blessings.[10] But however difficult it might be to obtain or control them, people wanted objects (herbs, water, bread, salt, prayer cards, pilgrim badges), not mere words. Moreover, there was, by the fifteenth century, a noticeable swing away from the recent tendency on the part of some spiritual directors and some of the devout to prefer reception of the Eucharist through viewing. The stress was now on physical reception of the Eucharistic elements: bread and wine.[11]

What is most striking for my argument, however, is the appearance of a new kind of miracle. To say this is not to claim that miracles generally increased after 1100. Miracles—particularly miracles of vengeance and miracles of healing or resurrection—were from the early Middle Ages associated with relic cult, and some scholars have argued (although this is debated) that there was a decline in such claims after the twelfth century.[12] I point rather to the emergence of a new type of miraculous occurrence: miracles of metamorphosis. By this, I mean miracles that involve the transformation (especially the lasting transformation) of holy matter. Stories of relics that bleed, or flower, or shine with light when fragmented are frequent in the later Middle Ages, although found earlier, and claims that Eucharistic elements turn into flesh or blood and endure as such seem to be new in the period after 1050. Miraculous branding or inscribing of wounds or signs on bodies occurs, seemingly for the first time. And as we will see in Chapter 4, the miracles discussed by university theologians were material miracles—that is, they tended to involve both the change or augmentation of matter and the arresting of the decay it was feared to represent. Hence, the problem and the opportunity posed by transformation miracles were special challenges of the later Middle Ages.

Second, I need to say a little more about how I use terms such as "elite," "learned," "intellectuals," "layfolk," and so forth. In the 1970s and early 1980s, a number of French scholars and others influenced by them tended to see a significant gap in medieval culture between popular and elite religion, which was sometimes equated with a split between folk or lay, on the one hand, and clerical or literate, on the other. Along with such an approach often went the assumption, sometimes unvoiced, that the culture of those who were not clergy, or not literate, or not "elite," was opposed or resistant to efforts by the powerful to impose Christian doctrine or practices upon them.[13] Since Peter Brown's *Cult of the Saints* (1981), with its frontal attack on such conceptualization, no one has held in any simple sense to such an assumption.[14] The reasons for rejecting it are many, but they boil down to the realization, first, that "elite" is not synonymous with "educated" or "literate" and certainly not with "clerical," and, second, to an understanding that the methods of recruitment of various groups in medieval society meant that people had complex and multiple loyalties. Hence, neither a division between clerical and lay nor one between elite and popular works very well to describe the basic contours of medieval culture, and any theory that a uniform Christian belief trickled down from church leaders—or trickled up from folk culture—must be roundly rejected.[15]

Education did not correlate closely with status, either ecclesiastical or secular. By the thirteenth and fourteenth centuries, as both the parish system and mendicant preaching spread, the laity absorbed a good deal of religious knowledge from sermons and the liturgy as well as from pilgrimage propaganda, liturgical drama, confraternity rituals, and so forth. By the fifteenth century, pious lay women might be better informed about matters of devotion than their husbands or even their confessors, who sometimes looked up to them for advice, especially advice obtained by prayer and visionary experience. Nor did ordination guarantee uniformity of belief or provide immunization against local practices. Clerical and monastic authors purveyed stories of quite astonishing marvels (including phenomena such as fairies and green men usually thought to be folkloric), often using them to induce in their readers or hearers a providential understanding of events but sometimes to titillate as well.[16] Moreover—and this is one of my fundamental points throughout this short book—our evidence suggests not only that there was no uniform "clerical culture" or "folk culture" but also that among every social group there tended to be both, on the one hand, confusion about and resistance to the sort of holy matter I am describing, and, on the other, acceptance, even appropriation and manipulation of it. My point is exactly that basic assumptions, shared by scholastics and villagers, margraves and parish clergy, pilgrims and cloistered women alike, led, as Steven Justice has recently argued, to a complex stance in which belief jostled constantly with interrogation of the holy.[17]

In what follows, I employ words such as "laity" or "university intellectuals" without the implication either that culture is created by social or ecclesiastical affiliation or that it trickles either up or down.[18] Moreover, as Chapters 3 and 4 make clear, I use such terms without any implication that a functionalist analysis is sufficient to explain the phenomena I discuss. The theologians whose ambivalences I analyze below were, as I will show, reacting to practices (such as relic cult or image veneration) they observed in churches; they were not creating them for the populace. They certainly were not merely deploying them to induce allegiance to sites or doctrines, although they were not unaware of the utility of miracle stories in pastoral care and ecclesiastical politics. Nor should we assume that the Christians of many social statuses who went on pilgrimages or worshiped in churches were either surreptitiously resisting or simply imbibing a culture provided for them by others. All this will become clearer below when I discuss holy matter as threat and opportunity, for I use this theme to describe not an opposition between social groups but rather a tension within religious reactions at every social level.

In what follows, I give, first, a definition of various types of holy matter and adduce some examples of each. Then I show how theological discussion about them paralleled some of the debates about images I looked at in Chapter 1. The parallel is important, for it demonstrates that anxiety about and enthusiasm for the power of matter was not just a characteristic of image theory, on the one hand, and iconoclastic polemic, on the other. It underlay many aspects of late medieval theology, which, as we will see, was marked by a paradoxical need to restrain (sometimes to the point of denying) and yet utilize (sometimes to the point of exaggerating) the transformative power of the material. Such anxiety was in no way old-fashioned, a mere vestige of earlier concerns. Rather, the conflict of approaches to holy objects intensified as more and more forms of holy matter were simultaneously flaunted and questioned. Third, I deal with the reflection of such enthusiasm and anxiety in praxis, with what we might call "the politics of holy matter." I also note that our understanding of this is always filtered through the agendas of those who provide the evidence, and this, too, must be explored.

Definitions and Examples: Bodily Relics and Contact Relics

Veneration of relics—the remains of holy people, first the martyrs and, later, spiritual figures such as miracle-working monks or female visionaries—originated in the third century, or perhaps even earlier.[19] The practice flourished through the Middle Ages, although (as I pointed out in Chapter 1) the form of the containers in which bodies were displayed changed.[20] From purse reliquaries and caskets (often shaped like churches) that stress the collection or gathering together of their contents to crystal monstrances and body-shaped vessels that flaunt the fragments of bone contained, relic holders developed in such a way as to make the stuff inside increasingly visible. (Compare fig. 16 with figs. 18, 19, 21, 38, 39, and 43.) Brought up from the crypts of the early Middle Ages, which were often visible to ordinary people only through holes (*fenestellae*) in the floor, tombs and their holy bodies also became more approachable and seeable in the ambulatories of Romanesque and Gothic churches.[21]

By the later Middle Ages, the division of holy bodies by church authorities and their display as parts was ever more frequent, even as both ecclesiastical institutions and secular elites came to place a premium on possessing collections—sometimes huge collections—of such holy pieces.[22] So important did bodily relics become that the faithful sometimes found it hard to observe a proper mourning period before they eviscerated the bodies of holy people to make relics.[23] Hagiographers report that after the death of Clare of Assisi, seven guards had to be posted over the body to keep the crowds who gathered from stealing bits.[24] In 1263, thirty years after the burial of Antony of Padua, his remains were translated into a raised marble sarcophagus, and his tongue (which was supposedly found incorrupt and beautiful), jaw, left forearm, and left hand were extracted and placed in separate reliquaries.[25] The forearm, which was preserved in a reliquary shaped like a head, was regularly chipped away in the sixteenth century to provide small pieces that were given to royalty and the Venetian Republic. Later inventories record relics of Antony's finger and skin in gorgeous containers that make the objects visible through crystal.[26] Some saints (Douceline of Marseilles is an example) even seem to have thought of themselves as healing bodies analogous to relics while still alive.[27]

The more bodies and objects were revealed in their bodiliness and materiality, however, the more they and their containers were encrusted with jewels and gold, underlining their permanence and closeness to—perhaps even their residence in—the heavenly Jerusalem.[28] The more they were fragmented, displayed, and circulated as parts, the more prestige was attached not only to their accumulation but also to exhibiting them in forms, such as reliquary altars or even the partly secularized wonder collections (*Wunderkammern* or *Kunstkammern*) kept by aristocrats, that make the multiplicity of items clear (figs. 38, 39, and 40). In the early sixteenth century, for example, the Elector of Saxony, Frederick the Wise (who became the protector of Martin Luther), had a collection of some 19,000 pieces, which included the supposed

Figure 38. Retable from the Cloister of St. Clare in Cologne, second opening, from about 1360. A collection of reliquary busts, each displaying its holy contents in the breast ornament, this altar groups the saintly body parts around a Eucharistic tabernacle where another form of holy matter dwelt. (Photo: © Dombauarchiv Cologne, Matz and Schenk.)

Figure 39. This fifteenth-century reliquary triptych from the Baptistry in Florence makes clear the late-medieval impulse to collect and assemble large numbers of relics.

Figure 40. This cabinet of fossils from Michele Mercati, *Metallotheca* (published in Rome in 1717) is a typical early modern "wonder cabinet" used to house a collection of rare natural specimens and other oddities. Such cabinets sometimes contained relics and supposedly miraculous objects or portents. The striking similarity between relic altars and these protomuseums shows the parallel impulses at work in various forms of collecting and wondering at powerful matter. (Photo: © British Library Board.)

body of one of the holy innocents slain by Herod.[29]

A second, closely related type of holy matter—contact relics—was also important throughout the Middle Ages. The faithful revered not only bodies and body parts but also pieces of cloth, dust, water, flowers, or herbs that had touched the saints or their tombs.[30] From distant places in the early Middle Ages come two stories of Christians making such contact relics for themselves. In a well-known passage, Gregory of Tours (d. 594) describes the practice by which pilgrims to Rome acquired cloth relics known as *brandea* from St. Peter's tomb.

> Whoever wishes to pray comes to the top of the tomb after unlocking the railings that surround the spot; a small opening is exposed, and the person inserts his head in the opening and requests whatever is necessary. No delay will result if only a just prayer of petition is offered. But if someone wishes to take away a blessed relic, he weighs a little piece of cloth . . . and lowers it into [the tomb]; then he keeps vigils, fasts, and earnestly prays. . . . [What happens next] is extraordinary to report! If the man's faith is strong, when the piece of cloth is raised from the tomb it will be so soaked with divine power that it will weigh much more than it weighed previously.[31]

At Thecla's shrine in Turkey in the same period, devotees not only carried dust from the tomb away in ampullae but also lowered objects on string through two holes in the floor so that they might be imbued with the presence of the saint.[32]

Nor did the importance of contact relics abate in the later Middle Ages. For example, Isabelle of France (d. 1270), younger sister of King Louis IX and founder of the abbey of Longchamp, was venerated after her death (although she was never canonized), and objects in contact with her were understood to possess power. Earth from around her tomb was said to heal; not only her hair but also her pillow, a goblet she drank from, and even a nightcap she knitted were treated as relics.[33] Among the relics of Antony of Padua preserved to this day is a tumbler that allegedly remained intact after being thrown from a window by a heretic who ridiculed the miracles of the saint.[34] Statues also provided objects analogous to contact relics. Cloths that had touched the statue known as the Schöne Maria in Regensburg were considered effective for curing sick cattle, and the nuns of Unterlinden in Alsace kept the hand of a Christ child statue, broken off by one of the sisters in ecstasy when the child came to life.[35] Even heroes and heroines of the Old Testament were sources of contact relics. Frederick the Wise's collection included a piece of the burning bush before which Moses stood and soot from the fiery furnace through which the three children Shadrach, Meshach, and Abednego passed unscathed.[36]

The faithful also revered contact relics of Christ and Mary (for example, pieces of Mary's mantle or straw from the manger at Bethlehem) and effluvial (that is, exuded) relics (such as Mary's milk).[37] Indeed, associated relics were particularly important in the case of Jesus and Mary, because their actual bodies were assumed to be unavailable, having been taken up into heaven. In the early Middle Ages, the "true cross" (that is, the cross of the Crucifixion) was especially venerated. Later, the sweat cloth or *sudarium* and other of the instruments (called *arma*—that is, weapons or arms) of the Crucifixion were added to it; together, these relics tended to eclipse the relics of saints. English relic lists from, for example, Exeter, Waltham, Abingdon, and Glastonbury claimed pieces of Christ's crib, bath, and cross, of the table from which he ate, of the seal from his tomb, of the sponge, nails, and thorns of the Passion, and even a vial of water from the River Jordan.[38]

The high and later Middle Ages saw unparalleled enthusiasm for transporting the Holy Land to Europe. Pilgrims took earth from the Holy Sepulcher to put under the floor of their chapels and brought home measuring sticks of the length of Christ's tomb that were then used to calculate numbers of intercessions owed. After the fall of the Latin Kingdom of Jerusalem made pilgrimage to the Holy Land more difficult, the Holy House of Nazareth and pieces of the manger of Bethlehem appeared miraculously in Italy so that the faithful could continue to make visits to the objects that had touched the bodies of Christ or his mother.[39]

By the twelfth century, effluvial and quasi-bodily relics, such as the holy foreskin from Christ's circumcision or the blood of Christ, also reached new prominence. In the north of Germany, for example, the transfer of particles of a blood relic between the cities of Lübeck, Cismar, and Braunschweig undergirded relations of filiation and loyalty between episcopal and monastic institutions. At the convent of Marienfliess, the nuns used their blood relic to compete with other houses for pilgrim revenues and perhaps fabricated documentary evidence to support it.[40] At Schwerin, the blood of Christ, preserved in expensive jasper, was supposedly acquired by Count Henry I from a papal legate while Henry was on crusade in 1219 and not only stimulated the building of a blood chapel with daily services revering it but also drew other relics to it. Louis IX of France sent a thorn from the crown of thorns to join it in 1260.[41]

Objects associated by tradition with the life of Christ often came to be seen as a kind of effluvial relic because of claims that they were soaked with Christ's blood. For example, the holy staircase in St. John Lateran in Rome was identified, at least from the mid-fifteenth century, with the marble steps Jesus climbed and descended on the way to trial before Pontius Pilate and hence was revered as stained with his blood. Supposedly brought to Rome by Constantine's mother as a gift to Pope Sylvester I (311–35), the twenty-eight steps are still today climbed by the faithful on their knees. The veil of the Virgin, enthusiastically venerated in late fourteenth- and fifteenth-century Bohemia, was holy less because of its intimate contact with Mary than because it was saturated with Christ's blood, which supposedly spilled on it at the Crucifixion.[42]

From the later Middle Ages also come our best-known stories of relics themselves undergoing or causing miraculous transformations. In the fourteenth century, for example, Pope Clement V granted an indulgence to those who viewed the liquefaction of the relic of Christ's blood at Bruges, which allegedly occurred every Friday between 1303 and 1309.[43] Claims for the liquefaction of the blood of St. Januarius also date from the fourteenth century, although the relic itself was said to derive from a fourth-century saint.[44] The hairs of the thirteenth-century holy woman Mary of Oignies, preserved apart from her corpse, supposedly came alive for an hour and cured the sick; the foot of Agnes of Montepulciano (d. 1317) rose from her bier to salute her saintly visitor, Catherine of Siena. On occasion, relics produced holy stuff themselves. The body of Agnes, for example, caused manna to fall from heaven and, like the bodies of several other medieval holy women, supposedly produced miraculous oil.[45] When a cross relic owned by Jane Mary of Maillé (d. 1414) bled upon division, the blood was collected and placed in the two cross reliquaries with the two pieces of wood. Even imitation contact relics could undergo transformation. The nail Alda of Siena (d. 1310) had carved to aid her meditations oozed sap three hundred years later.[46]

Definitions and Examples: Dauerwunder

A third type of holy matter, the Eucharist—understood to be Christ's body and blood present to the faithful in every mass—was treated throughout the Middle Ages as if it were a bodily relic of Christ.[47] Although theologians and ecclesiastical authorities were sometimes dubious about the practice, consecrated wafers were buried in altars, along with and in place of relics. They were used in healings and to authenticate oaths. As holy matter, the Eucharistic wafer was understood to cure sterility, drive away enemies, and control natural events, extinguishing fire or stilling hail and windstorms.[48] Indeed, one of the causes of *Dauerwunder*—the literal transformation miracles characteristic of late medieval piety—was the tendency of lay people to take the consecrated wafer away from church under their tongues in order that they might conjure with it or use it to heal disease or to increase the fertility of their flocks or produce. It was when the Eucharistic elements were thus "abused"—that is, when preachers convinced the populace that such practices were abuse—that the elements were rumored to protest, causing the bush or field, fishpond or beehive, into which they had been introduced to bleed, reverberate, or glow as reproach or revelation.[49]

From the twelfth century on (and despite the emphasis of many theologians on Eucharistic real presence as by definition invisible), visionaries came increasingly to see the figure of Christ—sometimes as a baby or a suffering man, sometimes as mutilated flesh—in the consecrated bread and wine. A number of Low Country women, denied the chalice because of illness or a tendency to extravagantly enthusiastic reception, by-passed their priests entirely and nursed from the crucifix. According to one of the versions of the revelations of the fourteenth-century Italian holy woman Angela of Foligno, the saint saw Christ "with the eyes of her spirit" at the moment of communion, first as living and then as dead on the cross.[50] The fifteenth-century French monastic reformer Colette of Corbie was said to have received, when she prayed to the Virgin, a vision of "a dish completely filled with carved-up flesh like that of a child. And she heard this reply: 'This is what I request of my beloved on account of the horrible sins, injuries, and offenses people do against him, offenses that tear him into smaller pieces than the flesh cut up upon this plate.'"[51] Although Colette's vision was not received during mass, the equation of Mary's son with macerated flesh on a dish is clearly based in a Eucharistic theology that materializes God into matter that is really flesh under the appearance of bread.

A winged altarpiece, probably painted about 1350/60 for a convent of Clarisse nuns in Nuremberg, presents a less disturbing revelation (fig. 41).[52] Clare of Assisi, crowned by an angel, receives a vision of Christ as a baby in the wafer (called in the banderol "the bread of heaven") and asks him to protect her and her sisters, which request he immediately grants (also in a banderol). The painting thus materializes still further what a visionary supposedly somatized and materialized (that is, experienced as bodily matter) in her devotion, and the materiality is here

Figure 41. This panel from a winged altarpiece, probably painted about 1350–60 for a convent of nuns in Nuremberg, shows Clare of Assisi receiving a vision of the Christ child in the consecrated wafer. In most late medieval Eucharistic visions given to women, the visible somatization and materialization of God is not so much a proof of the doctrine of the real presence as a gift of special grace to a devoted worshiper. (Private collection.)

associated with comfort, protection, and the glory of heaven. An altogether nastier and more sinister image is found in the late fifteenth-century *Siebenhirter Hours*, made for the first Master of the Order of St. George. On fol. 158v, priests administer the sacrament to, respectively, a devout believer, who sees a child on the paten; a conventional worshiper, or doubter, who receives bread; and a heretic, or lost soul (further denigrated by being depicted with black skin and skimpy attire), who receives a toad. The miniature may picture a vision, or it may simply visualize for us, the viewers, a theological argument, but it in any case graphically displays the sort of showings or revelations that are often reported in medieval vision collections.[53]

The visions of Angela, Colette, and Clare of Assisi were individual, and however lasting their importance to the recipient, ephemeral. In some cases, such as Angela's revelation or Gertrude of Helfta's reception of the golden tube discussed in Chapter 1, the text claims explicitly that they were seen only with the inner eye. But we know of a few early medieval cases of more material visions.[54] From the days of the Church Fathers, stories were told of doubters in Eucharistic presence—sometimes even groups of doubters—to whom blood or bleeding flesh appeared. Already in Paschasius Radbertus's *De corpore et sanguine Domini* (830–833), the author himself included the story of one Plecgils, rewarded with a vision of the Christ child because he wanted to see "the nature of Christ's body" in the wafer; he also included other, more threatening stories, supposedly of the Fathers Basil and Gregory the Great, in which a Jew and a doubting woman saw the flesh of Christ. Later manuscripts of Paschasius's work interpolate several more stories of doubting Jews who see flesh, including one whose tongue is paralyzed by Eucharistic reception, and a particularly graphic story, borrowed from the Lives of the Fathers, in which "a certain Scythian who was great in active life [i.e. in works of piety] and simple in faith" sees an angel descend to the altar, slaughter a boy spread out there with a knife, catch his blood in a chalice, and then break his body into pieces.[55] In all of these stories, however, emphasis is placed upon the return of the transformed elements to bread and wine, a result for which the officiant explicitly prays. Once the doubting Scythian has received his vision, he is instructed by his more sophisticated companions that God knows human nature cannot eat raw flesh; thus, this compassionate God transforms his body back into bread and his blood into wine so that faith can receive it. It is almost as if the reverse transformation is the important miracle.[56] In the later eleventh century, Guitmond of Aversa, reporting one of the stories also found in Paschasius, states that Pope Gregory stretched out his hand over a transformed host particle, imploring God to return it to its accustomed species of bread because the doubting woman, now faithful but suffering from a horror of flesh (*horrorem carnis*), did not dare to communicate.[57]

Although it is not certain when the first instances occur in which such caution and horror depart, a radical change in attitude is involved when the vision itself becomes enduring, preservable holy stuff such as the wondrous wafers of Wilsnack, Gottsbüren, and Andechs or the bloody altar cloths of Walldürn and Bolsena.[58] Such materialization and literalization of vision into object seems to have begun in the period around 1200.[59] There is at least one eleventh-century report of miraculous stuff preserved for veneration, although our account of it is at two removes from the supposed event.[60] But it is only later that such accounts become common and document identifiable cult sites. By the late twelfth century, sources refer to pilgrimages made to chalices that held Eucharistic blood or even to transformed hosts themselves. Both Heribert of Clairvaux and Gerald of Wales tell of a host in Flanders half of which changed into flesh, while the other half (the part held by the priest's fingers) retained the appearance of bread. Kept in a crystal container, it was verified, we are told, by "faithful and honest clerics of the French king." People streamed to the spot. Gerald reported that he journeyed through the region eight days after the miracle and scrutinized it for himself.[61] After the supposed host desecration in Paris in 1290, accounts in which

Jews were held to be responsible for producing the enduring miracle became popular in certain regions, especially southern—and a bit later northern—Germany. By Nicholas of Cusa's day, such miracles of enduring stuff were the focal point of pilgrimages in a number of places in Europe and provided for the faithful new sources of miracle-working matter and hence new foci for devotion. Famous sites included Daroca in Spain, where a blood-stained corporal, carried as a banner, supposedly repelled Muslim attack; the bleeding host in Brussels, allegedly the result of Jewish desecration in 1369–70; and the bloody corporal of Bolsena/Orvieto, first referred to in the fourteenth century and made famous by Raphael's paintings in the Vatican.[62]

It is clear that the ordinariness and easy availability of the matter animated in such *Dauerwunder* contributed to their proliferation. Especially for northern realms that were far from the Mediterranean cradle of early Christianity, the acquisition and importation of traditional relics from the Holy Land or from the places of early martyrdoms could be expensive, time consuming, or even impossible. Although difficult to induce or predict, the bleeding of hosts or altar cloths could occur locally and provide sudden and very useful competitive claims to prestige and cult. Such objects thus played an important role in changing the religious landscape, enabling new towns and hamlets to compete with established sites by offering their own goals of pilgrimage.[63]

Sometimes thought to be manifestations of God's power and love, enduring Eucharistic miracles were more and more frequently seen as divine responses to abuse of various kinds: theft by criminals, conjuring by ignorant women, ritual impurity on the part of priests. As they became more accusatory, they also became bloodier. Increasingly after 1290, *Dauerwunder* were anti-Jewish libels. Hosts were thought to erupt in blood because they had been stabbed and fragmented by Jews wishing to test or conjure with them.[64] Such hosts were understood as material objects by which Jews spread anti-Christian activity from town to town. They were even used in Christian judicial proceedings (ecclesiastical and secular) as physical evidence of Jewish misdeeds. At the trial of alleged desecrators in Sternberg in northern Germany in 1492, the nails and table supposedly used by the perpetrators were actually introduced as physical evidence against the accused.[65] Two decades later, after a trial in Brandenburg that resulted in the execution of forty-one Jews and a Christian thief, not only bits of the violated bread but also wood and a paint chip into which blood had allegedly soaked were translated to Berlin by the bishop and kept as relics.[66] Thus, in the same period in which statues and wall paintings were thought to come alive in order to bestow benefits or protest desecration, other physical objects, such as relics, contact relics, and consecrated wafers, increased in prominence and began in new and more literal ways to announce the holy within them. (See fig. 42.)

Definitions and Examples: Sacramentals and Prodigies

The Eucharist was not the only type of matter made holy by clerical act and carrying in its materiality intrinsic power. The other sacraments also were understood to be effective through a material object (for example, the water of baptism or the oil of last rites). Although sacramental theology was perforce complicated, since the water of baptism did not become the Holy Spirit in the same way the Eucharist became Christ's body and blood, the physical element or *materia* of the sacrament was crucial.[67] It was not just a signifier of grace; it made grace present. There was no baptism without water (unless it was the baptism of martyrs by blood—also a quite material presence). Moreover, there was the whole class of objects that were from the time of Alexander of Hales (d. 1245) denominated "sacramentals" (*sacramentalia*) in contrast to "sacraments" (*sacramenta*) but were often confused with them. Most of these went back to the early Middle Ages—a time before the number of sacraments was limited to seven or their effectiveness was defined by theologians as *ex opere operato* (that is, by the fact of the action being performed). Holy water, palms from Palm Sunday, candles blessed at the Feast of the Purification (known in

Figure 42. The miraculous bleeding host of Dijon in its monstrance. Folio 17v, Ogier Benigne's Book of Hours, Baltimore, Walters Art Gallery, MS W291. Given by Pope Eugene IV to Duke Philip the Good of Burgundy in 1433, the host (to which vague allegations of Jewish desecration had accrued) was housed in a magnificent gold monstrance made for it in 1454. This depiction of it was added to a Book of Hours around 1500 by the family of Ogier Benigne, comptroller of the Dijon waterways. (Photo: © Walters Art Museum, Baltimore.)

England as Candlemass), herbs from the Feast of the Assumption, St. Blaise water and St. Agatha bread from the feast days of their respective saints, pennies vowed to saints by bending or marking them, and wax from Easter candles known as *agni Dei* are only a few examples.[68] Objects such as spears and swords used in knighting rituals and on crusades were also blessed, as were the small arrows carried as talismans against plague.[69]

However much some theologians disapproved of the words some blessing formulae used to elevate such objects, most of the faithful clearly thought blessings added to the water, palms, candles, salt, or grain a physical efficacy that was conveyed to those who consumed or touched them. Blessing formulae expressed this: the objects acted *per virtutes*, *per vim benedictionis*, and so forth.[70] For example, a wine blessing of uncertain provenance from the fourteenth century reads: "God of Abraham . . . we pray that you will deign to pour into this wine creature the power of your perfume [*ut fundere digneris in hanc creaturam vini odoris tui virtutem*] that it may be an armor of defense for your servants, so that the ancient enemy may not enter their viscera or find entry or take up a seat there."[71] Not only the power poured in but also the nature of the defense is presented in strikingly physical terms.

A late-fifteenth-century blessing for radishes (long roots from a plant of the mustard family, used as relish) displays a similar sense of material power injected into the plant and of its consequently inherent efficacy. Although the Trinity is invoked, the root is expected, once blessed, to be useful in itself and to drive out demons.

> Let us pray. Oh God, who hast miraculously created all from nothing [*mirabiliter cuncta creasti ex nihilo*], who hast commanded the earth to produce different seeds . . . and hast implanted [*imposuisti*] different sorts of medicine in them, bless and sanctify this radish [*raphanum*] that it may be useful to all in soul and body.
>
> I exorcize you, creature radish, in the name of the Father, Son, and Holy Spirit that you communicate no evil spirit but rather [act]

> to the honor of the Father, Son, and Holy Spirit, that wherever you are dispersed, every unclean spirit is driven from the place.[72]

Given such understandings of efficacy, it is hardly surprising that the faithful used such things as medicine for humans and animals or aids in childbirth, carried them as protection against robbers and natural disasters, or put them in the beds of newly baptized children to ward off witches. As Walter Stephens has commented, many sacramentals were not so much countermagic as counterdemonic.[73]

Moreover, sacramentals, like relics, could perform transformation miracles, either inducing change or stilling its ordinary progress. A number of saints supposedly healed with bread they had blessed. In a striking miracle that associates holy bread with repelling decay, the story is told of the Danish Cistercian Eskil (d. 1181), who requested such bread from St. Bernard while on a visit to Clairvaux and wanted to toast it before returning to Denmark to protect it from corrupting. The saint forbade this, arguing that one should trust blessing more than toasting. Predictably for the genre, the story claims that the blessed and untoasted bread remained fresh and enjoyable for a long time.[74]

By the fifteenth century, other sorts of objects—parallel to sacramentals but not necessarily given their efficacy through clerical blessing—became popular as well and raised the anxiety of religious authorities because they seemed perilously close to amulets and hence to magical manipulation. An example, recently discussed by John van Engen, is the cult of the Holy Name, popular in the 1420s and 1430s, which led to use of tablets inscribed only with letters as aids in prayer. Some criticized such objects for scandalously erasing the cross and Christ; others doubted their spiritual efficacy. For my purposes, the objects are yet another example of the fusing of body, material, and sign that we see in Suso's action of carving the holy name in his chest as if he were parchment. But they are also an example of the threat and the opportunity of materiality.[75]

The Dominican Bartholomew of Florence, attacking the use of such tablets by Bernardino of Siena, made it clear that their very physicality was suspicious. However much Bernardino might insist that the tablets were only triggers of inner devotion, pointing to deep Christological secrets that needed to be glossed by priests, Bartholomew charged that their very gilding and roundness drew the people to idolatry. The church had ruled (warned Bartholomew) that the only circle the populace could adore was the host. Moreover, accounts of the origins of such tablets made it clear that the originator, Bernardino, had simply decided to have the tablets made. There was thus even a hint that objects, producible or reproducible by any Christian, could conjure up divine power or provide a dwelling place for the numinous.[76]

I close this catalogue of types of holy matter by pointing out that the fifteenth and sixteenth centuries saw the increased importance of objects that were on the border, so to speak, between the sacred and the anomalous: the prodigies and oddities collected by the faithful as signs—or more than signs—of divine favor or dismay. Although there was often debate about their status or nature, all sorts of things were preserved, by both Catholics and Protestants, as evidence of God's power and intent. Even objects of Muslim provenance such as ostrich eggs and crystal lamps entered such collections.[77] The Catholic Duke Albrecht V of Bavaria in the late sixteenth century had in his *Wunderkammer*—one of those special rooms filled with objects that foreshadow the modern museum—bread baked from grain that had miraculously fallen from heaven, the sleeve of a peasant stained by a rain of blood, and a piece of wood God had supposedly petrified when a man cut logs for his fireplace on Good Friday instead of going to church.[78] Albrecht's collection also included—alongside the gallstone of his uncle, a wooden pear, and several alimentary stones from cud-chewing animals—the branches and nuts of a tree that not only miraculously flowered on St. John's Day but also miraculously changed its flowering date upon the papal calendrical reform of 1582.

What is important about this and other wonder collections is the fact that objects such as the nut tree were accepted not only as the result of miraculous intervention by God but also as proof of it. In this, they are parallel to the girdles, candles, and stones received by Spanish visionaries from Mary and the saints as proof of their earthly visits and points of contact with their presence and power. Indeed, holy matter was increasingly seen as authentication of legal or doctrinal positions. After the Sternberg trial I mentioned above, not only the tabletop and awls or nails used to perpetrate the abuse but also a stone bearing the footprints of the rabbi's wife, the iron pot the priest allegedly tried to redeem by selling the hosts to the Jews, and the hosts themselves—in a painted and gilded tabernacle—were kept in the church.[79] The tabletop and stone survive to this day.

Further testimony to the prominence of objects in late medieval piety is the increasing use of *ex votos* by the faithful. Sometimes an actual body part (for example, a bladder stone), sometimes a replica of a miraculously healed body part (for example, a wax model of an eye or a formerly cancerous breast), sometimes a sort of mnemonic device (such as a crutch or the chains of redeemed or miraculously liberated prisoners), *ex votos* were material offerings that gave back to God the stuff, or a representation of the stuff, he created and cured. Occasionally, the object or matter (wax, for example, or a coin) was offered to God or the saint prior to the desired miracle, and the vowed material was then applied to the diseased or injured body part to produce a cure before being returned to God.[80] In *ex votos*, the miraculous and the everyday fused, as did image and object, object and proof, object and self. At Sternberg, *ex votos* were hung all round the tabernacle of the desecrated hosts, including chains of prisoners and a little silver model of the city of Kolberg.

As the case of *ex votos* suggests, the various types of holy matter I have discussed here are not easily separated from each other. To Frederick the Wise, the body of a holy innocent, the straw from Bethlehem, and soot from the fiery furnace were all relics. There are even cases where the form of a reliquary itself seems almost to confuse relic and contact relic, body and object. The fifteenth-century reliquary of the Merovingian goldsmith St. Eligius, for example, contains a bit of bone visible through a small crystal at the center joining, but the entire container is made in the form of the saint's attribute (fig. 43). The faithful who viewed it would have seen a small piece of St. Eligius *as his hammer.*[81]

Moreover, it would clearly be odd to insist on deciding whether the stone marked with an image of the Holy Family found in the heart of Margaret of Città di Castello after her autopsy was a bodily or a contact relic.[82] (The distinction used today between first-class, second-class, and third-class relics is postmedieval.) Cloth pieces from the Schöne Maria in Regensburg that allegedly imparted health to animals are analogous to both contact relics and sacramentals without being exactly either. Wax vowed to a saint and applied to a cancerous breast or throat was a sort of *ex voto* before the fact. Pennies bent in honor of a saint and then used for the cure of animals or humans functioned as sacramentals did, whether or not they were blessed by clergy. The oil-exuding Syrian icon described by Niccolò da Poggibonsi is parallel to Western relics and holy tombs that reportedly exuded healing oil or water; some Syrian devotees even thought the icon flowed with Mary's milk.[83] And theologians such as Aquinas who were suspicious of relics of Christ's blood alleged to descend from Golgotha admitted that *sanguis Christi* might flow from violated statues and crucifixes, hence conflating some very different liquids and making their sources analogous. To Albrecht V, a measure of the Virgin's body, earth from Jerusalem, stones of odd shapes, and wooden carvings of fruit were all collectibles; only some of them are relics or miracles or proofs of divine intent, but they tended to be jumbled together in Albrecht's displays. All carried something of an aura as wonder-inducing. If not exactly divine presences, they were not ordinary objects, either.

The faithful were often themselves confused about how religious objects related to the divine. Uncertain about the

Figure 43. Hammer reliquary of St. Eligius, East Flanders (?), fifteenth century. Brussels, Musées royaux d'Art et d'Histoire, Musée du Cinquantenaire, Inv. 4150. Made for a relic of the Merovingian goldsmith St. Eligius, which is visible through the rock crystal in its center, this golden hammer in the shape of the saint's attribute conflates the symbol of the saint with his physical remains. (Photo: © Royal Museums of Art and History, Brussels.)

difference—if any—between sacraments and sacramentals, they used both theurgically.[84] The woman who sprinkled ground-up host on her cabbages probably did not think she was behaving differently from the man who used blessed radish root or a marked penny to keep his livestock healthy.[85] To many, St. Agatha bread seemed no different from the consecrated Eucharist, just as the ablutions cup (which held wine the priest used to wash the chalice after consecration) was often taken to contain Christ's blood. Altar linen on which the host and chalice rested could be seen as a sort of contact relic, whether or not it miraculously displayed blood when wine was spilled on it. As I mentioned in Chapter 1, pilgrim trinkets from Erding were made of holy earth that was supposedly permeated with bread and wine transubstantiated into blood; they depicted and *were* the stuff of miracle. Votive tablets inscribed with "IHS" were (or so some authorities feared) a substitute for Christ and the cross. Lengths of linen or string brought back from the Holy Land and held to be the measure of Christ's body were not so much images as presences—relics that made the absent body tactile and visible. What modern historians call "images" of Christ's side wound, especially when they included such measures, were presences, too. And when people gave to God measures of wax calculated to the length or weight of their own bodies in thanksgiving for delivery from disaster, they were giving themselves.[86] Understood in this light, even the gallstone preserved in Albrecht V's *Wunderkammer* may have been not simply an odd bit of matter, but rather, as Katharina Kaliardos has argued, an object on the border between curiosity and *ex voto*.[87]

What all this makes clear is that the various types of holy matter I have classified here (mostly in an attempt at orderly exposition) were powerful because they were physical presences. It was *as objects* that they conveyed divine power. Moreover, they were complexly material and hence involved in transformation (whether miraculous or natural). Because matter was that which changed, miraculous matter could change miraculously—proliferating, metamorphosing, even facilitating the change or augmentation or repair of other matter. But because it was by definition that which changed, it was subject to passing away as well. Even blessed oats went sour, holy water vessels dried up, miracle hosts deteriorated into dust.[88]

The Theology of Holy Matter: Relics, Sacramentals, and Dauerwunder

Such things made learned theologians quite uneasy. As I explained in Chapter 1, the materiality of images was a problem. The Second Commandment, after all, warned against making as well as worshipping a "graven thing." Hence, despite the support some of them gave to certain miraculously animated statues or panel paintings, theologians and preachers, both orthodox and dissident, struggled to avoid the suggestion that images were or could be living per se. Images, they argued, are only signs pointing to an exemplar or triggers that directed the attention of the faithful to an ultimately *un*seeable divine.

In similar fashion, theorists jumped through intellectual hoops to avoid certain other implications of the idea that the holy is instantiated in matter. The discourse could become quite abstruse, as the examples that follow will demonstrate. In discussing such theories, I am, however, less concerned with the details of argumentation than with the ambivalence displayed. For the learned could not entirely dismiss a sense that the holy operates in and through matter. The doctrines of creation (that matter has been created by God), of the Incarnation (that God became human in the figure of Christ), of the resurrection of the body (that the material would in some sense be present in heaven at the end of time), and of divine omnipotence (that God could make matter behave in ways that violated the natural laws he also established) militated against such dismissal. Hence, we find even university professors talking out of both sides of their mouths or—to put it more elegantly—conceptualizing the world through paradox.

Thomas Aquinas, for example, explained that a relic is not the living body of the saint "on account of its difference of form"—

that is, it is no longer informed by the saint's soul, which is in heaven. Like the image, it should be venerated for that toward which it points—in this case, not the saint at all but God, who works wonders through it. Yet a relic *is* the saint, he says, "by identity of matter, which is destined to be reunited with its form."[89] In honoring bits of saints, we revere physical stuff that will be reassembled, resurrected, animated, and glorified at the end of time. In other words, the relic both is and is not the saint. Insofar as it is, what matters is its matter.

Aquinas and some who followed him (mostly members of the Dominican order) held that there could not be bodily or quasi-bodily relics of Christ, such as the holy foreskin or vials of his blood. Christ's whole body had already ascended into heaven; hence, no part could be left behind without threatening his perfection. Aquinas wrote:

> All the blood which flowed from Christ's body, belonging as it does to the integrity of human nature,[90] rose again with His body; and the same reason holds good for all the particles which belong to the truth and integrity of human nature. But the blood preserved as relics in some churches did not flow from Christ's side, but is said to have flowed from some maltreated image of Christ.[91]

In an earlier discussion, however, Aquinas himself admitted that there were plausible theories according to which bits might have been left on earth:

> What is assumed ... is never laid down, but the Word of God assumed in our nature not only body but also blood. Therefore his blood was never laid down and returns to him in resurrection. But [one can point to the contrary evidence, namely that] ... the blood of Christ is said to be preserved in several churches up to today.
>
> To this, the reply is that in resurrection, both Christ's and ours, all that is of the truth of human nature [*de veritate naturae humanae*] is restored but not those things that are not of the truth of human nature. And about this—that is, what is of the truth of human

> nature—there are different learned opinions, according to one of which not all nutritive blood [*sanguis nutrimentalis*]—that is, blood generated from food—pertains to the truth of human nature. Since therefore Christ ate and drank before the Passion, nothing prohibits there having been in him some nutritive blood that would not pertain to the truth of human nature and would not have to return to his body in resurrection.[92]

In other words, Aquinas admits there is an explanation of physiological processes that makes blood relics plausible. And we should note that even in his rejection of relics from the body of Christ, Aquinas accepts the miraculous production of holy matter—in this case, blood—from mutilated devotional objects such as crosses.

Moreover, despite Aquinas's dismissal of effluvial relics from Christ's body, a number of other theologians (many of them from the Franciscan order) defended blood relics, both ontologically and as supports to popular piety. They argued, in other words, that Christ could have left bits of his blood behind as traces to stir up enthusiasm at times of crisis or lukewarm religiosity, and they bolstered such reasoning with quite technical discussion of human physiology of the sort we see Aquinas summarizing in the second passage quoted above. (They asked, for example, whether blood provided at conception and blood from food were different bloods, how much blood was essential to the body's core [its *veritas humanae naturae*], whether all elements of human physiology were replaced over time, and so forth.) The later Middle Ages saw widespread enthusiasm for the sort of effluvial relics these theologians defended. A number of visionaries and devotional writers (especially but not exclusively women) revered with special intensity such somatic presences.[93] The nun Bridget of Sweden and the beguine Agnes Blannbekin were devoted to the relic of the holy foreskin.[94] Pope Innocent III (d. 1216) explicitly refused to doubt the foreskin relic, and later popes supported it with indulgences.[95]

Dauerwunder presented even more of a conundrum. Some scholastic writers went so far as to argue that the body and blood of Christ could never be seen. "Transubstantiation" as an explanation of Eucharistic change had been required at the Fourth Lateran Council in 1215 (although with considerably less precision than historians sometimes realize), and that definition meant that only the substance of the elements (what they were by definition) changed; the accidents (that is, the appearance) remained the same. Hence, if an individual or even a group saw a host or a communion cup change to blood, they were not (according to this theory) seeing what was really there. For essence or substance is not seeable; what is seeable is accidents. Appearances of blood or flesh in the Eucharist, whether transient or long-lasting, must be—if not illusions or frauds—either the result of special miracles worked by God in the imaginations of viewers or new "red things" created in bread and cup to enhance faith. The presence of the material, human, living Christ in the elements was (according to this interpretation) guaranteed by its *un*seeability.[96] Anything seen would by definition be accident, not substance.

From the Carolingian period to the end of the Middle Ages, there were, moreover, spiritual writers for whom presence was experienced and authenticated exactly by its beyondness, or (perhaps better put) its within-the-soulness, not its physical graspability.[97] Jean Gerson (d. 1429) wrote: "It is not what our bodily eyes see but what the eyes of our heart see that is God."[98] The author of the early fourteenth-century devotional dialogue *Schwester Katrei* remarked that if God were to reveal himself in the Eucharist as he truly is, "the eyes of the people would break."[99] A number of theologians and devotional writers hypothesized that God had chosen to hide Eucharistic presence in bread and wine exactly because of a natural human horror at blood (*horror cruoris*). Roger Bacon (d. 1294) claimed that the sacrament "is veiled . . . [because] the human heart could not endure to masticate and devour raw and living flesh and to drink fresh blood."[100] Nor was skepticism about the palpable presence of the divine in matter limited to intellectuals and contemplatives. There were ordinary Christians, too, who doubted the more extravagant claims for *Dauerwunder*, and not only because they suspected fraud. We find pilgrimage accounts from the later Middle Ages in which travelers expressed doubts about the claims of shrine attendants both to the possession of miraculous objects and to the healings they supposedly produced.[101]

Theologians and ecclesiastical authorities did not by any means always treat holy objects literally as loci of the divine. Like images and relics, the Eucharistic elements could be treated as signs or "similitudes." Liturgists often explained Eucharistic details allegorically. It was important for symbolic reasons, they argued, that the elements be *like* what they signified. Wine was red to look like blood. Bread was round and white, not only to evoke flesh but also to image body and community through the way it gathered pieces (grains) into one loaf. The species were of two kinds because humans are dual, body and soul, and Christ redeems both. Wine was distinct from bread (although each part includes the whole) because in sacrifice, blood is spilled, separated from body.[102] In such exegesis, likeness is crucial to the religious impact of objects; hence, the effect is anything but arbitrary. But likeness remains allegory or symbol.

Yet all orthodox theologians agreed that the holy did reside in matter. After consecration, the Eucharistic elements were not only signs or mementos. They were Christ: Christ human and Christ divine. Visionary nuns might be accused of hysteria or of faking specific revelations.[103] Individual local pastors might be convicted of fabricating *Dauerwunder* in order to promote pilgrimage and garner revenues.[104] But it was hard to reject all arguments for the authenticity of Eucharistic visions and miracles. The real presence of Christ in consecrated wafer and cup could not—at least not without coming under suspicion of heresy—be denied. Hence, if Christ were really present, an omnipotent God could surely signal or manifest this in a variety of ways, sometimes quite shocking and literal. Some theologians, such as the twelfth-century writer Gerhoh of Reichersberg, simply assumed that Christ sometimes chose to show himself in Eucharistic appearances.[105]

Indeed, even matter found in the penumbra of the Eucharist or associated with it came to seem more than ordinary. Although the Eucharist was sometimes allegorized, the obverse also occurred. Allegory was sometimes literalized into contact relic. For example, Archbishop Edmund Rich of Canterbury (d. 1240) poured wine over the wounds of a crucifix and drank it as if he were drinking blood. When the monks of the abbey of Weingarten spoke of "blood drinking," they meant a ritual imbibing of wine into which their own blood relic had been dipped.[106] In such practices, matter that is analogous to effluvial relics or the Eucharist, or in contact with them, fuses into and becomes the matter of Christ. Likeness—"similitude"—slips into presence.

Moreover, there were theologians and prelates (frequently those who also defended effluvial relics) who supported enduring Eucharistic appearances as such. An indulgence letter of Pope Innocent VIII in 1487 spoke of the corporal miracle of the Spanish monastery of Maria del Zebrero as if it were Christ's real blood: "Suddenly, in the aforesaid chalice, true blood miraculously appeared, visible to bodily eyes, and part of it flowed from the aforesaid chalice onto the linens that were on the altar, and this same blood remained visible and today is on view reserved as a relic, like the blood of a man or a goat recently spilled, although it appears coagulated [*coagulatus*—that is, sticky, not dried]."[107] There is no suggestion here of a bloodlike object or a specially created "red thing." What appears is "true blood" "today . . . on view," "visible" as if "recently spilled." Like real blood, the miracle coagulates, as the blood of a wounded man or a sacrificial animal does after its shedding.

Or to take a less straightforward example. The early sixteenth-century pastoral writer Johannes von Paltz, a member of Luther's own monastery at Erfurt, saw *Dauerwunder* as explicitly directed against unbelievers and heretics, who were thought to deny the sacrality and redeemability of the material. In a move that shows how complicated learned discussion of the issue had become, Paltz argued that the host miracle at Sternberg in 1492, supposedly the result of an attack on a Eucharistic wafer by Jews, was not a real manifestation of Christ's substance. But he acknowledged it to be a special creation by God, not only to refute the errors of Jews and Hussites but also to excite lukewarm Christians to increased devotion to the (unseen) blood of Christ.[108]

Theologians also tended to treat sacramentals with confusion and ambivalence. They sometimes suggested, as did the blessing formulae themselves, that sacramentals, like sacraments, acted *ex opere operato* (that is, by the fact of performance) and that power was inherent in their matter.[109] But they sometimes insisted that they were merely reminders of the power of the creator, dependent on the intentionality of the petitioner or even on the collective faith of the church.[110] The thirteenth-century theologian William of Auvergne, bishop of Paris, for example, stated that the idols of the heathen had a certain efficacy from "execrable consecration," just as the wax of an *agnus Dei* received power from papal blessing to halt lightning and salt gained the virtue of driving out demons. But he also said that the faithful should not pray that water vanquish demons or bells keep the weather fast, but should rather entreat God himself for these effects.[111]

Indeed, the fifteenth-century preacher Geiler von Kaisersberg discussed sacramentals in language that appears flatly self-contradictory.[112]

> You have heard that people should not use magic to drive out magic and what they should do when they are sick from magic.... But there are... things that are ordained that people should use against magic:... penance and sacramentals [*die sacramentaliche ding*] such as blessed salt, blessed candles, palms, Easter fire, and other holy things.... Now I want to talk about holy water.... And I say that the evil spirit has power over us because of sin, and not only over us but also over everything that pertains to our body, such as clothing, food, drink, house, etc.... If someone blesses something [that is, water] and attributes it to God, then you can drive out the evil spirit with it, just as when one wishes to consecrate a church or baptize a

child. So you exorcize the bad spirit with it [the water], just as you present the child before the church, which we call offering [*einsegnen*], so this is not other than what we do when we drive out evil spirits.... And in your houses you have blessed water, which you call "winewater," but you should not call it "winewater" but rather "blessed water," because these holy vessels can dry out, but wine vessels do not dry out [that is, one cannot add to a holy water container]. And in this way, we exorcize bad spirits from ourselves and from the things that belong to us.... And if you add much blessed salt to the holy water, it removes sin....

But I say that sacraments such as holy water and similar things (should I call them sacraments?) do not have their power from the institution as if they were true sacraments [*habent nit ir krafft von ir auffsetzunge, als die gewaren sacrament*], but from the devotion they receive. It is not the water you sprinkle on yourself that has the effect, but the devotion and your understanding of it and the faith with which you use the water. So it works not only by your belief but also by the faith of all Christendom and the holy Fathers who have prescribed such blessed water.[113]

Geiler here begins by recommending sacramentals as a kind of countermagic. Although he staunchly rejects magic and any suggestion that sacramentals might be categorized as magic, he identifies certain blessed objects as effective against magic. He initially suggests that once blessed, they work *ex opere operato*, as sacraments do, and seems to equate the water of baptism (a sacrament) with holy water (a sacramental), using the word "sacrament" for both. He then, however, feels compelled to question whether holy water is a sacrament and subsequently to deny it, asserting that its efficacy depends on belief—not only individual belief but the faith of the entire church as well. He even implies, in his reference to the Fathers, that an articulated theology of sacramentals is necessary to prevent abuse. Moreover, in that curious refutation of the custom of calling holy water "winewater," he perhaps suggests that the devout are simply adding water to the sacramental to keep it going, so to speak, just as they would add wine to a wine keg. Holy water should, however, be used up. The remark seems to reflect not just a sense of the impropriety involved in treating blessed objects like ordinary ones but also an anxiety that the blessed object might slip out of clerical control if the faithful could just keep topping up the container. One of the dangers of sacramentals was clearly the fact that objects, once blessed, could be used by the faithful for a wide variety of purposes far beyond what the clergy might originally have intended or prescribed.[114] This danger was only magnified if the faithful could multiply the substances for themselves.

A similar anxiety seems to lurk behind the fifteenth-century condemnation (later lifted) of the cult of the Holy Name. Authorities feared, somewhat inconsistently, that such objects were both too powerful and not powerful enough. In other words, they argued that veneration of letters on wood might be both idolatry (because inappropriate veneration of matter) and a waste of time (because tablets could not be effective as inducements of worship). But they also surely worried that such aids to devotion could be homemade.

Like the arguments against Holy Name tablets, the discussions of Geiler and William of Auvergne are cautious and contradictory. They argue that the power both is and is not in the object. Such ambivalence is clearly predicated on a need to maintain a clerical monopoly on the creation of holy matter. But it also goes deeper. It seems to involve a questioning of the extent to which power may reside in sacral objects, as well as a questioning of the recipient's response. Raised apropos holy water, the question—at least as posed by Geiler—seems to ask whether matter per se ever carries sacrality. Raised apropos Holy Name tablets, it suggests fear of such objects, even as it doubts the existence of the very power it fears. Nonetheless, there are also, in these discussions, vestiges of a quantitative and frankly materialist approach. Geiler, for example, remarks that "much" salt must be added to holy water to make it effective against sin. In other words, the more holy salt, the more holiness in the water.

Dissident and Heretical Critiques

The story of dissident criticism of Eucharistic theology, relic cult, and pilgrimage practices in the two hundred years before the Protestant Reformation has often been told. It, too, underlines the extent to which the problem of holy matter was at the center of theology and praxis in the high and later Middle Ages. Moreover, since these critiques are often described for us by their opponents, the very stereotyping of them as rejections of what I am calling Christian materiality tells us as much about the hopes and fears of the orthodox as about heretical or dissident practice. Whatever ordinary Cathars, Lollards, Waldensians, or Hussites thought, those who opposed them charged that they were rejecting the presence of the divine in the material.[115] This suggests both that such critiques were especially feared and that theologians and polemicists who defended the church against what they argued to be heresy suspected the paradox of holy matter to be a crux—perhaps *the* crux—of current problems.

In the eleventh and twelfth centuries, a number of dissidents, such as the group at Arras in the 1020s and the followers of Peter of Bruys a century later, were charged with rejecting all material objects of worship, even crosses, churches, and cemeteries. Writing against the Arras heretics, Gerard of Cambrai asserted, going beyond the group's own arguments: "You believe that nothing of a material nature should occur in church."[116] Peter reportedly burned crosses, charging that they were instruments of torture, argued that church buildings were mere heaps of stones, opposed alms giving, and denied any literalist interpretation of Eucharistic presence. Meanwhile, criticism of clerical wealth and power was increasingly conceptualized by opponents of such criticism as dualist or Manichean—that is, as rejection of the possibility of any goodness in matter. The Waldensians, who may not have held antimaterial opinions or objections to relics and realist Eucharistic theology per se, were charged with such because of their radical antisacerdotalism, which spilled over into opposition to the wealthy (and hence, to them, corrupt) clergy who consecrated the Eucharist, blessed sacramentals, and preached the resurrection of the body. By the thirteenth century, antiheretical polemics directed against the Cathars of southern Europe charged them with attributing evil to matter in any form and hence denying the humanity of Christ, the reality of the Crucifixion, bodily resurrection, the Eucharist, even burial rites for the dead. In the fourteenth and fifteenth centuries, as we have seen, Lollards and Hussites were understood to oppose relics and images and to hold a spiritualist interpretation of the Eucharist because they opposed what art historian Horst Bredekamp has astutely characterized as the idea of "wonder-producing, God-filled matter."[117] But it is important to note that neither group rejected the Eucharist as a rite, and indeed, the Hussites made central to their demands the reception of a kind of holy matter ordinarily denied to the laity—the wine of the chalice.[118]

Criticism and condemnation of criticism hardened during the fifteenth century, but the theology of holy matter remained ambiguous and confusing. Although Thomas Netter opposed the Lollard William Whyte when he rejected images because they were dead matter, the perfectly orthodox theologian Robert Holcot had said a century earlier that images were "dead."[119] The much-admired theologian and commentator Gabriel Biel (d. 1495), who argued for the physical reception of the Eucharist instead of spiritual communion, agreed with Holcot and Whyte that a living man was a better image of God than "dead matter." Orthodox preaching, such as the *Road to Heaven* I quoted in Chapter 1, warned as stridently against reliance on "pieces of wood" as any Lollard tract.[120]

Not only did orthodox defense of devotional objects often echo "heretical" concerns, those who rejected orthodox conceptualizing of Eucharist and image retained both some forms of holy matter and some earlier theorizing of it. In the early sixteenth century, part of the Protestant mainstream adhered to some sort of real presence in the Eucharist. Luther indeed defined it as "consubstantiation"—a theory some medieval theologians had held, three centuries before, to be an explanation philosophically preferable to "transubstantiation."[121] Moreover, sixteenth-century Protestants, despite opposition to relic cult and images, preserved accounts of prodigies as material signs of God's action in the world. Although Catholics were more apt to retain actual objects in *Kunstkammern* as proof of divine support, most written accounts of miraculous physical signs such as comets, rains of blood, or monstrous births were made by Protestant polemicists.[122] Such parallels make it clear that acute need for holy objects, combined with radical suspicion of them, was central to religious attitudes at the end of the Middle Ages, whether those attitudes were perceived to be superstitious, dissident, heretical, or at the very core of orthodoxy. Everyone condemned everyone else for misunderstanding how the divine intersected with the material, but no one denied that it did.[123]

The Example of Johannes Bremer

As a final example of how complex and ambivalent discussions of holy matter became over the course of the later Middle Ages, I turn to the learned German Franciscan Johannes Bremer. In 1455, in a short treatise called "magisterial" in several of the manuscripts, Bremer classified holy objects into three types, which parallel the categories I employ above. The reasoning behind his classification is important. Bremer wrote:

> There are, in the church militant, great and precious relics: the clothing of Christ, the cross, and other of his arms [*arma*—the instruments of the Passion]. And there are, so the pious believe, major and more noble relics, that is, the flesh and blood of Christ reserved under their proper species [presumably the foreskin and blood relics]. And there are the greatest and most noble relics, in which it is necessary to believe for salvation—that is, the flesh and blood of Christ under the sacrament of the Eucharist. The first are great, because they are Christ's *arma* and the instruments of our redemption, although separated. The second are greater, because

> they are something of the humanity of Christ and were joined to the divinity [*quia sunt aliquid humanitatis Christi et fuerunt divinitati coniunctae*].[124] The third are greatest and most precious, because they are united in the *supposito divino* by the act of divinity [that is, they are Christ's humanity assumed by his divinity].[125]

Bremer's highly technical language is typical of fifteenth-century discussions of relics and *Dauerwunder*, as is the hint of discomfort. There is, for example, a good deal of imprecision—even equivocation—in the phrase "something of the humanity of Christ" applied to relics of Christ's blood. Such relics were, in Bremer's day, fiercely contested, and he does not quite commit himself about their ontological status when he says *aliquid humanitatis Christi* (although as a member of the Franciscan order, which possessed a number of such effluvial relics, Bremer is not comfortable with rejecting them entirely). Moreover, Bremer does not here suggest that the greatest relic—the Eucharist—becomes visibly Christ's flesh and blood, although his area of Germany saw, in his own day, intense debate over *Dauerwunder*, and several of his fellow Franciscans supported such miracles. But Bremer does argue both that there can be degrees of instantiation of the holy in matter and that all three types of holy matter in some sense manifest the presence of God. It is crucial to the spirituality found in his sermons, as well as to his scholastic analysis, that the pieces (*particulae*) of—or associated with—Christ be whole (*totus Christus*). In other words, *sanguis Christi*, whether soaked into the cross, present in reliquaries, or consumed by the faithful in the Eucharist, is spilled by Christ in a going out of the godhead (*exitus*), yet returned to and joined with him in glory (*redditus*).

The hierarchical classification in Bremer's *questio magistralis* depends on the degree to which, and the method by which, the divine and the material make contact. Lowest are objects that touched Christ. Higher are material bits of his body preserved under their own species or appearance—that is, as flesh and blood. Or "so the pious believe." (Bremer's hesitation is clear.)

Highest is the Eucharist—ordinary matter (bread and wine) that becomes, in what it is, the union of humanity and divinity that is Christ. All three types are "relics." All are holy matter. But the highest is a union of the divine with the lowliest matter (bread and wine). Yet it is also the complete and miraculous, but invisible, transformation of that lowly matter into something else. The "something else" is, however, still matter—that is, body—but body that is itself inextricably united to the divine. Both in the hint of ambivalence and in the complexity of his analysis, Johannes Bremer displays the centrality of matter in fifteenth-century piety and the issues it so urgently raised.

Holy Matter in Social Context

The holy matter that proliferated in presence and in visibility in Europe on the eve of the Protestant and Catholic Reformations was not only an object of reformist and heretical attack or a conundrum for theologians such as Bremer. It was also—and most importantly—a central and insistent part of religious practice. As such, it was both problem and opportunity. For many ordinary lay people, cloistered monks and nuns, local clergy, and authorities (both ecclesiastical and secular), material miracles were the occasion for focusing personal piety, fomenting new pilgrimages (with their attendant economic benefits), and refuting criticism of established cults. But they were also, as many scholars have argued, a threat to ecclesiastical and secular lords, who found it difficult to manage images, relics, and bloody Eucharistic wafers that might crop up, or erupt into new forms, without any official prompting. In what prelates, preachers, and polemicists wrote, it is clear that they often saw such devotions as a threat to the church's control or even to local aristocratic power, however much they also attempted to use them to foster allegiance to specific monasteries, communities, or pilgrimage sites. Some claims to bleeding wafers and altar cloths (for example, Wartenburg bei Wittenberg, Pulkau, and possibly the Wilsnack miracle itself) seem to have been engineered, and the fact that there was spirited debate about such cases suggests both that fabricating a Eucharistic miracle could be useful to ecclesiastical and political authorities and that such miracles were powerful enough to be worth condemning and rooting out.[126]

At even the highest levels of the church, there was recognition that Christian materiality was simultaneously useful and threatening—both spiritually and politically. Popes regularly granted indulgences to sites of *Dauerwunder*, thus enhancing their drawing power.[127] But they also carefully investigated miracle claims, preferred to support long-established pilgrimages over new ones, and tried to circumvent the possibility of idolatrous worship—and spontaneous enthusiasm—by insuring that clerically consecrated hosts were displayed alongside miraculous stuff.[128]

Before I go further in considering the complexities of holy matter in praxis, a caveat is necessary. We cannot take stories of miraculous matter literally. This is not simply because we must bracket questions about their ultimate cause or because some miracles were manifestly fraudulent. It is also owing to the fact that the stories were often constructed—usually by clergy—to stereotype certain groups as impious or superstitious, or even as social and religious threats. The way in which shrine attendants recorded miracles or hagiographers and chroniclers wrote about saints suggests that authorities feared anticlerical or anti-Christian reactions and projected those fears onto outsiders, scapegoating lower-class women, working men, and religious dissidents. Stories about peasants who steal wafers to make their beehives or fishponds fertile may be morality tales constructed by clerics who fear lay religiosity.[129] Moreover, some of the surviving accounts of miracles were composed long after the supposed event. Indeed—a point seldom raised even today—a surprising number of the accounts were made in the sixteenth century by Protestant scholars who exaggerated the miraculous in order to accuse Catholics of credulity. Nonetheless, if we exercise proper caution, we can see that the stories fall into broad patterns that are suggestive of social facts.

Animated images were usually said to appear to people of lowly or marginal status, especially children, and frequently in out-of-the-way places. Eucharistic visions, received more often by women than by men, often functioned to point an accusing finger at licentious and corrupt priests and were frequently received when clergy withheld the sacrament or other sorts of spiritual comfort from the women. *Dauerwunder* were sometimes alleged to be the result of servants, especially female servants, criminals, or impure priests misusing the wafer.[130] Such stories suggest that transformation miracles were sometimes occasions on which ordinary Christians (shepherds, alewives, serving maids, traveling journeymen, and so forth) claimed to come into unmediated and awe-inspiring contact with the holy, thus bypassing clerical control.

Both theoretical discussions and miracle stories indicate that authorities worried about such subversive possibilities. When Geiler von Kaisersberg, for example, suggested that holy-water vessels should dry out, he was probably cautioning the populace against adding anything to a holy substance consecrated by the clergy.[131] When preachers warned their congregations against going on pilgrimage because, after all, the consecrated Eucharist was available at home, they were not just giving spiritual advice or attempting to keep ecclesiastical revenues in their own parishes, they were also asserting their own authority over Christian materiality. When bishops insisted on translating miracle hosts to episcopal sees or on reconsecrating dubious *Dauerwunder*, their actions not only asserted clerical control but also hinted at the possibility that such control might be lost if either the faithful or the holy matter itself took charge.[132]

Moreover, miracle stories do seem to reflect occasions on which Christians abused, stole, or attempted to work magic with relics or wafers. At Zehdenick in northern Germany, for example, a miracle supposedly occurred when a woman stole a host to bury under her beer keg so her beer would be better than that of her neighbors. Blood bubbled up from the earth where she buried it and was collected by the faithful as a relic. When a similar miracle occurred at Wasserleben, the ecclesiastical authorities tried to take the bloody chalice and cloth away to neighboring Halberstadt, but the blood allegedly flowed again to protest being moved.[133] Many of the details of such accounts are not, of course, historically verifiable. But a large number of such stories circulated, and taken together, they suggest both direct, lay encounters with holy matter and resistance on the part of some of the laity to clerical efforts to manipulate it in order to stimulate or repress devotion. Nor was lay enthusiasm for such miracles felt only by non-elites. Lords often supported miracles in their regions for reasons pious as well as political and economic, and resisted ecclesiastical efforts to repress or regulate them. In 1429, for example, when a canon of Magdeburg arrived in Wartenburg bei Wittenberg to investigate a miracle many alleged to be a fraud, he found that the supposed *Dauerwunder* had already been taken under the protection of the duchess.[134] Furthermore, it is clear that Waldensians and Lollards came to reject images, Eucharistic miracles, and other forms of holy matter in part because they objected to the wealth and power of the clergy who consecrated or managed them. Opposition to holy objects was often opposition to those who controlled or profited from them, just as enthusiasm for the same objects could be a way of bypassing rituals performed by the clergy.

Increasingly in the fourteenth and fifteenth centuries, host desecration stories were anti-Jewish libels. Often they stood alone; sometimes they merged with accusations of ritual murder.[135] Jews were said to stab not only the wafer but also the living child seen within it; they allegedly murdered Christian children to extract from their stomachs the consecrated hosts needed for various nefarious rituals. As the number of such charges increased, their function changed. From justification after the fact for persecution, expulsion, and extermination, host-desecration libels became excuses for legal charges against Jewish communities. Behind some late medieval accounts of Eucharistic miracles lie pogroms and Christian efforts (secular as well as ecclesiastical) to find excuses for them. A number of reports of *Dauerwunder* from the late thirteenth to the fifteenth century are stories fabricated significantly after lynchings of Jews and confiscations of Jewish property in order to justify the earlier events. But by the later fifteenth and sixteenth centuries, such stories were often circulated in preparation for judicial proceedings against Jews.[136] The trial in Brandenburg in 1510, which I cited above, is a particularly horrifying example.[137]

The politics of holy matter were thus complicated and sometimes indeed sinister. Accusing women, servants, petty thieves, or—increasingly and most perniciously—Jews, animations of objects provided opportunities for persecution as well as for access to succor and healing. Ordinary layfolk, secular political leaders, and clerical authorities were all involved in the vicious scapegoating.[138] Much has been written about this. What I stress here is merely one aspect: the role of material transformation in such events. Animated objects provided occasions for blame of self and blame of other; both could lead—the one by paranoid projection, the other by direct persecution—to the torture, expulsion, and murder of dissidents and outsiders.[139] Not only did holy stuff proliferate, its very lability became a mechanism of reproach and accusation.

The Case of Wilsnack

The miracle claimed by little town of Wilsnack in the Mark Brandenburg shows the ways in which animated matter was problematic, both in its perceived capacity to accuse and in its susceptibility to manipulation for ends pious and impious.[140] I have treated Wilsnack elsewhere in greater detail and in another context. I return to it briefly here because it provides our most fully documented case of the kind of controversy such sites of transformed matter engendered.

The originating event occurred in 1383 when three miraculously preserved and blood-spotted wafers appeared in the ruins of a village church that had been burned to the ground by a predatory knight. Offered as a promise of rebirth to the community by its priest, and perhaps indeed connected with a local harvest festival, the objects triggered an enthusiastic cult that lasted more than a hundred years and drew a wide variety of people from all over Europe. A range of evidence, including the distribution of its pilgrim badges, with their characteristic three red blood drops, argues that the site was the most popular northern European pilgrimage goal of the fifteenth century.

The hosts supposedly caused other animations and transformations. In early accounts, they were even said to raise the dead. Moreover, matter associated with the hosts and their altar was also claimed to be holy. A number of early miracles had to do with candles that lit miraculously or miraculously went out, and such candles were preserved for veneration by the faithful alongside the miraculous wafers.

Soon after 1383, however, the hosts were suspected by the authorities in Magdeburg of being a fraud. Conflict over their authenticity became the occasion both for sophisticated theological debate at several major synods and councils and for struggle over pilgrimage revenues, local security, and other matters of secular and ecclesiastical jurisdiction. Archepiscopal authorities in Magdeburg opposed the prestige and power given the little church of Wilsnack by its pilgrimage, but the bishop of Havelberg and the Electors of Brandenburg adamantly supported it. Arguments against the pilgrimage emanating from both the Archdiocese and the University of Prague to the south erupted repeatedly in the fifteenth century and were clearly, among other things, a contest between German and Czech nationalisms. Papal legations, led by such powerful figures as Nicholas of Cusa and John of Capistrano, became involved. Criticism of the cult came not only from the highest levels of the church but also from a number of ordinary pilgrims who, in the accounts of their journeys, tell of faked miracles and question improbable metamorphoses, such as the transformation of pilgrims' staves into swords when pilgrims were attacked by robbers.

Yet the Wilsnack miracle retained its power as holy matter well into the sixteenth century. The evangelical pastor Joachim Ellefeldt, appointed in the early 1550s, came into conflict with the Catholic canons over it. Convinced that the only sure way to end the sway of "the idol" was to destroy it entirely, Ellefeldt opened the monstrance in the presence of witnesses and burned the hosts, for which deed he found himself arrested, imprisoned for six months, and then expelled not only from his parish but from the Mark Brandenburg as well. Down into the nineteenth century, the pot in which he allegedly burned the hosts and the "sin scales" into which penitents supposedly put the price of their misdeeds while clever clergy manipulated the plates were preserved as Protestant relics of Catholic superstition.

What I wish to call attention to here is not only the political maneuvering of the many parties involved but also the arguments that were mounted for and against the hosts for over a hundred years after their supposed appearance. The most virulent phase of the controversy occurred in the 1440s. In addition to asserting that the former priest (by then deceased) had orchestrated the miracle—a charge that invited, of course, the countercharge that opponents had lied about the priest's confession—polemicists against the hosts claimed that there was "nothing red there" either in 1443, when they were inspected, or originally. The problem, they declared, was not so much moral turpitude and manipulation by the priest; it was that there was no miraculous matter at Wilsnack—only spiderwebs and mold. From Jan Hus to Nicholas of Cusa, many theologians asserted specifically that what was in the monstrance was at most only a "colored thing" (*talem rubedinem*), not Christ's blood. They inveighed against the revering of the Wilsnack candles as miraculous and against the making and purveying of the red-spotted badges taken away by pilgrims. Indeed, their critiques viewed matter's tendency toward deterioration as a threat not only to miracle hosts but even to ordinary consecrated ones. In the decree of 1451 that I quoted in my Introduction, Nicholas of Cusa warned that "transformed hosts should be consumed by the celebrating priest in communion, rather than that the sacred Eucharist... be permitted to disintegrate through the corruption of the species [*per specierum corruptionem desinere*]." But we note that, for all his opposition, Cusanus does call the wafers in question "transformed hosts."

And Wilsnack had its supporters, both politicians and theorists. They argued repeatedly and strenuously that such miraculous appearances stimulated faith, especially at a time when Eucharistic fervor seemed on the wane. The favorable economic impact of the flood of pilgrims was clearly one of the reasons the Elector of Brandenburg repeatedly sent delegations to Rome to argue for the miraculous hosts. Some supporters of the cult even suggested that pilgrimage increased efforts at peacekeeping and hence the safety of the region.[141] Moreover, there were theorists who held that Christ *could* have left blood behind at the Resurrection; hence, it could appear on consecrated hosts. Indeed, in a sort of desubstantiation, the blood on hosts could be present as accidents without substance, they argued. In other words, what the faithful saw in the host was the accidents left behind when the substance of Christ's blood ascended to glory.

To proponents of the miracle, such holy matter was useful exactly because it accused as well as revealed. One of the earliest stories connected to Wilsnack told of the miracle hosts bleeding again to ward off the injury of double consecration when the bishop arrived to say mass with them. Moreover, as the early sixteenth-century theologian Johannes von Paltz theorized in a general discussion of *Dauerwunder*, miraculous blood was useful to castigate both lukewarm Eucharistic observance and heresy. It cried out against sin and abuse because it was shed innocent.[142] Indeed Paltz, who rejected the claims of Wilsnack but supported the Sternberg host miracle of 1492 as God's accusation against Hussites and Jews, asserted that miraculous eruptions of blood on and in matter were in his own day "more numerous [*multiplicata*] than any other miracles."[143]

Conclusion

As the case of Wilsnack makes clear, material miracles were both problem and opportunity for religious authorities who wished to educate and control, just as they were both problem and opportunity for layfolk who wanted immediate and tangible access to God. Sometimes efforts to assert the cultural hegemony of orthodox Christianity, such events also sometimes involved—and were often feared to involve—resistance to ecclesiastical authority, orthodoxy, or orthopraxy. Moreover, for ecclesiastical authorities and laity (aristocrats, townspeople, and peasants), miraculous objects functioned to focus persecution, lynching, and judicial murder, as well as faith and pilgrimage. They were feared as reproaches by parishioners and their pastors, even as they were also used to punish dissidents, outcasts, and those seen as threatening or alien. Holy matter was a tool in both the deployment and the questioning of ecclesiastical and social power.

But the material Christianity of the later Middle Ages involved not only questions of power and control; it also involved questions of the meaning of human embodiment and its place in a material world. As I tried to suggest by my brief discussion of both technical theological debates and dissident critiques, holy matter was opportunity and threat at a metaphysical level as well. For matter is by definition locatable, divisible, temporal, changeable; the Christian God is by definition whole, immutable, and transcendent; yet that Christian God is understood to redeem, not merely to transcend, the material. Hence, corruptible matter must be—impossibly, inconceivably, paradoxically—capable of incorruption. By definition partible, matter must be capable of eternal wholeness, of achieving the promise of Psalm 15:10: "He will not give his holy one to see corruption."

In the next chapter, I treat this paradox by exploring what was perhaps its central consequence: medieval Christianity's insistence on material fragmentation as a way of conveying and distributing the holy while embedding this insistence in the idea of concomitance—the idea that part is whole. I focus on this because it is, for modern scholars, one of the most puzzling aspects of Christian materiality. After all, the cult of relics and animated images characterizes many of the world's religions,[144] and in many religions, apotropaic objects are crucial to ritual. But the insistent deployment of fragmentation—and the paradoxical claim that part is whole—is peculiarly prominent in medieval Christianity.[145] To explain the emergence of this improbable conception, I will describe in greater detail attitudes toward part and whole, corruption and incorruption, from the early years of Christianity down to the sixteenth century.

CHAPTER THREE

Holy Pieces

Holy matter provided religious opportunity and challenged religious authority in the later Middle Ages. It had long done so. The use of relics to undergird and create power was nothing new. But Christian materiality had, since antiquity, been a theological and philosophical problem as well, and the emergence of new kinds of transformation miracles only heightened awareness of and raised new questions about the nature of materiality itself. Hence I turn in Chapters 3 and 4 from politics to ontology.

The decay and partition of holy matter was an especially challenging conundrum. When the bodies of holy women were alleged to remain undecayed after death, what was supposedly being asserted was their victory over both physical and moral corruption. But did this mean that physical inviolability was proof of holiness of life? If so, why did some saintly bodies decay? When theologians in the eleventh and twelfth centuries answered those who worried that realist Eucharistic theories might expose the flesh of God to digestion and excretion, they accused such critics of heresy. But the accusation left the orthodox with the difficult and somewhat embarrassing question of considering whether at some point after consecration, the transubstantiated bread and wine might nonetheless cease to be Christ's body. When the faithful claimed to see relics flower or liquefy, statues cry, and wafers bleed, what they were claiming was that such matter manifested the holy by showing itself alive. Yet as the fate of numerous relics and miracle hosts made clear, such manifestations of life could dry into powdery dust or fade into cobwebs and mold, thus leaving the question of divine presence as acute as before.[1]

In Chapters 1 and 2, I discussed how images, relics, sacramentals, and *Dauerwunder* were used and responded to; this led quite naturally to a consideration of theological treatments of particular objects, which constituted, by the later Middle Ages, efforts to control or rein them in without denying their sacrality completely. I turn now to the deeper challenge holy matter presented in both theory and practice: the challenge of partition and decay.

Parts, Wholes, and Triumph over Decay

The conviction that God resides in and redeems the material he has created had long posed problems for medieval Christians. I begin with some background.

From the days of the early church, relics raised the problem of the material. In the first Western controversy concerning them to which we have detailed access, the charge against relic venerators was that they revere not just dead or inert stuff but stuff that, because dead, is preeminently friable, mutable, corruptible, and polluting. Defending relics against the charge of one Vigilantius that holy cadavers are merely and permanently vile dust, Jerome wrote in 404:

> Are bishops all to be adjudged sacrilegious, even idiotic, when they carry a vile object and dissolved ashes in . . . vessels of gold? Are the people of all the churches foolish who run to the holy relics and receive them with joy as if they discerned there a living and present prophet? . . . If the Lamb [i.e., Christ] is everywhere, those who are with the Lamb [i.e., the saints] should be believed to be everywhere. When the devil and demons go about all over the earth, how can the martyrs, after the pouring out of their blood, be left waiting, shut up under the altar . . . ? The saints are not called dead but sleeping.[2]
>
> We, however, refuse cult and adoration not only to the relics of the martyrs but also to the sun and moon, the angels and archangels . . . and to every name that is named in the present world and in the

> world to come, lest we serve the creation more than the Creator.... But we honor the relics of the martyrs that we may honor him whose martyrs they are.... Are the relics of Peter and Paul unclean? Is the body of Moses unclean, that body which, according to Hebrew truth, was buried by the Lord himself?... If the bones [of the holy] pollute what they touch, how did the dead Elias raise a dead man?[3]

Jerome here defends the saints as nonpolluting because nondecaying. They are alive and without spatial location or incarceration. Although their bodies are dust and ashes, the saints themselves are "not dead but sleeping." Jerome's defense adumbrates the later argument that relics should be honored not adored, and honored because of the creator whose glory they reflect. But he also protests against what he understands to be older Hebrew ideas of corpse pollution by refusing to associate the saints (whatever their remains may indicate visually) with dissolution or decay. Although he may seem to imply that the saints are souls in heaven, not remains incarcerated in earthly altars and tombs, he also suggests that their bodies are glorious, not "vile," as critics claim. Holy bodies are worthy of reverencing in golden vessels and powerful enough in themselves to raise the dead.

Victricius of Rouen, in a well-known text written just eight years before Jerome's, went further. Victricius argued that holiness makes the bodies of the saints in some sense already glorified, lifted to the immutability and impartibility of heaven. Relics are "jewels," whole and hard. The healings they perform cannot drain them any more than shining dims the sun.

> Let no one, deceived by vulgar error, think that the truth of the whole of their bodily passion is not contained in these fragments.... We proclaim, with all our faith and authority, that there is nothing in these relics that is not complete....
>
> The Passion of the saints is the imitation of Christ, and Christ is God. Therefore, no division is to be inserted in fullness, but in that division which is visible to the eye, the truth of the whole is to be adored....

> I touch remnants but I affirm that in these relics perfect grace and virtue are contained.... He who cures lives. He who lives is present in his relics....
>
> It is toward these jewels that we should set the sails of our souls; there is nothing fragile in them, nothing that decreases, nothing that can feel the passage of time.... The blood which the fire of the Holy Spirit still seals in their bodies and in these relics shows that they are extraordinary signs of eternity.[4]

Having received a shipment of holy body parts from the bishop of Milan, Victricius was worried that by accepting such a gift, he contributed to mutilating the saints. Hence, he argued that they are complete in every particle. But his argument goes further than practical concerns about the means by which he has acquired holy stuff. His position is Christological and soteriological. The wholeness of the saints lies in the fullness of Christ, who is whole and perfect because living, even in division and death.

Seven centuries later, Peter the Venerable (d. 1156), writing to honor the relics of St. Marcellus, possibly on the anniversary of their translation to Cluny or their transfer into a new reliquary, made the same argument. The cultural practices concerning relics were, of course, different in Peter's day. Jerome and Victricius had confronted bodies divided by persecutors and hence had argued, against the abusers, that God viewed his tortured and divided martyrs as if they were whole and already in heaven. In contrast, it was Peter's Christian contemporaries who were dividing holy bodies for distribution—a point to which I will return.[5] Nonetheless Peter's metaphors and the assumptions behind them are the same as Victricius's. Similar, too, is the subtext of potential criticism the text reveals. Those who are incapable of thinking in the categories of eternity might, Peter suggests, fear dead bodies as dead—inert or even contaminating. The charge that matter is dead (and not merely dead but slimy, friable, decaying, and polluting)—a charge familiar to us from attacks on images and miraculous objects—is here suspected to undergird skeptical attitudes toward the saints themselves.

> The divine dignity divides his martyr into equal parts, so that he may retain his soul for himself among the mass of the blessed and give, with marvelous largesse, the relics of his sacred body to be venerated by the faithful.... But suppose someone says: "What does it profit us to honor a lifeless body... bones lacking in sense?"... [But] we anticipate for them a future resurrection in their bodies with immortality and in every sense incorruptibility. For this reason we do not debase as inanimate, despise as insensate, or trample under foot, like the cadavers of dumb beasts, the bodies of those who in this life cultivated justice; rather we venerate them as temples of the Lord... hoard them as pearls... preserve them as vessels of resurrection....
>
> Behold whose bodies you venerate, brothers, in whose ashes you exalt, for whose bones you prepare golden sepulchers. They are the sons of God, equal to angels.... And in this hope I have confidence more certainly than in any human thing that you ought not to feel contempt for the bones of the present martyrs as if they were dry bones [*non uelut arentia contempnitis*], but should honor them now full of life as if they were in their future incorruption [*quasi future incorruptione iam florentia honoratis*].... Flesh flowers from dryness and youth is remade from old age.... Having therefore, dearest brothers, the author of the old law and the new grace, Jesus Christ... we ought to reverence with due honor the body of this blessed martyr as about to be resurrected, as it will be clothed in immortal glory [*ut resurrecturum, ut immortali gloria uestiendum honore*], although we see it as dead.... I say that the bodies of the saints live with God [*Uiuere, inquam, Deo sanctorum corpora*].[6]

Once again, we find images of jewels and flowers used to insist that part is whole, dead is not only incorruptible but also alive. Once again, as in Jerome and Victricius, we find the lurking fear that "someone," sunk in "vulgar error," might disagree. Throughout these seven centuries of discussion, bodily partition and decay are closely linked. Hence, in somewhat contradictory metaphors, holy matter is both hard (unchangeable and impartible) like jewels, and yet blossoming (alive and growing into glory) like flowers. The threat to be warded off is the threat that fragmentation constitutes a corruption of being—a corruption that not only destroys but also pollutes.

By the high Middle Ages, concern to remove from relics any implication that partition is pollution seems to have underlain the way both texts and objects represented the saints. Authors of saints' lives frequently spoke of the bodies and bones of holy people as jewels in life as well as in death. Walter Daniel wrote that Aelred of Rievaulx (d. 1167) glowed like the sun while still a baby; in death, his flesh was "clearer than glass, whiter than snow," shining like a carbuncle.[7] Peter Damian described St. Romuald as, on earth, "a neglected pearl of heaven"; thus, after death, he "shines ineffably among the living stones of the celestial Jerusalem."[8] James of Vitry reported that the thirteenth-century holy woman Mary of Oignies appeared to him in a dream after her death "as if transformed into a very brilliant precious stone."[9] Mechtild of Magdeburg (d. ca. 1282) saw in a vision the body of St. John in heaven, whole in every detail and unchangeable, like a crystal, but apparently asleep, awaiting the general resurrection.[10] In such accounts, bodies reflect graphically and exactly the virtues of persons; virginity or ascetic denial is manifested as literally pure flesh (like clear crystal). Indeed, in many of the descriptions (Damian's and James of Vitry's are examples), body, separated soul, and saint fuse. On earth and in heaven, both before and after the coming resurrection, holy bodies are living but hardened against the change of corruption. Hence, stones and metals were a telling analogy to such bodies, for minerals were understood by medieval theorists to be decay resistant but alive (or quasi-alive), growing organically in the earth and manifesting powers of attraction and repulsion rather like desire.[11]

In the later Middle Ages, hagiographers and advocates for the canonization of holy people increasingly made the claim that their bodies or body parts in fact defied corruption. The tongue of St. Antony of Padua was alleged to remain incorrupt for hundreds of years after his death. The hand of the fourth-century martyr St.

Quentin, separated from his body (as was his cranium) when the relics were translated in 1228, is still displayed today with its flesh intact.[12] More than half of the universally venerated saints from the period 1400 to 1900—and all of the female saints—are said to have incorrupt bodies or to demonstrate odd phenomena that imply nondecay.[13]

Hagiographical accounts often insisted in other ways on the "life" of relics. For example, another of Mary of Oignies' hagiographers, Thomas of Cantimpré, claimed that her hair wrought cures after her death and on one occasion "came alive" for an hour.[14] Two centuries later, a relic of the true cross, possessed by the holy woman Jane Mary of Maillé, spilled fresh blood as if alive when it was cut in two.[15] The point of fourteenth-century accounts of blood relics that liquefied—as the blood of St. Januarius in Naples and that of St. James the Lesser in the Church of the Holy Apostles in Rome, or the vials of Christ's blood at Bruges and Weingarten, were said to do—was to demonstrate that the blood was living because red and fluid, not dried.[16] A similar point is made in stories from the Eastern church that relics from the crown of thorns were often found green and blossoming, especially on Good Friday.[17]

Such miracles are complicated, because implicit in them is anxiety about and resistance to partition, as well as manifestation of life. When Jane Mary's cross relic bleeds, it can be seen as objecting to division, just as the chalice of Halberstadt-Wasserleben filled with blood to protest being moved and the host supposedly mutilated by Salomon of Spandau bled when fractured. The well-known tenth-century story of the healing of a fissure in the Gero crucifix when a consecrated wafer was inserted into it is often interpreted as a case of implanting a relic in the carved corpus of a cross. But it is also a case of one kind of holy matter healing another, and it clearly suggests that any breach in a devotional object is a defect. The host in the Gero crucifix disappears into wholeness. But the mutilated wafer at Spandau allegedly chose to divide and bleed; Jane Mary's relic produced not only two cross relics but also a multiplication of blood that was itself a holy presence.[18] Such miracles are to be understood not only as resistance to destruction but also as manifestation of its opposite: life. Paradoxically, then, both miraculous return of wholeness and miraculous division are signs of resistance to violation and decay.

Reliquaries made the same argument. From the central Middle Ages on, these containers both displayed the stuff holy bodies had become in death and lifted that stuff to eternal life by cloaking it in incorruptible metal and gems. The reliquary of Thomas Becket's blood shown in figure 15 (p. 72), for example, substitutes a shimmering red stone (itself ingeniously constructed to look like blood) for the relic within, which is not seen. But the stone's shining redness clearly makes the claim that what is inside is blood—liquid, glowing, alive. It is even possible to argue that reliquaries literalize Peter the Venerable's text or James of Vitry's vision by transforming bones and dust into jewels and gold, alive with God.[19] Or one might reverse the argument and suggest that Mechtild's vision of John's body is a textual version of a reliquary monstrance. Indeed, all bodies seem to become reliquaries in Mechtild's vision of last things. After the resurrection, we will be (she says) "of human form," bearing within ourselves the "godly flame" of the soul, which will shine through our bodies "as luminous gold shines through a clear crystal."[20] In Mechtild's poetic vision, we all become "speaking reliquaries" at the end of time.

By the later Middle Ages, the bodies lifted into incorruption by the gorgeousness of reliquaries were often parts. The reliquary of John the Baptist shown in figure 17 (p. 74) is clearly a head, but it is golden and with hair, not a skull. Art historians suggest that it perhaps contained a tooth of the saint.[21] Hence, the reliquary presents the body as not decayed, though it is divided. Moreover, if it did contain a tooth or small bone particle, the form of the container makes that particle into a far larger body part. Even in containers where the fragment within is visible, it is often presented not as a mere sliver or bit but as a recognizable part (arm, foot, rib, etc.). And such parts tend to be clothed, as

1 Corinthians 15:53 put it, "in incorruption." For example, the bone inside the Prague reliquary later ascribed to St. George, like that in the reliquary of St. Nicholas of Myra, is clearly visible, yet it is displayed to the viewer garbed for heaven. (See figs. 18 and 19, pp. 75 and 76.) The reliquary of St. Basil shown in figure 20 (p. 77) clothes the hand in a liturgical glove, a sign of the saint's position as bishop. Lines in the lower part imitate the folds of material, and wrinkles around the fingers also suggest the fabric or cured skin of a fine glove. But the glove fits so tightly that the thumb at least appears to have a nail. Even visually, therefore, the image confuses us, conflating fabric covering, cured glove skin, and flesh—all silvered or gilded. We, the viewers, are not sure whether such relics are overclothed with glory or have become it.[22]

Thus, despite the anxiety about division suggested in early texts such as those of Jerome and Victricius, what is denied in body-part reliquaries—as in Peter the Venerable's text or Thomas of Cantimpré's account of Mary's hair—is not partition but decay. Indeed, by the later Middle Ages, the division attendant upon death is displayed, even in some ways celebrated. Although recent work has demonstrated that body-part reliquaries do not necessarily contain the specific part they illustrate, they certainly call attention to parts qua parts. It is hard not to see the St. Basil reliquary, for example, as underlining armness, especially when we realize that such objects were used as arm extenders or prostheses to perform liturgical blessings.[23] Reliquaries glorify and sublimate partition. What they deny is putrefaction.

The fairly frequent claim in saints' lives and canonization proceedings that holy bodies do not corrupt after death also suggests that what was feared and almost obsessively denied in rhetoric and reliquary was not so much death as decay.[24] Death was after all conceptualized as the gateway to heaven, and saints' lives, especially those from the fourteenth to the seventeenth centuries, often glory in accounts of heroic dying carried to excruciating lengths. This stress on dying as the crucial life event is seen not only in the great popularity of martyr accounts from the early church, often retold in the vernacular for a wide audience in the high Middle Ages, but also in the emergence of lengthy deathbed reports, such as the so-called "Life" of Catherine of Genoa (d. 1510), as a new hagiographical genre.[25]

All this suggests that to medieval Christians, putrefaction was more horrifying than partition or death. That is why it became (as it does in *transi* tombs and *memento mori*) a metaphor for and warning against worldliness, pride, sin, and damnation. (See fig. 22, p. 80.) It is not a coincidence that at this period, the conceptualizing of leprosy as living decay achieved new prominence in European consciousness. Leprosy was understood to be literal fragmentation by corruption; as the disease advanced, body parts fell off. Associated with sexual transgression, which was thought to be the occasion for its transmission, leprosy was seen not merely as sickness but also as a particularly virulent manifestation of sin and of God's wrath at sin.[26] The figure of Frau Welt makes the connection of corruption and evil clear. (See fig. 23, p. 81.) Elegantly dressed when viewed from the front, the worldly woman is already eaten by worms from behind. Decay is an erupting on the body of moral decadence and damnation.

Indeed, medieval burial practices (like burial practices in most cultures) manifest a palpable anxiety about the corruption and slime immediately attendant upon death. Christians hid the putrefaction of bodies by reducing them to the hard stuff as quickly as possible (through boiling, for example, or through first burial in the ground before removal to a charnel house).[27] The bones that were then displayed might be manifestly divided, but they appeared to be beyond decay. The holy bodies contained in reliquaries, like bones in the charnel house, were explicitly body—often explicitly body parts—but body removed as far as possible from the abhorrent change of corruption. It is worth noting that on the rare occasions when soft tissue was displayed as a relic (for example, the tongue of St. Antony of Padua), it was claimed to be hard and incorrupt.[28]

Theologians and the Problem of Putrefaction

Theological texts suggest a similar concern with and fear of putrefaction. When Peter the Venerable glorified St. Marcellus, he nonetheless betrayed an underlying worry that some might feel unease, or even skepticism, about relics as unclean. Insisting that holy flesh and bones are dry and jewel-like (that is, not putrefying), he is not content with their cleanness, but feels compelled to see them as "flowering," alive, and young, "in every sense incorruptible" as well.

Writing two generations before Peter, Thiofrid of Echternach went so far as to argue that the saints, if dominated by the spirit in this life, might be rendered incorrupt after death. Subject "by nature" to decay, the body can nonetheless "by grace and merit" repel the attacks of worms and rot. "The flesh of the saints," writes Thiofrid, is

> born to glory...although what is conceived and engendered from the worm is eaten by worms, and dust reverts to dust.... [B]ut it is one thing from nature and another from grace and merit. From nature it is putrid, but from grace and merits it remains for a long time without rot even contrary to nature, and it repels the greedy worms.... [F]or he who puts away from himself worms (that is, nasty thoughts) will not be sweet to the worm.... Sanctified flesh, through nature *clothed with rottenness* [Job 12:5]...rises again from the dust through grace and merit.... And this is greatly to be marveled at, for it feeds worms yet heals men, it is putrid yet it puts off putrefaction...it is crushed into ashes yet it shines among the stars of the morning.[29]

What is striking for my purposes about this panegyric to the saints is not only Thiofrid's confidence that body can mirror spirit, and outer inner, both before and after death, but also his quite graphic disgust at the rot flesh "naturally" experiences in the grave—a disgust carried to the point of conflating earthly triumph over it in saintly bones with the moral triumph of saintly souls. Indeed, it is difficult to tell exactly what Thiofrid's soaring rhetoric claims. Like those reliquaries that make body fragments gold and crystal (while still parts), Thiofrid's prose describes the flesh of the tomb both as "crushed" and "putrid" and as having "put off putrefaction." What is clear, however, is that the putting off of putrefaction is of tremendous concern.

Such unease with decay is carried even further in a text contemporary with Thiofrid's: Guibert of Nogent's well-known *De pigneribus*, often said to be one of the first rationalist critiques of relics. At the heart of Guibert's argument, however, is not the critical sense of evidence nineteenth-century historians attributed to him, but rather a concern to keep putrefaction at bay. It is for this reason that he categorically denies the possibility of any bodily or effluvial relics of Christ. The blood and water shed from Christ's side at the Crucifixion were not absorbed by the earth, asserts Guibert, because they would face decay there. Any particle of Christ that remained behind—even his baby teeth—would eventually perish. Yet God cannot decay. Therefore, nothing of Christ can be left behind. The words of Psalm 15:10 promise: "He will not give his holy one to see corruption." Guibert argued: "We are promised that he 'will reform the body of our lowness, made like to the body of his glory' [Phil. 3:21]. How will he raise the despicableness of human corruption to conformity to his glory if he left behind a part of his body . . . without any rational cause and showed himself powerless to take up again something that was of himself?"[30] A stark fear of the bodily division he finds imaged in body parts lurks behind Guibert's strident opposition to relics of Christ.[31] Any partition seems, to him, a prelude to decay and dissolution. His is not a rationalist critique of relics as inauthentic or fraudulent but a statement: God redeems matter from corruption.

Much antiheretical literature from the central and later Middle Ages manifests a similar anxiety concerning decay. Repeatedly, the authors of treatises against heretics—whether Cathars, Free Spirits, Lollards, or Hussites—attributed to Christian dissidents an inability to accept the redemption of matter implicit in the Incarnation, Resurrection and Assumption of Christ as well as in saint cults and the Eucharist. Writing against the Cathars in the early thirteenth century, for example, James Capelli charged that heretics denied the Eucharist because they thought food to be evil, "having its origin from the earth." They held (he said) that "the devil divided the elements" and "gave fertility to the earth."[32] Another polemicist, Rainer Sacconi, wrote that Cathars deny Christ's human body to be glorified. Although it will be briefly assumed for the Day of Judgment, after the judging "it will [so the heretics argue] be resolved into pre-existent matter like a putrid corpse."[33] Whether or not dissidents actually expressed disgust at the organic processes of matter, their orthodox opponents understood their rejection of body to equate body with putrefaction.[34] It is thus clear that much of this polemic projects onto dissidents exactly the fear of bodily corruption that animates Guibert's rejection of relics of Christ. Whatever the Cathars actually taught (and we know of them mostly from hostile sources), Christians accused them of what they feared they themselves might believe. The conception of matter that informs such accusations is one in which matter is assumed to be that which changes, divides, and decays.

A curious university text from the late thirteenth century suggests the extent to which even learned theologians and natural philosophers found decay problematic. Hence, they dragged it, along with all its most graphic consequences, into discussions where it seems to modern tastes singularly inappropriate, yet they somehow managed simultaneously to deny what would seem, to modern assumptions, its full implications. In his *Quodlibet* 10, *questio* 6, Henry of Ghent (d. 1293) raised the question whether one could adore [*adorare*] a dead body (that is, a relic). Henry was responding to certain unnamed English thinkers who had apparently raised objections to the veneration of relics by arguing that if dead bodies were adored, it would be because something living remained in them. But, said these theorists, something living does remain in a dead body: namely, the worms it engenders, which are in turn nourished from its matter. In other words, its matter "remains in worms." It would however, they asserted, be improper to adore worms.[35]

In answer, Henry of Ghent argued that there are four kinds of adoration (*propter se*, *per se*, *propter aliud*, and *per accidens*).[36] The fourth, adoration *per accidens* (that is, because of something accidental to what the object is intrinsically), can be of six types: because of what the thing signifies, as in the water of baptism; because of what it imitates or is like, as in images; because of what it contains, as in the case of the dove of the Holy Spirit; because of contact, as in contact relics (Henry gives the examples of clothes or hair cut from holy people or the cross, which had touched Jesus); because of descent or actual coming from, as in the case of dead bodies of the saints coming from living bodies; and by what Henry calls "conaturality." The list serves as a catalogue of types of what we might call "associated" holy matter; this is what Henry means by *per accidens*. And these associated things receive simple *dulia* (veneration) not *latria* (full adoration) or *hyperdulia* (special veneration). The argument is an example of those theological positions (discussed in Chapter 2 above) that theorize objects as pointing to something beyond themselves—as holy because of contact with or gesturing toward the sacred, rather than by virtue of divine indwelling.

What interests me particularly here is Henry's fifth type, "conaturality," for it is his answer to the problem of the worms who share matter with the saints. By it, Henry means that worms from the cadavers of saints will have material from the saints' bodies inside, and these worms can be adored *per accidens* with simple veneration, just as relics are. What is adored is not, however, the worms, but the matter of the saints they contain, which is conatural with the saints.

> For the matter that is under the form "worm" can be considered in two ways. In one way, it is ordered to the form of worm.... In the other, it is ordered to the form of the saint, under which it was

> in life and to which it has a habitude.... In the first way, it is not to be adored...just as the cadaver of Peter is not to be adored qua cadaver.... But in the second way—I speak here of that matter which will have been under the form of worms or cadaver or something else—it can be adored according to conaturality.[37]

Thus, adoration is not offered to the cadaver, or ashes, or worm food per se, but to it insofar as it is associated with the saints whose matter it is. And this matter (whether ashes, or a corpse, or bits consumed by worms) is associated with the saints because it is the material that will rise as their bodies at the end of time.[38] Moreover, the veneration to which the worms are entitled should be purely "interior" or spiritual (*mente sola*), not done with bodily gestures, such as genuflexions, for gestures might give the impression that the worms themselves were being venerated. In other words, Henry argues that the lowly worms that contain the matter of the saints are still in some kind of *per accidens* relationship to the holy—a relationship analogous to that of the water of baptism, or the mantle of the Virgin, or an image, or a body-part relic. But all such associated objects are venerated because of that to which they refer.

Especially striking for my purposes is the attitude toward matter and decay revealed in the arguments of both Henry and his unnamed interlocutors. The actual process of putrefaction—the sliminess out of which worms erupt—seems eclipsed even in being described. A line is drawn between dead and living bodies, it is true, but the worms of putrefaction are in some sense a continuation of the living body. Even dead matter is thus alive in the worms of putrefaction; decay is not really decay but continuation, if not of self or even of body per se, at least of life. Even in extreme partition, matter carries—if not the saint's identity—at least something identifiable as the matter of that saint.[39] If it were not that saint's matter, it would not be conatural with that saint. Hence, decay is not complete disappearance or destruction. Moreover, there is even a hint here that the dead body of the saint and the living body of the worm in some sense fuse. Although

Henry speaks of dead bodies (relics) coming from living saints, there is a suggestion here that the bodies of the saints might live on in the worms who eat them. Thus, we might say that, on the one hand, Henry's analysis protects all matter—especially matter as it is afflicted with decay and dissolution—from being worshipped per se. Hence, it reflects the suspicion of materiality we have found in many other theologians of the period. On the other hand, Henry sees even matter we would call dead as continuing to live in what are to us odd ways and associates such material with the holy even to the point of permitting its veneration.

The argument between Henry and his interlocutors is, to be sure, the sort of bizarre and hypothetical reasoning favored by scholastics. As such, it is hardly a guide to common assumptions. Nonetheless, like Guibert's argument about the relic of Christ's baby tooth or Thiofrid's panegyric to incorrupt saints, Henry's quodlibet is an example of the way concern for both confronting and denying decay continued to crop up in medieval Christianity. The more fragmentation and corruption were repressed or explained away, the more they intruded into technical theological and devotional discourse. Matter and its attendant processes of change and fragmentation remained an insistent threat.

The Contradiction: Fragmentation as Opportunity

It is thus clear that behind texts such as Henry's and Guibert's and objects such as the St. Basil reliquary lay a gigantic oxymoron. Decay was feared, repressed, denied; partition was sublimated. Yet fragmentation was central to the Christian cult of holy matter. However much Christians might disclaim or obfuscate the disintegration brought by putrefaction and partition, they were busy dividing bodies for religious purposes. Over the course of the Middle Ages, actual and metaphorical partition of holy objects became central to piety.

Moving and dividing bodies had been problematic in the early church.[40] The Romans had legislated against burying within the city walls, against moving, fragmenting, or selling bodies, and the earliest Christian sermons repeated such prohibitions. But the premier Christian heroes and heroines—the martyrs—were divided in the arena and torn apart by wild beasts. Thus, Jerome, Victricius, and others of the Fathers had perforce to argue for a kind of heavenly wholeness in bodies violated by persecutors. And the idea of wholeness in partition caught on. By the high Middle Ages, holy matter of all sorts was enthusiastically divided. Pieces of the true cross were spread across Europe. The faithful sat by the beds of dying holy people, hoping to get a fragment of the body as soon as the bones were prepared for distribution.[41] Monasteries created networks of affiliation by sending bits of their own precious relics to daughter houses as gifts, and religious authorities took bodies and body parts on processions around towns and fields in order to provide protection, mark out boundaries, or enhance fertility. Sacramentals were divided—even swallowed—to multiply and focus their power. Holy matter traveled and thereby spread its effects.[42]

We find even secular cases of body division and distribution in the Christian West. From the tenth century on, the aristocracy and royalty of Europe (and by the fourteenth century, the princes of the church as well) left instructions in wills to have their bodies divided after death and buried in widely scattered places in order not only to garner prayers from diverse ecclesiastical establishments but also to spread their power throughout the area of their jurisdiction.[43] Here, too, there was an assumption that matter carries presence. Paradoxically, then, matter's partibility became the key to its efficacy.

We see the assumption that partition spreads presence operating in sinister ways in the case of anti-Jewish host-desecration libels. Among the nastiest aspects of such libels are the repeated charges that Jews not only stab but also divide the host and carry the pieces from town to town. For example, in the anti-Jewish hysteria in the neighborhood of Berlin in 1510, the Jew Salomon of Spandau was accused of mishandling a host, which then miraculously sprang into three pieces, each marked with blood.

Salomon was alleged to have subsequently sent the pieces to the towns of Brandenburg and Stendal for further abuse. Such charges reflect not only an anti-Jewish paranoia that aided Christians in spreading persecution from one region to another but also a conviction that holy matter is whole in every part. Manifesting itself as powerful and alive by bleeding, each piece of the wafer is understood to be the whole Christ, who is executed again in every fragment.[44]

A Comparison with Jewish Practice

Those Jewish communities Christians feared and periodically attacked struggled with certain parallel questions concerning the place of body and matter in the divine economy. A comparison of Christian and Jewish discourse is therefore useful in clarifying what exactly was characteristic of late medieval Christian assumptions.

We are usually told that European Jews, at least before the emergence of Hasidism and various forms of messianism after 1492, did not revere saints. "With rare exceptions, Jewish graves did not become shrines, and relics are unheard of."[45] Those rare exceptions are usually said to be found in the Middle East, where Jews and Muslims sometimes made pilgrimages to the same shrines, such as those dedicated to the biblical figures Elijah, Ezekiel, and Abraham. At such shrines, talismanic objects rather like contact relics are found, and Eastern Jews, like Muslims, sometimes thought holy earth from graves had curative powers.[46] Nonetheless, comparativists have usually claimed that Jews had no saint cult, partly because of Judaism's strong emphasis on community rather than exemplary individuals, partly because of a deep Jewish sense of the impurity of corpses.[47] The Palestinian Talmud asserted: "One erects no grave monuments to the dead; their lives perpetuate their memory."[48]

Jews in Ashkenaz in the late Middle Ages did, however, sometimes perform pilgrimage to holy grave sites—a practice that perhaps emerged under Christian influence. Manifesting a fear of decay parallel to that of their Christian counterparts and deeply rooted in the Jewish tradition, rabbis therefore found it necessary to theorize that such pilgrimage was not the revering of dead and polluting cadavers. That, they said, was what Christians did, above all in the abuse of putting a dead body—Jesus—at the heart of their religion. If Jews paid honor to the burial sites of holy people, it was (they argued) because some element of the person's spirit or "psyche" hovered around the tomb. Therefore, a living person, not a body, was revered at Jewish grave sites.[49] In a twist on the text from the Palestinian Talmud just quoted, these rabbis insist that even if monuments are erected, it is life (that is, spirit) that is revered at Jewish graves.

This interpretive move of the rabbis may seem exactly parallel to certain Christian interpretations of the same phenomenon. After all, Thomas Aquinas argued that Christians give adoration not to the bodies of the saints but to God, who works miracles through them (and the rabbis did not deny that miracles happened at tombs). But there is an important difference. Whereas the rabbis denied that what is visited is the body at all, Aquinas held that holy bodies are worthy of a lesser kind of veneration because they are matter that will rise to glory at resurrection. Henry of Ghent even argued, as we have seen, that the material of saints' bodies could be venerated in worms. Matter is more central in these Christian conceptualizations, and that fact accounts in part for the tortured quality of the argumentation. Moreover, although Jews in Europe may have adopted the practice of pilgrimage to grave sites, the bodies to which they journeyed were not raised out of the grave, divided, and displayed as pieces.

The Iconography of Parts and Wholes: The Example of the Side Wound

The oxymoron that lurks behind relic cult—the need, that is, both to use and to sublimate fragmentation, or even in some cases to resist it—is mirrored in physical objects. Although reliquaries increasingly underlined and exhibited holy bodies as parts, reliquary altars and relic collections gathered the pieces into displays that suggest communities of believers. (See figs. 38 and 39, pp. 133–34.) Twelfth-century reliquaries already implied community by their very shape as churches (see figs. 15 and 16, pp. 72–73), but such containers did not make the pieces visible. Later reliquary altars, triptychs, and cabinets, however, insisted visually that what is assembled is bits. Hence, the partition that body-part reliquaries asserted was transcended not only in the precious containers that spoke of resistance to change but also in the propensity of the faithful to collect parts and exhibit them as gathered into wholes.

The Five Wound images I spoke of in Chapter 1 manifest a similarly paradoxical tendency: fragmenting and quantifying the body of Christ, they simultaneously deny the partition they represent and indeed enact.[50] I return to this now as an illustration of the complexity of the notion of "holy pieces."

As I pointed out earlier, the account of the Crucifixion in John 19:31–36 stressed that Christ's body was not broken. Even his cloak remained undivided. But by the fifteenth century, the poetry and iconography of the devotion known as the Five Wounds fragmented Christ rhetorically and visually. Veneration of his wounds (two in the hands, two in the feet, one in the side) was articulated not only in prayers to the parts of Jesus, addressed one after another, but also in paintings and woodcuts. (See figs. 29, 30, 32, 33, 44, and 46.) In such iconography, the crucified figure disappears, to be replaced by hands, feet, and heart, standing alone. Although the pieces are gathered by various framing devices into a whole, the visual presentation also stresses parts as parts.[51]

In this devotion, the wound in Christ's side acquired special prominence. (See figs. 12, 31, 44, 45, and 46.) Sometimes it replaced Christ's body visually, as it does in the late fifteenth-century woodcut analyzed by David Areford (fig. 30, p. 96). Sometimes it was turned horizontally, as if it were a mouth, and this presentation tended to echo the theme of guilt and divine anger we saw in some of the polemic surrounding the Wilsnack hosts.[52] For example, in a page from the devotional miscellany found in Brit. Lib. Add. MS 37049, the wound appears to speak to sinners the very reproach that is inscribed around it (fig. 44).[53] Christ displays the side wound with one hand and with the other almost seems to sprinkle blood on the enlarged heart toward which he gestures. The heart becomes the whole Christ as all five wounds are transferred onto it. The prayer transcribed to the left refers directly to humankind's responsibility: "O man unkynde, hafe in mynde, my paynes smert." And the guilt-inducing words around the wound, which opens like a mouth, speak pointedly of Christ suffering for our redemption.

Sometimes the wound was depicted vertically in a presentation that has reminded modern critics of a vagina. (See, for example, fig. 45).[54] Nor is there reason to think this is just a modern projection. Medieval texts speak of entering into Christ's side as if into a womb and thus make the sexual reference clear.

The point is more complicated than is sometimes understood. Explicitly female images of Jesus in the Middle Ages stress gestating, birthing, and lactating, not sexual union. Nestling within is usually an image of conception or reconception. When apostrophized, the breasts of Jesus are explicitly identified with food, not erotic stimulation. For example, the topos of mother Jesus used by the fourteenth-century English anchoress Julian of Norwich—a medieval figure on whom there has been very extensive modern commentary—is a locus for discussing creation. The blood Christ shed on the cross is analogous to the blood of birthing, and this birthing, paradoxically, precedes conception. To Julian, Christ is mother in feeding but above all in giving the very matter of existence to the child. Salvation is resting within. We may read this as sexual union, but in Julian's own verbs and adjectives, mothering denotes and connotes giving life.[55]

Moreover, direct visual identification of the side wound with the vagina is most obvious in objects such as birthing girdles that use it as an amulet against difficult childbirth.[56] Such girdles,

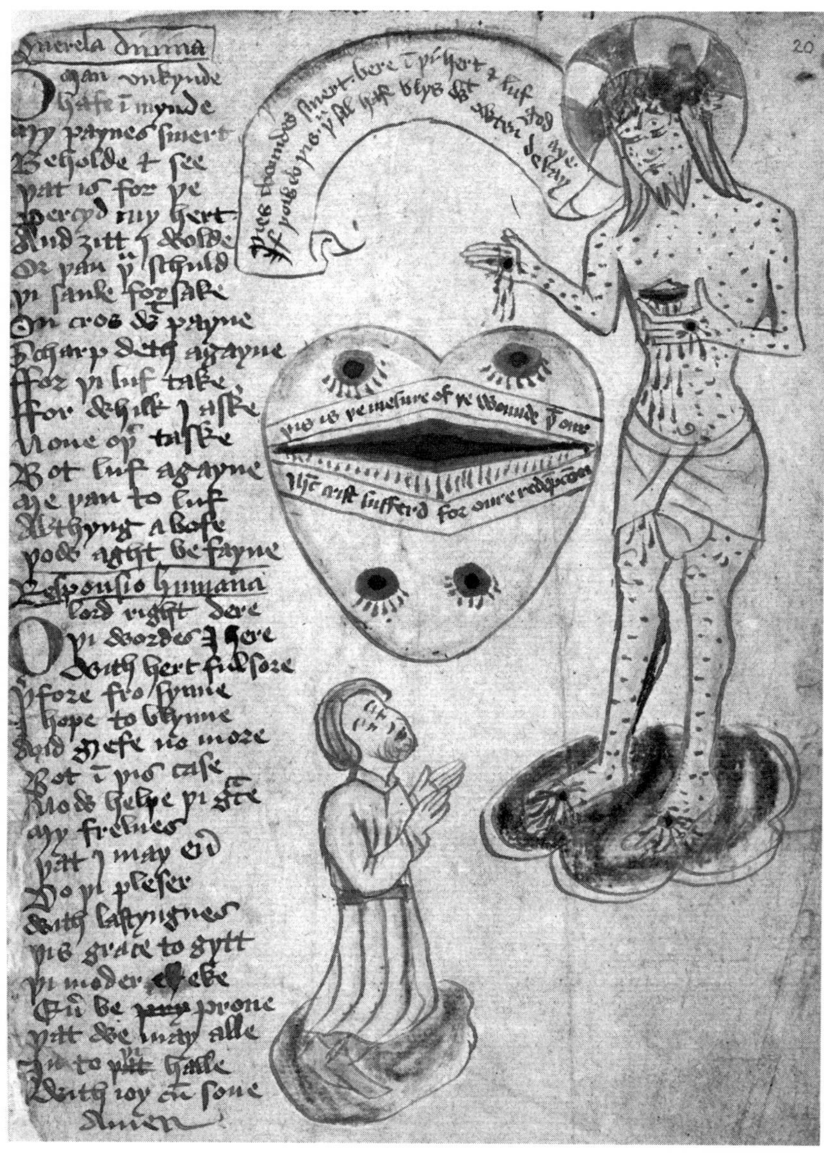

Figure 44. Folio 20r, Brit. Lib. Add. MS 37049, fifteenth century. Illustrating the idea that Christ's blood offers both salvation and reproach, the miniature shows the bleeding Man of Sorrows, who offers his heart to a little lay figure and complains: "O man unkynde, hafe in mynde, my paynes smert. Beholde and see, that is for the, percyd my hert." Bearing all five wounds, the heart becomes Christ's whole body. The side wound, placed horizontally, becomes a mouth, speaking the accusatory text it bears, but it also announces itself to be the wound Jesus suffered in a literal sense, because it is the wound's exact "mesure." (Photo: © British Library Board.)

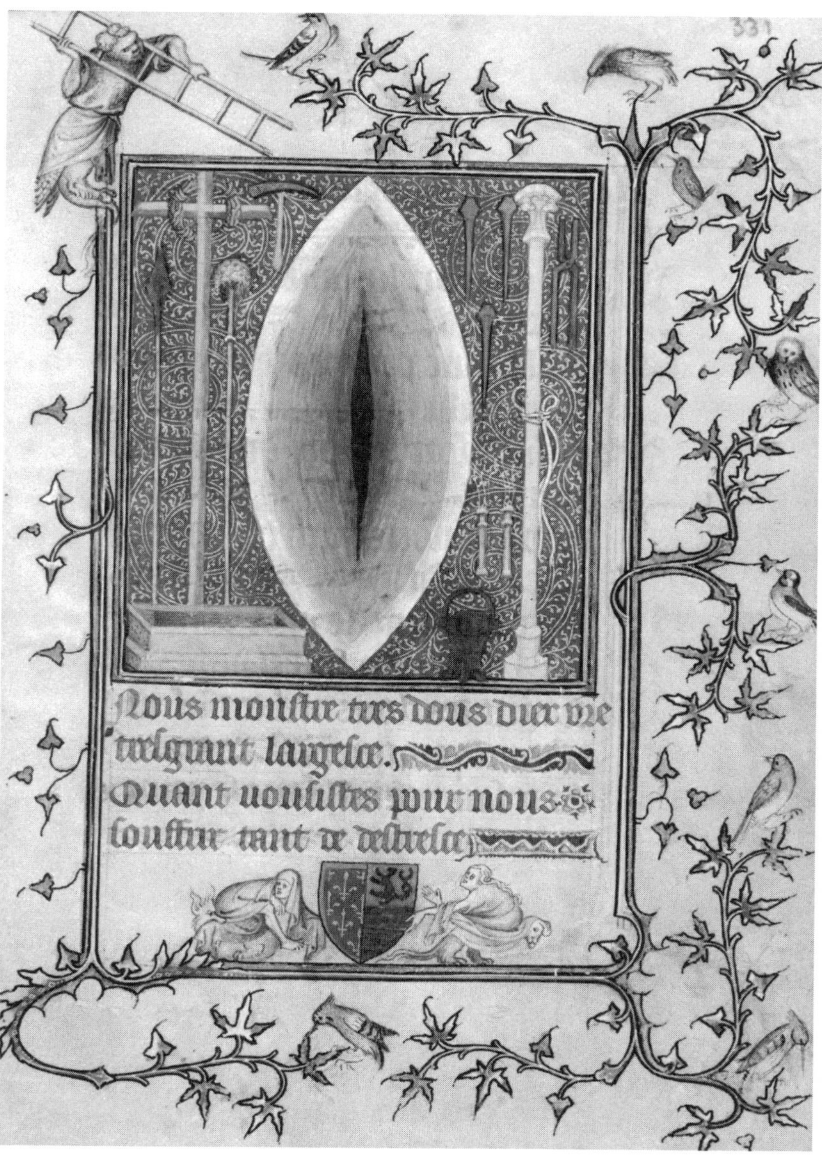

Figure 45. Folio 331r, Psalter and Hours of Bonne of Luxembourg, The Metropolitan Museum, The Cloisters Collection 69.86, from before 1349. Surrounded by the *arma Christi*, the vertically presented and flamboyantly red side wound has been interpreted by some modern scholars as drawing a parallel between Christ's gift of salvation and a vagina, understood as the opening from which the salvation of the world was born and into which saved souls return to rest in the center of Christ. (The Metropolitan Museum of Art, The Cloisters Collection, 1969 [69.86]. Image: © The Metropolitan Museum of Art.)

bearing depictions of the side wound, were bound onto the laboring mother in the hope that one gaping slit would aid another in opening (fig. 46). It is the age-old principle of *similia similibus*—like controls and counters like—that is at work.

The apotropaic power of the wound as vagina on birthing girdles parallels its power as a bearer of indulgences when it serves as the measure of Christ.[57] As I discussed in Chapter 1, the wound as measure of the length of Christ served not only as a formula for exactly how many prayers would earn a given number of indulgences but also as a kind of protective amulet. Just as people could understand themselves as giving self to God when donating a length or weight of candle wax equivalent to their own measures, so they felt in contact with the actual body of Christ when they prayed according to—or actually kissed—an image of the wound that exactly calculated his stature. Images such as the woodcut in figure 30 (p. 96) exhort devotees not just to measure the length of Christ's body by multiplying the little cross inside the wound but also to kiss the wound itself. (And we know that kissing occurred; figure 12 on p. 64 shows an image almost completely abraded by rubbing and kissing.)[58] In such depictions, the wound *is* the body, both because multiplication of its contents gives the full stature of Christ and because it is, visually, the connecting tissue holding together hands, feet and head. Those depictions of the side wound that appear to us to be like vaginas are most often, in their medieval visual contexts, explicitly connected with birthing, measuring, or the obtaining of indulgences.

Nonetheless, there is reason to think that medieval authors, craftspeople, and worshippers did see the sexual and fetishizing overtones of such devotions. Certain conservative theologians were made uncomfortable by what they felt to be an odd interest in the interior of the Virgin's body.[59] And there are surviving examples (which must be only a fraction of what once existed) of objects that appear to mock both Holy Wound piety and relic devotion and thereby suggest that the sexual overtones were apparent to contemporaries.[60] A little lead badge, cast about 1400 and now in the Cluny Museum in Paris (one other example, from Rotterdam, is known), shows three penises carrying a vagina in procession, just as reliquaries of holy arms, feet, and ribs were carried (fig. 47).[61]

The little badge is certainly bawdy. We cannot, however, be certain that it was intended to be a parody of contemporary piety, because we know nothing about its reception. No images survive of people wearing such sexual badges.[62] Most surviving lead badges are religious—the pilgrim badges so familiar to scholars from deposits in riverbeds and along roads and depicted in paintings of saints.[63] And "parody," like caricature and satire, is notoriously difficult for one culture to recognize and identify in another. At least one recent critic argues that such bawdy depictions are themselves apotropaic, rather than erotic, although this is difficult to prove (or indeed to refute).[64] The visual parallels between the Cluny badge and such images as the Bohun Book of Hours or the Hours of Bonne of Luxembourg are, however, striking. (See figs. 30, 31, and 45, pp. 96–97 and 199.) The vertical, mandorla-shaped wound in the Bohun Book (see fig. 31, p. 97), lifted upward in resurrection by angels as if it were the body of Christ, bears a striking resemblance to the little vagina borne by penises in the badge now at Cluny.

Moreover, a number of examples survive (mostly from Holland) of badges in which vaginas are dressed as female pilgrims and a few in which both penis and vagina are depicted as going on pilgrimage.[65] A fabliau such as *Du Prestre crucifié*, analyzed by Howard Bloch, draws an explicit parallel between a tumescent priest-lover and the corpus of Christ on the cross. Yet another fabliau recounts the story of three male pilgrims who find a penis along their pilgrimage route and are puzzled about what to do until a clever abbess claims to identify it as the abbey's stolen door knocker.[66] Three German tales from the fifteenth century, recently discussed by Ann Marie Rasmussen, feature wandering genitalia, both male and female.[67] Such images clearly mock pilgrims and priests, as does a good deal of late medieval literature,

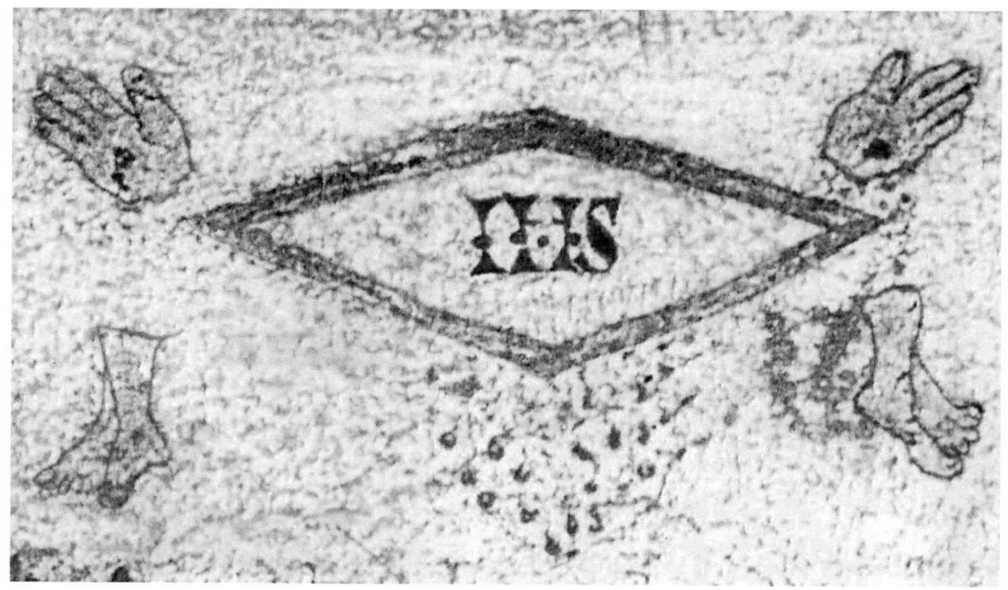

Figure 46. Portions of a birthing girdle, Wellcome MS 632, computer-generated simulation by Stephen Morse, created by permission. Very worn from use, this narrow (10 cm) scroll, sewn together from four pieces of vellum, was bound onto the body of a mother in labor to ease the birth. It bears the *arma Christi* and the five wounds, of which the largest, the side wound, sheds blood drops and was believed to have the apotropaic quality of inducing the vagina, to which it bears a close resemblance, to open. Few such girdles survive, but it is clear, from the urgency of the need, that they were numerous. (Photo: Wellcome Library, London.)

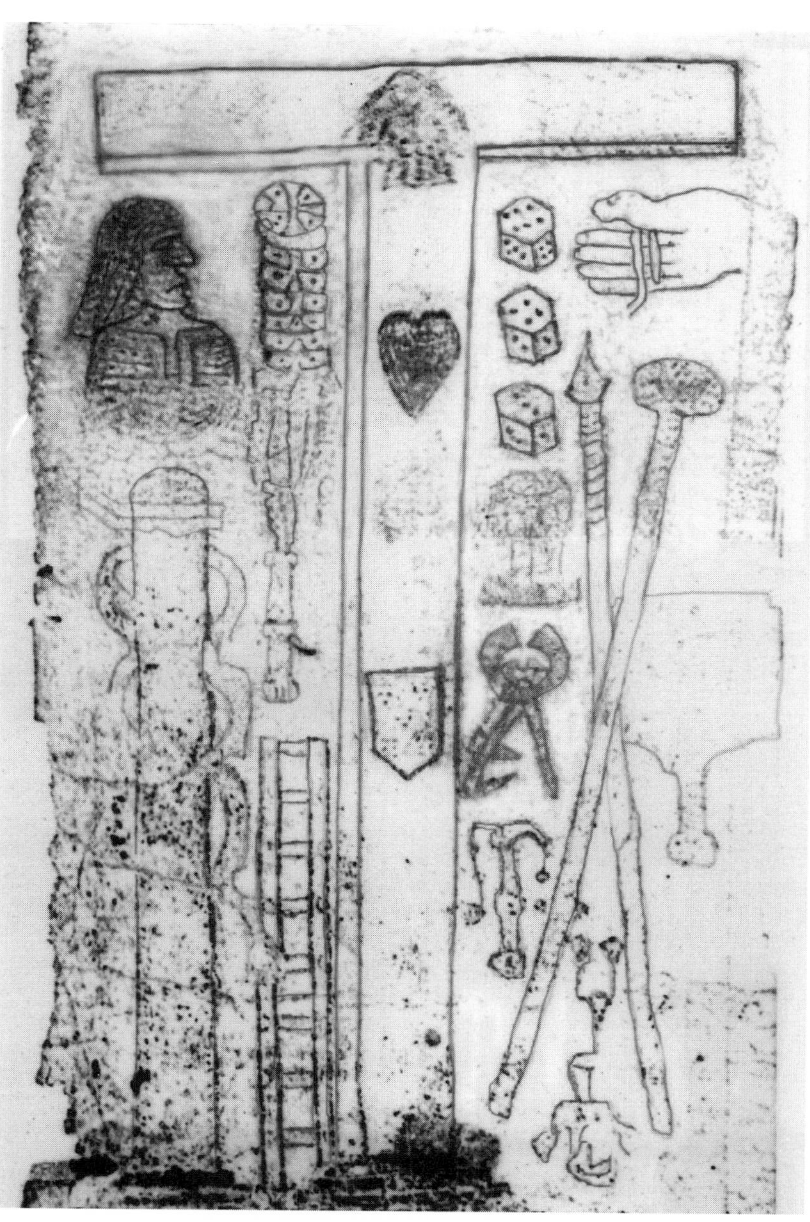

Figure 47. Three penises carrying a vagina in procession. Lead badge, 5.4 x 4 cm, end of the fourteenth or beginning of the fifteenth century. Such bawdy badges, which have been found in relatively large numbers in Holland, parallel the insignia collected by pilgrims to memorialize their journeys and often suggest mockery of pilgrim hypocrisy by portraying priests and nuns as wandering genitals. It is rare to find what might be taken as parody of actual holy objects, but this badge is clearly a visual take-off of holy-wound devotion such as is seen in Figures 31 and 45. (Photo: Réunion des musées nationaux/Art Resource, NY.)

both moralizing and otherwise. Parodying those who engage in religious behavior (cynically or profanely) is not, of course, as radical or transgressive as mocking a holy object itself. Nonetheless, the existence of such bawdy depictions of clerics, nuns, and pilgrims of both sexes suggests that it was quite possible for medieval devotees and critics to see—and use satirically—the sexual overtones of devotional objects. In one of the stories analyzed by Rasmussen, a dialogue between a lady and her vulva, the lady is depicted in an enclosed garden; the parallel to the Virgin Mary is unmistakable.[68]

We know that secular and religious love poetry tended to use the enumeration of body parts to underline devotion. A manuscript of the lives of the saints from 1320 includes a long poem in seven sections addressed to the "members" of Christ: feet, knees, hands, side, breast, heart, and face. The so-called Lentulus Letter, known from the middle of the fourteenth century, describes the beauty of Christ's facial features and body, part by part.[69] Troubadours hymned their ladies—and the Virgin Mary (Lady above all others)—in songs that counted their physical attributes (forehead, lips, neck, breasts, etc.), dwelling on each.[70] They apparently saw nothing sacrilegious or even peculiar in doing so. But we sometimes find hints in fabliaux and romances that authors were aware of how shocking or entertaining it might be to draw parallels between the body parts of lovers and those of saints. In the fifteenth-century *Das Nonnenturnier*, the second part of which is devoted to the adventures of a knight's severed penis, nuns are described as carrying the penis on a litter in what is at least partly a reversal of the little badge from Cluny and Rotterdam.[71] And to cite another example, the Jewish poet Isaac haGorni produced a parodic last will and testament in which his body was bequeathed to friends and former lovers. Isaac makes the analogy to Christian relic cult explicit and thus indicates that there was a general cultural awareness of—and amusement at—the parallel between literal and metaphorical, secular and religious, fetishizing of body parts.[72]

A famous passage in the thirteenth-century *Romance of the Rose* makes the parallel even clearer. When the author finally reaches the point in his long story at which the lover has sexual intercourse with his "rose"—an allegorical figure that signifies both the lady and the female genitals—he speaks of uncovering the vagina as revealing "the relics." Whether the language is a parody, intended to shock or amuse, we can never be sure, but the analogy to Christian devotion is explicit.[73] In a manuscript illumination of the scene (Biblioteca Històrica de la Universidad de València MS 387 fol. 147v), discussed by Michael Camille, the lover's sword penetrates these "relics," located between the lady's legs, but the legs have become the pillars of a temple; her unveiling and sexual initiation is explicitly rendered as a tearing of the temple curtain and entry into the tabernacle (fig. 48). It is impossible not to think that the author—like the manuscript illuminator who illustrates the scene—notes and uses the oddness of his religion. Similarly, it is difficult not to think that those who made and wore badges such as the one now in the Cluny Museum saw the humor as well as the possible blasphemy in certain lush and graphic depictions of Christ's side wound and in the devotional frenzy that led to passionate kissing of it.

But the parallel of the little badge of penises and vagina with images such as those in Paris BN MS Fr. 574 (fig. 12, p. 64) and the Bohun Book of Hours (fig. 31, p. 97) not only raises questions about sexuality, humor, parody, and cultural reception. It also underlines my general argument. For the parallel is incomplete. Images of the side wound go more explicitly toward visual synecdoche than does the badge. We have, of course, our modern suspicions, but the extent to which the bawdy badge reduces women to vaginas and men to penises is open to debate. Even in fabliaux, as in the fifteenth-century German stories of wandering genitalia, the vulvas and penises seem to achieve their literary power to represent transgressive acts or individuals exactly as fragments.[74] They are shocking or funny because they are *parts* that fly or walk; whole figures chase or manipulate them, desiring

Figure 48. In this illustration of the climax of Jean de Meung's *Romance of the Rose*, the successful lover finally penetrates the "rose" (symbol for both the lady and the vagina) he has long sought. The poet's imagery is explicitly religious: "I partly raised the curtain which covered the relics and approached the image to know the sanctuary more intimately." Visually, the moment is rendered by the sword's penetration between the columns of the temple, which are also the lady's legs. (Photo: Biblioteca Històrica de la Universidad de València, MS 387 fol. 147v.)

to possess these body parts almost as if they were sex toys. There is, however, no question that depictions of wound devotion make the side wound the whole body. What angels in the Bohun Book of Hours raise on high when Christ rises from the sepulcher *is* the side wound. In late medieval devotion, part *is* whole.[75]

Concomitance as Theory and Habit of Mind

Much of the oddness of such devotion was theorized in what theologians called the doctrine of concomitance, which argued that, with Christ, part is whole. Concomitance was worked out in the eleventh century in the context of a controversy over the real presence of Christ in the Eucharist.[76] Those theologians who emerged on the winning side in this conflict charged that some of their opponents held a heresy these theologians labeled "stercoranism" (from *stercus*, "excrement").[77] Its proponents supposedly argued that if the bread and wine really became flesh and blood at the consecration, Christ would then be macerated and crushed, even digested, by believers, or multiplied into a mountain of matter by the celebration of countless masses. Theologians who supported real presence countered such interpretation by explaining that Christ is totally present in every mass and in every particle of the fragmented host. Hence, if each part is the whole Christ, he is not damaged, divided, or chewed. As Hugh of Lincoln supposedly said, about 1200, when offered the opportunity to behold a host that bled miraculously when divided: we see Christ in the Eucharist perfect and complete. Only those of immature spirituality see parts. "Why should we gape at a sensory image of this divine gift when every day we behold by faith this heavenly sacrifice, whole and entire? Let that man look with his bodily eyes on the minute fragment who cannot by faith internally behold the whole."[78] The truth beyond the appearance of division is wholeness and immutability.

Such theological use of synecdoche had broad implications, both theoretical and practical. As far as the theology of the mass was concerned, concomitance theory meant that Christ could bilocate. Eternally present at the right hand of the Father in resurrected glory, Christ was also present on the altar at every celebration of the Eucharist. No matter how many services were sung or consecrations performed, there was only one sacrifice offered to God for humankind, and it was offered simultaneously on earth and in heaven.

Concomitance theory had practical applications as well. In the thirteenth century, when the clergy moved to deny the communion cup to the laity (largely because of fear that the devout would spill it in their eagerness for it), the doctrine was used to justify such withdrawal. By the fifteenth century, when the followers of Jan Hus in Bohemia made a demand for the return of the lay chalice their rallying cry, miracles of the host were said to justify the idea of concomitance almost as often as they were said to demonstrate transubstantiation. Johannes von Paltz, for example, argued that the supposed *Dauerwunder* at Sternberg was produced by God both in order to show Jews and Christian doubters that Christ was really present in the consecrated wafer and in order to refute Bohemian (that is, Hussite) claims to the cup. The Hussites were wrong to demand the chalice, Paltz argued, because every Christian already had blood in the wafer. To demand communion in both kinds was to hold a mistaken Eucharistic theology, one that denied concomitance.[79]

Concomitance doctrine was also employed in debates over effluvial and quasi-bodily relics. In the thirteenth century, one Gerhard of Cologne was asked by the abbot of the monastery of Weingarten to defend its venerable relic of the blood of Christ against the criticism made by theologians such as Aquinas that effluvial relics were impossible because all of Christ's blood had ascended into heaven. Gerhard wrote:

> Just as he [Christ] could make his subtle and glorified body touchable and visible to his disciples, so he could not do without one and the same blood in heaven and yet left it behind as a comfort for his believers here on earth. Cannot one and the same all-powerful

> Savior in one and the same moment be changed into the sacrament in the hands of a thousand priests, really here present and undivided, and yet not be absent there [in heaven]?[80]

Concomitance theory is used here, somewhat torturously, to defend the bilocation—or perhaps even trilocation—of the blood of Christ. If all Christ is in every particle, then Christ's blood can be totally in heaven, glorified (almost immaterial), and yet present on earth both in the Eucharist and as the palpable drops (seeable, touchable, even drinkable) of the Weingarten relic. Gerhard's near contemporary, Thomas of Chobham, in his treatise on preaching, made similar use of the Eucharistic analogy. Discussing how Christ's foreskin can both remain on earth and be resurrected, Thomas asserted: "Just as by a miracle the body of Our Lord can be at one and the same time in several places, so that body can exist in several forms.... Christ's foreskin, glorified as part of his integral body, may exist in another place unglorified."[81] In such arguments, we find the Christian understanding of holy matter taken to its improbable yet logical conclusion. Sacrality is conveyed, not diminished, by material partition, because part is forever part yet forever whole.

Concomitance theory was even used in anti-Jewish propaganda. The published account of the fact-finding commission concerning the events of 1510 in the Berlin area stressed that the Jew Salomon "pierced and stabbed [the host] many times but could not harm it [*jedoch nit verwunden mögen*]." The host was then reported to have divided itself into three pieces, as if at the consecration, with bleeding along the cracks. Salomon was said to have sent two fragments to friends in other towns before attacking the remaining particle again. The language of the report makes it clear that the host took it upon itself to divide. Thus, however counterintuitive the claim, division is taken here to be proof of indestructibility; bleeding is not only protest against violation but proof of continuing life as well. The report also clearly suggests that the distribution of pieces through the Mark Brandenburg was perpetrated by the Jews in order to render Christ liable to further abuse. The abuse, although heinous, was forever ineffective, because host fragments, "although drowned, burnt, and in other ways persecuted," cannot be "destroyed [*umbringen*]."[82] In such propaganda, the idea that part is whole, and that life and power perdure beyond and indeed by means of division, becomes the basis for fantasies about Jewish conspiracy. It is because the bits remain Christ that they are alleged to carry with them the possibility of continued (but forever unsuccessful) Jewish attack against him; hence, they also continue and indeed multiply the possibility of Christian attacks against Jews.

We find such theories used even more explicitly in another anti-Jewish libel that emerged in the wake of the Berlin trial. At the cloister of Heiligengrabe not far from Wilsnack, there seems to have been some sort of pilgrimage before 1300, and it may have been to an alleged blood miracle. But the host-desecration legend was constructed only in the early sixteenth century by the abbess, who wished to capitalize on the hatred of Jews unleashed by the trial of 1510 and to preserve old belief in the face of encroaching reform. In propaganda for the cult, which included German and Latin broadsides as well as panel paintings depicting the host desecration and the execution of its alleged Jewish perpetrators, a good deal of theological ingenuity is employed in discussing both the mutilation of the host and its subsequent adventures. For example, the author of a Low German version of the founding legend written in 1521 describes how the smaller of the two hosts, pulverized and hence collected as red dust in a feather quill, is the undivided godhead. The healing of a possessed peasant woman with this dust is said to demonstrate that "without any doubt or fraud this was God [*unde ane allen twyuel unde bedroch de ware god*]," who is present "no less in the little pieces of bread than in the whole [*nicht weniger jn den brockessen dan yn deme gantzen*]."[83] In this polemic, an anti-Jewish libel becomes the occasion for offering a bit of theological education. A supposed desecration years before the moment of writing is used not only to foment outrage against Jewish crimes and to encourage pilgrimage to the spot where the marvelous object had performed its miracles but also to illustrate the abstruse theological doctrine that a living God resides not less in part than in whole.

What we can perhaps call the assumption of concomitance undergirded some of the disciplinary conundrums concerning *Dauerwunder* and relics we find expressed in the fourteenth and fifteenth centuries. For example, at Cismar in the far north of Germany, the bishop—worried because he could not find documentation for the monastery's blood relic—opened the monstrance in 1467 in the presence of the abbot and brothers to find that what was there was crumpled crimson silk. The silk was not then burned, however; it was placed with the other relics. The cult was suppressed, but the object itself was treated as if it retained some aura from the veneration it had previously received.[84] Or to take another example: at the shrine of Deggendorf in Bavaria, the supposed miracle host was replaced several times over the course of its history, and church authorities disagreed right down into the 1990s over whether such substitution was acceptable or not.[85]

As these cases make clear, historical documentation and authenticity of provenance were taken seriously. Authorities did not want the faithful venerating mistakes or frauds; indeed, they warned that veneration of nonholy matter was idolatry. But the absence of authenticating documents, even the absence of the original substance, was not quite enough to leave them comfortable with simply deaccessioning matter that had long been venerated. When bishops and shrine attendants substituted new hosts for supposedly miraculous ones (as was done repeatedly at Deggendorf) or attempted to camouflage the deterioration or disappearance of relics (as someone may have done at Cismar), their motives could have been as much devout as fraudulent. By the doctrine of concomitance, Christ was wholly present in every host; hence, one could replace another. And by the same doctrine, his blood could be simultaneously present in particles on earth (perhaps even vanishing particles) and yet whole in heaven. Why risk scandalizing the faithful by allowing them to see a miracle overlaid with spiderwebs and mold? Indeed, the bishop of Passau in 1338 and Popes Eugene IV and Nicholas V in the fifteenth century insisted that "ordinary" consecrated hosts be displayed alongside supposed miraculous ones exactly so that the faithful would not be committing idolatry if the miracle was a fraud in the first place or had decayed into mere matter.[86]

As employed by Gerhard of Cologne, Thomas of Chobham, Pope Eugene IV, and the author of the Heiligengrabe pamphlet, concomitance doctrine led to remarkably convoluted argumentation. Many parts are all one part, and each part is the whole. The blood of Christ can simultaneously be present in a vial at Weingarten, on a miraculous host at Wilsnack, and pleading for sinners before the throne of heaven. A consecrated wafer, such as the one supposedly attacked at Spandau, might choose to fragment itself in order to manifest its wholeness. The cultural practices I have discussed above—relic partition and distribution, host-desecration charges, partible burial of kings and cardinals as well as saints, the fragmentation of Christ's body into five wounds in poetry and visual presentation—all suggest that such thinking was more than a theological doctrine. Concomitance was a habit of mind.[87]

The habit of concomitant thinking was deeply embedded in medieval assumptions about what the material is. Because it was understood to be that which changes, matter was threat and opportunity: a threat because it decays, an opportunity because change is manifestation of the new. Matter is the place where what was seems to depart, yet it is also the place where life can be born. Astonishing things erupt in it. It can renew itself (as, for example, in miracles of the repair of eyes or fingernails), generate new matter (as in miracles of holy bodies calling down manna from heaven), or return from decay to life in resurrection miracles.[88] The assumption that part is whole is closely connected to this understanding of the material. For concomitance is a way of defeating the threat of matter while making explicable, even profiting from, the occasion it provides for new life. Concomitant thinking assumes that division does not destroy what was; partition does not kill; distribution does not dissolve identity. The cardinal or king whose head is in one church while his bones are in another is the same cardinal or king, present in two places. Mutilated bread is not so much injured as the locus of new life. Part is not inert; it is potentially alive as well as potentially whole. Hence, partition and distribution can proceed, for each part carries the fullness of power. When people behaved as if hosts or wood bled, just as when they theorized that Christ or the saint resided in every fragment of itself, they were, so to speak, performing the habit of concomitance.

I have not intended to imply, by what I have said above, that theories cause attitudes or, conversely, that behaviors are simply rationalized or reflected in theories. Nor am I suggesting that all medieval theologians held one theory. In fact, as I have shown, they disagreed widely about what I am calling Christian materiality—about relics, contact relics, and sacramentals, about Eucharistic theory and *Dauerwunder*, about visions and images. Moreover, I am not maintaining that all people behaved in similar ways toward relics and images. Cathars, Lollards, and Hussites rejected certain material objects to which other groups enthusiastically adhered. Nonetheless, I do suggest that a wide variety of people expressed, in word, ritual, and daily life, the attitudes I have explored in these chapters and that the attitudes were in a number of ways self-contradictory. Those who attacked images as dead and/or rotten, like those who revered them as holy presences, in fact acted as if they were alive. Those who launched proceedings against Jews for desecrating the Eucharist believed the holy was there to be desecrated and in some cases welcomed the supposed abuse as the revelation of holy stuff (and hence the occasion for new pilgrimage). Those who rejected or ridiculed effluvial relics, like those who defended them, betrayed an uneasy suspicion that there was something deeply sinister if they decayed. The very vehemence of the attacks on supposed relic fraud, faked pilgrimages, or animated statues indicates that the assumptions of what I am calling Christian materiality were sources of acute anxiety for some, even as they were opportunity for others. Indeed for many, they were both.

Conclusion

The habit of thinking concomitantly did not resolve the anxieties to which assumptions about matter gave rise. Despite the enthusiasm of pilgrims, mystics, and devotional writers for revelation through images or the conviction of Aristotelians such as Thomas Aquinas that we need objects because we, as humans, must acquire knowledge through the empirical world, the coming of the transcendent into matter was deeply problematic. I have cited throughout these chapters many writers (both orthodox and dissident) who expressed ambivalence over the material location of the holy. I remind you only of Guibert of Nogent's obsession with protecting every particle of Christ's body from division and putrefaction or William Whyte's objection that images cannot be worshiped because they are dead wood, even if carved in the likeness of living men.

Yet the problem of matter was even more complex than the texts of Guibert and William Whyte, Thomas Aquinas, and Gerhard of Cologne, suggest, and to this I turn in Chapter 4. To adumbrate the deeper problem, I return for a moment to the case of miracle hosts. Lurking behind the opposition to these objects as both improbable and dangerous was the question: can Christ be present not just in matter but in enduring matter—in this case, red spots on a piece of bread? The problem was not merely disciplinary, although there is evidence that host miracles were sometimes frauds. The problem was ontological—that is, it concerned the very nature of things, both physical and divine. Could the Eucharistic blood of Christ be visible? And—an even greater problem—if it was, how long would it remain? For matter changes. Even if the divine does appear in bread, making it holy and empowering it to spread holiness wherever it goes, how long will it remain vivid and red? It seems that repeated miracles will be necessary, lest the miraculous object fade, giving way to another, and another, and yet another.[89] The fact that sites of animated images, or bleeding hosts, or liquefying and oozing relics tended to emerge in competition with each other in a given region in the later Middle Ages was not owing only to calculation by authorities desirous of maintaining pilgrimage revenues (although there was a certain amount of fostering and even inducing of miracles). Competition and resacralization was a necessity lodged in the nature of matter itself. Since matter changes, it must be reanimated if it is to endure as the locus of the divine.[90] The nature of matter makes the eruption of miracles possible, but the nature of matter also makes the repetition of miracles necessary. Assertions of concomitance notwithstanding, many feared that miraculous apparitions in bits of matter could not endure forever, incorruptible and whole.

Hence, materiality itself was the problem. In my next chapter, I move beyond the assumptions about part and whole that underlay specific instances of holy matter (images, relics, and *Dauerwunder*) to consider the opportunity and threat of materiality in another way—through medieval theories of matter itself.

CHAPTER FOUR

Matter and Miracles

In their theoretical discussions of images, relics, sacramentals, and *Dauerwunder*, medieval theologians vacillated between explaining, even supporting, such holy objects, on the one hand, and dismissing or explaining them away, on the other. In a sense, then, the simultaneity of threat and opportunity offered by holy matter in the practices of ordinary Christians and of authorities, secular and ecclesiastical, was mirrored in the writings of intellectuals when they explicitly addressed the use and meaning of material objects. Preachers, spiritual directors, scholastic theologians, and ecclesiastical leaders inevitably felt pressure from those who revered relics and images and from those who condemned them—a pressure that led to attempts both to orchestrate and to limit such veneration by careful definition. Whether one considers Lollard attacks against images, scholastic debate over the ontological status of blood relics, or the polemics surrounding pilgrimages to sites of moving statues and bleeding bread, holy matter as threat and opportunity is a theme that runs through praxis and theory in the later Middle Ages.

But in reading discussions of specific objects by theorists and polemicists (the sort of texts I considered in Chapters 1 and 2), one cannot help feeling that there is a broader context. I began to explore this context in Chapter 3 by considering views of part and whole that peek up into explicit theorizing but seem only the tip of semiconscious assumptions. In this chapter, I try to dig down even deeper to such assumptions by considering what philosophers and theologians said about holy matter itself. I do so by looking especially at some of the many places where they treat the topic of miracles—that is, cases where matter, under the direct action of God, ruptures the order of nature God himself has established. In scholastic theories of matter and miracle, we find the same sense of simultaneous threat and opportunity, and the same paradox of change and triumph over change, that we found in assumptions about part and whole.

The natural-philosophical understandings I look at here may seem as self-contradictory as the concomitance theory I explored in Chapter 3. Both before and after the recovery of Aristotelian physics and biology in the thirteenth century, matter was understood under the paradigm of generation and corruption. Thus, a sense of its lability and propensity for extravagant change undergirded, albeit to a varying extent, learned discussion throughout the later Middle Ages. At the same time, scholastic theorists, ecclesiastical authorities, and devotional writers employed various more specific theories of matter (ranging from seminal reasons, atomism, and Galenic medicine to Aristotelian ideas of substance or Neoplatonic understandings of a world soul) to harness the very sense of lability their assumptions also fostered. The entry of Aristotelian biological, physical, and metaphysical texts in the thirteenth century and their sophisticated use in the fourteenth introduced genuinely new tools for conceptualizing change as anything but arbitrary or random. Although it is not correct to say that natural philosophy and theology were one and the same in the thirteenth and fourteenth centuries, scholastic thinkers came increasingly to explore and elaborate questions about religious and theological issues, such as the natures of Adam, Mary, and Christ, and indeed of creation and God's power over it, with natural-philosophical material.[1] The scholastic tendency to understand matter as the locus of generation and decay—of coming to be and passing away—therefore cut in two opposing directions: both to control matter and to unleash it.

Medieval understandings of miracle may also seem self-contradictory. No medieval thinker could completely deny the possibility of miracles—that is, of occurrences that were by definition not just beyond our current understanding but also outside the ordinary workings of nature. God was omnipotent. Creation was filled with signs of his power and splendor. Both human and natural phenomena, such as war, plagues, or earthquakes, could be understood as expressions of divine providence or displeasure.[2] But because miracles were beyond natural explanation, they were ipso facto regarded as rare and established as miracles only when other understandings failed. How else would one know they were miracles?[3] Not only pilgrims, shrine attendants, and authors of briefs for canonization but also natural philosophers who studied astronomy or psychology were pulled by their assumptions about divine power both to believe that it could erupt unexpectedly in matter and to utilize their theories to explain away some such eruptions completely, as well as to analyze others as cases where matter cooperated with God.

Such opposing impulses at the heart of understandings of both matter and miracle are contradictions, not paradoxes in the sense in which I have been using this word as an analytical tool. Theories of matter led philosophers both to understand it as by definition corruptible and to assert that something (a nature or identity) could persist in it; theories of miracle led philosophers and theologians to a sense that the order of the world was only very occasionally violated but was nonetheless by definition capable of violation. These contradictory implications of basic assumptions led to a good deal of both confusion and creativity, which I will discuss below. The true paradox lay beneath them, however. It was the paradox of creation itself: the presence of the eternal and immutable in the transient and corruptible. In a sense, then, the paradox of creation is the conjunction of the two sets of assumptions I explore here: matter (and its contradictions) with miracle (and its). The paradox of creation is the simultaneous existence of change (in all its opposing yet productive implications) and the

Unchangeable (which can create or impose miraculous survival in the midst of ordinary demise).

Three Examples

I begin with three very different theorists, whose treatments of matter show the slippages, fissures, and confusions inherent in or resulting from medieval assumptions. These confusions are very different from each other, and I do not conflate them here. Rather, I intend them as examples of the kind of issues I will be focusing on in what follows.

First, I return to Peter the Venerable's praise of the relics of St. Marcellus, which I discussed in my third chapter. What I underlined there was Peter's sense that part is whole, that dead and dry are nonetheless fertile and flowering. But if we consider the text again, we note something else. Not only do we sense a defensive note in Peter's *laudatio*—someone might say (and seemingly has said) that these relics are "bones lacking in sense," "lifeless," "dry," contemptible, "cadavers like those of dumb beasts"—but we are also struck by the slippage in Peter's own language between "is" and "as if." We are not to think of the saints "as if [*uelut*]" dry bones, says Peter. But he also says that they are only "as if [*quasi*]" in future incorruption.

> And in this hope I have confidence more certainly than in any human thing that you ought not to feel contempt for the bones of the present martyrs as if they were dry bones [*non uelut arentia contempnitis*] but should honor them now full of life as if they were in their future incorruption [*quasi future incorruptione iam florentia honoratis*].... Flesh flowers from dryness.... [W]e ought to reverence...the body of this blessed martyr as about to be resurrected, as it will be clothed in immortal glory [*ut resurrecturum, ut immortali gloria uestiendum honore*], although we see it as dead.... [T]he bodies of the saints live with God [*Uivere, inquam, Deo sanctorum corpora*].[4]

Are the bones alive with God, then, or are they awaiting their resurrection? Are they temples (that is, containers) and pearls (that is, hard defenses against decay), or are they "now" full of life, flowering, remade, and living with God. In other words, is their "as if"—their analogous—quality attributable to their boneness or to their saintness, to their hardness or to their fertility? Peter seems, oddly enough, to say both. The sacred slips between animate and inanimate, bodily and heavenly, present and eternal, as if the poles were simultaneous, rather than dichotomous. Yet behind it all is a nagging worry that someone may not understand.[5]

Many texts from the later Middle Ages suggest such confusion or slippage. My second example is a passage from Nicole Oresme's *Livre du ciel et du monde*, a commentary—which is far more than mere commentary—on Aristotle's *De caelo*. Oresme (d. 1382) is one of the fourteenth-century figures most sympathetic to modern readers for his self-confident naturalizing of marvelous phenomena and his creative advances in the science of graphing and in cosmology. In the *Livre du ciel*, Oresme considered a topic that loomed large in late medieval discussions both because of a Neoplatonizing Aristotelianism imparted to western Europe, above all via Islamic philosophy, and because of pressing questions raised by astrology, which many intellectuals supported.[6] Asking whether heavenly bodies are alive or not, Oresme maintains that the heavens are not alive, because if they were, the fact would give support to idolaters, who worship matter as if it were living.[7] Since to be material means, to Oresme, to be altered, he actually argues that the heavens are not a material thing (*chose materielle*). Or if they are matter (*ou se il est de materie*), it is matter of another nature (*d'autre nature*) from the matter here below that is subject to generation and corruption.[8]

Hence, it is clear that Oresme defines matter as the subject of change. And his own sense of it is quite dynamic.[9] Elsewhere, he tends to use paradigms of the animate for the entire material world, analogizing (for example) the poisonous gases of mines to the stench of corpses or the powers of plants to those of stones—a point to which I will return.[10] Nonetheless, Oresme clearly fears (as did the Lollard polemicists I considered in Chapter 1) that Christians fall all too easily into treating certain kinds of matter (heavenly bodies and representations of them) as alive. Several different understandings of *materie* are clearly in play here, as are a number of different attitudes toward it.

As a final example, I return to the debate over the Wilsnack hosts that took place in the 1450s. In a treatise titled "Concerning Adoration and Against the Blood [*contra cruorem*]," Eberhard Waltmann, reforming Premonstratensian and provost of the Archdiocese of Magdeburg, reacted to the supposed miracle of 1383 by rejecting the church's claim to possess a miraculously preserved wafer or wafers on which the blood of Christ had appeared.[11] But in doing so, he did not contest the possibility of material miracles (although he asserted that the Wilsnack hosts themselves were not miraculous); rather, he contested the appropriate devotional response.

When I discussed the Wilsnack controversy in Chapter 2, I called attention to the political maneuvering of many parties—local and international, secular and ecclesiastical. I also mentioned the charge of opponents that the event was a fraud and the problems, ontological as well as political, posed by the deterioration of holy matter. What interests me here in Waltmann's text are the ambiguities and anxieties evidenced in the specific arguments he mounted against the hosts almost seventy years after their supposed appearance.[12] Wishing to discredit them and their powers, Waltmann first states that this particular miracle cannot be the natural remains of Christ because it is dead stuff. In this, we hear—as we did in Oresme's text—echoes of exactly the sort of arguments I discussed in Chapter 1. Like Lollards in England arguing against panel paintings and statues as dead stones and rotten sticks, Waltmann here suggests that a preserved wafer is dead, inert, or (even worse) decaying stuff—that it is, in other words, mere matter. To adore specks on it is to adore flyspots or mold, not God. Yet, Waltmann admits, God *can* create matter miraculously. Indeed, he did so in the famous account of a finger appearing in the chalice when Pope Gregory the Great celebrated mass.[13] But, argues Waltmann, coming to the crux of the issue: even if God does perform such miracles, they are horrible (*horribilis*). Change done by God is terror-inducing. Like the blood plague inflicted on the ancient Egyptians (Exod. 7:17–21), such miracles show God's wrath at sin or disbelief. Pope Gregory responded to the miracle of the chalice, says Waltmann, by praying that God immediately reconvert it into wine and wafer. This is what the priest at Wilsnack should have done as soon as the miracle hosts were found. The Magdeburg provost's ultimate argument is, therefore, not that the host is a fraud or that the local clergy are misusing it, although he suggests both. His argument is also not that God does not, or cannot, make dead matter live. Rather, Waltmann argues that if God does perform such miracles, they are a reproach, or worse, to his people. Holy matter is not so much to be dismissed and disbelieved as avoided and feared. The proper response to the manifestation of the holy in matter might well be Gregory's—to pray to God that he return to invisibility and immateriality as quickly as possible.

The confusions and slippages revealed in these texts are quite diverse. And their contexts are different: a monastic author of the twelfth century eulogizes a valued relic; a natural philosopher two hundred years later relates Aristotle's view of the heavens to the problem of idolatry; a theologian and polemicist of the fifteenth century attempts to rein in pilgrimage enthusiasm. My point is simply that all three of these authors—and those for whom or about whom they write—reflect some uncertainty about the nature of matter.

No one of the three authors rejects the possibility of miraculous occurrences. Peter the Venerable penned a miracle collection, although he occasionally expresses the typically monastic sentiment that the highest glory lies not in miracle working but in virtue.[14] Waltmann disclaimed not miracles in general but the Wilsnack hosts. Even Oresme did not deny that an omnipotent God could act *supra naturam*.[15] Indeed, he used the miracle account in Joshua 10:13 of the sun standing still in the sky during battle to provide support for his famous argument for the diurnal motion of the earth.[16] Although both astronomical models of the event involved the transgression of natural laws, it would be easier, said Oresme, for God to stop the movement of the earth for a day than to hold still the entire rotation of the heavens.[17] What we find in the texts of these three authors is not, however, either the simple affirmation or the occasional denial of the possibility of miracles. Rather, it is a probing discussion of the potentialities and dangers inherent in matter itself—that very matter in which the sacred was understood to lodge in such disparate ways.

Elite and Popular: Again a Caveat

Before I move further into the attitudes toward matter and miracle found in such texts, a final word of introduction is necessary. Although I focus in this chapter on intellectual elites, I am not arguing, either explicitly or by implication, that their theories about miracles or about matter were the cause of cultural practices. Ambivalence about miraculous transformations—skeptical denial as well as staunch support—is found at every cultural level in the later Middle Ages.

We have plenty of evidence that ordinary people as well as religious authorities and intellectuals questioned specific miracles, just as they questioned Christian doctrines concerning God's relationship to the material.[18] Some Christians seem to have doubted the resurrection of the body; many transformation miracles (for example, the pilgrim staves supposedly turned into swords and hung in the church at Wilsnack) were ridiculed;[19] even holy women, such as Gertrude of Helfta, worried that their visions might be self-induced.[20] As Steven Justice has perceptively argued, the medieval belief that miracles are manifestations of both the extraordinary and the unseen led to repeated interrogation—and sometimes rejection—of the supposedly miraculous.[21] The artisans, housewives, and peasants who testified in canonization processes or trials of heretics were operating with the assumption that supernatural events are violations of the ordinary; a workaday understanding of a distinction between natural and supernatural was clearly part of their intellectual apparatus.[22]

Evidence of doubt is often provided exactly by those who wrote against it. For example, in circa 1200, Peter of Cornwall prefaced his vision collection with a warning to those who do not believe in God, in the survival of the soul after death, or in the providential direction of the universe. Rejecting good and bad angels, "consider[ing] only what they can see," such people (so he asserts) think the world has always existed and is ruled by chance, not God.[23] Indeed, it was usually doubt (or improper belief resulting in misuse) that occasioned the miracles of host and chalice I discussed in Chapter 2. Concern on the part of pastors and monastic supervisors about faked miracles and feigned sanctity shows that assumptions, both about the presence of God in creation and about the rarity with which he acts to rupture ordinary processes and provide special graces, were widely shared. Walter Stephens has in fact argued that the underlying motivation of witchcraft theorists was not so much their own belief in witches as resistance to skepticism about them.[24]

A number of the devout moved from disillusionment with specific saints or images to antagonism toward relics and images generally. As we have seen, movements such as the Waldensians, Lollards, and Hussites, not to mention the Cathars, opposed in various ways the particular forms of holy matter supposedly found in statues, relics, or the transubstantiated Eucharist. The theologian Giles of Rome (d. 1316) asserted that the Eucharist was doubted more than any other sacrament.[25] A Cathar woman who expressed abhorrence at the idea of transubstantiation because of a sense that the matter of the human body is threatening and unclean can stand for others whose voices have not survived. Aude of Montaillou told her inquisitor: "One day as I was going to the church of the Holy Cross to hear mass . . . I thought of the disgusting afterbirth that women expel in childbearing and whenever I saw the body of our Lord raised on the altar I kept thinking, because of that afterbirth, that the host was something polluted. That's why I could no longer believe it was the body of Christ."[26] Aude's assimilation of the supposedly miraculous change of transubstantiation to the possible pollution of ordinary organic process reminds us of Guibert of Nogent's questioning of Christ's bodily relics or the connection between fragmentation and evil suggested in contemporary attitudes toward leprosy.

There is thus little indication that the arguments of intellectual elites caused popular resistance to or compliance with cult. Exactly the opposite was often the case. In many instances where Christian theorists discussed such objects as effluvial relics or *Dauerwunder*, practice seems to have pressured theorizing—sometimes in the direction of rejecting, sometimes of accepting, the miraculous. When Johannes Bremer categorizes types of holy matter, for example, he is clearly skirting certain issues made pressing by the practices of his region and his order.[27] For Bremer, the highest manifestation of Christ is not visible; the miracle of miracles is the ordinary consecration in the mass. But he cannot simply dismiss relics of Christ's blood. Nor does he want to. The objects exist and induce piety; moreover, fundamental religious assumptions about creation and salvation, parts and wholes, make such presences possible. The equivocation reflected in his reasoning, as in that of his contemporary Franciscans, stems from core beliefs about the power of God in creation but also from objects he encounters.

Indeed, as some scholars of comparative religion have suggested, it is of the nature of objects to carry practices with them; theologians and ideologists can only accommodate or resist them. In a certain sense, then, objects such as contact relics or the materials theologians denominated "sacramentals" have an agency of their own. When such objects are widespread and long-standing, it is likely, as Nile Green has argued, that theology becomes "the servant of pre-existing practices."[28]

The understanding of matter—both its power and its threat—that theorists such as Guibert, Waltmann, or Oresme articulated was not limited to intellectual elites or generated by their theories. Hence, I do not look at their ideas about matter and miraculous transformation, any more than I earlier explored their theories about specific objects, because I think philosophy is the engine of cultural change. Rather, I explore these texts in order to ferret out slippages and silences, unconscious inconsistencies and contradictions, that reflect that subterranean place where lie the assumptions that undergird acts as well as ideas.[29]

Theories of Miracle as a Way of Accessing Assumptions about Matter

University theologians and natural philosophers spilled a good deal of ink discussing the miraculous.[30] But their focus seems to us an odd one. From the twelfth century on, and especially after the papacy took over canonization, the miracles actually recorded as worked by holy people during their lives and at their tombs or by their relics after death were overwhelmingly miracles of healing. As Benedicta Ward has shown, these healing miracles tended to replace the paradigmatic early medieval miracle: the miracle of vengeance.[31] The healing miracles of the high Middle Ages did sometimes involve the creation or transformation not merely of body but also of matter. Earth from around the tomb of Isabelle of France, for example, was reported to have provided a new fingernail for someone who had lost one.[32] And miracles of incorrupt bodies, characteristic of women saints in the later Middle Ages, can be understood as miraculous cessations of the decay matter is prey to.[33] But many healing miracles involved restoring life or bodily balance or casting out evil spirits, rather than increasing or transforming or controlling matter. What is interesting for my purpose here is the fact that—despite the overwhelming predominance of healing miracles in later medieval hagiographic collections—the paradigmatic miracles discussed by intellectuals were miracles of material transformation, especially the wedding at Cana, where Christ changed water into wine (John 2), and the contest between Aaron and Pharaoh's magicians in Exodus 7.[34]

Indeed, healings, resurrections, and exorcisms were themselves often treated less as questions of restoring the balance of bodies than as questions of the manipulation of bodily stuff. And delineating exactly how spirits (either angels or demons) might interact with and employ bodies received a great deal of attention.[35]

Peter the Venerable argued that the distinction between counterfeit miracles (such as those of Pharaoh's magicians) and true Christian ones was not only that magic has a natural cause and miracle a cause beyond nature, but also that counterfeit miracles vanish quickly and take much education to perform, whereas Christian ones are solid and real, firmly fixed in matter.[36] A century later, Albert the Great (d. 1280) explained that both "the marvelous" and "the miraculous" result in real transformation and stated decisively: "The method of miracles is this: the transformation of matter."[37] Thomas Aquinas (quoting Augustine) echoed this opinion, saying: "True miracles are done by some change of bodies."[38] To Aquinas, it is exactly because demons cannot fundamentally alter bodies that the rods made by Pharaoh's magicians were only "magic" and manipulations of natural change, whereas Aaron's seemingly exactly similar rods were "miracles"—that is, real and *praeter*-natural transformation of matter. Nicholas of Autrecourt (d. 1369), one of the very few medieval thinkers to espouse atomism, used a complex argument about balance in the universe to suggest that bodily resurrection is possible because "if a man who exists now ceased to exist here in our hemisphere and were caused elsewhere, and again ceased to exist there some time later, and then were caused here, he would be said to have risen."[39] Autrecourt's discussion is not so much a fully naturalized explanation of resurrection—which almost all theologians took to be a miracle—as an analysis of the particulate nature of, and eternity of, matter.[40]

Even effects we would not consider to be physical were understood as such. Nicole Oresme, fascinated as were other medieval thinkers by examples of action at a distance (such as the influence of the skies on weather, the attraction of iron to a magnet, or—that nasty example given throughout the Middle Ages—the power of a menstruating woman to cloud a mirror at a glance), argued that only bodies can act on bodies. If a body acts on another body across intervening space, what really happens, says Oresme, is that the configuration (the geometrical pattern) of the first body or its member is altered; that configuration then alters the medium between it and the affected body, which is then itself altered.[41] Alain Boureau has recently demonstrated that a group of theologians in Paris around 1300 held a theory according to which the human imagination could cooperate with the grace of God to produce physiological effects such as stigmata.[42] The formulae of sacramentals suggested, as we have seen, that the blessed salt or grain, palm or water, was impregnated with a physical power that it conveyed to those who touched or consumed it.[43] By the fifteenth century, much of the discussion of witches, which had earlier involved the charge that it was heresy to believe witchcraft possible, came to focus on ways in which witches might manipulate alien bodies (without actually becoming them) to achieve physical results, such as riding animals or collecting sperm and impregnating women.[44] In the same period, Jean Gerson described the great twelfth-century saint, Bernard of Clairvaux, as invaded by some kind of "breath or odor" when the power of miracle came over him, just as Jesus felt something go out of himself when the hemorrhaging woman touched the hem of his garment (Luke 8:46).[45] It is as if Gerson, in a parallel to medieval vision theory, which understood sight as involving the encounter of rays sent out from the eye with those emitted by objects, has to think of spiritual power as something quasi-physical entering and exiting the body.[46] My point is not that all these theorists were making the same argument. Oresme's theory of configurations, for example, was almost unique in the fourteenth century, significant though modern historians find it as a step toward the mathematizing of explanation. My point is rather to underline that events and objects understood as unusual or miraculous tended to be analyzed in the late Middle Ages as material changes. To intellectuals, the question of miracles was a question of matter.

The Historiography of Matter

Modern historians have been very interested in the categories used by medieval theorists and have paid a great deal of attention to the emergence of clear conceptual differences between "magic" and "marvel" (natural although not fully understood), on the one hand, and "miracle" (beyond or contrary to the laws of nature), on the other. (Recent scholarship notes that, despite theoretical distinctions, the terms were actually used fairly fluidly to designate extraordinary events.[47]) The assumptions about matter that lie at the heart of medieval treatments of miracles have, however, been little studied, in part because studies of medieval conceptions of matter have gone in two very different directions, and neither line of interpretation has received much attention recently.

Philosophers have studied "matter" and its companion concept "form" in the hylomorphic thinking (the adjective comes from the Greek for matter, *hylē*, and shape, *morphē*) that derived from Aristotle and dominated medieval metaphysics. In such thinking, especially in its Thomistic version, "matter" was the capacity to be something else that, standing between A and not-A, made true change possible. As such, it tended to be equated with potency, and discussions of the nature of things focused on its companion concept "form."[48] Historians of science have concentrated on what we might call a "fuller" conception of "matter," understanding it as a kind of substratum, indeed, as material substance itself.[49] But until quite recently, they have been interested primarily in its mathematization—that is, in the way in which an idea of something called by fourteenth-century natural philosophers the "quantity of mass" or "elemental mass" emerged out of discussions of motion, rarefaction, and condensation, leading toward (but not yet arriving at) the modern scientific notion of mass.[50] Neither of these lines of investigation gets us very far in thinking about the assumptions behind treatments of miracle, except by helping us to note that there was no one medieval conception of *materia*.[51]

Nonetheless medieval theorists of miracle did talk about the transformation of matter as lying at its heart, and the materiality of miracles did provide incentive to sophisticated probing both of the natural world and of the sacred. If we prescind from questions about hylomorphism in philosophy or quantification in science, we can see, lodged at the heart of the major treatments intellectuals drew on, certain assumptions about matter that made miracles both possible and problematic. Thus, discussion of miracle had to limit and control the lability and corruptibility such understandings of matter made all too likely.

Conceptions of Matter and Change

I cannot in a brief chapter give a summary of medieval conceptions of matter. But I need to say a few words about the principal texts natural philosophers and theologians drew on. I begin, where medievalists' treatments of concepts almost always begin, with Isidore of Seville, the seventh-century Spanish encyclopedist whose etymological dictionary provided basic definitions for the entire Middle Ages. Isidore's definition of matter, which is itself derived from much earlier texts, occurs in his discussion of wood and woodworkers. He says: "All wood is called matter because from it something is made, so if you refer to a door or a statue, it will be matter." Matter is "always accepting [*semper accipienda*] with regard to something"; hence, we say "the elements are the matter of things that are made from them." The elements are called *silva* (woods) because woods are the "matter of forests."[52]

"*Materia* [matter] is named from *mater* [mother]," says Isidore. That is, *mater* is in *mater-ia*. In such etymologizing, the structure of the word is understood to *be* the structure of the reality it refers to. Hence, to Isidore, matter is, in its essence, maternal—that is, fertile and capable of becoming.

Moreover, discussing *corpus* (body), Isidore distinguishes it thus from *caro* (flesh):

> *Corpus* is called from the fact that something, being corrupted [*corruptum*], perishes; for it is soluble and mortal and able to be dissolved. *Caro*, however, is called from creating [*creando*]. . . . *Corpus* and *caro* signify differently, for there is always body in flesh but flesh is not always in body. Body can be said of something that is dead after life has departed or of something that has been brought forth without life. And sometimes there are bodies with life but without flesh, as, for example, grass or trees.[53]

It is of the nature of body and flesh to be passing away and coming to be; *cor-pus* contains *cor-rup-tum*; *caro* contains *cre-are.*

Isidore's discussion of the distinction between *corpus* and *caro* is also important because (as I mentioned in my Introduction) the recent flood of attention to "the history of the body" has obscured for us the extent to which medieval discussion of "body" is discussion of "matter."[54] As we see in Isidore, *corpus* in medieval theology meant something closer to "living thing" or even "thing" than to "human being." Cadavers, grass, and wood are all bodies.

Such understandings of both matter and body operated throughout the Middle Ages. This is especially clear in discussions of alchemy. For example, when, in a scholastic debate, Giles of Rome (d. 1316) asked whether men can make gold, the possible arguments he gives *for* the proposition include both the fact that human beings can make glass and electrum and the fact that Pharaoh's magicians made serpents from staves.[55] Giles then goes on to classify different forms of generation: horses from equine *menstruum*, bees from the decaying carcasses of cattle, wine from grapes, and gold from other metals deep in the earth. The difference is, he says, the place and form of generation. Giles himself (like most Western thinkers before him) decided against the possibility of alchemical transmutation. But what interests me here are not the arguments for and against alchemy or the question of the nature and inviolability of species. What is telling for my analysis is that, in Giles' elucidation of the issue, the process we would call normal physiological production (fetus from uterine material), what we would call spontaneous generation (bees from decaying flesh), and what we would call mechanical production (glass from sand or—if possible—gold from lead) are treated as parallel cases as far as the production of body is concerned, and that production is conceptualized as generation.[56] An even clearer example of the understanding of all matter as in essence fertile—both generative and decaying—is found in the Paduan doctor and alleged magician Pietro d'Abano, who probably died in the same year as Giles of Rome. Pietro spoke of the matter of alchemy as *menstruum mulieris*—the menstrual or uterine stuff of a woman—and compared the transmutation of metal by the alchemist to the cure of the human body by a physician, as if both were changes of organic matter.[57] Although neither Giles (who rejected alchemy) nor Pietro (who accepted it) went so far as to equate metallic bodies with human, the assumption that all change is analogous to organic generation clearly underlies their arguments and their metaphors.

The complex sense we find in Isidore and much later in Pietro d'Abano and Giles of Rome that matter is fertile, maternal, labile, percolating, forever tossing up grass, wood, horses, bees, sand, or metal, was enhanced in the high Middle Ages by the enormous influence of two works: the opening and closing books of Ovid's *Metamorphoses*, a paean to "bodies changed into new forms," and Aristotle's essentially biological model of change in his *On Generation and Corruption* (better translated as *On Coming to Be and Passing Away*).[58] Following these ancients, medieval thinkers assumed that at least in the sublunar world, to be was to be-about-to-change. I give three examples: Bernard Sylvestris, Nicole Oresme, and Niccolò Tignosi da Foligno.

In the twelfth century, Bernard Sylvestris's magisterial allegorical poem, the *Cosmographia*, gave a very Ovidean account of creation. Indeed, as Brian Stock remarks, matter is the heroine of the *Cosmographia*.[59] Sometimes a chaos of primitive and warring elements longing to be reborn, sometimes a more abstract substratum, Bernard's matter draws from two rather different treatments in Ovid. It is both the rough and teeming mass of Ovid's book 1 and the perduring reality of the more Pythagorean account in Ovid's book 15. Because ever-flowing matter (*silva*) lies beneath, Bernard's universe contains the seeds of its own creativity.[60] Procreation is seen as fighting death by perpetuating species.

Ovid's matter, as described in book 1 of the *Metamorphoses*, accounts for the fecundity of things; it is forever breaking out in new forms. But it can also be understood, as it is in Pythagoras's great speech in book 15, as that which underlies change—that is, as an eternal return or a guarantee of some enduring identity for the universe. What is important about the Ovid reception of the twelfth century, of which Bernard's poem is probably the single best example, is the fact that poets, natural philosophers, and commentators persistently emphasized the two parts of Ovid that dealt with matter and change over the more moral (or immoral) stories that come in between. Moreover, the part of book 15 that was echoed, used, and absorbed by poets and grammarians was not the doctrine of metempsychosis per se but the celebration of fertility.[61] They saw eternal return less as a Neoplatonic ascent of the soul to exemplar (although it was sometimes read this way) than as the story of form impregnating chaos. Indeed, they tended to interpret as natural philosophy, especially natural philosophy having to do with fertility and change, many of Ovid's stories that seem to modern readers to deal with quite other questions. For example, they related the sex change of Tiresias to the germination of seeds and took the story of Phaëthon and the horses of the sun as a description of sunlight and harvest.[62] It is thus possible to argue both that Ovid profoundly influenced the medieval conception of material change and that a concern with change led to a particular way of reading Ovid.

In the later thirteenth and fourteenth centuries, new conceptions of matter, very different from the teeming mass of Ovid or the maternal *corpus* of Isidore, became commonplace among intellectuals. Change came to be understood in line with Aristotle's doctrine of contraries—that is, the idea that material qualities come to be and pass away within a narrow range defined by the contraries. Both a principle of change and a limitation of change, Aristotle's matter is what accounts for going from one thing to another: caterpillar to butterfly, ice to water, whole log to cut wood. To Aristotle, change is real because matter is not a thing itself. (If it were, it would endure, and change would be only superficial.) But because a potency to be something else accounts for particular changes, change is not inexplicable or arbitrary. Hence, Aristotelian concepts rein in a sense that change might be completely random.

Nonetheless, understanding change continued to be a major metaphysical worry for those who studied Aristotle. Nicole Oresme, for example, pointed out that we cannot even think without the concept of transmutation.[63] Commenting on the treatise *On Generation and Corruption*, Oresme (like a number of his contemporaries) gave a strictly Aristotelian theory of change, making matter a potentiality to be not-A that guarantees identity in the change of A to not-A:

> We say that the fact of contraries [*contrarietas*] is the cause of corruption.... And this is proved because all corruption is by alteration of the previous.... [T]herefore it follows that every thing having a contrary is at some time corrupted.... And thus because the same thing is the matter of contraries, therefore they succeed to each other in the same matter. And thus matter which is under one contrary is in potency to this—that it can be under another contrary—which, unless it occurs, it would follow that this potency would be frustrated [*esset frustra*].[64]

Such an interpretation might seem to suggest that unlike Ovidean matter, Aristotle's matter has no characteristics. It would then be only that which accounts for the fact that we can say we are dealing with "the same thing" when a previous something becomes a posterior something. All the essence, definition, "whatness" of a thing would be accounted for by form. But, as Zoe Bosemberg has pointed out, this is not really Oresme's understanding. Matter to Oresme is far from "empty" potency. The use of the word "frustrated" in the passage I just quoted suggests, indeed, that matter has a certain dynamic quality; it is characterized, on the one hand, by a privation or lack (*turpitudo*), which is a sort of desire for form, and on the other hand by a tendency toward persisting (*conatus*).[65]

Hence, it would seem that even after the reception of Aristotle, natural philosophers continued to have a sense of matter as more labile and fertile than the Aristotelian texts would, taken strictly, suggest. And as Christof Lüthy has pointed out, Aristotle himself was less consistent than is sometimes thought. When writing about biology, he did distinguish animate from inanimate morphologically. Animate matter has *entelechy* (an inherent directing and regulating form) and organs; inanimate matter does not. But on the phenomenological and ontological level, the distinction is less clear. Aristotle is sometimes imprecise about whether all matter might be able to move or reproduce, and he does include all matter under the theory of hylomorphism (that is, the general ontological categories of form plus matter). Thus, he could be read as encompassing what we would call the living and the inanimate in one physics.[66]

Many of those who used and commented on Aristotle spoke, as did Oresme, of a kind of propensity or yearning in matter. Albert the Great held, for example, that there is an *inchoatio formae*, a kind of confusion in the heart of *materia*, that can cooperate in the generation of creatures. Although some Aristotelians, such as Aquinas, rejected this, a number of theorists, such as Bonaventure and Henry of Ghent, continued to hold to a sort of autonomy or actuality or desire in matter.[67] In the thirteenth and fourteenth centuries, then, even Aristotelian matter had certain affinities with the percolating stuff of Ovid and Bernard Sylvestris.

Moreover, in the fifteenth century, Neoplatonic interpretations, which had always accompanied Aristotelian texts in the high Middle Ages, contributed to the tendency to give the whole material world a labile, dynamic, even animate quality. Although alchemical theory in the thirteenth and early fourteenth centuries saw what we would call inert as analogous, not equivalent, to the living, by the fifteenth century, authors began to see all matter simply as animate. Confidence in the possibility of the transformation of species increased. The development of the idea of a philosophical stone found in all bodies, like the idea of an alchemical quintessence, led to theories of a vital stuff diffused throughout the cosmos. Marsilio Ficino (d. 1499), for example, related alchemical quintessence to a *spiritus mundi* (soul or spirit of the universe).[68]

Using Neoplatonic theories, intellectuals also debated the relationship of heavenly bodies to the earth. It was after all clear that the heavens do influence earthly change and fertility: Tides correlate with the phases of the moon; seeds need sunshine to germinate; tadpoles appear quite suddenly in apparently empty ponds after rain.[69] Not all worldly change is as obviously the production of like by like as is the birth of puppies from dogs. Moreover, theories of astral determinism, derived directly from the ancients or from Neoplatonizing Arab texts, contributed to a heightened and anxious interest in the role of the heavens in worldly affairs. Hence, philosophers asked whether earthly changes occur through the induction or eduction of forms by celestial intelligences—that is, through a process whereby these intelligences impregnate matter with forms or draw forms out from matter—and queried whether something like a Platonic Idea might be a necessary intermediary in this process.

Two treatises on Platonic Ideas, attributed to a certain Niccolò Tignosi da Foligno (d. 1474), who was a physician and teacher of both logic and medicine at Florence, provide an example.[70] At issue was the question of whether things generated in cases where like does not produce like are generated by the heavens acting directly or involve the Ideas. The examples given in both treatises are the birth of a mouse from putrefaction and the generation of fire by striking stone and iron together. What interests me are not the details of Tignosi's abstruse discussion about the Ideas, but rather his queries about and his definitions of change.[71]

First, we should note Tignosi's assumption that a wide variety of changes are parallel and can be explained by a single understanding of form acting on matter. There is no theoretical difference for this author between the production of fire from flint and the birth of an animal from slime: both are generation. What needs explaining is the emergence of not-like from like–that is, of not-A from A–and how the stars produce it.

Second, we should note the actual definitions of matter at play here. Attempting to sort out the very complicated issues raised along the way, the author concludes:

> If anyone wants to interpret rightly the statement "form is educed from the potency of matter" other than it is commonly understood, he must say that "matter" is subsumed under three headings: first, for that which is pure potency–which is the non-existent part of a natural thing–; second, for a thing which is opposite–that is, for that from which something is made so that that from which it is made is not non-existent, as for example fire is made from air–; and third for a natural agent.

In the ensuing explanation, the second meaning of matter is the four elements. The third refers to that from which the form is made in the process of generation

> ...so that the substantial form which is generated is educed from the potency of matter–that is, from the active potential of the material agent, and by this material agent I understand, in the way of the theologians, every agent which includes in itself imperfection, which are all agents except the first [God].[72]

Matter is clearly understood here not only as stuff, rather than simple potentiality, but also as dynamic stuff. Indeed, matter is all the stuff of creation, forever in motion exactly because imperfect, in contrast to the perfection of God.

The understanding of matter as in some sense dynamic, as possessing power or desire within it, does not run in a straight line from the Neoplatonic and Ovidian writings of Bernard Sylvestris and his contemporaries to fifteenth-century figures such as Tignosi and Ficino. The thirteenth-century recovery of Aristotle did make a difference. And as I have suggested, Aristotle's "matter" is not a substance; hence, it is less labile in itself than the matter of twelfth- or fifteenth-century theorists. Moreover, fourteenth-century scholastics such as Oresme were less concerned with matter per se than was, for example, Bernard Sylvestris. They were suspicious of ideas of animate matter, whether alchemical or cosmological, although change, especially in the form of local motion, remained a pressing question for them. The theories of matter we find in natural philosophy from the twelfth to the sixteenth century were not all the same, nor do they show a continuous development from the "world soul" of some twelfth-century commentators on Plato to Ficino's "soul of the universe." Nonetheless, even those theorists of the thirteenth and fourteenth centuries who opposed the possibility of living stars or alchemical manipulation tended to assume, almost in spite of themselves, a basic dynamism lurking in matter.

Change as Threat and Opportunity: A Reprise

Such an understanding of materiality was, theologically speaking, both an opportunity and a problem. If matter was by definition the great roiling mass of Ovid's *Metamorphoses* or even the "active potential" of Niccolò Tignosi's "material agent," then the eruption of the sacred in *Dauerwunder*, for example, or in animated statues was easy to envision. Its continuing presence (its stasis or endurance) became difficult to explain, however. If things were always coming to be, were they not also always passing away? To Isidore, after all, *corpus* was related etymologically—and thus ontologically—to *corruptum*.[73] And was not such passing on, such *corruptio*, a problem if it touched the divine?[74] In Guibert of Nogent's attacks on relics in the early twelfth century, as in the fifteenth-century debate over the Wilsnack hosts, the issue of corruption was in fact key. Guibert's opposition to relics of Christ (teeth, foreskin, blood, etc.) was not a rationalist skepticism about the authenticity of relic provenances; rather, it was rooted in a frantic desire to protect Christ's body parts from the putrefaction they would inevitably experience if left behind on earth. In the Wilsnack controversy, there were theorists such as James of Klusa who claimed not only that the deteriorated stuff revered in the 1450s could not be sacred because it had decayed but also that if it later decayed, it could never have been holy matter in the first place.[75] When Nicholas of Cusa accepted the miraculous hosts of Andechs, after fulminating against other cases of holy matter, his reaction was perhaps more than mere political expediency. Ignoring claims that blood spots had appeared on them, Cusanus referred to the incorruptibility of the wafers as support for their extraordinary sacrality. Behind such reactions lay an obvious question. God cannot change; how then can matter, if it has been impregnated by the divine? As the treatment of relics such as the blood of Cismar or hosts such as the Deggendorf miracle suggests, the fact that sacred things pass away was a devotional and disciplinary conundrum. But it was also a metaphysical one.

Moreover, even coming to be was a problem. Materiality needed to be controlled conceptually and ecclesiastically. Church authorities and theorists could hardly tolerate a world in which anything might erupt anywhere. Hence, they attempted to direct attention to the God who operated through the saints' relics, the God toward whom images gestured. In such theories, holy matter was a means of access, not itself divine. Nonetheless, people continued to act as if statues wept and walked, relics came alive on Good Friday, holy dust conveyed sacred action at a distance. Even Lollard and Hussite objections to holy matter hammered home its dangers. The very iconoclasts who denied images hacked them to pieces as if they were living enemies. Some Lollard propaganda stressed with triumph (and what feels to a modern reader like genuine surprise) the fact that torched or fragmented statues did not cry out or weep in protest.[76] A way of reining in the miraculous was clearly needed. It was needed all the more because in an intellectual world where philosophers and theologians stressed ever more stridently the absolute power of God (*potentia absoluta Dei*), the miraculous could not be simply denied.[77]

And a partial solution was available in exactly the understanding of matter that was also the problem. Scholastic theories, especially Aristotelian theories, circumscribed change within fairly narrow parameters without denying its reality. Conceiving matter as the substratum for generation and corruption provided resources for understanding in naturalistic—or almost naturalistic—terms the particularly immediate encounter of God with matter called miracle. Even Ovidian and Augustinian notions of the seeds of change in things could be utilized to limit change. What we find from the twelfth to the sixteenth century in discussions of miracles is both a concern with material change and a series of efforts, intellectual as well as administrative and political, to contain it as much as possible without denying the ability of God to act *supra*-naturally. The theories of theologians and natural philosophers controlled (that is, limited) miraculous change in a variety of ways, sometimes by reducing it to the mere appearance of transformation, sometimes by admitting it but hedging it about with explanations that involved as little change as possible. In what follows, I discuss each of these strategies in turn.

Reducing Change to Appearance

As I explained in my second chapter, a number of theologians held that *Dauerwunder*, in which consecrated wafers and wine supposedly changed visibly into flesh and blood and endured as such, were not real change of accidents (that is, appearance). The real change in the Christian Eucharist was, of course, the substantial change of bread to flesh, but this miracle of miracles was invisible. It was part of the very definition of transubstantiation that the accidents do not change. Hence, most theologians held that, if an individual or a group saw a host or communion chalice change to blood, they were seeing not the substance of Christ in the Eucharist but an effect produced by God in their imaginations.[78] *Dauerwunder* might be miracles but they were not miracles of seeing God directly.

Building on theories that went back to the Church Father Augustine of Hippo (d. 430), theologians by and large made similar arguments about the bodily metamorphoses that so fascinated late medieval people: the changes of men into animals or werewolves, supposedly caused by witches, demons, heredity, sin, or the moon.[79] For example, Heinrich Kramer (Istitoris), in the notorious *Malleus maleficarum* (1486), argued that witches could make men believe that they had lost their genitals by hiding them from view or act on the senses and imagination to delude people into "think[ing] they see marvellous things, such as beasts and other horrors, when in actual fact they see nothing."[80] But witches—although they cause real evil—cannot turn people into beasts.

> For we are told of a girl who was turned into a filly, as she herself and, except S. Macharius, all who looked at her were persuaded. But the devil could not deceive the senses of the holy man; and when she was brought to him to be healed, he saw a true woman and not a horse.... And the Saint, by his prayers, freed her and the others from that illusion.[81]

Convinced that spirits manipulate bodies, producing marks such as stigmata or the bites of incubi and succubi, theorists nonetheless strained to keep spirit and body conceptually separate, no matter how much they might stress the body as the mechanism of contact, either immediate or at a distance, or theorize as bodily effects occurrences we would see as psychological. The thirteenth-century collector of moral tales Caesarius of Heisterbach, for example, held that spirits occupy spaces in the bowels of those whose bodies they use but do not pass into the flesh.[82] Nicole Oresme, in his commentary on Aristotle's *De caelo*, argued that angels cannot inhere in or appropriate bodies but they can move with bodies. Angels occupy space by moving from one body to another but they do not transmute corporeal things.[83]

Explaining Miracles by Limiting Change

Even more important for my argument than theories that hold miracles (and marvels) to be merely appearances of material change are the wide-ranging efforts of theologians and natural philosophers to explain them in ways that, while leaving them as material transformations, nonetheless limit or naturalize the physical change involved. We see this in several moves made by intellectuals: to explain physical change by internal mechanisms (even if used supernaturally), to mathematize physical and psychological change, and to explain human bodies, even Christ's body, by natural physiological processes as far as possible.

The first move made use, from the twelfth to the fourteenth century, of an idea, inherited from Augustine of Hippo, that fit particularly well with an Ovidean sense of nature as a percolating mass of forms.[84] This was the idea of seminal reasons: seeds of later things or incipient forms or patterns of development implanted by God at creation. The idea that bodies bear seeds of other bodies they might generate or become was used by a number of intellectuals to explain miracles or elucidate doctrines such as transubstantiation. It was an idea that closely controlled the nature and direction of change without naturalizing the miraculous completely. In the twelfth century, Peter Lombard, and in the thirteenth Thomas Aquinas, argued that Pharaoh's magicians created serpents and frogs by manipulating the seeds in things; hence, these acts were magic, not miracle. Thomas, however, insisted (as we have seen) that the manipulation by Moses and Aaron was a miracle. Both John of Salisbury and Rupert of Deutz explained the miracle at Cana similarly. There are seminal reasons in things that unfold in preordained time. Trees draw up water into grapes and make wine. If God speeds this up and turns water into wine without the intervening step, we call this a miracle.

Peter the Venerable used the speed-up argument to explain the change of substance in the Eucharist: the transformation of wine into blood is possible, he argued, because it happens in our bodies.[85]

Theories of seminal reasons lasted into the fourteenth century. Henry of Langenstein (d. 1397) posited, for example, that there were in prime matter seeds or seminal bodies (*corpora quasi seminales*), not actually existent forms but rather a "natural aptitude and potency" toward certain forms and away from others.[86] But there were also other concepts that could be employed to limit change. Hugh of St. Victor seems to have had a theory of atoms that explained the production of Eve from Adam's rib, although it made all growth in a sense miraculous; and (as we have seen) Nicholas of Autrecourt explained resurrection atomically.[87] Both Albert the Great and Roger Bacon used the biological principle "like produces like" to describe (and limit) miracles. Although Albert held that there are certain senses in which we cannot say that seeds are planted in bodies from the beginning, he also observed that there is in things a "potency to similar species." Miracles may produce the *mutatio* of matter, but "every miracle . . . tends to some similar species of nature." What the blind man receives is eyes, not an extra ear.[88] Bacon gave an analysis of resurrection as the reduction of body to prime matter and the induction of the same form again.[89] Although not denying the miraculous nature of the event entirely, this discussion analyzes it in terms of a natural process like that debated by contemporary alchemists. Oresme, commenting on Aristotle's *On Generation and Corruption*, naturalized the effects of the Eucharist, if not the Eucharist itself, arguing: it is a miracle that accidents are present without a subject but not, however, a miracle that these accidents act on other accidents or substances.[90] Hence, the Eucharist can feed those who eat it. Indeed, Oresme's mathematicizing—or, better said, geometrizing—of a wide range of processes in the remarkable and anomalous *De Configurationibus* clearly entails a naturalizing of the miraculous, although he is elsewhere careful to assert that there are some "marvelous and miraculous" things that are "so dissimilar to and far from the natural that they cannot in any way be reduced to a natural cause."[91] However unprovable, undetectable, and unmeasurable the configurations (or geometrical patterns) that Oresme proposes for everything from motion and rarefaction to magic, visions, otherworld journeys, and the emotions, his is a remarkable effort to explain extraordinary and completely unpredictable change by mathematical structures embedded in things.

Jan Hus's two treatises on Christ's blood from 1406–1407 provide rather different examples of limiting without denying miraculous change. Hus dismissed effluvial relics such as the holy foreskin, labeling them mere "visible signs" for the faithless; he rejected as fraudulent the transformation miracles associated with the Wilsnack hosts (resurrections from the dead, staves turned into swords, and so forth); and he suggested that preserving supposed blood relics and host miracles was akin to venerating horses' blood or "red stuff" smeared on wafers by "lying priests." To revere such bits of mere matter was to desecrate God. Yet Hus admitted that the absolute power of God *could* cause Christ's blood to remain behind on earth. It is after all, by concomitance, wholly present in every celebration of the sacrament; hence, it could be on earth while also in glory. And Hus employed Aristotelian terminology and natural-philosophical analogies to explain the possibility both of blood relics and of another singularly unnatural occurrence: the resurrection of the body at the end of time.[92]

Apropos blood relics, Hus asserts that redness might remain on tunic, bread, or sweat cloth apart from the substance of Christ's blood, just as accidents remain in the Eucharist when substance changes. He insists, however, that if such redness appears, it is only "left *in memoriam*." In other words, he has to admit the possibility of blood relics (which he clearly prefers to dismiss), but he uses technical substance-accident language both to explain the possibility and to claim that the present redness—even if created or permitted to persist by God—is not the substance of Christ.

Apropos the blood of Christ's circumcision, Hus writes:

> And it is possible that the blood of Christ, which flowed out from his body in the circumcision, was substantially converted into something else according to form, or that the blood if drained out on the cross and converted to vapor by the heat of the sun . . . reverted then by his power on the day of resurrection to its proper form and this was the same blood in number as in form. . . . Nor should the faithful fear that they will not receive again their bodies because wild animals have eaten them and drunk their blood. For in the resurrection all will be glorified.[93]

In this passage, we see Hus using both Thomistic notions of formal identity and natural-philosophical understandings of vaporization to render the miracle of bodily resurrection as credible as possible, logically and scientifically. Because form carries what a thing is, the return of substantial form to matter that has in the meantime had another substantial form can make an entity the same thing it was before.[94] Things converted to gas or vapor by the sun can recondense. Hence, even blood shed in crucifixion days before (or in circumcision years before) can be reassembled for resurrection, just as moisture returns out of the air, and it will in a technical sense be the "same" salvific blood of Christ.

Hus's point is not, of course, to limit material change or to rein in the miraculous per se. To him, the devotional and theological agenda is paramount. What he wants to restrain is false piety. What he asserts most passionately is the soteriological significance of the resurrection of the dead. He uses the natural analogy of vaporization to assert that all Christ's blood rose with Christ because he wants to limit pilgrimage to blood relics and *Dauerwunder*. He uses Thomistic language of form and substance because, to him, the return of bodies at the end of time is central to the Christian hope for individual, personal salvation. His argument constrains one kind of miraculous change (the eruption of blood on sacred objects) but supports another (the resurrection of every bodily particle). Moreover, he uses the language of formal identity to bolster faith in God's power to do the truly astonishing–raising the dead–although he denies that God did so at Wilsnack. By such arguments, Hus restricts certain kinds of miraculous change while supporting others. Displaying the by now familiar late medieval tendency to consider devotional issues in metaphysical and scientific language, he demystifies, makes intellectually accessible, even naturalizes certain aspects of holy matter. What he does not do is either deny God's power to transform matter or leave it without explanation.

Using Physiological Theories to Contain Miracles

In addition to ideas such as formal identity, seminal reasons, atoms, and configurations that could be employed to explain extraordinary or miraculous change, a number of late medieval theologians and natural philosophers employed physiological theories such as the traditional Galenic idea of the humors to categorize anomalous bodily events. The increasing interest in the physiology of holy figures such as Christ and his mother, Mary,[95] and a growing desire for precision about exactly which occurrences in Christ's body were natural and which miraculous make clear what I have been calling the need to control change conceptually. Around 1300, there was, for example, discussion of whether the bloody sweat Christ shed on the Mount of Olives was naturally or supernaturally produced,[96] and at least from the mid-thirteenth century on, theologians discussed whether the death on the cross was a natural consequence of the Crucifixion or the result of divine choice, since, as Robert Grosseteste argued in his *De cessatione legalium*, the piercing of hands and feet would not have caused enough bleeding to kill a healthy young male in three hours.[97] Debates about the relics of Christ's blood at places such as Westminster, Weingarten, Schwerin, and La Rochelle entailed determining whether the blood Christ shed on Golgotha was superficial nutritional blood, generated from food, or blood of the so-called core of human nature (*veritas humanae naturae*).[98]

As I explained in Chapter 2, some theologians denied entirely that the blood of Christ could remain on earth, since Christ's body was resurrected and had ascended into heaven, but others held that nonessential blood might remain behind.[99] Such discussion involved detailed consideration of the production of bodily fluids from food and of the relationship between a physiological core that endured and bodily matter that turned over through natural processes of digestion and excretion—all such discussion applied enthusiastically and unashamedly to the body of Christ himself.

Theorizing the relationship between the natural and the supernatural spilled over into devotional literature as well. Discussing the spiritual significance of Christ's salvific blood, shed when the soldier named in medieval legend Longinus thrust a lance into his side, the German mystical writer David of Augsburg (d. 1272) said:

> That [the blood] flowed from a glowing heart... was for us a living witness. For if the body there had been cold and dead, the blood could not have flowed; it would have stood and coagulated as is usual in nature as one sees it with the dead. But this did not happen to you [Christ].... [T]he love's glow of your heart was so strong that a sweet stream ran down from your wounded side.[100]

Stressing that the gush of blood from Christ's wounded side was demonstrably miraculous exactly because Christ was dead and dead bodies don't bleed, David seems almost to give a physiological cause for the miraculous occurrence. The blood stayed uncoagulated because Christ's heart, aglow with love, kept it warm. Scientific understanding both explains that the occurrence is miraculous (dead bodies don't bleed) and suggests a natural mechanism for it—one that functions, however, unnaturally (a heart remains hot and glowing after death). David's pride in his medical learning is as striking here as his confident and graceful spirituality.

In a later devotional treatise attributed to Dionysius the Carthusian (d. 1471), the dichotomy between natural and supernatural is even more emphasized.

> [The soldier with clouded eyes] took the lance and pierced [Christ's] heart.... When the blood reached his hands he touched his eyes and immediately received his sight.... And thus...there were two miracles relating to Christ's dead body, first, that at the touch of that noble liquid the blind soldier received his sight, and, second, that blood and water came out from a dead body [*de corpore mortuo*], which was done miraculously and contrary to nature, because naturally blood coagulates in a dead body so that it is not able to flow out naturally [*quod factum fuit miraculose et contra naturam, quia naturaliter in quolibet corpore mortuo sanguis coagulatur, ut naturaliter fluere non possit*]. And there was a watery element...for the body of Christ was composed of four elements.... Thus Christ had a true human body not a celestial or fantastical one as the heretics say.... For a fantastical body does not give forth blood and water. And he chose to pour out this blood from his dead body [*de corpore suo mortuo effluere voluit*] so that he might show the full and perfect love which he had for the redemption of the human race; hence he wished to retain no blood within his body [*nullum sanguinem in corpore suo retinere vellet*] but to pour it all out for our reconciliation [*sed totum pro nostra reconciliatione effundere*].[101]

In this passage, we hear the unattractive us/them rhetoric of the late Middle Ages—the defining of one's own position by projecting its contrary onto an "other" (in this case, heretics).[102] But we also see a stunning acceptance of the natural world, explored in the physiology of Jesus. Christ's body was composed, we are told, of four elements. It was matter, like the rest of creation. There was nothing celestial or fantastical—nothing illusory—about its materiality. The flow from a dead body is a miracle, but that the flow is water and blood is explained by natural philosophy. Moreover, if the matter of Christ's body behaved in a radically unnatural way for a spiritual reason, we can understand the unnaturalness only by understanding how matter behaves naturally. The repetition of references to what is natural or unnatural three times in one sentence (*contra naturam*...*naturaliter*...*naturaliter*) shows the importance of the natural/miraculous distinction to the author, for whom it is equally important that Christ's body is fully normal physiologically and that both his death and his blood flow are, by choice, miraculous and beyond nature. "He *chose* to pour out his blood from his *dead* body." For this devotional writer, then, it is necessary to know what the rules of natural change are in order to understand exactly when they are transgressed by the power of God. But the power is also stressed. Blood does not simply erupt, even from God's own body; his control and choice are underlined.

Matter as Dynamic Substratum

I hope I have now demonstrated that behind the discussions of university theologians and natural philosophers about miracles lay a certain fascination with material change that parallels the proliferation of images, relics, and *Dauerwunder* I spoke about in earlier chapters. However much theorists might describe relics and images as merely pointing beyond their own materiality to heaven or posit transubstantiation as by definition unseen, neither in theory nor in practice were things so simple. Direct encounter with an unseen divine was not the primary devotional goal of the later Middle Ages. Encounter was through visible, tangible things. Ecclesiastical authorities, intellectuals, and the ordinary faithful lived in a world where blood erupted on wafers, images changed color and descended from walls, bodies broke out in stigmata. Such events were both troubling and exhilarating. Whereas Guibert of Nogent abhorred relic devotion because no body part, no matter how hard, can ultimately resist corruption, his contemporaries Thiofrid of Echternach and Peter the Venerable saw in the bones of the saints a suggestion of flowering and life already begun. The blood hosts of Passau, Wilsnack, and Sternberg, castigated by some, were held by others to be manifestations of God's power. But such objects presented, as we have seen, spiritual, disciplinary, and ontological problems to the theologians, the ecclesiastical authorities, and the ordinary faithful who supported them: spiritual because such eruptions might be signs of divine anger instead of comforting presences; disciplinary because it was difficult for church leaders to predict, let alone control such eruptions; ontological because even holy matter tended to dissolution.

Moreover, religious objects were not the only matter that was thought to undergo and to cause stunning change. Magnets drew iron particles across space; decaying logs and animal carcasses seemed to give birth to worms and mice; fermentation changed the liquid of grapes into wine. Despite the suspicion felt by many intellectuals about the popular enthusiasm for magical incantation, many also held that plants and jewels could be used to cure the sick if they were not inscribed with or accompanied by magic spells.[103] Roger Bacon protested—no doubt too much—that incantations were not magic. But "[by] words uttered in accordance with the intention of the rational soul, which receive in the mere act of pronouncing them the force of heaven . . . the matter of the world is changed to many wonderful forms [*alteratur enim mundi materia ad multas passiones mirabiles*]."[104] Matter was per se both powerful and labile, susceptible to influence. Confidence in metamorphosis increased.

The chronology is important, although for such basic changes in attitude, it is necessarily imprecise. In the same period in which *Dauerwunder* and other transformation miracles proliferated—accompanied by theological efforts to deal with them—we find a shift in other sorts of theorizing. Whereas in the twelfth and early thirteenth centuries, the newly received alchemical texts were accompanied by glosses that suggested that species might be inviolable, by the fourteenth and fifteenth centuries, there was growing confidence that species could be transmuted.[105] Gold could be made if only the correct formula were found. Twelfth-century ideas of a world soul or of matter as Ovidian fecundity were succeeded in the late thirteenth and fourteenth centuries by a more Aristotelian focus on local motion and an opposition to ideas of a living heaven, but these were followed in the fifteenth century by a return of Neoplatonic ideas of a soul of the universe.

Twelfth-century stories of werewolves and other bodily transformations, although very popular, insisted that such changes were only apparent; a human being, with human emotions and mores, remained under the fur. By the later fifteenth century, some theorists hinted that people really became wolves.[106] Although, as we have seen, there continued to be resistance to the idea that witches actually turn people into beasts or snatch away their body parts, they were increasingly persecuted for creating widespread illusions of change; some among them and among their persecutors did believe they could cause such metamorphoses. By the later Middle Ages, astrology flourished, and intellectuals devoted a great deal of discussion not only to ways in which the stars controlled earthly events but also to material changes they caused here below, such as the birth of hermaphrodites and monsters. Teratology, as well as alchemy, was a characteristic early modern science.

The case of the magnet, studied recently by Nicolas Weill-Parot, provides an example of this chronological shift. Following Aristotle and Averroes, thirteenth-century scholastics rejected the idea that the magnet managed to induce movement in iron because it was living. Walter Burley (d. 1344) explicitly remarked on the earlier rejection, attributing the local movement of the iron to a change of quality in it caused by the magnet. But William Gilbert (d. 1603), often credited with the first modern theory of magnetism, approved the theory of Thales, as reported by Aristotle, that the magnet is a living stone insofar as it rejects its living mother, the earth.[107] Gilbert wrote:

> Wonderful is the loadstone shown in many experiments to be, and, as it were, animate.... The ancient philosophers... all seek in the world a certain universal soul, and declare the whole world to be endowed with a soul. Aristotle held that not the universe is animate, but the heavens only; his elements he made out to be inanimate; but the stars were for him animate.... As for us, we deem the whole world animate, and all globes, all stars, and this glorious earth, too....

> ... Pitiable is the state of the stars, abject the lot of earth, if this high dignity of soul is denied to them, while it is granted to the worm, the ant, the roach, to plants and morels; for in that case worms, roaches, moths, were more beauteous objects in nature and more perfect, inasmuch as nothing is excellent, nor precious, nor eminent, that hath not soul. But since living bodies spring from earth and sun and by them are animate, and since in the earth herbage springs up without the sowing of seeds (e.g., when soil is taken out of the bowels of the earth and carried to some great elevation or to the top of a lofty tower and there exposed to the sunshine, after a little while a miscellaneous herbage springs up in it unbidden), it is not likely that they (sun and earth) can do that which is not in themselves; but they awaken souls, and consequently are themselves possessed of souls.[108]

Or to take another example. In the opening decade of the sixteenth century, Symphorien Champier attacked magic that verged on demonolatry or idolatry but wove into his *Hermetic Theology* borrowings from Ficino that defended man as the worker of material transformations.

> The other animals live either without art or each with one art in particular ... men, on the contrary, are the discoverers of countless arts, which they pursue as they will. In these crafts one can see how man handles all the world's materials from everywhere as if all were subject to man. I tell you he handles elements, stones, metals, plants, and animals, and he changes them into many forms and figures as the beasts never do. Nor, like the brutes, is he satisfied with one element or several; he uses them all as if lord of all. He tramples the land, oppresses the water, mounts the air.... And it is not that man merely uses the elements—he embellishes them unlike any of the animals.... Since man knows the order of the heavens, whence they are moved, whither they are moving, in what measure and what they engender, who will deny that in his talent he is, if I may so put it, almost like the maker of the heavens?[109]

The very heavens move, make, and engender; cooperating with and mimicking them, man does the same. In Champier, these ideas were connected to a desire to escape the limits of corporeality that I cannot consider here. But as Brian Copenhaver has emphasized, the denial of the body characteristic of Renaissance Neoplatonism and occultism is intimately connected to exploration of the world and the body and to confidence in their power. What I stress here is that to the more learned as well as the less learned, the stuff of the world was alive. In its constant coming to be and passing away, it was promising as well as threatening. And this sense increased markedly in the late Middle Ages.

There was, as we have seen, no one medieval understanding of matter. From Isidore's *materia* as *mater* and Bernard Sylvestris's teeming *silva* to Nicole Oresme's and Niccolò Tignosi's several different understandings of matter as potency, there was a wide range. But most medieval theorists assumed a material substratum with some dynamic aspects. Moreover, for all their efforts to categorize objects, effects, and types of generation, their primary distinction in treating the natural world was not, as the texts I have considered make abundantly clear, that between animate and inanimate matter. Not only was matter understood as by definition that which changes; the paradigm for change was biological process. The word "digestion" was, for example, the common designation for the production of blood from food in the stomach and gold from lead in the bowels of the earth.

Theorists did, of course, sometimes distinguish living from nonliving and, more frequently, artificial from natural or human from nonhuman. The debate over images I discussed in Chapter 1 used the distinction between natural and man-made objects, living and dead matter, as fundamental, even as it made these distinctions problematic. For example, we see such categories operating in Caesarius of Heisterbach's description of an image of the Virgin that struck a nun on the head to prevent her from succumbing to temptation. "Amazement overcomes me when I hear a voice speaking in wood, a hand lifted to strike, a body curving down, then lifting itself up, then sitting and showing other living movements. Indeed this causes me more wonder than the ass that spoke to Balaam. For that was a being with motion and a soul, but in wood, stone, and metal there is no living spirit."[110] Caesarius's words utilize the same contrast of dead sticks and living flesh that would be so prominent later in Lollard anti-image polemic. Yet the discussion undercuts exactly the distinction it uses. What the author underlines is that wood *can* speak and move. In Caesarius's accounts, the inanimate is capable—one might almost say frequently and easily capable—of animation. Lollard anti-image propaganda fears that this might be so; Caesarius's pro-miracle propaganda rejoices that it is so. But the distinction between human and nonhuman dissolves even as it functions.

Later writers also utilized such distinctions while in some ways obfuscating them. Aristotle's biological writings had, of course, differentiated the animate from the inanimate morphologically, and medieval commentators took note of this or used it. In his commentary on Aristotle's *On Generation and Corruption*, for example, Oresme asks whether there is a periodicity to the process of corruption and cites four distinctions, the fourth of which is the distinction between living and nonliving.[111] In the passage I quote above, Champier uses, as grouping terms, the elements, stones, metals, plants, and animals and makes much of the contrast of animal and human. Niccolò Tignosi da Foligno, in a eulogy to Cosimo de' Medici, exclaimed: "However much the soul is separate from bodies, man from other creatures, animate things from metals, so much is reason deemed more noble than the corporeal, sensible, transient."[112]

But when intellectuals wrote more freely and generally about the world, they tended to speak as if all change was what we moderns call "organic" generation and decay. My point is not that there was no use of such categories as animal and mineral, vital and inert, and no distinction of natural organic process from radical, seemingly *praeter*-natural transformation. Nor is it that there was no difference between the twelfth and the fifteenth centuries. My point is rather that—despite great differences in the ostensible topics treated—discourse slipped easily from category to category. John of Salisbury saw the miraculous production of wine from water at Cana as merely a speed-up of natural fermentation. Albert the Great and Thomas Aquinas analogized (if not completely) the serpents of Pharaoh's magicians to those of Aaron. Nicholas of Autrecourt and Jan Hus understood as parallel the condensation of bodies and their resurrection. Nicole Oresme analogized gases in the earth to vapors from decaying corpses. Although he did not equate animals, plants, and minerals, the alchemist Petrus Bonus (fl. 1330) spoke of the growth of worms from carcasses, chickens from eggs, and gold from base metals as if they were analogous processes.[113] Tignosi saw the production of fire from stone by flint as parallel to the generation of mice from putrefaction. And even in the encomium to Cosimo quoted above, his basic point is not so much to differentiate between categories of beings as to place them on a spectrum, within each category of which there is wide diversity. Symphorien Champier was sure the heavens "engender" things on earth and that for this reason, men could use their power to transmute matter.

Ironically enough, intellectual efforts to control change conceptually by using natural models to explain even supernatural processes could contribute to a sense of all bodies as a flow of generation and corruption. And understanding matter under the template of generation encouraged the expectation that blood, motion, life, or intentionality might erupt from deep within it.

Holy Matter as Triumph over Matter

Yet the eruption of the holy in matter was more than mere change. Whether in statues that spoke, hosts that turned suddenly to blood, or relics and images that induced fertility or health, the bursting forth of life could be understood as matter triumphing over exactly the change it represented. A miracle was, after all, a miracle—as Caesarius of Heisterbach underlined. At the moment of miraculous change, objects bodied forth transcendence and eternity as well as materiality. When a statue of the Virgin at Neukirchen bei Heiligenblut in Bavaria bled in response to attack by a Hussite sword in 1450, it was not merely protesting desecration. It was also asserting that it lived on unharmed.[114] When relics flowered on Good Friday or the blood of St. Januarius or St. James the Lesser liquefied, such objects were announcing that holy matter is eternally alive, not subject to the *corruptio* of evil, death, and putrefaction.

Blood, sweat, and tears were particularly appropriate for expressing the enduring life of matter, because they could not—except under extraordinary (marvelous or miraculous) circumstances—be produced by corpses, as David of Augsburg and Dionysius the Carthusian emphasized. It is significant that accounts of such miracles underline repeatedly that the stuff emitted is liquid, fresh, wet, not long coagulated or dried—that is, it is not something that normally arises from death or decay. It is also important to consider that the red silk at Cismar, like the artificial ruby on the Becket blood casket (see fig. 15, p. 72), may have been deliberately placed to assert the life of what was supposedly within. The blood of Christ and of the martyrs cries out, forever fresh.

Such assertions—textual and visual—underlined the essential paradox of eternal life. For there is a contradiction implicit in the idea that eternal (perduring) salvation is lodged in the historical (hence momentary) event of Calvary. Indeed, the contradiction is even starker: life, which can be understood only by analogy to the organic and thus changeable, must, if eternal, never undergo the change of generation and corruption that, however, defines it.

The author of the Middle English *Prickynge of Love* underlines this paradox when he exhorts: "Open . . . with full faith the mouth of thy heart and let this blood drop into the marrow of thy soul, for know thee well that Christ's blood is yet as hot and as fresh [*als hot . . . als fresch*] as it was when he died on Good Friday and shall be so in holy church unto the day of doom."[115] The event of Christ's sacrifice lasts until Judgment Day—and even beyond. In much late medieval art, the scars on Christ's body are unhealed after the Resurrection and Ascension—bleeding freshly or emitting a ghostly glow. And even where the artist shows them as healed, they are not erased. When images of Christ's body parts depict the pieces streaming with blood (as in figs. 32, 33, and 46, pp. 100 and 202), they make the same point. Christ is not only whole in every fragment, he is also alive in death. Both sacrifice and triumph over it are real and eternal. Christ's bodily matter lives at the moment he expires—and forever.

Understood this way, miracles in which stones bleed or rods turn into serpents are both change and assertions of triumph over change. They, too, insist on the *life* of holy stuff. Indeed, even miracles in which the earth rested or particles of bodies came together again in resurrection were, in an ontological sense, similar. In all such occurrences, matter contradicts matter by stilling for a moment its own *corruptio*, its decay and passing away.

For a moment. But even holy matter—matter that triumphs over materiality—cannot, exactly because it is material, last. It needs in fact to be renewed. And if the faithful were not convinced by its regular renewal at moments of Eucharistic consecration or ritual display of reliquaries, desecration might compel its more irregular and extraordinary appearance. The proliferation in the late Middle Ages of anti-Jewish host-desecration libels suggests that the need for a God immanent in matter could have sinister implications. If holy matter both had to—and could not—perdure, then something was necessary to induce or sustain its presence. Yet Christians who desired its appearance under more than the invisible form of the Eucharist or the traditional stuff of relic and statue could not be certain of inducing this by prayer. And they dared not produce it themselves by desecration. Hence, the scapegoats who were said to cause its eruption might be horribly necessary to the practice of devotion. Jews who supposedly violated hosts, like dissidents who did in fact occasionally attack statues, were in this sense essential to a religion that needed a divine that was visibly, suddenly, and often violently present in the stuff of the physical world. Even the theologians Eberhard Waltmann and Johannes von Paltz, who wished to claim that specific *Dauerwunder* were not true miracles, found it difficult to deny that such events were possible—even educational.

Popes and preachers did occasionally point out that nothing in Jewish practice or theology suggested that Jews in fact desecrated Christian hosts or murdered Christian children.[116] Yet charges of Jewish host desecration continued into the sixteenth century. Where they had earlier triggered pogroms or justified them after the fact, they were now pursued with all the apparatus of the law. As Heiko Oberman has pointed out, the rise of legal process changed lynchings into judicial murder; as far as anti-Semitism was concerned, the onset of modernity changed methods, not beliefs.[117] Behind the particular nature of the anti-Jewish libels of the fourteenth to sixteenth centuries lay the same need for holy matter that resulted in more innocent sightings of blood at places such as Wilsnack, Orvieto, or Walldürn. The assumptions that made possible not only the fact of holy matter but also the sophisticated theorizing of it were a burden and a horror as well as an opportunity in the years around 1500.

The Materiality of Creation

Anthropologists and students of comparative religion tell us that all religions make some use of the material to represent or lead to something beyond. After all, as the twentieth-century mystic Simone Weil once said, we use stone, paint, and body to image the transcendent because it is all we have.[118] But not all religions emphasize materiality qua materiality. Christianity does—and never more so than in its late medieval version. The images, relics, and miracles of which I have spoken were not illusions to be passed beyond; they were holy matter. They were not so much symbols of the divine as "God with us." There were, of course, in the same period, mystics such as Hadewijch, Eckhart, Margaret Porete, and Nicholas of Cusa who stressed God's radical otherness and unrepresentability. Creation had an "as if" quality; a powerful negative theology was elaborated. I have mentioned this in my Introduction and will return to it briefly in my Conclusion. My point in this chapter has been, however, to underline the extraordinary way in which late medieval Christianity encouraged intellectual exploration of a matter it both affirmed and feared.

We are usually told that the doctrine of the Incarnation is at the heart of Christian belief. And it is often understood to be the root of Christian materiality.[119] But the doctrine of creation was more important in late medieval theological discussions and pious practice than is usually recognized. (See figs. 49 and 50.) Hexaemeral commentaries (that is, commentaries on the Genesis account of the six days of creation) were a persistent genre.[120] The formulae for blessing sacramentals not only invoke a God named as creator but also stress that grain, water, and so forth carry his power *as his creatures*. Indeed, it was the doctrine of creation that underlay technical discussions of miracles, especially transformation miracles. God had made the world ex nihilo. If he could create, he could certainly re-create. All things were possible to God.[121] Although Christian theologians did formulate an understanding of miracle as that which occurs above, beyond, or counter to the regularities of nature God himself established, they also continued the New Testament tradition of understanding miracles as "signs" of God, "holy works," presences, disclosures, manifestations. Many followed Augustine of Hippo in seeing everything in creation as "miraculous" because everything is ultimately dependent on divine providence.[122] This conviction in no way meant that miracles in a technical sense were common or that all matter was holy matter (in the sense in which I have been using the term). Indeed, it meant that a seemingly unusual material event had to be interrogated for its significance; such events might or might not be disclosures of the sacred. But it also meant that God's power over and presence in nature could not be denied.

It is therefore hardly surprising that Bonaventure held all creation to be God's footprints; Francis of Assisi saw the creator in stars, birds, and even wolves; the holy women Margery Kempe and Gherardesca of Pisa contemplated God in a workaday carthorse or a piece of straw.[123] When the nun Mechtild of Hackeborn (d. 1298/99) saw a vision in which the vestments of a celebrating priest were covered with every blade and twig, every hair and scale, of the flora and fauna of the universe, she expressed surprise. But as she looked, she saw that "the smallest details of the creation are reflected in the holy Trinity by means of the humanity of Christ, because it is from the same earth that produced them that Christ drew his humanity."[124] Nothing could make it clearer than do the words of Mechtild's sister nun, who describes her, that the body of Christ includes not merely his senses and suffering, flesh and blood, but the fur and feathers, sticks and stones, of the earth as well.

The doctrine of the Incarnation had implications for more than what modern criticism means by "the body." As medieval theorists from Isidore to Guibert of Nogent, Nicole Oresme, and Marsilio Ficino make clear, *corpora* referred not just to the physical element of the human self but to logs, trees, comets, and so forth as well. Incarnated in matter, Christ rose from the dead, taking matter to heaven; while still on earth, he healed the bodies of others and raised them from the dead. The early fourteenth-century Provençal mystic Margaret of Oingt saw Christ's humanity as a clear mirror in which was reflected all the beauty of creation.[125] The author of the nuns' book of Unterlinden commented explicitly that *homo* (our humanity) includes all creatures.[126] Nicholas of Cusa, the towering intellectual figure with whom I began this book, saw Christ's humanity as a *manductio* leading all creation back to God. Cusanus's idea of "learned ignorance" was, after all, as H. Lawrence Bond elegantly puts it, the idea not only of the enfolding of the finite in the infinite but also of the unfolding of the infinite in the finite and particular.[127] In his *De visione Dei*, Nicholas wrote: "[O God] . . . no one can approach you because you are unapproachable. . . . [H]ow will you give yourself to me if you do not at the same time give me heaven and earth and

Figures 49 and 50. God creates the world. Meister Bertram, 1379–1383. Two panels from the Grabow altar of the St. Petri Church, Hamburg. Hamburger Kunsthalle, Inv. 500. The theme of God's power to create and re-create in miracle and resurrection was an important one in late medieval art and devotion. It underlined the role of matter itself as means of access to salvation. (Photo: Bildarchiv Preussischer Kulturbesitz/Art Resource, NY.)

all that are in them? . . . [H]ow will you give me yourself if you do not also give me myself?"[128] Such statements are not animism or pantheism but rather a radical understanding of the paradox of the material. They assert that in giving us his unknowable self—a self beyond and other than creation—God gives us creation and all that is in it, down to the smallest fleck of ash or slime.

In this context, it is important to remember that the doctrine of the resurrection of the body was intimately linked in fifteenth-century theology to the doctrine of creation. Resurrection at the end of time was interpreted as the re-creation by God of the exact physical body possessed before death—that is, as the reassemblage of material particles, even after they had been rolled by the seas or ground into dust. Material re-creation was a miracle paralleling material creation.[129] It was such an understanding that made the relics of the saints or the contact relics of Christ so powerful. Theorists such as Jan Hus, who opposed Christ's effluvial relics, argued that he must have risen whole, since we are promised integral and complete resurrection. If he left pieces behind, we would lose confidence in the promise that we will achieve such salvation at the end of time. Those such as Johannes Bremer who supported blood relics argued that they were left on earth exactly in order to give us visual evidence of God's power for our future redemption. Whichever interpretation one espoused, it was as pieces of matter, adumbrating future physical resurrection, that the relics were powerful.

As much recent scholarship reminds us, the religious culture of late medieval Europe was characterized by a new attention to the body of Christ—and hence to the bodies of his faithful. But in medieval theology, the term "bodies" (*corpora*) referred to things—things both promising and threatening in their constant coming to be and passing away. For over a thousand years, the wood of the cross on which Christ was executed spread all over Europe, standing in, so to speak, for his departed body. From at least the twelfth century on, the bread and wine blessed by Jesus at his Thursday celebration of Passover were understood not only to be the hidden presence of God but also to look like body and blood when they erupted in host and chalice miracles. God's saints were thought to be present not just in their tombs but also in their bones and ashes, which were avidly divided and sent around Europe. Images were venerated—or feared—as alive, both because they sometimes fused literally with other sorts of holy matter (such as relics, bleeding earth, or miraculous bread) and because they called attention to their plasticity and tactility. Understood as physical stuff ("dead stones and rotten sticks"), images nonetheless became the focal point of both private and public worship to such an extent that reformation outbreaks of iconoclasm had little long-term effect on European artistic development. The Christianity of the later Middle Ages was a matter of bodies in the larger sense of objects—the stuff of the universe. It was, in other words, a matter of matter. It entailed both a radical awareness of the corruption and transience of all that is not God and a radical conviction that God, immanent and immediate in the stuff of the world, might for a moment lift that stuff to exactly the eternity and transcendence it could by definition never fully be.

Conclusion

In these four chapters, I have explicated one aspect of late medieval Christianity: the intense concern, in theology and practice, both heterodox and orthodox, with materiality. From blessed radishes and oats that protected livestock, to images that stepped down from walls in order to protest their neglect, to bones of the saints or consecrated wafers that manifested sacred presence by oozing or bleeding—objects were central. Altarpieces and devotional statues conflated depictions of Christ or the saints with the real presence of the consecrated wafer or relic. Distinctions between living and dead, body and thing, presence and mimesis, part and whole, animate and inanimate, tended to blur; all of creation could convey and reveal God.

Yet as I have emphasized repeatedly, theorists, church authorities, spiritual advisors, and the ordinary faithful were all ambivalent about exactly the materiality they utilized and venerated. Popes, bishops, and legates promoted some miraculous objects with indulgences while attempting to suppress others. Theorists from a variety of perspectives crafted ingenious explanations of how matter might be marvelously and quite astonishingly transformed yet tended to argue that the material simply pointed beyond itself rather than enfolding or incorporating the divine. Externalized practices that depended on objects—practices such as telling rosary beads or using a measure of Christ's body to calculate prayers owed or indulgences granted—multiplied alongside expressions of radical interiority and mystical encounter that alleged all external religiosity to be of naught. Dissidents who defied both standard practice and mainstream theology focused on relics and images an exaggerated attention that suggests the power of these objects at least as much as rejection of them; to the Bohemian Hussites, for example, access to a physical object, the chalice, became a rallying cry against the established church.

I have characterized the Christian materiality of the late Middle Ages as a paradox exactly because of this ambivalence. And a paradox is, as Nicholas of Cusa put it, the "coincidence of opposites." It is not a combination or synthesis of differing aspects, nor is it a violation of the integrity of opposing concerns through compromise. It is the simultaneous assertion and performance of opposing values.[1]

As this understanding of paradox suggests, fifteenth-century attitudes toward the matter of creation were radically disjunctive and contradictory, and this radical ambivalence—the simultaneous embracing and rejecting of material religiosity—increased in the years between 1300 and 1500. Nicholas himself, with whose decree at Halberstadt I began this book, encapsulates such paradox in his life as well as his writing. Holding Christ's glorified blood to be completely unseeable, he nonetheless approved pilgrimage to the miracle hosts of Andechs. His articulation of the utter unknowability and beyondness of God was harnessed to a sense that that same God gives himself to human beings by giving them creation and all that therein dwells.

My purpose in this book has been to focus on a better understanding of the late medieval period, which is all too often reduced to a preparatory stage for the changes of the sixteenth century because it is seen to be characterized either by an externalized piety in need of reform or by a growing internalization of religion that led to the *sola fides* of the mainstream Protestant Reformation. I have wanted to give back to this period its own complexity.[2] Nonetheless, it may be helpful in closing to ask what difference it makes to our understanding of Western history if we take the paradox of materiality to be a basic characteristic of the later Middle Ages. Briefly put, such an interpretation contributes three larger insights, or perhaps, to put it more accurately, raises three larger questions: how understanding the material Christianity of the later Middle Ages might help us to reinterpret not only the fifteenth but also the sixteenth century; how such understanding contributes to the comparative study of Judaism, Islam, and Christianity; and how my conclusions relate to the current theoretical concern with material culture and the "agency" of objects.

Reinterpreting the Fifteenth and Sixteenth Centuries

Understanding the paradoxical focus of the later Middle Ages on materiality casts both the reformations of the sixteenth century and the mystical theology and reform concerns of the fifteenth in a new light. Although I have concentrated in this book on only one side of the late medieval paradox, elucidating it elucidates the whole. Thus, I suggest here that the increasing emphasis in fourteenth- and fifteenth-century theology on the power of God as explanation, like the new stress in spirituality on interior response cut free from any necessity to conform that response to outer gesture or speech, is one pole of a paradox whose other pole is an increasing sense that the sacral is manifested and conveyed in matter. The God whose will might account for anything was theorized by natural philosophers such as Albert the Great or Oresme as a God whose own rules for matter could be used to understand and limit its anomalous behavior. Fear and rejection of images were in part reactions to renewed instances of their animation. The increased emphasis on interiority was not merely a reformist response to an old-style religion of mechanical and "superstitious" spirituality but rather the uneasy complement to a new enthusiasm for matter that disclosed the divine. Indeed, what scholars have seen as a quantifying tendency in late medieval spirituality—a desire to accumulate merit through the repetition of practices—was often neither mechanical nor externalized. Rather, it was an assertion of personal religious agency by individual Christians that was facilitated by the multiplication of devotional objects.

To return for a moment to a single example. The Holy Name tablets created by Bernardino of Siena and extremely popular in the 1420s and 1430s were also attacked as idolatry, heresy, or witchcraft. Tactile and visual aids to prayer, they could be assimilated to magical talismans and amulets, understood to act apotropaically, even mechanically, or adored as if the sacred were revealed in the gilded letters and rays. Their sheer materiality was powerful. Yet preachers who glossed them defended them not only as presences but also as aids to inner response. The tablets might carry the one praying to a quiet space beyond images where lodged unutterable secrets. But they might also *be* the burst of grace encountered. A simple object was both presence and absence.[3] The two complemented each other, but they also competed. Exactly the insistent materiality that attracted adherents pressured the Franciscan preachers who promoted it to increasingly mystical and interiorized interpretations of its meaning.

In short, interior and individualized religious response grew apace with exterior practices, partly as criticism, partly as complement.[4] Suspicion—even rejection—of material objects was stimulated by proliferating claims to the power of their presence. An intense need to make the holy "other" grew along with an equally intense need to find it immanent, and confidence in immanence was accompanied by efforts to control it conceptually. Each need stimulated its opposite.[5]

Although lodged in doctrinal formulations such as bodily resurrection, the full humanity of Christ, transubstantiation, concomitance, and a theology of sacrifice, such needs were not the result of theological formulations.[6] In many cases, the formulations were the result of religious needs.[7] And those needs were engendered by the increased Christianization of European society at the local level—that is, the spread of the parish system in the countryside and of mendicant preaching in towns and the growing eagerness of cities and local rulers to foster devotion and pilgrimage, for reasons economic and political as well as religious. Popular and folk practices and beliefs fused with clerically defined rituals as Christianity spread. Some objects that gained both increased popularity and increased criticism (blessed herbs, bread and water, for example; wall paintings that protested earlier neglect; pilgrim badges, amulets such as Holy Name tablets, and religious souvenirs such as the Walldürn silks) may have been older phenomena newly yet questionably energized by the efforts of preachers to provide a focus for pious practice.[8] The proliferation of devotional materials and their increased vibrancy and plasticity were made possible both by the economic resources of a church that could increasingly afford to hire carvers and painters and by technical changes that gave craftsmen access to new pigments, woods, and metals, some of which were cheaper than before.

In situating the broad changes I have described, we should not forget that the assumptions—and the anxiety—about materiality that we find in religious discourse and religious behavior can be seen in scientific thought and vernacular literature as well. After questioning or even rejecting such conceptualizations in the thirteenth and fourteenth centuries, natural philosophers came to theorize objects as mundane as the magnet or as broad as the cosmos under the category of animation. The move on the part of fifteenth-century intellectuals and poets as well as the populace to accept tales of metamorphosis as literal, rather than illusionary, went hand in hand with greater concern about and persecution of those such as witches who might cause such transformations. There are parallels historians have not sufficiently noticed among Lollards who smashed statues in order to show that they were not alive, pilgrims who journeyed to bleeding bread yet were suspicious of the healings it allegedly produced, alchemists who strove to transmute metals with occult formulae as well as chemicals but repeatedly failed to do so, poets who wrote of werewolves and fairies, philosophers who disputed whether the heavens are living, and theologians who crafted explanations of *Dauerwunder* and witch effects while doubting specific cases.

In a sense, then, the iconoclasm of some fifteenth-century dissidents and its intensification in sixteenth-century radical reform, the more moderate distrust of the visual we find in Martin Luther, the Tridentine decrees prohibiting unusual images and mandating increased episcopal control of iconography, and the rejection in sixteenth-century Catholic art (at least in the Old World) of many motifs extraordinarily popular in the fifteenth century[9] were all responses to the increasingly paradoxical sense of the material, as were, of course, the changes and reformulations of Eucharistic theology found among Catholics and Protestants and new hesitations about relic cult and objects such as sacramentals. It would be wrong to see such moves as continuations of either fifteenth-century reform or of the varieties of fifteenth-century piety that such reform both created and criticized. Instead, the point and counterpoint of attitudes toward the material that had been present since the twelfth century seem to have led to a crisis of confidence in Christian materiality, out of which came a multitude of responses, no one of which merely continued the motifs of late medieval devotion or theology. That crisis was at least as much a result of the confusion induced by the increasing ingenuity with which local populations used and theologians discussed eruptions of the sacred in matter as it was of doubts concerning the eruptions themselves.

If I am right in this characterization, then several older interpretations fall away as too simple. The upheavals of the sixteenth century cannot be seen either as rejections of earlier "corruption" or "superstition" or as reactions against a spirituality that has sometimes been described as freezing or literalizing religious practice into desiccated, lifeless externals. Nor can they be seen as simple extrapolations from late medieval interiority or from the "voluntarism" or "radical mysticism" of late medieval theology.

In the past three or four decades, scholars such as Eamon Duffy and John Bossy have argued in new ways against older ideas of the externalized nature of late medieval religion, and Bossy has suggested that some of its vitality and sense of community continued into the sixteenth century. Literary scholars such as David Aers and James Simpson have stressed anew the ways in which a rupture between the medieval and reformation periods is a creation of Reformation attacks.[10] John van Engen has eloquently articulated the case for understanding the period from 1350 to 1500 in its own terms. Constantine Fasolt has objected to taking "the Reformation," or indeed any of the reform movements and the confessionalization that followed, as major breaks in European history, arguing that the real breaks in religious and social history come with Gregorian reform in the eleventh century and the Industrial Revolution in the nineteenth.[11]

Although I agree with all of these interpretations, my claim in this book is not about periodization. In fact, I suggest that an awareness of the radically paradoxical nature of late medieval religion frees us from the rather sterile debates of the past about whether the sixteenth century is a growth from or a break with earlier Christianity.[12] Depending on what we look at, it is both and neither.

Nonetheless, if I am right about the intense pressure exerted on fifteenth-century Christians by the paradoxical nature of their religious concerns, the pressure of paradox may need to be itself understood as one of the often-discussed "causes of the Reformation."

Jews, Muslims, and Christians

The argument of this book not only suggests that we need to reconceptualize the nature and hence the consequences of fourteenth- and fifteenth-century Christianity. It also raises questions for the study of comparative religion. Understanding the full materiality of Christian belief and practice may help to clarify at least one of the ways in which medieval Christianity (and, in certain aspects, its modern descendants) is similar to, yet differs from, its sister religions, Islam and Judaism.

There are, of course, parallels between the practices of medieval Muslims, Jews and Christians, as there are in the attitudes toward objects of many of the religions of the world. The offering of material objects as gifts and the theft or looting of objects from enemies or subordinates is never simply a political or economic act. Things carry many sorts of power. When exchanged or given, they create social, emotional, and religious bonds; when stolen or destroyed, they signify disrespect for and triumph over those who are dispossessed.[13] This is especially so when the objects given, captured, or obliterated are objects made significant by their role in religious ritual. Moreover, the handing on of objects within cultures and their borrowing across cultural boundaries conveys and supports rituals, beliefs, and assumptions. For example, as Nile Green has pointed out, Muslims and Christians in the Mediterranean basin have long shared the practice of hanging ostrich eggs in shrines.[14] Such practices not only have a similar functional purpose (to prevent mice from running down the chains of hanging lamps to drink oil) but also express similar and very complex religious values. Across Mediterranean cultures, eggs symbolize fertility and resurrection; they continue to be used to do so even when various religious groups voice the suspicion that the practice is an importation from an alien culture.[15] As this example demonstrates, objects are remarkably consistent and resilient in signification as well as remarkably labile, multivalent, and adaptive. In their apotropaic and theurgic qualities, they pass easily between cultures, often retaining similar power and meaning even when situated in very different theologies or ideologies.

In addition to such general similarities among all religions in the deployment of the material, it is important to note that there is something parallel to the Christian relic in many cultures[16] and that the three religions of the Mediterranean basin shared many cultic practices. There was some Jewish pilgrimage to tombs both in Syria and in Ashkenaz during the Middle Ages, as we have seen, and we very occasionally find Jewish reverencing of objects or their use as talismans, although there was no bodily division or relic cult per se.[17] Islam did have active pilgrimage to the shrines of holy people, although it was never required, as was the pilgrimage to Mecca. What we might call "bodily relics" were occasionally revered: the hair and nails of the Prophet, for example, and the head of the martyred Husayn.[18] And there are occasional stories of objects seeming alive at shrines visited by Jews and Muslims alike.[19] But early stories of the Prophet's nails and hair clippings see them as stuff to be pulverized and buried with the dead, not as objects to be preserved. The relocation of bodies was very rare, and anxiety was expressed about even architectural renovations that might expose bones.[20] Objects that had been in contact with the Prophet—his footprints, sword, kohl pencil, and so forth—were venerated, and even the washwater of holy people was understood to convey sacrality. But the most important relics of the Prophet were textual. Hadith reports—accounts of his sayings handed down and spread by migration and conquest—were called "relics" and were more widely distributed and religiously important than any physical object.[21]

The rabbis of medieval Ashkenaz, like Muslim theologians, often disapproved of tomb veneration or attempted to reinterpret and redirect it. Jews differentiated themselves from Christians by claiming that it was not bodies that were venerated at Jewish shrines, but rather the souls that might hover there.[22] The thirteenth-century Jewish poet Isaac haGorni understood Christian relics as fetishes and found them funny.[23] Ibn Taymīya, an early fourteenth-century Muslim theologian, argued that Jews and Christians worship tombs, but Muslims do not. If prayers made at such shrines are answered, it is not because the dead are useful, but rather because God has mercy on living ones who pray for the dead.[24]

There are clearly similarities between such arguments and those of Christian writers who asserted that bodily relics were not worshipped; rather, they pointed toward the God beyond, who loved and empowered the saints. Nonetheless, in neither Judaism nor Islam did theologians spill so much ink delimiting, without denying, the status of miraculous objects while insisting on their power as material. Aquinas, as we have seen, felt compelled to argue not just that the relic was not the saint, but that it *was*. Moreover, like Nicholas of Cusa and Johannes Bremer, he admitted that the "Blood of Christ" preserved in churches was or might be miraculous blood, even if it did not originate in the body crucified on Golgotha.

Nor, despite what is sometimes argued, do we have a situation in which popular practice was the same around the Mediterranean but theology was different. Clearly, the doctrines of the Incarnation of Christ and of transubstantiation impelled Christian theologians toward more tortuous arguments about matter than are found in their Jewish and Islamic counterparts, even if all three traditions had to deal with questions of divine power and the miraculous.[25] But praxis was also not the same. Neither the Islam nor the Judaism of the later Middle Ages saw anything like the eruption of transformed images and objects—the weeping statues and bleeding bread—that characterized late medieval Christianity. Neither saw the proliferation of an increasingly tactile and insistent visual matter—winged altarpieces, opening statues, Braille-like prayer cards, oozing wall paintings—that, to the horror of some Christians and the delight of others, hovered so often on the brink of animation, occasionally tipping over into life. Despite the fact that early Islam, rabbinic Judaism, and medieval Christianity shared the doctrine of the resurrection of the body and hence a certain predisposition to value the physical and somatic, Christian materiality is quite different from anything we find in Judaism or Islam.[26] We can see the difference clearly when we compare the Christian sense of space with that of Jews and Muslims.

In Judaism and Islam, place is crucial. As Josef Meri puts it: "Whether actual or perceived, [to Jews and Muslims] holiness was a feature of the land."[27] In the Middle East (and very occasionally in northern Europe) Jews did make pilgrimage to tombs and performed rituals there. Texts from the Cairo Geniza attest to the importance of such practices, and stories survive of adherents lying on and rubbing against graves or bringing home talismans from them.[28] But both in northern Europe and in the Middle East, as we have seen, tomb veneration was regarded by the rabbis with suspicion. After all, God himself (Deut. 34:6) had concealed the location of Moses' grave in order to ward off idolatry. For Jews, holiness lay more in places where events had occurred or memories were condensed than in bodies or their burial places per se. However complex the theological interpretation of exile and return may be, it is safe to say that even today, Jews return to the Holy Land because the space itself is in some sense sacred.[29]

Muslims, too, revered and traveled to holy places. Although objects such as the black stone at Mecca or the throne of the Queen of Sheba sometimes focused cult, the memory of historical or prehistorical events was often enough to create sacred space.[30] Around Damascus, for example, Islamic pilgrimage sites included the place where Cain slew Abel, the place where Abraham was born, and the place where Mary and Jesus took refuge as well as the tombs of the saints.[31]

Muslims did sometimes revere contact relics, as we have seen. Cenotaphs were reproduced. But there is no real cult of body parts in Islam, deliberate and sanctioned bodily division being inconceivable. (The head of Husayn is a body fragment only because it was cut off in martyrdom.) And it is clear that where saint cult did emerge, it was place of burial and not any visible presence of body that drew devotees.[32] The black stone of Mecca did not itself voyage abroad, carrying sacrality. And where effluvial and contact relics such as footprints or whiskers did spread power in Islam, they operated at the borders of Islamic territory, not at the center.[33] Like Jerusalem to Jews, Mecca to Muslims was not primarily a place where objects were (although this was sometimes claimed). Rather, place seems to have preceded objects or bodies, to have been itself a locus of the holy and hence a magnet drawing devotees to it. However hard it may be logically to separate the sacred space of burial place or biblical event from physical tomb, the centripetal force of certain spots seems to have been, for medieval Jews and Muslims, more powerful than any particular object that resided there.

In contrast, it was overwhelmingly objects that conferred and conveyed sacrality in medieval Christianity. Sites that became holy and miracle working were those to which relics had been translated or those where images animated and hosts erupted in blood. Matter created place rather than place sacralizing matter. Rome, Santiago, Orvieto/Bolsena, and Wilsnack became centers of pilgrimage because bodies or objects were located there. Dust and cloth from tombs worked miracles because they had been in touch with bodies. Apparitions were pinned down by being solidified into objects, which were then themselves revered.[34] Although indulgences could be earned by visiting holy sites, they were more often given for viewing or even making tactile contact with specific objects and body parts. Even when transformed walls or crosses, wafers, chalices, or bodies faded into the ordinary, it was the ordinary object that became the goal of pilgrimage and not the place where the event had allegedly occurred. People went to Wilsnack not because something had happened there but to see the hosts (even if what was in the monstrance was no longer red); they went to Santiago not because a peasant had had a vision of St. James but in order to kiss James's head.

Even in that most sacred of places, Jerusalem, it was matter that, for Christians, conferred holiness. As early as the fourth century, piety focused on stones that had been in contact with Christ.[35] And throughout the Middle Ages, Christian pilgrims felt confident that they carried something of Christ home when they carried measures of his tomb, just as they felt that they visited Jerusalem when they prayed before a piece of the crib of Bethlehem in a Roman church. To Christians today, Protestant as well as Roman Catholic and Orthodox, what is crucial above all else about Jerusalem is the Holy Sepulcher—an empty place for the body that, in its very gone-awayness, confers presence.[36] As Eusebius argued in the fourth century—and Christians have repeated many times since—the empty tomb "by its very existence bears clearer testimony to the resurrection of the Savior than any words."[37] The focus is not so much on place as on the absence of an object.

Moreover, sacrality in medieval Christendom was spread by parading, dividing, and distributing holy objects (much as Muslims distributed hadith reports). In the Eastern church, images as well as relics created holy space as they moved through cities in procession. For example, when the icon of the *Hodegetria* whirled miraculously through the air (as it was reported to do regularly between the eleventh and fifteenth centuries), it was enacting at every street corner the saving of Constantinople half a millennium before.[38] In other words, it was the icon that, going out, re-created the event. At Weingarten, near Lake Constance, a relic of the blood of Christ is, still today, borne around the fields to guarantee their fertility.[39] From the early Middle Ages on, body parts and associated objects were enthusiastically divided, not only for transfer to new or frontier areas but also to solidify bonds in the Christian heartland by a kind of gift exchange. Sometimes the goal was simply to make more foci of worship within a given space. When the jaw, left forearm, and left hand of the body of Antony of Padua were extracted and placed each in its own reliquary, the point seems to have been to proliferate sacred objects per se. In a number of regions of late medieval Europe, as we have seen, even Jewish desecrators were understood to spread sacrality (albeit in evil ways) when they transported pieces of abused hosts from one venue to another. The objects carried and created in a new place both Christ and the Jewish plot against him.[40] J.M. Minty has argued that it was easy, relatively speaking, for Christians to deconsecrate and reuse Jewish space (synagogues) after pogroms or forced exiles because they did not have a particularly developed sense of perduring holy space.[41] In comparison with other religions that, like it, emerged in the Middle East, medieval Christianity (and in certain parts of the world its Roman Catholic descendants) gave a more intense and paradoxical role to material objects.

Theories, Medieval and Modern

Finally, there are methodological implications of my study that are worth spelling out. Historians, historians of science, art historians, anthropologists, archaeologists, classicists, scholars of comparative religion, and sociologists have recently been interested in what Lorraine Daston calls "things that talk."[42] The study of objects, often denominated "material culture," is one of the new trends in historical studies, so much so that Randolph Starn, in a recent issue of the *American Historical Review*, could speak of a turn, or re-turn, "from the primacy of discourse to the priority of object."[43] The general thrust of such work has been to insist that things are not merely or primarily symbols or signifiers but that they act. The image revered or the plow used by medieval peasants, like the curling iron or the typewriter employed by twentieth-century women, shapes its users as much as it is shaped by them. A great deal of sophisticated theorizing has recently been devoted to formulating exactly how objects have this capacity to shape, often called "agency," and how they carry meaning by what they *are* rather than, and indeed sometimes despite, what people attribute to them. Behind such theorizing, whether it be the sociology of Bruno Latour, the anthropology of Alfred Gell, or the art history of Günter Bandmann and David Freedberg, lies both a generalizing impulse—the search for a universal theory of how things act—and a concomitant need to differentiate things from persons, as found, for example, in Barbara Johnson's recent *Persons and Things*.[44]

Such modern theorizing is helpful in understanding medieval objects, but two points need to be made—points that are comprehensible only now that the end of my analysis has been reached. First, modern theorists sometimes neglect to consider the theories of those contemporary with the objects. Yet such contemporary theorizings are not just meanings attributed to objects—and even if they were, they would be at least as important to take into account as modern theories used to understand these same objects. But contemporary theories are evidence about the attitudes and assumptions of those who shaped and were shaped by the objects themselves, and they offer a sort of evidence modern theories cannot provide. The ambivalence of Thomas Aquinas, Johannes Bremer, Jan Hus, William Whyte, Nicole Oresme, or Johannes von Paltz about the various categories of religious objects they must, as theologians or philosophers, consider is itself evidence about the objects in a way that the ambivalence of modern viewers, be they theorists, worshippers, or voyeurs, is not. The point is an obvious one. But it is often quite deliberately ignored, not only because the turgid reasoning of medieval scholastics is unattractive to some modern interpreters but also because earlier work on such theories often looked to them to give *the* explanation for medieval objects (which of course they do not do), rather than understanding them to provide one kind of evidence, among others, about basic assumptions. Rejecting older approaches that assumed the theories of scholastics to be the best—or indeed the only—way of characterizing medieval attitudes should not mean, however, that we fail to take scholastic theories seriously as evidence or simply substitute modern theory for them.[45]

Second. Although modern theories raise the right questions, they sometimes give the wrong answers—wrong about medieval objects and hence perhaps even wrong about objects more generally. The current theories that have mostly been used to understand medieval objects are right to attribute agency to objects, but it is an agency that is, in the final analysis, both too metaphorical and too literal.

The agency of which theorists such as Latour and Gell speak is, finally, a metaphorical agency; it is *like* that of human actors. Typewriters, keys, plows, statues, and relics shape those who employ them. They come closest to acting when they come closest to living—that is, to being like a human agent. To Barbara Johnson, building on formulations that go back at least to the eighteenth century, the Pygmalion story is paradigmatic. But it is still a fable—one that is diagnostic of our attitudes. In this understanding, the closer something is to resembling the living—that is, to naturalism—the more agency, or life, it has. "Things that talk" are metaphorical people.

But medieval cult objects had agency in a more literal sense. They were not like life; they (at least sometimes) lived. And they were not more apt to come alive or animate—bleed, weep, move, glow with light—the more they approached resemblance to human beings. Pieces of wood or bone, bread, wine, bits of wall or paint animated. It seems that their life or agency lay not in their naturalism or similitude but in their materiality.[46] The capacity of medieval objects to represent or imitate the divine did not rest in mimetic likeness. To Johannes Bremer, the "relics" that were closest to God and acted most effectively to bring him to humankind were not wood that had touched Christ or vestiges of his physiological blood but bread and wine.

At the same time, many modern theories of objects tend, by medieval standards, to be too literal. Such theories freeze objects into stuff. Whether in asserting that things carry significance across cultural boundaries but resist theorizing, or in asserting that objects are most thingy when most resistant to change, such positions make objects by definition static.[47] Objecthood is therefore the opposite of change. Although the most sophisticated current theorizing goes beyond this, recognizing the paradoxical nature of those objects most likely to "talk," sometimes to the point of seeing them as "athwart the person/thing divide,"[48] even such formulations perforce utilize the divide as if it were the basic ontological distinction. No wonder, then, that articulating the agency of objects becomes both so difficult and so urgent for modern theorists. In their various formulations, it is in the nature of an object to resist change, even when it shapes others and manages metaphorically to "talk" itself.

Yet medieval objects, both in how they behaved and in how they were theorized by those who pondered them, were labile. In a world increasingly convinced of the possibility of literal (not metaphorical) metamorphosis, whether of lead to gold, human to wolf, or pond water to frog, matter was that which changed. And matter included the human body as well as the animal body, the body of the stars, or the body of wood, ash, and bone. Medieval theorists, such as Aquinas, Oresme, Hus, and Bremer, who discussed miracles or glossed Aristotle, like medieval pilgrims to Walldürn, Andechs, Orvieto, or the Madonna of the Prison in Prato, were perfectly aware of the difference between a bucket and a person. But their assumptions about matter were not ones that made the problem of the agency of objects or the boundary between person and things a primary one. For them, the primary problems were, on the one hand, controlling the agency objects literally had and, on the other, preserving access to the truly transcendent (that beyond all change) when the only stuff available to humans was matter—by definition labile, changeable, and capable of act. To oversimplify a bit, one might say that to a modern theorist, the problem is to explain how things "talk"; to a medieval theorist, it was to get them to shut up. Hence the insistence with which Eberhard Waltmann urged priests confronted with *Dauerwunder* to pray that God reconvert the miraculous stuff to ordinary as soon as possible.

A large body of recent interpretation relies on the assumption that a difference between living and not living, between animate and inanimate, is central to cultures and that the power of objects increases as they approximate persons. Images come alive because they represent the human form. They live when their eyes make contact with yours.[49] Even sophisticated analyses of the relationship between images and objects often use the difference between life and lifelessness as basic. To Robert Sharf, for example, fascination with relics is basically a fascination with—and a need to bridge (both in concept and in praxis)—the fundamental and threatening line between being alive and being dead.[50] Yet this does not seem to have been the basic concern or the basic problem for those medieval adherents who journeyed to shrines where images sweated, bled, or glowed with light, where candles burned without losing wax and girdles eased the pains of birthing. It was not the "more realistic" images that came to life, nor did the enthusiasm for relics manifest much of a sense that bodiliness was more valuable than stuffness. A drinking cup that failed to crack was as miraculous as a bit of tongue that refused to decay. The problem for medieval worshippers and theorists, both those who doubted and those who believed, was change – not the line between person and thing, or the line between life and death, but the divide between what something is (its identity) and its inevitable progression toward corruption.

I raise these differences between medieval and modern assumptions not in order to suggest that medieval ones should be adopted. That would be impossible. Nor do I explain them in order to undercut modern theorizing. I am, after all, modern and would not be able to ask questions about difference at all without modern theories to think with. I do, however, suggest that acquaintance with medieval assumptions – and attention to the ways in which they are different from ours – not only produces a more nuanced understanding of the Middle Ages but also unsettles some modern theorizing, at least insofar as that theorizing takes as self-evident the boundary between human and thing, part and whole, mimesis and material, animate and inanimate. Medieval theories, like medieval praxis, operated not from a modern need to break down such boundaries but from a sense that they were porous in some cases, nonexistent in others.

Perhaps it is worth noting that some contemporary work in the life sciences or on the mind/brain problem has a similar sense of these boundaries as porous or nonexistent.[51]

Again the Paradox

What I have argued in this book suggests that the understanding of the material with which medieval people lived produced no less unease than modern theories about objects and persons produce for moderns, but the unease was different. In conclusion, then, I return to matter as medieval people confronted it. For that is the focus and burden of these chapters, not the three rather epiphenomenal conclusions I have sketched above.

I have argued not only that the late Middle Ages saw both an intensifying rejection and an intensifying revering of matter as the locus of the divine but also that such simultaneous intensification of contrary responses was located in the very nature of matter. As a religion at whose heart lie the doctrines of incarnation, creation, and the re-creation of resurrection, Christianity has to take matter seriously. Yet whether in Isidore's formulation or Aristotle's, *materia* was understood to be that which, by definition, comes to be, generates what is other than itself, and passes away. How, then, was it to manifest the eternal changelessness of God? The paradoxical religious practices, attitudes, and theories of late medieval Christians reflect a struggle to live in and understand a world in which physical stuff announces and discloses a creator whose nature (eternal, immutable, and unknowable) is the opposite of matter.

The paradox of fourteenth- and fifteenth-century devotion lies not only in the prevailing assumption that matter is essentially animate and labile. Nor is it merely the simultaneous assertion of the eternally unknowable and the this-worldly material. Rather, it is the assertion by miraculous matter itself of life in death, eternity in change, ever-living blood in ever-decaying bread, wood, or bone. Transformation miracles were moments in which matter contradicted itself. But it could do so only in material ways. Hence, if matter transcended its own ordinary changeability by denying decay, it could do so, it seemed, only by yet another change. Such extraordinary change could, however, last only a moment. Bleeding hosts, glowing relics, and weeping statues inevitably faded. Other miracles were then necessary. But the recurrent eruption of miraculous stuff was threatening to ecclesiastical authorities, to philosophers theorizing the natural world, and to ordinary Christians who wished either to adhere to traditional cult objects or to worship by inner response rather than external pilgrimage.

The paradox of late medieval devotion rested in sophisticated assumptions about the stuff of the world, which were ultimately assumptions about survival and decay, meaning and meaninglessness. I have tried to show what these assumptions were by considering specific examples from medieval practice as well as medieval theology. In closing, however, I must state again that paradox is by definition impossible to explain in discursive language. One cannot simultaneously assert contraries. Rude, other-denying facts such as identity and annihilation, or the haunting presence and yet utter beyondness of ultimate meaning, cannot be spoken together. Yet together is how they must be lived. Their simultaneity cannot be stated; it can only be evoked—and even this only inadequately. If I have not, in this book, succeeded in simultaneously asserting the mutually contradictory, I hope I have provided a sufficient number of examples to evoke for my readers the paradox of Christian materiality in the later Middle Ages.

Notes

ABBREVIATIONS USED IN THE NOTES

AASS Johannes Bollandus and Godefridus Henschenius (eds.), *Acta sanctorum quotquot toto orbe coluntur, vel a catholicis scriptoribus celebrantur quae ex latinis et graecis, aliarumque gentium antiquis monumentis collegit, digessit, notis illustravit*, new edition edited by J. Carnandet et al. (Paris: V. Palmé, 1863–1940). Not all the volumes in this series are in their third edition, but the series as a whole is the third edition.

DTC A. Vacant et al. (eds.), *Dictionnaire de théologie catholique*, 15 vols. and Tables générales (Paris: Letouzy et Ané, 1909–50).

PG J.-P. Migne (ed.), *Patrologiae cursus completus: Series graeca*, 161 vols. in 167 (Paris: J.-P. Migne, etc., 1857–[1905?]).

PL J.-P. Migne (ed.), *Patrologiae cursus completus: Series latina*, 221 vols. (Paris: J.-P. Migne, etc., 1841–64).

INTRODUCTION

1. See Adolph Friedrich Riedel (ed.), *Codex diplomaticus Brandenburgensis: Sammlung der Urkunden, Chroniken und sonstigen Quellenschriften für die Geschichte der Mark Brandenburg und ihrer Regenten*, 41 vols. in 32 (Berlin: Morin, 1838–69), A (= first section) 2, document 17, pp. 152–56, for the archbishop of Magdeburg's reissue of the decree. See also Anton Joseph Binterim, *Pragmatische Geschichte der deutschen National-, Provinzial- und vorzüglichsten Diöcesanconcilien vom vierten Jahrhundert bis auf das Concilium zu Trient*, 7 vols. (Mainz: Kirchhein, Schott und Thielmann, 1835–48), vol. 7, pp. 257, 278, 474,

486, 541, and 548. Unless otherwise indicated, all translations are mine. On Cusanus as legate, see Donald Sullivan, "Nicholas of Cusa as Reformer: The Papal Legation to the Germanies, 1451–1452," *Mediaeval Studies* 16 (1974): 382–428, and Erich Meuthen, "Die deutschen Legationsreisen des Nikolaus von Kues 1451/1452," in Hartmut Broockmann, Bernd Moeller, and Karl Stackmann (eds.), revised by Ludger Grenzmann, *Lebenslehren und Weltenwürfe im Übergang vom Mittelalter zur Neuzeit: Politik-Bildung-Naturkunde-Theologie* (Göttingen: Vandenhoeck & Ruprecht, 1989), pp. 421–99.

2. I have discussed these sites in Caroline Walker Bynum, *Wonderful Blood: Theology and Practice in Late Medieval Northern Germany and Beyond* (Philadelphia: University of Pennsylvania Press, 2007), pp. 26–45, 54–55, and 293–94 n. 121. See also Kristen Van Ausdall, "Doubt and Authority in the Host-Miracle Shrines of Orvieto and Wilsnack," in Sarah Blick and Rita Tekippe (eds.), *Art and Architecture of Late Medieval Pilgrimage in Northern Europe and the British Isles*, 2 vols. (Leiden: Brill, 2005), vol. 1, pp. 513–38; and Felix Escher and Hartmut Kühne (eds.), *Die Wilsnackerfahrt: Ein Wallfahrts- und Kommunikationszentrum Nord- und Mitteleuropas im Spätmittelalter,* Europäische Wallfahrtsstudien (Frankfurt: Peter Lang, 2006).

3. Rudolph Haubst, *Die Christologie des Nikolaus von Kues* (Freiburg: Herder, 1956), pp. 276–98, and see Bynum, *Wonderful Blood*, pp. 125–27 and 142–43.

4. In addition to Haubst, *Die Christologie*, see Nicholas of Cusa, *De visione Dei*, chapters 19–21, in *Nicholas of Cusa: Selected Spiritual Writings*, trans. and ed. H. Lawrence Bond (New York and Mahwah, NJ: Paulist Press, 1997), pp. 272–78. And on Nicholas, see also Bernard McGinn, *The Harvest of Mysticism in Medieval Germany (1300–1500)* (New York: Crossroad, 2005), pp. 432–83.

5. Peter Browe, "Die eucharistischen Verwandlungswunder des Mittelalters," *Römische Quartalschrift* 37 (1929): 148, and Romuald Bauerreiss, "Der 'gregorianische' Schmerzensmann und das 'Sacramentum S. Gregorii' in Andechs," *Studien und Mitteilungen zur Geschichte des Benediktiner-Ordens und seiner Zweige* NF 13 (44) (1926): 57–78. Although the hosts were not in fact new when Nicholas of Cusa came to examine them, they undoubtedly do not go back to Gregory the Great (d. 604), to whom some legends attributed them. Their chronology is very badly documented, but they are known to have attracted excitement and veneration since the twelfth century. The story of their miraculous transformation was probably grafted onto earlier claims

that they were wafers that had been consecrated by two saintly early medieval popes.

6. See, for example, Jean Louis Schefer, *L'Hostie profanée: Histoire d'une fiction théologique* (Paris: P. O. L., 2007), pp. 99–113; Derek A. Rivard, *Blessing the World: Ritual and Lay Piety in Medieval Religion* (Washington, D.C.: The Catholic University of America Press, 2009), pp. 12–17, and the earlier literature cited there.

7. As many scholars have pointed out, the nature of the sources that survive is such as to exaggerate these aspects of the period.

8. Thomas Lentes, "'Andacht' und 'Gebärde': Das religiöse Ausdrucksverhalten," in Bernhard Jussen and Craig Koslofsky (eds.), *Kulturelle Reformation: Sinnformationen im Umbruch, 1400–1600* (Göttingen: Vandenhoeck & Ruprecht, 1999), pp. 26–67; Robert W. Scribner, "Popular Piety and Modes of Visual Perception in Late-Medieval and Reformation Germany," *The Journal of Religious History* 15 (1989): 448–69.

9. Pierre-André Sigal, *L'Homme et le miracle dans la France médiévale (XIe–XIIe siècle)* (Paris: Éditions du Cerf, 1985); Philip M. Soergel, *Wondrous in His Saints: Counter-Reformation Propaganda in Bavaria* (Berkeley: University of California Press, 1993), pp. 20–30; and Mitchell B. Merback, "Channels of Grace: Eucharistic Imagery, Architecture and Purgatory Cult at the Host-Miracle Pilgrimages of Late Medieval Bavaria," in Blick and Tekippe (eds.), *Art and Architecture*, vol. 1, pp. 587–646.

10. The classic study is Edouard Dumoutet, *Le Désir de voir l'hostie et les origins de la dévotion au Saint-Sacrement* (Paris: Beauchesne, 1926), and see Chapter 1, n. 43, for bibliography on ocular communion.

11. André Vauchez, "Les Images saints: Représentations iconographiques et manifestations du sacré," in *idem*, *Saints, prophètes et visionnaires: Le Pouvoir surnaturel au moyen âge* (Paris: Albin Michel, 1999), pp. 79–91.

12. Jeffrey F. Hamburger, *The Visual and the Visionary: Art and Female Spirituality in Late Medieval Germany* (New York: Zone Books, 1998); Lentes, "'Andacht' und 'Gebärde'"; Robert W. Scribner, "Vom Sakralbild zur sinnlichen Schau," in Klaus Schreiner and Norbert Schnitzler (eds.), *Gepeinigt, begehrt, vergessen: Symbolik und Sozialbezug des Körpers im späten Mittelalter und der frühen Neuzeit* (Munich: Wilhelm Fink, 1992), pp. 309–36; *idem*, "Popular Piety and Modes of Visual Perception"; and Chapter 1, nn. 92 and 93.

13. For interpretations that stress vision and visuality in the period, see Chapter 1, nn. 1 and 43. The fact that my own earlier article about the iconographical theme of the Gregory Mass is titled "Seeing and Seeing Beyond: The Mass of St. Gregory in the Fifteenth Century," in Jeffrey F. Hamburger and Anne-Marie Bouché (eds.), *The Mind's Eye: Art and Theological Argument in the Middle Ages* (Princeton, NJ: Department of Art and Archaeology in cooperation with Princeton University Press, 2006), pp. 208–40, makes it clear that I am not opposing the line of interpretation that stresses the way in which all sorts of images in the later Middle Ages are understood to point beyond themselves. I have, however, changed somewhat the emphasis of my interpretation.

14. See Peter Brown, *The Cult of the Saints: Its Rise and Function in Latin Christianity* (Chicago: University of Chicago Press, 1981); Patrick Geary, *Furta sacra: Thefts of Relics in the Central Middle Ages*, rev. ed. (Princeton, NJ: Princeton University Press, 1990); Victor Saxer, *Morts, martyrs, reliques en Afrique chrétienne aux premiers siècles: Les Témoignages de Tertullien, Cyprien et Augustin à la lumière de l'archéologie africaine*, Théologie historique 55 (Paris: Beauchesne, 1980); Cynthia Hahn, "Seeing and Believing: The Construction of Sanctity in Early-Medieval Saints' Shrines," *Speculum* 72, no. 4 (1997): 1079–106; and the works cited in Chapter 2, n. 19.

15. See Johannes Fried, *Das Mittelalter: Geschichte und Kultur* (Munich: C.H. Beck, 2009), p. 148 and plate 23. For controversies about the dating of the Gero crucifix, see Annika Elisabeth Fisher, "Cross Altar and Crucifix in Ottonian Cologne: Past Narrative, Present Ritual, Future Resurrection," in Søren Kaspersen and Erik Thunø (eds.), *Decorating the Lord's Table: On the Dynamics between Image and Altar in the Middle Ages* (Copenhagen: Museum Tusculanum Press, 2006), p. 28 n. 13. There has recently been lively debate about several other crucifixes whose wood can be dendrochronologically dated to earlier than the Gero crucifix. Although several scholars have claimed them to be Carolingian, it is not clear to me that the carving is earlier than the early twelfth century, no matter what the date of the wood. See Heribert Meurer, "Karolingische Monumentalskulptur? Die romanischen Kruzifixe von Schaftlach, Enghausen und Schlehdorf revidiert? Expertengespräch am 30.5.2005 im Dombergmuseum Freising," *Kunstchronik: Monatsschrift für Kunstwissenschaft, Museumwesen und Denkmalpflege* 58, no. 12 (December 2005): 613–16; and Gerald Dobler, "Anmerkungen zu dem Bericht von Heribert Meurer über das

Expertengespräch zu den Kruzifixen von Schaftlach, Enghausen und Schlehdorf am 30.5.2005 im Dombergmusuem Freising," *Kunstchronik* 59, no. 6 (June 2006): 303–305. I am grateful to Shirin A. Fozi for information about recent research on monumental crucifixes.

16. Peter Damian, *Opusculum* 19: *De abdicatione episcopatus* [Letter 72], chapter 5, PL 145, col. 432. Peter Dinzelbacher, "Das Blut Christi in der Religiosität des Mittelalters," in Norbert Kruse and Hans Ulrich Rudolf (eds.), *900 Jahre Heilig-Blut-Verehrung in Weingarten 1094–1994: Festschrift zum Heilig-Blut-Jubiläum am 12. Marz 1994*, 3 vols. (Sigmaringen: J. Thorbecke, 1994), vol. 1, p. 425 n. 147, says this is the first such vision. The famous Anglo-Saxon poem "The Dream of the Rood," in which the cross appears spotted with blood, is a dream vision, not a literal animation such as Damian supposedly experienced.

17. See Giles Constable, "The Cross of the Crusaders," in *Crusaders and Crusading in the Twelfth Century* (Farnham, UK: Ashgate, 2008), pp. 67–79, and *idem*, *Three Studies in Medieval Religious and Social Thought* (Cambridge: Cambridge University Press, 1998), p. 200. The Life of the eleventh-century pope Leo IX by Wibert of Toul claims that the body of the child was marked with crosses; see *ibid.*, p. 200. Crosses were also understood to be inscribed within; see Jean-Claude Schmitt, *Le Corps des images: Essais sur la culture visuelle au moyen âge*, Le Temps des images (Paris: Gallimard, 2002), pp. 80–81, for Gerard of Cambrai arguing, against the heretics of Arras, that the crucifix inscribes itself on the heart.

18. See Chapter 1, pp. 112–13.

19. For background to the 1290 miracle, see Gilbert Dahan, *Les Intellectuels chrétiens et les juifs au moyen âge* (Paris: Éditions du Cerf, 1990), pp. 546–53; Nicole Bériou, "Entre sottises et blasphèmes: Échos de la dénonciation du Talmud dans quelques sermons du XIIIe siècle," in Gilbert Dahan et al. (eds.), *Le Brûlement du Talmud à Paris 1242–1244* (Paris: Éditions du Cerf, 1999), pp. 211–37; and Elsa Marmursztejn, "Du Récit exemplaire au *casus* universitaire: Une Variation théologique sur le thème de la profanation d'hosties par les juifs (1290)," in *La Rouelle et la croix destins des juifs d'Occident*, coordinated by Dominique Iogna-Prat and Danièle Sansy, *Médiévales* 41 (Autumn 2001): 37–64. For the later miracle host given by Eugene IV to Duke Philip the Good of Burgundy in 1433, see figure 42, p. 146, and Miri Rubin, *Gentile Tales: The Narrative Assault on Late Medieval Jews* (Philadelphia: University of Pennsylvania

Press, 2004), p. 168 plate 24.

20. See Jean-Paul Roux, *Le Sang: Mythes, symboles et réalités* (Paris: Fayard, 1988), pp. 202–203.

21. Adolph Franz, *Die kirchlichen Benediktionen im Mittelalter*, 2 vols. (Freiburg: Herder, 1909), vol. 1, pp. 381–85. On the care with which one must use terms such as "popular" and "folk," see Chapter 2, pp. 129–30.

22. Franz, *Die kirchlichen Benediktionen im Mittelalter*, *passim*. See also Rivard, *Blessing the World*, esp. p. 278. This may be due in part to the vagaries of the survival of evidence but cannot be owing entirely to this.

23. See Erik Thunø and Gerhard Wolf (eds.), *The Miraculous Image in the Late Middle Ages and Renaissance*, Analecta Romana Supplement 35 (Rome: "L'erma" di Bretschneider, 2004).

24. See Vauchez, "Les Images saints."

25. As examples of recent work on medieval and early modern pilgrimage, see Merback, "Channels of Grace"; Soergel, *Wondrous in His Saints*; and Robert Maniura, *Pilgrimage to Images in the Fifteenth Century: The Origins of the Cult of Our Lady of Częstochowa* (Woodbridge, UK: Boydell Press, 2004).

26. For examples of the materializing of the peasant's vision into a standardized image, see *The Arts in Latin America 1492–1820*, catalogue of the exhibit organized for the Philadelphia Museum of Art by Joseph J. Rishel with Suzanne Stratton-Pruitt (Philadelphia: Philadelphia Museum of Art, 2006), pp. 340 and 393. No matter how much they are enjoined even today to direct their prayers to Mother Mary in heaven, many contemporary Christians make pilgrimages to that image and take *it* away with them as little medallions and prayer cards. William Christian, Jr., *Apparitions in Late Medieval and Renaissance Spain* (Princeton, NJ: Princeton University Press, 1981), shows how often the experience of collective or group visions led to the finding of a holy image or to the providing of other sorts of material traces, such as footprints; hence, even the visionary experience tended to result in holy matter. See Chapter 1 at nn. 111 and 120.

27. Classic here is Michael Baxandall, *The Limewood Sculptors of Renaissance Germany, 1475–1525: Images and Circumstances* (New Haven, CT: Yale University Press, 1980). See also Anton Legner, "Bilder und Materialien in der spätgotischen Kunstproduktion," *Städel-Jahrbuch* N.F. 6 (1977): 158–76; Günter Bandmann, "Bemerkungen zu einer Ikonologie des Materials," *Städel-Jahrbuch*

N.F. 2 (1969): 75–100; and David Park, "The Polychromy of English Medieval Sculpture," in Stacy Boldrick, David Park, and Paul Williams (eds.), *Wonder: Painted Sculpture from Medieval England* (Leeds, UK: Henry Moore Institute, 2003), pp. 31–54. And see Chapter 1, n. 47.

28. For analysis of the winged altar shown in figures 13 and 14, see Chapter 1, pp. 67–70.

29. See Chapter 1, pp. 101–104.

30. See the images in Jeffrey F. Hamburger, *The Rothschild Canticles: Art and Mysticism in Flanders and the Rhineland circa 1300* (New Haven, CT: Yale University Press, 1991), plates 4 and 12 and pp. 118–54. And see figure 2 above. Here the viewer is invited to penetrate through to nonrepresentational presentations of the Trinity. Paradox is signaled by the very confusion of forms. But ironically, this conjuring up of the triune beyond anthropomorphic figures issues in images that are even more material in the substance depicted; in fol. 84r, the Trinity is a folded cloth. Even in fol. 106r, where the cloth is drawn aside, it still appears as a frame for the central image, which is a scintillating star.

31. Herbert Kessler, *Seeing Medieval Art*, Rethinking the Middle Ages 1 (Peterborough, Ontario: Broadview Press, 2004); Baxandall, *The Limewood Sculptors*, esp. pp. 53–94.

32. Some work in the anthropology of art suggests that it is in the nature of all "art objects" to do this. Alfred Gell, for example, who uses the word "index" for the sort of objects I am talking about here, argues that art objects are "devices for securing the acquiescence of individuals in the network of intentionalities in which they are enmeshed." See Nicholas Thomas, "Foreword," in Alfred Gell, *Art and Agency: An Anthropological Theory* (Oxford: Oxford University Press, 1998), p. viii, quoting Gell from 1992. This idea, with which I basically agree, makes the materiality of art itself effective more by what it does than by what it "means" or "communicates" or "says." I am, however, making an argument here for historical difference, not proposing a general theory of objects or art objects. I would also not go so far as Gell in rejecting altogether the notion that things "talk" and prefer Daston's formulation: "thickenings of significance are one way that things can be made to talk. But their utterances are never disembodied. Things communicate by what they are as well as by how they mean.... Thinking with things is very different from thinking with words, for the relationship between sign and signified is never

arbitrary—nor self-evident." Lorraine Daston, "Introduction: Speechless," in Lorraine Daston (ed.), *Things That Talk: Object Lessons from Art and Science* (New York: Zone Books, 2004), p. 20. See Chapter 1, nn. 1, 7, 9, and 47, and Caroline Walker Bynum, "The Presence of Objects: Medieval Anti-Judaism in Modern Germany," *Common Knowledge* 10, no. 1 (2004): 26–31, where I try to work out a general theory of medieval holy objects.

33. Not entirely, of course. Schmitt points out that they are different as well as related. *Le Corps des images*, pp. 274–94.

34. See Dagmar Preising, "Bild und Reliquie: Gestalt und Funktion gotischer Reliquientafeln und -altärchen," *Aachener Kunstblätter* 61 (1995–97): 13–84. On Throne of Wisdom statues, which sometimes contained relics, see Chapter 1, pp. 88–89 and n. 78.

35. On the Karlštejn Chapel, see Barbara Drake Boehm and Jiří Fajt (eds.), *Prague: The Crown of Bohemia, 1347–1437*, exhibition catalogue (New York and New Haven, CT: The Metropolitan Museum of Art and Yale University Press, 2005), pp. 10–15. On the Crucifixion, see Jiří Fajt (ed.), *Magister Theodoricus, Court Painter to Emperor Charles IV: The Pictorial Decoration of the Shrines at Karlštejn Castle*, exhibition catalogue (Prague: National Gallery, 1998), pp. 320–21. According to the catalogue entry, the relics were perhaps placed after the painting was completed. It is also worth noting that a quite graphic Man of Sorrows located on the wall directly under the Crucifixion has a large opening for a relic container in the sarcophagus; see *ibid.*, pp. 318–19. Unfortunately, the central image has been badly damaged and heavily restored; moreover, it is not possible to ascertain what was in the reliquary aperture. I am grateful to Nino Zchomelidse for discussions of this Crucifixion. For other examples of objects with relics embedded, see Chapter 1, nn. 137–40.

36. I avoid here the question of how far the medieval attention to the materiality of "art" is like the concern of certain twentieth-century artists with materials. There are some obvious parallels between the medieval approach and works, such as those of Barnett Newman or Joseph Cornell, that explore the nature of paint and paper or the irreducibility of objects. But medieval artists do not attempt to strip away the multiple significances of materials in the way some contemporary artists do. Some current discussion in the anthropology of art and in anthropology generally deals with this; see the works by Gell, Osborne and Tanner, and Miller cited in n. 40 below. And see n. 32 above and

Chapter 1, n. 1.

37. Johan Huizinga, *The Autumn of the Middle Ages*, trans. Rodney J. Payton and Ulrich Mammitzsch (1919; Chicago: University of Chicago Press, 1996). For the standard (and somewhat unfair) take on Huizinga, see John Kieschnick, *The Impact of Buddhism on Chinese Material Culture* (Princeton, NJ: Princeton University Press, 2003), p. 20.

38. I have dealt with these trends recently in "Perspectives, Connections, and Objects: What's Happening in History Now?" *Daedalus* (Winter 2009): 1–16. For an excellent brief overview of recent work on material culture, see Kieschnick, *The Impact of Buddhism*, pp. 15–23.

39. See above, n. 27.

40. See Daniel Miller, "Materiality: An Introduction," in Daniel Miller (ed.), *Materiality* (Durham, NC: Duke University Press, 2005), pp. 1–50, esp. pp. 6–15; Arjun Appadurai, "Introduction: Commodities and the Politics of Value," in *The Social Life of Things: Commodities in Cultural Perspective* (Cambridge: Cambridge University Press, 1986), pp. 3–63; Gell, *Art and Agency*; Robin Osborne and Jeremy Tanner (eds.), *Art's Agency and Art History*, New Interventions in Art History (Oxford: Blackwell, 2007), esp. pp. 1–27; Bruno Latour, "The Berlin Key or How to Do Words with Things," in Paul M. Graves-Brown (ed.). *Matter, Materiality and Modern Culture* (London: Routledge, 2000), pp. 10–21; and Daston (ed.), *Things That Talk*. Especially useful is Daston's "Introduction: Speechless," in *ibid.*, pp. 9–24. For the argument that things have not "agency" but rather processual and relational attributes, see Tim Ingold, "Materials against Materiality," *Archaeological Dialogues* 14, no. 1 (2007): 1–16.

41. On this, see n. 44 below.

42. See n. 32 above and Chapter 1, nn. 13 and 106–107. Crucial here are Hans Belting, *Likeness and Presence: A History of the Image before the Era of Art*, trans. Edmund Jephcott (Chicago: University of Chicago Press, 1994), and Gell, *Art and Agency*.

43. See Daston (ed.), *Things That Talk*. See also Randolph Starn, "A Historian's Brief Guide to New Museum Studies," *American Historical Review* 110, no. 1 (2005): 68–96; and Leora Auslander, "Beyond Words," *American Historical Review* 110, no. 4 (2005): 1015–45.

44. See John Onians, *Neuroarthistory: From Aristotle and Pliny to Baxandall*

and Zeki (New Haven, CT: Yale University Press, 2007); Hans Belting, *Bild-Anthropologie: Entwürfe für eine Bildwissenschaft* (Munich: Wilhelm Fink, 2001); *idem*, "Image, Medium, Body: A New Approach to Iconology," *Critical Inquiry* 31, no. 2 (2005): 302–19; and David Freedberg and Vittorio Gallese, "Motion, Emotion and Empathy in Esthetic Experience," *Trends in Cognitive Science* 11, no. 5 (May 2007): 197–203. And see David Freedberg's now classic *The Power of Images: Studies in the History and Theory of Response* (Chicago: University of Chicago Press, 1989). For reservations about the recent move to the psychology or anthropology of response, see Robert Suckale's review of Belting in *Journal für Kunstgeschichte* 11, no. 4 (2007): 351–60.

45. The epigraphs come from David Shulman, *Spring, Heat, Rains: A South Indian Diary* (Chicago: University of Chicago Press, 2009), p. 30, and Daston, "Introduction: Speechless," p. 24. See also Chapter 4, n. 29, and the section "Theories: Medieval and Modern" in the Conclusion.

46. Such usage seems to me confused. See, for example, Philip Hancock et al., *The Body, Culture and Society: An Introduction* (Buckingham, PA: Open University Press, 2000). The introduction speaks of struggles for citizenship as waged by "excluded bodies" and medicine as focusing on "healthy bodies" (*ibid.*, p. 1). "Body" clearly does not mean the same thing in these sentences. It is also important to point out here that I am not sympathetic to current moves that reduce processes once considered aesthetic, ethical, spiritual, or intellectual to locations in the brain. On this, see the charming essay by Fernando Vidal, "*Eternal Sunshine of the Spotless Mind* and the Cultural History of the Self," *WerkstattGeschichte* 45 (2007): 96–109.

47. As Esther Cohen has recently observed, much work inspired by *Holy Feast and Holy Fast* and *The Resurrection of the Body* seriously misrepresents both their arguments and medieval anthropological theory by equating body with person. In medieval anthropology, person was a psychosomatic unity. See Esther Cohen, "The Animated Pain of the Body," *American Historical Review* 105, no. 1 (2000): 41; Caroline Walker Bynum, *Metamorphosis and Identity* (New York: Zone Books, 2001), p. 222 n. 7; and *eadem*, s.v. "Soul and Body," in Joseph R. Strayer (ed.), *Dictionary of the Middle Ages, Supplement*, ed. William Chester Jordan (New York: Charles Scribner's Sons–Thomson/Gale, 2004), pp. 588–94. On the relationship of this to theories of what modern people call identity, see *eadem*, *Metamorphosis and Identity*, pp. 19–21.

48. Recent work in medieval cultural history has moved away from stereotypes of the "self" as mind/body or soul/body dualism. Although work in the early and mid-twentieth century tended to see medieval Christianity as dualistic and anti-body, scholars in the past few decades have agreed that Christianity actually emphasizes the body and sees the person as a mind-body unit. For the older view, see Jacques Le Goff, "Body and Ideology in the Medieval West" and "The Repudiation of Pleasure," in *The Medieval Imagination*, trans. Arthur Goldhammer (Chicago: University of Chicago Press, 1988), pp. 83–85 and 93–103. For recent views, see Bynum, "Soul and Body." It is important to note, however, that this does not mean that medieval theorists equated body with person. In glossing medieval texts, we cannot substitute "body" for "person." When Bernard of Clairvaux says "no one can hate his own flesh, much less his soul," for example, he accepts body as a component of self but within an understanding of self as bipartite or hybrid. See Bernard of Clairvaux, *De conversione*, chapter 3, paragraph 4 to chapter 4, paragraph 5 in *Sancti Bernardi opera*, ed. Jean Leclercq, C.H. Talbot, and H.M. Rochais, 8 vols. (Rome: Editiones Cistercienses, 1957–77), vol. 4, pp. 74–77. Moreover, the modern tendency to treat the body mostly as a locus of sexual expressivity, gender, or sexual orientation is clearly anachronistic when applied to medieval texts; see Caroline Walker Bynum, "Why All the Fuss about the Body? A Medievalist's Perspective," *Critical Inquiry* 22 (Autumn 1995): 1–33. And see n. 47 above.

49. See Schmitt, *Le Corps des images*, and Vauchez, "Les Images saints," pp. 90–91. In a felicitous phrase, Schmitt speaks of images as "justifiées par la logique de l'Incarnation" (*Le Corps des images*, p. 209). The attitudes toward matter per se that I explore in Chapter 4 have not been connected in previous scholarship to attitudes toward the body or visual images or even to relic cult. For an odd and quite polemical exploration of the role of the material in Christianity, see Arthur G. Gibson, *The Voices of Matter*, compiled and edited by Lorine M. Getz (Lewiston, NY: Edwin Mellen Press, 1996). For a popularizing and not very accurate description of the material nature of premodern Christianity (which I cite here only as an indication of how widespread the generalization has become), see Meredith B. McGuire, "Why Bodies Matter: A Sociological Reflection on Spirituality and Materiality," in Elizabeth A. Dreyer and Mark S. Burrows (eds.), *Minding the Spirit: The Study of Christian Spirituality* (Baltimore, MD: Johns Hopkins University Press, 2005), pp. 118–34. The

standard complaint against the neglect of objects in the study of Christianity links this neglect to Protestantism; see Colleen McDannell, "Interpreting Things: Material Culture Studies and American Religion," *Religion* 21 (1991): 371–87.

50. Euan Cameron, *Interpreting Christian History: The Challenge of the Churches' Past* (Malden, MA: Blackwell, 2005), pp. 57–59 and 80–90. See also Euan Cameron, "The Power of the Word: Renaissance and Reformation," in Euan Cameron (ed.), *Early Modern Europe: An Oxford History* (Oxford: Oxford University Press, 1999), pp. 63–101.

51. See the citations from Jan Hus and Johannes Bremer in Chapter 4, p. 264.

52. For more on this, see Chapter 4, p. 219, and Conclusion, pp. 284–86.

53. It is obviously crucial in Christianity that matter and body are redeemed through a human figure. For example, to Nicholas of Cusa, it is Christ—the God-man—who leads all of creation back to God. See Chapter 4, p. 261.

54. For the very old interpretation that sees late medieval religiosity as simply corruption, see Constantin Fasolt, "Hegel's Ghost: Europe, the Reformation, and the Middle Ages," *Viator* 39, no. 1 (2008): 349–54. Fasolt argues for a new and very much broader periodization. See Conclusion, pp. 270–73.

CHAPTER ONE: VISUAL MATTER

1. On the ocularity of the later Middle Ages, see, for example, Robert W. Scribner, "Popular Piety and Modes of Visual Perception in Late-Medieval and Reformation Germany," *The Journal of Religious History* 15 (1989): 448–69; *idem*, "Vom Sakralbild zur sinnlichen Schau," in Klaus Schreiner and Norbert Schnitzler (eds.), *Gepeinigt, begehrt, vergessen: Symbolik und Sozialbezug des Körpers im späten Mittelalter und der frühen Neuzeit* (Munich: Wilhelm Fink, 1992), pp. 309–36; and Henning Laugerud, "Visuality and Devotion in the Middle Ages," in Henning Laugerud and Laura Katrine Skinnebach (eds.), *Instruments of Devotion: The Practices and Objects of Religious Piety from the Late Middle Ages to the 20th Century* (Aarhus, Denmark: Aarhus University Press, 2007), pp. 173–88. Basic still is Anton Mayer, "Die heilbringende Schau in Sitte und Kult," in *Heilige Überlieferung: Ausschnitte aus der Geschichte des Mönchtums und des heiligen Kultes. Festschrift für Ildefons Herwegen* (Münster: Aschendorf, 1938),

pp. 234–62. For reactions to this recent emphasis, see Paul Binski, "The English Parish Church and Its Art in the Later Middle Ages: A Review of the Problem," *Studies in Iconography* 20 (1999): 1–25, esp. pp. 13–14, and Jeffrey F. Hamburger, "Seeing and Believing: The Suspicion of Sight and the Authentication of Vision in Late Medieval Art," in Alessandro Nova and Klaus Krüger (eds.), *Imagination und Wirklichkeit: Zum Verhältnis von mentalen und realen Bilder in der Kunst der frühen Neuzeit* (Mainz: Philipp von Zabern, 2000), pp. 47–70. Hamburger also provides a positive assessment of medieval writers' own theories of seeing in Jeffrey F. Hamburger, "Speculations on Speculation: Vision and Perception in the Theory and Practice of Mystical Devotion," in Walter Haug and Wolfram Schneider-Lastin (eds.), *Deutsche Mystik im abendländischen Zusammenhang: Neu erschlossene Texte, neue methodische Ansätze, neue theoretische Konzepte, Kolloquium Kloster Fischingen 1998* (Tübingen: Niemeyer, 2000), pp. 353–408. On the privileging of sight in Western culture before the twentieth century, see the well-known study by Martin Jay, *Downcast Eyes: The Denigration of Vision in Twentieth-Century Thought* (Berkeley: University of California Press, 1993). A recent trend in art history does, however, involve an emphasis on materials. See, for example, Herbert Kessler, *Seeing Medieval Art*, Rethinking the Middle Ages 1 (Peterborough, Ontario: Broadview Press, 2004); Monika Wagner, *Das Material der Kunst: Eine andere Geschichte der Moderne* (Munich: C. H. Beck, 2001); and Thomas Raff, *Die Sprache der Materialien: Anleitung zu einer Ikonologie der Werkstoffe*, Kunstwissenschaftliche Studien 61 (Munich: Deutscher Kunstverlag, 1994). Michael Baxandall, in *The Limewood Sculptors of Renaissance Germany, 1475–1525: Images and Circumstances* (New Haven, CT: Yale University Press, 1980), says: "The very materiality of the image encouraged the viewer to see it as pure object, as mere material" (p. 90). Although I agree with this stress on the materiality of the object, I give it a different interpretation, since, as I will argue in this chapter, I do not think there was a concept of "pure object" or "mere material" in the later Middle Ages.

2. A great deal of this interpretation draws on sophisticated studies of medieval symbolism, such as Marie-Dominique Chenu's justly famous essays on symbolic mentalities and Platonism in *Nature, Man, and Society in the Twelfth Century: Essays on New Theological Perspectives in the Latin West*, ed. and trans. Jerome Taylor and Lester K. Little (Chicago: University of Chicago Press, 1968), or Friedrich Ohly's *Zur Signaturenlehre der Frühen Neuzeit: Bemerkungen*

zur mittelalterlichen Vorgeschichte und zur Eigenart einer epochalen Denkform in Wissenschaft, Literature und Kunst, ed. Uwe Ruberg and Dietmar Peil (Stuttgart: Hirzel, 1999). I am aware that some art historians feel that it is impossible to interpret medieval art without invoking medieval symbolism, epistemology, and exegetical theory as a habit of mind against which attitudes toward art objects (which we call "images") must be set. There is much truth to these claims. But I find that such discussions sometimes slip from discussions of textual "images" (that is, semantics, epistemology, and allegory) to visual objects in ways that are to me disconcerting, or they assume that viewers' reactions are best understood through the highly theorized texts of the educated. In this book, I've worked the other way, starting with the objects and how they themselves induce us to see them. This means that much of what follows in this chapter begins in formal analysis of the objects themselves or in reactions to their materials, not in texts. I do, however, devote significant attention in Chapter 2 to medieval treatments of devotional objects, and I argue in my Conclusion, pp. 280–81, that such attention must be given. Although my argument is not the same as his, I am partly in agreement with Thomas Raff in *Die Sprache der Materialien*.

3. For more on this, see the Introduction, nn. 32, 36, and 40 and this chapter, n. 34 below.

4. See, for example, Johannes Tripps, *Das handelnde Bildwerk in der Gotik: Forschungen zu den Bedeutungsschichten und der Funktion des Kirchengebäudes und seiner Ausstattung in der Hoch- und Spätgotik* (Berlin: Gebrüder Mann, 1998). On the objects in my figures 1 and 3, see *Krone und Schleier: Kunst aus mittelalterlichen Frauenklöstern*, exhibition catalogue published by the Kunst- und Ausstellungshalle der Bundesrepublik Deutschland, Bonn, and the Ruhrlandmuseum, Essen (Munich: Hirmer, 2005), pp. 371 and 372. Michael Camille, *The Gothic Idol: Ideology and Image-Making in Medieval Art* (Cambridge: Cambridge University Press, 1989), p. 219, speaks of an "image explosion" in the period.

5. Baxandall, *The Limewood Sculptors*, pp. 60–70. For a study of an early winged altar, see Donald L. Ehresmann, "The Iconography of the Cismar Altarpiece and the Role of Relics in an Early Winged Altarpiece," *Zeitschrift für Kunstgeschichte* 64 (2001): 1–36. On possible Italian forerunners in the late twelfth or thirteenth centuries (although without carved inner shrines), see Nino Zchomelidse, "The Aura of the Numinous and Its Reproduction:

Medieval Paintings of the Savior in Rome and Latium," *Memoirs of the American Academy in Rome* 55 (2010), forthcoming.

6. Horst Appuhn and Christian von Heusinger, "Der Fund kleiner Andachtsbilder des 13.–17. Jahrhunderts im Kloster Wienhausen," *Niederdeutsche Beiträge zur Kunstgeschichte* 5 (1966): 91–132. And, for an example, see Jeffrey F. Hamburger, *The Visual and the Visionary: Art and Female Spirituality in Late Medieval Germany* (New York: Zone Books, 1998), pp. 366–67. For how such objects were used, see *ibid.*, pp. 78, 84–85, and 323.

7. Obvious modern parallels are Mark Rothko and Jackson Pollock. Barbara Johnson comments on this in *Persons and Things* (Cambridge, MA: Harvard University Press, 2008), p. 61. But no contemporary theory would treat modern painting as simply a piece of evidence or an object. The very word of choice used by contemporary art historians—"images"—suggests some vestige of "representation" in the sense of presenting something in a medium it isn't. Paint, wood, steel, and so forth present to us as if they were, for example, apples or the color red, but they are not, and thus they call attention to the "not-ness." Even minimalist or pop art calls attention to the gap between itself and objects by in some sense questioning—or even insulting (by mimicking)—their objecthood. See Michael Fried's classic essay, "Art and Objecthood" (1967), reprinted in *Art and Objecthood: Essays and Reviews* (Chicago: University of Chicago Press, 1998), pp. 148–72. On this, see also Caroline Walker Bynum, "The Presence of Objects: Medieval Anti-Judaism in Modern Germany," *Common Knowledge* 10, no. 1 (2004): 27.

The point about an analogous medieval concern for the materials of images is made best by the cover of Herbert Kessler's *Seeing Medieval Art*, which shows a medieval miniature that depicts simply color. The image is also reproduced here in figure 6. In underlining the medieval concern for materials, I do not want to go so far as some anthropologists of art who attempt a general theory of all "art objects," from a West African nail fetish to Marcel Duchamp, as a realization of social agency. See Robin Osborne and Jeremy Tanner (eds.), *Art's Agency and Art History*, New Interventions in Art History (Oxford: Blackwell, 2007), p. 3, summarizing the work of Alfred Gell. My argument is historical—that is, I am interested in the specific ways in which late medieval devotional objects called attention to their materiality—and I argue that this awareness, and indeed manipulation, of materiality is more prominent than in other periods.

8. See Horst Appuhn, "Altardecken und Fastentücher, Weissstickereien," in *Bildstickereien des Mittelalters im Kloster Lüne* (Dortmund: Harenberg, 1983), pp. 27–52.

9. Useful here is Alfred Gell's point that all art objects are in some sense "representation," but not all representation is mimetic. "Representing" as a portrait does and "representing" as an ambassador or a seal does are not the same thing; the seal or the ambassador does not look like, for example, Sweden. But in no case is the object simply itself without conveying some sort of power beyond itself. See Alfred Gell, *Art and Agency: An Anthropological Theory* (Oxford: Oxford University Press, 1998), pp. 97–98. For a splendid treatment of the materiality of icons in the Eastern Christian tradition, see Bissera V. Pentcheva, "The Performative Icon," *Art Bulletin* 88, no. 4 (2006): 631–55.

10. In saying this, I do not mean to participate in any way in the current tendency to dismiss or denigrate the iconological approach of the great historian Erwin Panofsky. For an example of what can be accomplished by a very different approach to iconography, one that takes seriously the material subjects of medieval art *as objects*, see Marilyn Lavin, "The Mystic Winepress in the Mérode Altarpiece," in Irving Lavin and John Plummer (eds.), *Studies in Late Medieval and Renaissance Painting in Honor of Millard Meiss* (New York: New York University Press, 1977), pp. 297–301.

11. See Caroline Walker Bynum, "Patterns of Female Piety in the Later Middle Ages," in Jeffrey F. Hamburger and Susan Marti (eds.), *Crown and Veil: Female Monasticism from the Fifth to the Fifteenth Centuries*, trans. Dietlinde Hamburger (New York: Columbia University Press, 2008), pp. 172–90.

12. See, for example, Suzannah Biernoff, *Sight and Embodiment in the Middle Ages* (New York: Palgrave Macmillan, 2002).

13. See Introduction, nn. 32, 40, and 44. It seems to me that David Freedberg, in *The Power of Images: Studies in the History and Theory of Response* (Chicago: University of Chicago Press, 1991), has in fact extrapolated much of his general theory from specifically late medieval phenomena. Indeed, admitting as much, he says: "The ontology of holy images is exemplary for all images." David Freedberg, "Holy Images and Other Images," in Susan C. Scott (ed.), *The Art of Interpreting*, Papers in Art History from the Pennsylvania State University 9 (University Park, PA: Department of Art, The Pennsylvania State University,

1995), pp. 69–89, esp. p. 69. See also Robert H. Sharf, "On the Allure of Buddhist Relics," *Representations* 66 (Spring 1999): 97 n. 37. Sharf's essay has been reprinted in David Germano and Kevin Trainor (eds.), *Embodying the Dharma: Buddhist Relic Veneration in Asia* (Albany: State University of New York Press, 2004), pp. 163–91. And see John Kieschnick, *The Impact of Buddhism on Chinese Material Culture* (Princeton, NJ: Princeton University Press, 2003), pp. 48–49. As I conclude at the end of this book, however, I think the argument that people respond to certain images as animate because those images "look like people" is, at a basic level, too simple. See the Conclusion at nn. 49–51.

14. Insistent materiality is clearly not enough: Rothkos and Jackson Pollocks do not literally come alive for modern viewers. Medieval devotional objects sometimes came alive or were feared to do so (or to be misunderstood as doing so) because they proliferated in a world where other sorts of matter came alive and where both theories of matter, such as were found in alchemy, and theories of miracle suggested that this was possible. See Chapter 4 of this volume.

15. To say this is not, of course, to deny that representation of the holy was also an issue. See the passage quoted at n. 20 in this Chapter.

16. All biblical references are to the Vulgate, and all translations of the Bible are from the Douay-Rheims English translation.

17. The iconoclastic inscription is from Alain Besançon, *The Forbidden Image: An Intellectual History of Iconoclasm*, trans. Jane Marie Todd (Chicago: University of Chicago Press, 2000), p. 124. The passage from Claudius of Turin, as summarized by his opponents, is found in Jean-Claude Schmitt, *Le Corps des images: Essais sur la culture visuelle au moyen âge*, Le Temps des images (Paris: Gallimard, 2002), pp. 71–73. On Western attitudes toward images during the iconoclastic controversy in the East, see Celia Chazelle, "Matter, Spirit and Image in the *Libri Carolini*," *Recherches Augustiniennes* 21 (1986): 163–84, and David F. Appleby, "Holy Relic and Holy Image: Saints' Relics in the Western Controversy over Images in the Eighth and Ninth Centuries," *Word and Image* 8 (1992): 3–43.

18. John of Damascus, *Orationes pro sacris imaginibus*, *Oratio* 2, PG 94, cols. 1300B–D, cited by Freedberg, *The Power of Images*, p. 404. It is worth noting that flesh, bread, ink, and paper are grouped together here as matter.

19. John of Damascus, *Pro sacris imaginibus*, *Oratio* 2, PG 94, col. 1300B,

and *Oratio* 3, col. 1337c.

20. *Opus Caroli regis contra synodum (Libri Carolini)*, book 2, chapter 27, ed. Ann Freeman with Paul Meyvaert, Monumenta Germaniae historica: Concilia, vol. 2, supplement 1 (Hannover: Hahn, 1998), pp. 290–94.

21. On Arras, see Schmitt, *Le Corps des images*, pp. 79–82; on Peter of Bruys, see Walter L. Wakefield and Austin P. Evans (eds. and trans.), *Heresies of the High Middle Ages: Selected Sources Translated and Annotated* (New York: Columbia University Press, 1969), pp. 118–21.

22. I have made this point in Caroline Walker Bynum, *The Resurrection of the Body in Western Christianity, 200–1336* (New York: Columbia University Press, 1995), pp. 214–20. For doubts about whether there really were Cathars, see Mark Pegg, *A Most Holy War: The Albigensian Crusade and the Battle for Christendom* (Oxford: Oxford University Press, 2008). On anti-Cathar literature as primarily evidence for the minds of those producing it, see Uwe Brunn, *Des contestataires aux "Cathares": Discours de réforme et propagande antihérétique dans les pays du Rhin et de la Meuse avant l'Inquisition*, Collection des Études Augustiniennes: Série moyen âge et temps modernes 41 (Paris: Institut d'Études Augustiniennes, 2006). On the question of medieval heresy, see the excellent article by Peter Biller, "Christians and Heretics," in Miri Rubin and Walter Simons (eds.), *The Cambridge History of Christianity*, vol. 4, *Christianity in Western Europe c. 1100–c. 1500* (Cambridge: Cambridge University Press, 2009), pp. 170–86.

23. "Der Spiegel des Sünders," edited in Johannes Geffcken, *Der Bildercatechismus des fünfzehnten Jahrhunderts und die catechetischen Haupstücke in dieser Zeit bis auf Luther*, vol. 1: *Die zehn Gebote, mit 12 Bildtafeln nach Cod. Heidelb. 438* (Leipzig: T. O. Weigel, 1855), Anhang, col. 52. Passage translated in Baxandall, *The Limewood Sculptors*, p. 54.

24. Stephan von Landskron, "Die Hymelstrasse," edited in Geffcken, *Der Bildercatechismus*, Anhang, col. 115. Passage translated by Baxandall, in *The Limewood Sculptors*, p. 53.

25. William R. Cook, "The Question of Images and the Hussite Movement in Prague," *Cristianesimo nella storia: Ricerche storiche, esegetiche, teologiche* 3 (1982): 329–42; Thomas A. Fudge, "The 'Crown' and the 'Red Gown': Hussite Popular Religion," in Robert W. Scribner and Trevor Johnson (eds.), *Popular Religion in Germany and Central Europe, 1400–1800* (New York: St. Martin's

Press, 1996), pp. 38–57; and Margaret Aston, *England's Iconoclasts*, vol. 1, *Laws against Images* (Oxford: Oxford University Press, 1988), esp. chapter 4. For a recent and exciting treatment of the English debate over images, see Sarah Stanbury, *The Visual Object of Desire in Late Medieval England* (Philadelphia: University of Pennsylvania Press, 2008).

26. Aston, *England's Iconoclasts*, pp. 115–16.

27. Camille, *The Gothic Idol*, p. 30.

28. See Ephraim Shoham-Steiner, "'For a Prayer in That Place Would Be Most Welcome': Jews, Holy Shrines, and Miracles—a New Approach," *Viator* 37 (2006): 376.

29. This idea is also reflected in the passage from the *Libri Carolini* quoted at n. 20 above.

30. Pedro Garcia, summarizing for the commission, rejected the implication. I cite the commission's reading of Pico not because it was the majority position, but because it is significant that some idea of a difference between a living man and dead matter was operating. See Richard Trexler, "Florentine Religious Experience: The Sacred Image," *Studies in the Renaissance* 19 (1972): 40–41. For others making this argument (including perfectly orthodox theologians), see Jean Wirth, "La Critique scolastique de la théorie thomiste de l'image," in Olivier Christin and Dario Gamboni (eds.), *Crises de l'image religieuse de Nicée II à Vatican/Krisen religiöser Kunst vom 2. Niceanum bis zum 2. Vatikanischen Konzil* (Paris: Fondation Maison des Sciences de l'Homme, 1999), p. 107, and Aston, *England's Iconoclasts*, p. 117.

31. See Chenu, *Nature, Man and Society*, pp. 49–145. Jean Louis Schefer, in *L'Hostie profanée: Histoire d'une fiction théologique* (Paris: P. O. L., 2007), sees the loss of such an understanding of symbol as fundamental to Western understandings of images and relics, as opposed to Eastern. While there is much about his study that I think problematic, I find this insight basically correct.

32. The classic citation for a sense of God's footprints in creation is Bonaventure, *The Journey of the Mind to God*, trans. Philotheus Boehner, ed. Stephen F. Brown (Indianapolis, IN: Hackett, 1993). Hildegard of Bingen's understanding of *viriditas* is also a locus classicus for the sense of God in creation; see Gabriele Lautenschläger, "'Viriditas': Ein Begriff und seine Bedeutung," in Edeltraud Forster and the nuns of Eibingen (eds.), *Hildegard von Bingen: Prophetin durch die Zeiten. Zum 900. Geburtstag* (Freiburg: Herder, 1997), pp. 224–37.

For Mechtild's vision, see Chapter 4 at n. 124. And see, generally, Ohly, *Zur Signaturenlehre der Frühen Neuzeit*.

33. As will be clear by the time I get to Chapter 4, medieval understandings of matter and body were such that even a dead body or dead matter was understood under the paradigm of generation and corruption; therefore, even dead matter was in danger of erupting into life.

34. See Herbert L. Kessler, *Spiritual Seeing: Picturing God's Invisibility in Medieval Art* (Philadelphia: University of Pennsylvania Press, 2000), p. xv: "Art fully was a means to realize the central claim of medieval theory: to show the invisible by means of the visible." Kessler also elegantly emphasizes the importance of materiality: "Works of medieval art... were devised to engage the viewer in an anagogical process, offering spiritual readings of texts, elevating established categories of objects and iconographies, and deploying materials in such a way that physical presence is simultaneously asserted and subverted."

35. Besançon, *Forbidden Image*, pp. 149–51; Daniele Menozzi, *Les Images: L'Église et les arts visuels*, Textes en mains (Paris: Éditions du Cerf, 1991), p. 20; Chazelle, "Matter, Spirit and Image," p. 179. The position of the Council of Trent (session XXV, tit. 2) was essentially similar: images are to be retained and due honor given to them, but not worship, because there is no divinity or virtue in them. Honor shown to them is referred to the prototypes they represent. See Anthony Blunt, *Artistic Theory in Italy, 1450–1600* (Oxford: Oxford University Press, 1962), pp. 107–108.

36. Thomas's position was actually a good deal more complicated than the standard account indicates. In a move to which many later theorists objected, he held that *latria* could be offered to the cross because of what it refers to and even hinted, apropos both images and relics, at some kind of participation of image in exemplar. As Menozzi observes (*Les Images*, p. 34), there is a basic contradiction in Thomas's position; he condemns the idolatrous use of images, but encourages their veneration: "Ce n'est pas là l'unique aporie de son opération intellectuelle pourtant brillante. Comme le notera le nominaliste Durand de Saint-Pourçain au début du XIVe siècle, si l'image est un signe arbitraire n'ayant aucun rapport avec le prototype divin, elle ne peut être objet de latrie; mais si l'image matérielle a quelque rapport avec le prototype divin, le culte de l'image est alors idolâtrie." Jean Wirth, in "La Critique scolastique," points out that fourteenth-century theorists widened the gap between image and that

to which it refers.

37. Aquinas, *Summa contra Gentiles*, book 3, part 2, chapter 104, in *S. Thomae Aquinatis opera omnia*, ed. Roberto Busa, 7 vols. (Stuttgart–Bad Cannstatt: Frommann-Holzboog, 1980), vol. 2, p. 95.

38. Aquinas, *Summa theologiae*, part 1, question 1, article 9, in Busa (ed.), *Opera omnia*, vol. 2, p. 187; *Summa theologica*, trans. the Fathers of the English Dominican Province, (New York: Benziger, 1947–1948; reprint, Westminster, Maryland, 1981), vol. 1, p. 6. It is important to note that "image" here means any similitude.

39. Luther, sermon for March 12, 1522, quoted in Menozzi, *Les Images*, p. 167. The Catholic Thomas More made the same argument: see Aston, *England's Iconoclasts*, p. 32. Luther does, however (as is well known), stress hearing and texts more than seeing and images; see Thomas Lentes, "'Andacht' und 'Gebärde': Das religiöse Ausdrucksverhalten," in Bernhard Jussen and Craig Koslofsky (eds.), *Kulturelle Reformation: Sinnformationen im Umbruch, 1400–1600* (Göttingen: Vandenhoeck & Ruprecht, 1999), pp. 26–67, esp. pp. 44–53.

40. On prohibitions in the Hebrew Scriptures, see Besançon, *Forbidden Image*, pp. 63–82; Kessler, *Spiritual Seeing*, pp. 2–13 and 29–33. For various Christian uses of Jews as prototypes and antitypes, see Kessler, *Seeing Medieval Art*, pp. 67–70; Morten Steen Hansen, "Parmigianino and the Defense of a Miraculous Image," in Erik Thunø and Gerhard Wolf (eds.), *The Miraculous Image in the Late Middle Ages and Renaissance*, Analecta Romana Supplement 35 (Rome: "L'erma" di Bretschneider, 2004), pp. 200–202; Schmitt, *Le Corps des images*, pp. 82–84; Chazelle, "Matter, Spirit and Image," pp. 181–82. Some later reformers, such as Calvin, thought all human beings inevitably slip into idolatry if offered material things; see Menozzi, *Les Images*, pp. 172–79; Aston, *England's Iconoclasts*, p. 34.

41. Useful in such polemics was John 14:8–9: "He that seeth me seeth the Father also." But this was always understood in tandem with passages asserting the impossibility of seeing God himself: John 1:18, "No man hath seen God at any time," and Exodus 33:20, "Thou canst not see my [God's] face; for man shall not see me and live."

42. See the phrase from Michael Camille quoted in n. 4 above. For another and quite convincing approach to the question, see James Simpson, "The Rule of Medieval Imagination," in Jeremy Dimmick, James Simpson, and Nicolette

Zeeman (eds.), *Images, Idolatry, and Iconoclasm in Late Medieval England: Textuality and the Visual Image* (Oxford: Oxford University Press, 2002), p. 23: "Whereas... the reformers repeatedly deny that the images have life in them, the ferocity of the attack, and the often precise legal tortures to which the images are subjected, expose the suggestion that the images still have power to move.... The very act of iconoclasm reaffirms and reactivates, even if it imprisons, the imaginative power of the image and the saint it represents. Whether adored or reviled, then, images are dangerously vivacious. The iconoclasts' work can never finally be done, for once the physical images are broken, one must begin on the trickier business of purging the inner temple of the psyche."

43. Particularly relevant here is the large amount of recent literature on ocular communion. See, for example, Charles M. A. Caspers, "*Meum summum desiderium est te habere*: L'Eucharistie comme sacrement de la rencontre avec Dieu pour tous les croyants (ca. 1200–ca. 1500)," in André Haquin (ed.), *Fête-Dieu (1246–1996)*, vol. 1, *Actes du Colloque de Liège, 12–14 Septembre 1996*, Publications de l'Institute d'Études Médiévales 19 (Louvain-la-Neuve: Institute d'Études Médiévales de l'Université Catholique de Louvain, 1999), pp. 127–51; *idem*, "The Western Church during the Late Middle Ages: *Augenkommunion* or Popular Mysticism," in Charles Caspers, Gerard Lukken, and Gerard Rouwhorst (eds.), *Bread of Heaven: Customs and Practices Surrounding Holy Communion; Essays in the History of Liturgy and Culture* (Kampen, the Netherlands: Kok Pharos, 1995), pp. 83–97; and Judith Oliver, "Image et dévotion: Le Rôle de l'art dans l'institution de la Fête-Dieu," in Haquin (ed.), *Fête-Dieu*, vol. 1, pp. 153–72. See also Biernoff, *Sight and Embodiment*. For the stress that intellectuals placed on the gap between image and exemplar, see Wirth, "La Critique scolastique." On fear of the visual as reflected in the inner panels of altarpieces, see Reindert Falkenburg, "Hieronymus Bosch's *Mass of St. Gregory* and 'Sacramental Vision,'" in Andreas Gormans and Thomas Lentes (eds.), *Das Bild der Erscheinung: Die Gregorsmesse im Mittelalter*, KultBild 3 (Berlin: Reimer, 2007), p. 181, and the material he cites there.

44. Kessler, *Seeing Medieval Art*, p. 19; and see Jérôme Baschet, "Introduction: L'Image-objet," in Jérôme Baschet and Jean-Claude Schmitt (eds.), *L'Image: Fonctions et usages des images dans l'Occident médiéval* (Paris: Léopold d'Or, 1996), pp. 7–57, to which Kessler refers. Jacqueline Jung comments on the "*material* aspects of 'visual culture'" in "Crystalline Wombs and Pregnant

Hearts: The Exuberant Bodies of the Katharinenthal Visitation Group," in Rachel Fulton and Bruce Holsinger (eds.), *History in the Comic Mode: Medieval Communities and the Matter of Person* (New York: Columbia University Press, 2007), p. 233.

45. Another example of the interest of this art in itself—its own colors and shapes—is the Bamberg Apocalypse, folio 16v, where if one removed the figures of the Lamb of God, the throne, and the martyrs, one would have an exploration of colored squares rather like a modern painting by Rothko. Of course, one cannot just remove the figures. Nonetheless, the interest in color and pattern is striking. See Gude Suckale-Redlefsen and Bernhard Schemmel (eds.), *Das Buch mit 7 Siegeln: Die Bamberger Apokalypse; Eine Ausstellung der Staatsbibliothek Bamberg in Zusammenarbeit mit dem Haus der Bayerischen Geschichte: Katalog* (Lucerne and Wiesbaden: Harrassowitz, 2000), plate 10. See also plates 12, 16 and 17.

46. For the dressed Christ child, see Henk van Os with Eugène Honée, Hans Nieuwdorp, and Bernhard Ridderbos, *The Art of Devotion in the Late Middle Ages in Europe, 1300–1500*, trans. Michael Hoyle (Princeton, NJ: Princeton University Press, 1994), p. 99, figure 45; and Hamburger and Marti (eds.), *Crown and Veil*, p. 165. For an example of a dressed Madonna, see *Krone und Schleier*, pp. 411–13, and figure 311. On the form of the Madonna statue, see Susan Verdi Webster, "Shameless Beauty and Worldly Splendor: On the Spanish Practice of Adorning the Virgin," in Thunø and Wolf (eds.), *The Miraculous Image*, pp. 249–71. A better example than the one I reproduce here is in *ibid.*, p. 254, figure 3; the object is in private hands. On medieval art as brightly colored, see Herman Pleij, *Colors Demonic and Divine: Shades of Meaning in the Middle Ages and After*, trans. Diane Webb (New York: Columbia University Press, 2004). On decorating statues with jewels, see Robert Suckale, "An Unrecognized Statuette of the Virgin Mary by a Vienna Court Artist, ca. 1350," *Res* 53/54 (Spring/Autumn 2008): 107.

47. According to Pliny the Elder (*Natural History*, book 35, chapter 36), Zeuxis and Parrhasius held a contest to discover who was the greater artist. Zeuxis painted grapes, which the birds attempted to eat. But when Zeuxis asked Parrhasius to pull aside the curtain over his painting, he discovered that the curtain was the painting and was forced to concede defeat. I have discussed the issue of Renaissance illusion/realism further in Bynum, "Presence of

Objects," p. 27. See also Günter Bandmann, "Bemerkungen zu einer Ikonologie des Materials," *Städel-Jahrbuch* N.F. 2 (1969): 75–100, esp. 75. And note the nice distinction of Rico Franses in "When All That Is Gold Does Not Glitter: On the Strange History of Looking at Byzantine Art," in Anthony Eastmond and Liz James (eds.), *Icon and Word: The Power of Images in Byzantium: Studies Presented to Robin Cormack* (Aldershot, UK: Ashgate, 2003), p. 22, where he says: "To paint in gold is to paint in light rather than to represent it, as Renaissance painting does." And see above, n. 7.

48. On the principle of *similia similibus*—that is, that like not only signals but even controls or coerces like—see Stephen Wilson, *The Magical Universe: Everyday Ritual and Magic in Pre-Modern Europe* (London: Hambledon and London, 2000), p. xxiv. The principle was prominent in medieval folk remedies, especially those concerned with bleeding, where red cords were understood to induce or control blood flow. See Danielle Buschinger, "Sang versé, sang guérisseur, sang aliment et sang du Christ dans la literature médiévale allemande," in Marcel Faure (ed.), *Le Sang au moyen âge: Actes du quatrième colloque international de Montpellier, Université de Paul Valéry (27–29 novembre 1997)*, Cahiers du C.R.I.S.M.A. 4 (Montpellier: Université Paul Valéry, 1999), pp. 257–66; Peggy McCracken, *The Curse of Eve, the Wound of the Hero* (Philadelphia: University of Pennsylvania Press, 2003), pp. 1–2 and 47–50; Walter Michel, s.v. "Blut und Blutglaube im Mittelalter," in Gerhard Krauss, Gerhard Müller et al. (eds), *Theologische Realenzyklopädie*, 36 vols. (Berlin: de Gruyter, 1977–2004), vol. 6, pp. 737–38; and Johannes Heuser, "'Heilig-Blut' in Kult und Brauchtum des deutschen Kulturraumes: Ein Beitrag zur religiösen Volkskunde," Dissertation, Bonn, 1948, pp. 127–29. Bettina Bildhauer, in *Medieval Blood* (Cardiff: University of Wales Press, 2006), has a great deal on blood as healing (see esp. pp. 66–70, 83, 96–103, and 140–47) but does not treat the *similia similibus* phenomenon. See also Chapter 3, n. 56 below on the use of Christ's wound on birthing girdles.

49. See Raff, *Die Sprache der Materialien*. On the significance of gold, see Dominic Janes, *God and Gold in Late Antiquity* (Cambridge: Cambridge University Press, 1998), esp. pp. 139–52; Franses, "When All That Is Gold," pp. 13–24; and Pentcheva, "Performative Icon," pp. 639–644. On both red and gold, see Glenn Peers, *Sacred Shock: Framing Visual Experience in Byzantium* (University Park: Pennsylvania State University Press, 2004), pp. 35–58, 117,

and 126–30. On gems (although mostly in texts), see Christel Meier, *Gemma spiritalis: Methode und Gebrauch der Edelsteinallegorese vom frühen Christentum bis ins 18. Jahrhundert* (Munich: Wilhelm Fink, 1977).

50. See, for example, Albertus Magnus, *Book of Minerals*, trans. Dorothy Wyckoff (Oxford: Oxford University Press, 1967), and below, Chapter 3, n. 11.

51. Although, as I suggest here, the question of the effect of reproduction is an important one, Walter Benjamin's theory of reproducibility as diminishing the "aura" of a work of art puts the late medieval situation exactly backwards. Hence, I agree with the criticism of Horst Bredekamp, "Der simulierte Benjamin: Mittelalterliche Bemerkungen zu seiner Aktualität," in Andreas Berndt, Peter Kaiser, Angela Rosenberg, and Diana Trinkner (eds.), with the collaboration of Julia Feldtkeller and Christine Wahn, *Frankfurter Schule und Kunstgeschichte* (Berlin: Reimer, 1992), pp. 117–140, esp. pp. 125–34, but I think that he goes too far in equating images and relics. See below, n. 114.

52. The point I make here parallels that of Alfred Gell, who distinguishes between "representation" as looking like something and "representation" as standing for something. Gell, in considering idols, uses this point to argue that both iconic and aniconic objects can represent—that is, convey—the divine. See above, n. 9. Indeed, it is worth pointing out here that medieval images not only stood in for but even acted for—sometimes in startling ways. For images acting, see this chapter, p. 111.

53. See Caroline Walker Bynum, *Fragmentation and Redemption: Essays on Gender and the Human Body in Medieval Religion* (New York: Zone Books, 1991), pp. 230–35. In *The Resurrection of the Body*, pp. 118–21, 162–63, 174–76, 220–21, 309, and plates 19–22, I point out that such images also reassemble the saint.

54. See Peter Kidson, "Architecture and the Visual Arts," in David Luscombe and Jonathan Riley-Smith (eds.), *The New Cambridge Medieval History*, vol. 4: *c. 1024–1198*, part 1 (Cambridge: Cambridge University Press, 2004), p. 699.

55. On the Fritzlar pietà and related devotional images, see Walter Passarge, *Das deutsche Vesperbild im Mittelalter, mit 40 Abbildungen* (Cologne: F. J. Marcan, 1924), pp. 99 and 120; Wolfgang Krönig, "Rheinische Vesperbilder aus Leder und ihr Umkreis," *Wallraf-Richartz-Jahrbuch: Westdeutsches Jahrbuch für Kunstgeschichte* 24 (1962): 97–192; and Uta Reinhold, "Das Fritzlarer Vesperbild: Ein Meisterwerk mittelalterlicher Schnitz- und Fasskunst," *Denkmale*

und Kulturgeschichte 2 (2000): 33–38.

56. Ulinka Rublack, "Female Spirituality and the Infant Jesus in Late Medieval Dominican Convents," in Scribner and Johnson (eds.), *Popular Religion in Germany and Central Europe*, pp. 23–25, points out that these dolls tended to come alive in the nuns' visions when they touched the figures' feet or bodies.

57. For an example of an osculatory—a little parchment or leather flap placed in books explicitly for people to kiss—see the leather *sudarium* (Veronica) inserted in a sixteenth-century prayerbook, Staatsbibliothek zu Berlin/ Preussischer Kulturbesitz MS germ oct. 191, fol. 10v, in Hamburger, *The Visual and the Visionary*, p. 325. There are more examples in Jeffrey F. Hamburger, *Nuns as Artists: The Visual Culture of a Medieval Convent* (Berkeley: University of California Press, 1997), p. 194. For a miniature from a missal that has been abraded by the thumb of the priest who reads the missal and blesses it, see *Kreuz und Kruzifix: Zeichen und Bild*, exhibition catalogue (Freising: Diözesanmuseum Freising and Josef Fink Verlag, 2005), p. 310; the image is from the Upper Rhine about 1340. For an example of the holy wound abraded by kissing, see the manuscript folio in figure 12, from circa 1320, which is discussed in David Areford, "The Passion Measured: A Late-Medieval Diagram of the Body of Christ," in A. A. MacDonald, H. N. B. Ridderbos, and R. M. Schlusemann (eds.), *The Broken Body: Passion Devotion in Late-Medieval Culture* (Groningen: Egbert Forsten, 1998), pp. 220–21 and 238.

58. Suckale, "An Unrecognized Statuette," pp. 107–109. Sara Lipton's overview of late medieval images stresses, among other things, tactile reactions to them; see Lipton, "Images and Their Uses," in Rubin and Simons (eds.), *The Cambridge History of Christianity*, vol. 4, pp. 254–82, esp. pp. 280–81.

59. See this chapter, pp. 94–98. It is worth noting that in Buddhism, the religion closest to Christianity both in relic cult and in image practice, there seems to be much less tactile interaction with both sorts of object. For example, as Kevin Trainor puts it (summarizing an argument of John Strong): "Christian relics are commonly venerated in very physical terms (e.g., a kiss), while Buddhist relics tend to be mirage-like (evoking the presence of the Buddha's absence)." Kevin Trainor, "Introduction: Beyond Superstition," in Germano and Trainor (eds.), *Embodying the Dharma*, p. 21.

60. Hans Georg Gmelin, *Spätgotische Tafelmalerei in Niedersachsen und Bremen* (Munich and Berlin: Deutscher Kunstverlag, 1974), pp. 636–40; Günther

Robra (ed.), *Mittelalterliche Holzplastik in Ostfriesland* (Leer, Germany: Gerhard Rautenberg, 1959), pp. 32–35, plates 60–67; Caroline Walker Bynum, "Seeing and Seeing Beyond: The Mass of St. Gregory in the Fifteenth Century," in Jeffrey F. Hamburger and Anne-Marie Bouché (eds.), *The Mind's Eye: Art and Theological Argument in the Middle Ages* (Princeton: Department of Art and Archaeology, Princeton University, and Princeton University Press, 2006), pp. 218 and 231–32; Esther Meier, *Die Gregorsmesse: Funktionen eines spätmittelalterlichen Bildtypus* (Cologne-Weimar-Vienna: Böhlau, 2006), pp. 140–44 and plate 49; and Ulrich Schäfer, "Innen wie aussen fast immer im Zentrum. Die Messe des heiligen Gregor innerhalb der komplexen ikonographischen Bezugssysteme Antwerpener Retabel," in Gormans and Lentes (eds.), *Das Bild der Erscheinung*, pp. 376–80. As Meier points out, the Ihlower/Aurich altar is the earliest known representation of the Gregory Mass theme on a carved altar from the Antwerp workshop. As such, it is typical of much that is found in such altars, but the placement of the Man of Sorrows so high up is a "unique solution." Nonetheless, as Meier and I both point out, there are many such representations in which the scene is divided and on outer wings; there are also many cases in which the sight lines indicate that the pope and attendants are not "seeing" the vision. On Gregory Mass retables as exploration of visions, see David Ganz, "Christus im Doppelblick. Die Vision Papst Gregors und die Imagination der Betrachter," in Gormans and Lentes (eds.), *Das Bild der Erscheinung*, pp. 209–57.

61. See Bynum, "Seeing and Seeing Beyond," pp. 208–40, which gives earlier bibliographical references.

62. I know only three depictions of the early legend, in which a bloody finger appears in the chalice in response to Gregory's concern about the woman's doubt. See M. Heinlen, "An Early Image of the Mass of St. Gregory and Devotion to the Holy Blood at Weingarten Abbey," *Gesta* 37 (1998): 55–62, and G. de Tervarent, "Les Tapisseries du Ronceray et leurs sources d'inspiration," *Gazette des Beaux-Arts* 6th period, vol. 10, 75th year (1933): 80–83. A folio from the Book of Hours (sometimes inaccurately called a breviary) made for Johann Siebenhirter, first Master of the Order of St. George (founded in 1468), seems to depict the same event. On folio 173r (for Prime) of the *Siebenhirter Hours*, Stockholm, Royal Library MS A 225, we see a red finger appear on the paten before the celebrant. The text of the Hours does not explain the miniatures. See

Jeffrey F. Hamburger, "Bosch's *Conjuror*: An Attack on Magic and Sacramental Heresy," *Simiolus: Netherlands Quarterly for the History of Art* 14, no. 1 (1984): 12–14, and Karl-Georg Pfändtner, "Das Gebetbuch des Johann Siebenhirter in Stockholm: Geschichte—Ausstattung—Bedeutung," *Carinthia I: Zeitschrift für geschichtliche Landeskunde von Kärnten* 197 (2007): 124–26 and plate 29. I am grateful to Prof. Hamburger for calling my attention to this image. The story of Gregory, the woman, and the bloody finger was repeated in the treatise by Paschasius Radbertus discussed in Chapter 2 at n. 55.

63. Bandmann, "Bemerkungen," pp. 91–94. Although Bandmann is making an argument about materials that is somewhat different from my own, he also calls attention to the materiality of the central scene. His idea of a hierarchy of materials is, however, to my mind, too a priori; on this, see Raff, *Die Sprache der Materialien*, p. 11. Winged altars with central feast-day panels that were three-dimensional and gilded were very popular in the fifteenth century; see n. 5 above.

64. See Holger A. Klein, *Byzanz, der Westen und das 'wahre' Kreuz: Die Geschichte einer Reliquie und ihrer künstlerischen Fassung in Byzanz und im Abendland*, Spätantike—Frühes Christentum—Byzanz: Kunst im ersten Jahrtausend 17 (Wiesbaden: Reichert, 2004), plates 94, 107, 115, and 116, and see p. 267.

65. For a particularly graphic example, see Bynum, *Fragmentation and Redemption*, p. 261, fig. 6.10, a seventeenth-century monstrance from Bavaria. In this case, the materiality of what was behind the crystal is underlined by the fact that the container is an image of Mary, the Mother of God. The wafer here is a body, occupying a womb. For examples from the New World of monstrances, reliquaries, and other devotional objects of the type I treat in these chapters, see *The Arts in Latin America 1492–1820*, catalogue of the exhibit organized for the Philadelphia Museum of Art by Joseph J. Rishel with Suzanne Stratton-Pruitt (Philadelphia: Philadelphia Museum of Art, 2006), pp. 186, 194, 205–207, 209–10, 213, 231, 236, 239, and 316.

66. See Anton Legner, *Reliquien in Kunst und Kult zwischen Antike und Aufklärung* (Darmstadt: Wissenschaftliche Buchgesellschaft, 1995); Cynthia Hahn, "The Voices of the Saints: Speaking Reliquaries," *Gesta* 36, no. 1 (1997): 20–31. I argued the point about gold and gems denying decay in *The Resurrection of the Body*, pp. 200–25 and 318–29. And see Ellert Dahl, "Heavenly Images: The Statue of St. Foy of Conques and the Signification of the Medieval

Cult-Image in the West," *Acta ad archaeologiam et artium historiam pertinentia* 8 (1979): 175–92, esp. p. 186. It is worth noting that medieval burial practices also reduced the body to the hard stuff—bones and ashes—sometimes by artificial means. See Bynum, *The Resurrection of the Body*, pp. 203–204.

67. Kathleen Cohen, *Metamorphosis of a Death Symbol: The Transi Tomb in the Late Middle Ages and the Renaissance*, California Studies in the History of Art 15 (Berkeley: University of California Press, 1973), and Françoise Baron, "Le Médecin, le prince, les prélates et la mort: L'Apparition du transi dans la sculpture française du moyen âge," *Cahiers archéologiques: Fin de l'antiquité et moyen âge* 51 (2003–4): 125–58.

68. See, for example, the fourteenth-century reliquary bust from Utrecht that I discuss in *The Resurrection of the Body*, p. 211.

69. Dante, *The Divine Comedy*, translated with a commentary by Charles S. Singleton (Princeton, NJ: Princeton University Press, 1970–1975), *Inferno*, 2 vols., vol. 1, *Text*, cantos 24–25, pp. 247–69.

70. Mitchell Merback, *The Thief, the Cross and the Wheel: Pain and the Spectacle of Punishment in Medieval and Renaissance Europe* (Chicago: University of Chicago Press, 1999), and Valentin Groebner, *Defaced: The Visual Culture of Violence in the Late Middle Ages*, trans. Pamela Selwyn (New York: Zone Books, 2004).

71. Although general historical writing frequently connects late medieval use of death as a cultural motif to the Black Death, it is worth pointing out that epidemics do not automatically translate into iconographic obsession. More people died in the influenza epidemic of 1918 than in World War I, but it is the war not the disease that has dominated not only literature and art but also historical memory.

72. For very perceptive remarks on how the lack of perspective in much medieval art makes the subject more present to us—indeed, makes it "jump out at us"—see Schmitt, *Le Corps des images*, pp. 24–29. See also Hans Belting, *The Image and Its Public in the Middle Ages: Form and Function of Early Paintings of the Passion*, trans. Mark Bartusis and Raymond Meyer (New Rochelle, NY: Caratzas, 1990), pp. 80–83 and passim, on the mutuality of image and viewer, and Biernoff, *Sight and Embodiment*, pp. 133–64, on "spectorial reciprocity." Relevant to this, it is worth pointing out that a good deal of recent work on materiality stresses the reciprocity of user and object, thus denying in some

sense a clear division between matter and culture; see P[aul] M. Graves-Brown, "Introduction," *Matter, Materiality and Modern Culture* (London: Routledge, 2000), pp. 1–7 and the works cited in my Introduction, nn. 32 and 40.

73. See Jos Koldeweij, "'Shameless and Naked Images': Obscene Badges as Parodies of Popular Devotion," in Sarah Blick and Rita Tekippe (eds.), *Art and Architecture of Late Medieval Pilgrimage in Northern Europe and the British Isles*, 2 vols. (Leiden: Brill, 2005), vol. 1, pp. 493–519, esp. pp. 498–99 and 506.

74. *Sacrosancti et Oecumenici Concilii Tridentini Paolo III, Julio III et Pio IV, pontificibus maximis, celebrati canones et decreta: pluribus annexis ad idem concilium spectantibus* (Mechelen: J. Hanicq, 1862), pp. 270–74. The council also legislated against new miracles and new relics unless investigated by a bishop. On the council and its effects, see Anthony Blunt, *Artistic Theory in Italy, 1450–1600* (London: Oxford University Press, 1962), pp. 103–36, and Aston, *England's Iconoclasts*, pp. 43–46.

75. Alois Thomas, s.v. "Mühle, mystische," in Engelbert Kirschbaum et al. (eds.), *Lexikon der christlichen Ikonographie*, vol. 3 (Freiburg: Herder, 1968), cols. 297–99; A. Weckwerth, "Christus in der Kelter: Ursprung und Wandlung eines Bildmotives," *Beiträge zur Kunstgeschichte: Festschrift für Heinz Rudolf Rosemann zum 9. Oktober 1960* (Munich: Deutscher Kunstverlag, 1960), pp. 95–108; and Alois Thomas, *Die Darstellung Christi in der Kelter: Eine theologische und kulturhistorische Studie...*, Forschungen zur Volkskunde 20/21 (Düsseldorf: L. Schwann, 1936). For a fascinating variant on the iconography (which combines the *Hostienmühle* with the *Gnadenstuhl*), see Christiane Rossner, "Die Sakramentsmühle in der Dorfkirche von Loffenau: Christus im Mahlwerk," *Monumente: Magazin für Denkmalschutz* 7/8 (2009): 16–17. Robert W. Scribner, "Cosmic Order and Daily Life: Sacred and Secular in Pre-Industrial German Society," in Kaspar von Greyerz (ed.), *Religion and Society in Early Modern Europe, 1500–1800* (London: George Allen and Unwin, 1984), p. 26, calls these motifs a "grossly materialistic representation" but does not mean what I mean here.

76. Although general historical writing often attributes medieval iconography and miracle accounts to the definition of transubstantiation at the Fourth Lateran Council in 1215, scholarship makes it clear that there was no generally agreed upon definition after 1215 and that the Aristotelian language of substance and accidents was interpreted in widely different ways by

theologians. See Hans Jorissen, *Die Entfaltung der Transsubstantiationslehre bis zum Beginn der Hochscholastik* (Münster: Aschendorff, 1965); J. F. McCue, "The Doctrine of Transubstantiation from Berengar through the Council of Trent," *Harvard Theological Review* 61 (1968): 385–430; David Burr, *Eucharistic Presence and Conversion in Late Thirteenth-Century Franciscan Thought*, Transactions of the American Philosophical Society 74, no. 3 (Philadelphia: American Philosophical Society, 1984); Gary Macy, "The Dogma of Transubstantiation in the Middle Ages," *Journal of Ecclesiastical History* 45, no. 1 (1994): 11–41, reprinted in *idem*, *Treasures From the Storeroom: Medieval Religion and the Eucharist* (Collegeville, MN: Liturgical Press, 1999), pp. 81–120, and *idem*, "Reception of the Eucharist According to the Theologians: A Case of Diversity in the Thirteenth and Fourteenth Centuries," in John Apczynski (ed.), *Theology and the University*, Proceedings of the Annual Convention of the College Theology Society, 1987 (Lanham, MI: University Press of America, 1990), pp. 15–36, reprinted in *Treasures from the Storeroom*, pp. 36–58.

77. See Barbara Newman, *God and the Goddesses: Vision, Poetry and Belief in the Middle Ages* (Philadelphia: University of Pennsylvania Press, 2003), pp. 269–72, 283–84, and 313; Gudrun Radler, *Die Schreinmadonna "Vierge ouvrante": Von den bernhardinischen Anfängen bis zur Frauenmystik im Deutschordensland mit beschreibendem Katalog* (Frankfurt: Kunstgeschichtliches Institut der Johann Wolfgang Goethe-Universität, 1990); and Renate Kroos, "'Gotes tabernackel': Zu Funktion und Interpretation von Schreinmadonnen," *Zeitschrift für Schweizerische Archäologie und Kunstgeschichte* 43 (1986): 58–64. For new discussion of the "opening Virgin," see Marius Rimmele, "Die Schreinmadonna: Bild-Körper-Matrix," in Kristin Marek, Raphaèle Preisinger, Marius Rimmele, and Katrin Kärcher (eds.), *Bild und Körper im Mittelalter* (Munich: Wilhelm Fink, 2006), pp. 41–60, who points out (p. 44) that the use as a tabernacle was not the central function. Rimmele stresses the *Schreinmadonna* as container in another sense—as bearer of the Logos/image and therefore the authorization, so to speak, of image making.

78. Ilene H. Forsyth, *The Throne of Wisdom: Wood Sculptures of the Madonna in Romanesque France* (Princeton, NJ: Princeton University Press, 1972). For plates that show the figure from the side and therefore make her thronelike presentation clear, see plates 59, 64b, and 74. One of the conundrums concerning such statues is that some do not contain relics, a point Forsyth was

making over against the theory of Hagen Keller. But this is a question I cannot address here.

79. The role of processing, opening and closing, veiling and unveiling, in making images "live" deserves more attention than I have been able to give it in these chapters.

80. On Christ as charter, see Marlene Villalobos Hennessy, "Aspects of Blood Piety in a Late Medieval English Manuscript: London, British Library Additional 37049," in Fulton and Holsinger (eds.), *History in the Comic Mode*, pp. 186–90. On vellum pages covered with pen marks as a "recapitulation of the Incarnation," see Kessler, *Seeing Medieval Art*, p. 89. A lengthy and graphic treatment of Christ as charter inscribed by blood as ink is the fourteenth-century Middle English poem the *Charter of Christ*; see M. C. Spaulding, *The Middle English Charters of Christ* (Bryn Mawr, PA: Bryn Mawr Monographs, 1914), and Hennessy, "Aspects of Blood Piety in a Late Medieval English Manuscript," p. 347 n. 40. On the theme of writing with blood, see David Biale, *Blood and Belief: The Circulation of a Symbol Between Jews and Christians* (Berkeley: University of California Press, 2007), pp. 1–8. On allegorical use of the idea of parchment preparation, see Dieter Richter, "Die Allegorie der Pergamentbearbeitung," in Gundolf Keil et al. (eds.), *Fachliteratur des Mittelalters: Festschrift für Gerhard Eis* (Stuttgart: J. B. Metzler, 1968), pp. 83–92, and, more generally on metaphors of writing on skin or body, see Hildegard Keller, "Kolophon im Herzen: Von beschrifteten Mönchen an den Rändern der Paläographie," in Martin J. Schubert (ed.), *Das Mittelalter: Perspektiven mediävistischer Forschung; Zeitschrift des Mediävistenverbandes* 7, no. 2, *Der Schreiber im Mittelalter* (Berlin: Akademie Verlag, 2002), pp. 157–82. On Suso, see Jeffrey F. Hamburger, "Medieval Self-Fashioning: Authorship, Authority, and Autobiography in Suso's *Exemplar*," in *The Visual and the Visionary*, pp. 233–78, and Hildegard Keller, "Kolophon im Herzen."

81. Brit. Lib. Add. MS 37049, fol. 23r; fifteenth century, Carthusian; from James Hogg (ed.), *An Illustrated Yorkshire Carthusian Religious Miscellany: British Library London Additional MS. 37049*, vol. 3 (1981), *Analecta Cartusiana* 95, p. 27. And see n. 83 below. On the manuscript, see James Hogg, "Unpublished Texts in the Carthusian Northern Middle English Religious Miscellany British Library MS. Add. 37049," in James Hogg (ed.), *Essays in Honour of Erwin Stürzl on His Sixtieth Birthday*, Salzburger Studien zur Anglistik und Amerikanistik

10, 2 vols. (Salzburg: Institut für Englische Sprache und Literatur, Universität Salzburg, 1980), vol. 1, pp. 241–84. And note the Holy Name of Jesus on the seal. On the popularity of Holy Name devotion in the fifteenth century, see Chapter 2, nn. 75–76 below.

82. The reference in John is to Exodus 12:46; Numbers 9:12; Psalms 33:21.

83. See fig. 44, p. 198, another image from Brit. Lib. Add. MS 37049. Here Christ's wounded heart becomes a synecdoche for the whole body. Not only a heart, it is also a mouth. And the mouth is materialized into the paper on which it is drawn; it *is* the text it bears, speaking what one reads on it. "O Man Unkynde," Brit. Lib. Add. MS 37049, fol. 20r; fifteenth century, Carthusian; from Hogg (ed.), *An Illustrated Yorkshire Carthusian Religious Miscellany*, p. 22. On heart symbolism generally, see Hamburger, *Nuns as Artists*, pp. 137–75, and Henrik von Achen, "Piety, Practise and Process," in Laugerud and Skinnebach (eds.), *Instruments of Devotion*, pp. 23–44.

84. Areford, "The Passion Measured."

85. *Ibid.*, pp. 220 and 222, and Lucy Freeman Sandler, *Gothic Manuscripts 1285–1385*, 2 vols. (London: Oxford University Press, 1986), vol. 1, plate 365, and vol. 2, pp. 155–57.

86. Paul Sartori, "Zählen, Messen, Wägen," *Am Ur-Quell: Monatschrift für Volkskunde* 6, no. 2 (1896): 59 says about such measures of Christ: "Das Mass einer Person schliesst ihr ganzes Wesen in sich, es ist oft identisch mit der Person selbst und mit der ihr innewohnenden Kraft." See also Adolf Jacoby, "Heilige Längenmasse: Eine Untersuchung zur Geschichte der Amulette," *Schweizerisches Archiv für Volkskunde* 29, no. 4 (1929): 206. The translations of the scroll texts are Areford's, "The Passion Measured," pp. 223 and 225.

87. Areford, "The Passion Measured," pp. 223–25; Flora Lewis, "The Wound in Christ's Side and the Instruments of the Passion: Gendered Experience and Response," in Lesley Smith and Jane H. M. Taylor (eds.), *Women and the Book: Assessing the Visual Experience* (London: The British Library, 1996), pp. 204–29, esp. p. 208; Louis Gougaud, "La Prière dite de Charlemagne et les pieces apocryphes apparentées," *Revue d'histoire ecclésiastique* 20 (1924): 211–38; and Jacoby, "Heilige Längenmasse," *Schweizerisches Archiv für Volkskunde* 29, no. 1 (1929): 1–17, and no. 4: 181–216.

88. See the many prayers given in Jacoby, "Heilige Längenmasse," especially the seventeenth-century text on pp. 1–3, which, however, echoes many

earlier ones.

89. The length of the body or the length or circumference of a body part (sometimes the girth of a pregnant woman's belly) was measured with a cord, which then became the wick of a candle made to the measure. Adolph Franz, *Die kirchlichen Benediktionen im Mittelalter,* 2 vols. (Freiburg: Herder, 1909), vol. 2, pp. 456–57; and, for examples, see John Shinners (ed.), *Medieval Popular Religion, 1000–1500: A Reader* (Ontario, Canada: Broadview Press, 1997), pp. 161, 165, and 259–60, and Carl S. Watkins, *History and the Supernatural in Medieval England* (Cambridge: Cambridge University Press, 2007), p. 123.

90. Eamon Duffy, "Devotion to the Crucifix and Related Images in England on the Eve of the Reformation," in Robert W. Scribner (ed.), *Bilder und Bildersturm im Spätmittelalter und in der frühen Neuzeit*, Wolfenbütteler Forschungen 46 (Wiesbaden: Harrassowitz, 1990), figures 1 and 2, pp. 33–34.

91. See Chapter 3, p. 196.

92. See Thomas Lentes, "'As far as the eye can see . . .': Rituals of Gazing in the Late Middle Ages," in Hamburger and Bouché (eds.), *The Mind's Eye*, pp. 360–73; Biernoff, *Sight and Embodiment*, pp. 31–39 and passim; and nn. 1 and 43 in this Chapter.

93. Nancy Caciola, *Discerning Spirits: Divine and Demonic Possession in the Middle Ages* (Ithaca, NY: Cornell University Press, 2003); Dyan Elliott, *Proving Women: Female Spirituality and Inquisitional Culture in the Later Middle Ages* (Princeton, NJ: Princeton University Press, 2004); Barbara Newman, "What Did It Mean to Say 'I Saw'?: The Clash between Theory and Practice in Medieval Visionary Culture," *Speculum* 80, no. 1 (2005): 1–43; *eadem*, "The Visionary Texts and Visual Worlds of Religious Women," in Hamburger and Marti (eds.), *Crown and Veil*, pp. 151–71. André Vauchez, "Introduction," in *The Miraculous Image*, notes that visions increased from the fourteenth century on. Elliott, *Proving Women*, rightly stresses the persecution of visionary activity, especially women's visions.

94. Gertrude, *Le Héraut*, book 3, chapter 26, in Gertrude of Helfta, *Oeuvres spirituelles*, vol. 3, *Le Héraut (Livre III)*, ed. Pierre Doyère, Sources chrétiennes 143 (Paris: Éditions du Cerf, 1968), pp. 122–27; trans. Margaret Winkworth, *Herald of Divine Love* (New York: Paulist Press, 1993), pp. 190–91. On the collective authorship of the Helfta treatises, see Anna Harrison, "'Oh! What Treasure Is in This Book?': Writing, Reading, and Community at the Monastery of

Helfta," *Viator* 39, no. 1 (2008): 75–106.

95. Gertrude, *Le Héraut*, ed. Doyère, vol. 3, p. 127; *Herald*, trans. Winkworth, p. 191; this passage occurs just after the description quoted in n. 94 above. The sister who wrote the first book of Gertrude's *Herald* used Augustine's theory of three categories of vision (corporeal, spiritual, and intellectual) to categorize Gertrude's visions, asserting that "the loving Lord" flooded her soul with grace every day, "sometimes through the means of sensible corporeal similitudes, sometimes through the purer intellectual visions." But this same sister, although asserting intellectual *visio* to be higher, makes it clear that what she describes is the second category, spiritual vision, and implies that it is more useful for the education of others, saying "he [the Lord] wanted images of bodily likenesses, appealing to the human understanding, to be described in this little book." Gertrude, *Le Héraut*, book 1, prologue, in Gertrude, *Oeuvres spirituelles*, vol. 2, *Le Héraut*, ed. Doyère, Sources chrétiennes 139, p. 114; *Herald*, trans. Winkworth, p. 49. To this author, then, what Gertrude sees is not a gold tube really "out there" in the air, but it is nonetheless a set of visualizations with real (that is ontologically grounded) and good (that is, moral) meaning, really sent from God.

96. Caroline Walker Bynum, *Holy Feast and Holy Fast: The Religious Significance of Food to Medieval Women* (Berkeley: University of California Press, 1987), p. 86.

97. Gertrude's editor points out the parallel to the liturgical straw; Gertrude, *Herald*, trans. Winkworth, p. 248 n. 50. But it is not clear that nuns were in fact receiving the chalice at communion in the late thirteenth century; thus, there may be elements here of compensation for experience denied. On the senses in Gertrude's visions, see Hamburger, "Speculations on Speculation," p. 392.

98. Rublack, "Female Spirituality and the Infant Jesus," pp. 26–7; Gertrud Jaron Lewis, *By Women, for Women, about Women: The Sister-Books of Fourteenth-Century Germany*, Studies and Texts 125 (Toronto: Pontifical Institute of Mediaeval Studies, 1996), pp. 21–25 and 112. We can compare Adelheid's meditation with a prayer Henry of Nördlingen recommended to his spiritual advisee, the nun Margaret Ebner. Henry described the Christ child as demanding from Margaret "your soul as a cradle, your heart for a pillow, your blood for my bath, your skin for a blanket, and all your limbs as a living offering for all my

suffering." Once again we find the intensely material imagery: the soul is a cradle, the heart a pillow, the skin a blanket. See Margot Schmidt and Leonard P. Hindsley, "Introduction," Margaret Ebner, *Major Works* (New York: Paulist Press, 1993), p. 54. Note the parallel to Suso, who inscribed a name in his chest as if on parchment; see n. 80 above.

99. Quoted by Jeffrey F. Hamburger from the *St. Katharinentaler Schwesternbuch* in Hamburger, *The Visual and the Visionary*, pp. 85 and 495 n. 243.

100. Cited in John van Engen, "Multiple Options: The World of the Fifteenth-Century Church," *Church History* 77, no. 2 (2008): 279.

101. See, for example, Ursula Peters, *Religiöse Erfahrung als literarisches Faktum: Zur Vorgeschichte und Genese frauenmystischer Texte des 13. und 14. Jahrhunderts* (Tübingen: Niemeyer, 1988), and *eadem*, "Vita religiosa und spirituelles Erleben: Frauenmystik und frauenmystische Literatur im 15. und 16. Jahrhundert," in Gisela Brinker-Gabler (ed.), *Deutsche Literatur von Frauen*, 2 vols. (Munich: C.H. Beck, 1988), vol. 1, pp. 88–112. See also Susanne Köbele, *Bilder der unbegriffenen Wahrheit: Zur Struktur mystischer Rede im Spannungsfeld von Latein und Volksprache* (Tübingen: Francke, 1993), pp. 21–26.

102. Peter Dinzelbacher, "Zur Interpretation erlebnismystischer Texte des Mittelalters," *Zeitschrift für deutsches Altertum und deutsche Literatur* 117 (1988): 1–23.

103. Agathe Schmiddunser, *Körper der Passionen: Die lebensgrosse Liegefigur des toten Christus vom Mittelalter bis zum spanischen Yacente des Frühbarock* (Regensburg: Schnell & Steiner, 2008).

104. See Bynum, "Seeing and Seeing Beyond," and Reindert Falkenburg, "Hieronymus Bosch's *Mass of St. Gregory* and 'Sacramental Vision,'" in Gormans and Lentes (eds.), *Das Bild der Erscheinung*, pp. 179–206, esp. pp. 182, 188, and 194. In a brilliant analysis, Falkenburg points out that in the later altarpieces, the Christ figure is a visionary manifestation, a particular medium (painting or sculpture), and a concrete object or person (Christ); the indeterminacy suggests an oscillation between them. But the Mass of St. Gregory was so widespread as a motif, and so complex, that no generalization fits all cases. See Meier, *Die Gregorsmesse*, and n. 60 above.

105. For some examples, see Richard Kieckhefer, *Magic in the Middle Ages* (New York: Cambridge University Press, 1989), and Caroline Walker Bynum, *Metamorphosis and Identity* (New York: Zone Books, 2001), pp. 59–93.

106. It is this living quality of cult images that has led the German scholar Hans Belting to argue that there was no art per se in the Middle Ages: Hans Belting, *Likeness and Presence: A History of the Image Before the Era of Art*, trans. Edmund Jephcott (Chicago: University of Chicago Press, 1994). To Belting, the objects with which I have been concerned were not *Bilder* (images), intended for aesthetic purposes or to be viewed for their own sake. What we call "art" was a plethora of objects with which religious devotion (*Kult*) was performed and experienced. Hence, such objects, sometimes thought to descend from heaven or to have been made by other than human agency, were very close to having a divine spark within them. That some manifested this life occasionally in more explicit ways was hardly surprising.

Recent scholarship has criticized Belting's definition of "art" and his chronology. For the argument that he tends to overemphasize images as cult objects, see Schmitt, *Le Corps des images*, pp. 51–54. And it is important to note that there were, in the later Middle Ages, many crafted and beautiful objects that were neither cult objects nor in any sense religious objects. On chronology, see Thunø et al., who argue that, contrary to Belting's chronology, supposedly living cult objects were more common in Catholic Europe in the early modern period than in the Middle Ages: Thunø and Wolf (eds.), *The Miraculous Image*. William Christian Jr., in *Apparitions in Late Medieval and Renaissance Spain* (Princeton, NJ: Princeton University Press, 1981), supports this chronology. I should make it clear here that I think Belting's work has been enormously important in putting on the table exactly the right question about medieval devotional objects, despite the fact that both the dichotomy he draws between art and cult object and the chronological break he suggests between Middle Ages and Renaissance are surely too stark.

107. Erik Thunø, "The Miraculous Image and the Centralized Church: Santa Maria della Consolazione in Todi," in Thunø and Wolf (eds.), *The Miraculous Image*, p. 30. On animated images, see also Freedberg, *The Power of Images*, pp. 283–316, where he raises many of the important questions but does not emphasize chronology. André Vauchez, in "Les Images saints: Représentations iconographiques et manifestations du sacré," in Vauchez, *Saints, prophètes et visionnaires: Le Pouvoir surnaturel au moyen âge* (Paris: Albin Michel, 1999), pp. 79–91, argues that animated images increased from the twelfth century and to some extent replaced relics. He relates this increase to a "skeptical ambiance"

among Christians, especially about the Eucharist, and to attacks by heretics and argues that church authorities responded to such skepticism by stressing a sort of "real presence" in statues.

108. Thunø, "The Miraculous Image and the Centralized Church," p. 33; Robert Maniura, "The Images and Miracles of Santa Maria delle Carceri," in Thunø and Wolf (eds.), *The Miraculous Image*, pp. 81–96. For a Spanish example, see the case of a sexton who claimed that a crucifix bled when whipped by a thief; Christian, *Apparitions*, p. 184. Christian calls the claim a concoction.

109. For the Italian cases, see Thunø and Wolf (eds.), *The Miraculous Image*. On Grimmenthal and Regensburg, see Euan Cameron, *The European Reformation* (Oxford: Oxford University Press, 1991), p. 14. For Welsh examples, see Jane Cartwright, *Feminine Sanctity and Spirituality in Medieval Wales* (Cardiff: University of Wales Press, 2008), pp. 33 and 61–62. And see Chapter 2, n. 35 below for a statue that allegedly came to life in Unterlinden.

110. Niccolò da Poggibonsi, *A Voyage Beyond the Seas (1346–1350)*, chapter 154, trans. T. Bellorini and E. Hoade (Jerusalem: Franciscan Press, 1945), p. 78, cited (with incorrect page number) by Josef W. Meri, *The Cult of Saints among Muslims and Jews in Medieval Syria* (Oxford: Oxford University Press, 2002), pp. 210–11.

111. Christian, *Apparitions*, pp. 15–19. And see *ibid.*, p. 8, which points out that the proof of apparitions was "characteristically the weeping, sweating or bleeding of images."

112. For a stunning example from the New World of an image protesting violation, see *The Arts in Latin America 1492–1820*, p. 429. The image is a seventeenth-century oil painting of "The Miracles of the Wounds" from the series "The Life of St. Francis of Assisi" from the workshop of Basilio de Santa Cruz Pumacallao. An irreligious man who is offended at a depiction of Francis's wounds scrapes them out with a knife, only to find that they reappear. One day, after he scrapes at the wounds, five streams of blood from them spurt out so forcefully that they knock him on his back. The painting shows both the way in which the physicality of images can offend viewers to the point of attacking them and also the material force sometimes attributed to an object, which here projects out a stream that knocks a man to the ground. We have here a case in which image, object, and body are completely conflated.

113. On Neukirchen, see Horst Bredekamp, *Kunst als Medium sozialer*

Konflikte: Bilderkämpfe von der Spätantike bis zur Hussitenrevolution (Frankfurt am Main: Suhrkamp, 1975), p. 300, and Karl Kolb, *Vom Heiligen Blut: Eine Bilddokumentation der Wallfahrt und Verehrung* (Würzburg: Echter, 1980), p. 80. The longer story makes this even clearer. The statue survived when the church was burned and then sprang out again when thrown into a well. The original devotional object was displayed with the sword in its head; later, the sword was removed and the statue was crowned. *Ibid.*, pp. 79–80. On Gervase, see Gervase of Tilbury, *Otia imperialia: Recreation for an Emperor*, ed. and trans. S. E. Banks and J. W. Binnes (Oxford: Oxford University Press, 2002), p. 607 n. 7. Gervase writes as if the event is contemporary. Hence, although it clearly has an earlier model in the Eastern iconoclastic controversy, it is possibly an early Western example of an animated image. I thank Brigitte Bedos-Rezak for this reference.

114. Maniura, "Images and Miracles," pp. 81–95, esp. pp. 87–89 and 95. On images distributed as keepsakes, gifts, and amulets, see Hamburger, *Nuns as Artists*, p. 197. It is worth noting that when reproduced images are touched to the originals, this is usually done by shrine attendants and is thus part of their control of the power of the image. It is also worth noting that in contradistinction to what Walter Benjamin argues about modern reproduction, especially photography, in his often-quoted essay, "The Work of Art in the Age of Its Technological Reproducibility," reproduction in these cases *conveys* power rather than attenuating it. See n. 51 above.

115. Baxandall, *The Limewood Sculptors*, p. 84.

116. Jane Garnett and Gervase Rosser, "Translations of the Miraculous: Cult Images and Their Representations in Early Modern Liguria," in Thunø and Wolf (eds.), *The Miraculous Image*, pp. 205–22, esp. pp. 206–207.

117. See Mitchell B. Merback, "Channels of Grace: Eucharistic Imagery, Architecture and Purgatory Cult at the Host-Miracle Pilgrimages of Late Medieval Bavaria," in Blick and Tekippe (eds.), *Art and Architecture of Late Medieval Pilgrimage in Northern Europe and the British Isles*, vol. 1, pp. 604–609 and esp. n. 67; and Anton Bauer, "Eucharistische Wallfahrten zu 'Unserm Herrn,' zum 'Hl. Blut,' und zum 'St. Salvator,' im alten Bistum Freising," *Beiträge zur altbayerischen Kirchengeschichte* 21, no. 3 (1960): 37–71. Holy earth was not a new phenomenon in the later Middle Ages. Soil from the base of the column of Simon Stylites was distributed and later used to make images; see Gary

Vikan, "Sacred Image, Sacred Power," reprinted in Vikan, *Sacred Images and Sacred Power in Byzantium*, Variorum Collected Studies Series (Aldershot, UK: Ashgate, 2003), essay 1, pp. 6–7.

118. See Kolb, *Vom Heiligen Blut*, pp. 163–67. For an Eastern example, see Alekseĭ Lidov, "The Flying *Hodegetria*: The Miraculous Icon as Bearer of Sacred Space," in Thunø and Wolf (eds.), *The Miraculous Image*, pp. 273–304, describing the regular miracle performed by the icon every Tuesday in Constantinople and recorded by travelers from the eleventh to the fifteenth century. After the icon "flies," the clergy touch cotton wool to it to absorb the oil (and presumably also the power) that oozes from it; the wool is distributed to the people. It is also worth noting that one of the charges made against icon worshipers in the East at the time of the iconoclastic controversy was that shavings from icons were thought to work miracles and were sometimes even added to the Eucharistic species; see Besançon, *Forbidden Image*, p. 114.

119. On medieval badges with mirrors, see Eli Heldaas Seland, "Nineteenth Century Devotional Medals," in Laugerud and Skinnebach (eds.), *Instruments of Devotion*, p. 163. On measures, see Jacoby, "Heilige Längenmasse," pp. 190–94 and passim.

120. Christian, *Apparitions*, pp. 53 (on Tortosa) and 159–85 (for Francisca); for handprints and footprints, see pp. 24–25, 70, 75–76, 80, and 100–102.

121. Vauchez, "Les Images saints," in *Saints, prophètes et visionnaires*, pp. 81–82, and see n. 107 above. For an emphasis on miracle hosts replacing relics, see Merback, "Channels of Grace." For discussion of imprinting, see Freedberg, *The Power of Images*, pp. 2–3. For other examples, see Pleij, *Colors Demonic and Divine*, p. 11.

122. See above, pp. 53–58.

123. Alfred Gell, in his general theory of the agency of art objects, makes the same point; see Nicholas Thomas, "Foreword," in Gell, *Art and Agency*, p. viii. And see nn. 124 and 125 below.

124. Social historians and anthropologists increasingly stress that objects do not by themselves live or work miracles. It takes a participating audience to bring a statue to life in vision and cult or to experience healing or other changes understood to violate natural processes. See André Vauchez, "Introduction," in Thunø and Wolf (eds.), *The Miraculous Image*, pp. 9–14; Richard Trexler, "Being and Non-Being: Parameters of the Miraculous in the

Traditional Religious Image," in *ibid.*, pp. 15–27; and Maniura, "The Images and Miracles of Santa Maria delle Carceri," in *ibid.*, pp. 81–95. Nonetheless, the result of the interaction between audience and object was often that images acted as if alive or that miraculous changes were experienced.

125. To put it this way may seem to contradict Maniura's point, in *ibid.*, which is to argue against notions of "sympathetic magic" and suggest, rather, that miracle is created in the space between image and audience. His point about miracles is of course correct, and I have no wish to return to rather crude notions of magic. But the physicality of the contact in at least some cases is important. See nn. 114 and 120 above.

126. See Introduction, n. 9.

127. On the cross, see Klein, *Byzanz, der Westen und das 'wahre' Kreuz*; Barbara Baert, *A Heritage of Holy Wood: The Legend of the True Cross in Text and Image* (Leiden: Brill, 2004); and Antony Eastmond, "Byzantine Identity and Relics of the True Cross in the Thirteenth Century," in Alekseĭ Lidov (ed.), *Eastern Christian Relics* (Moscow: Progress-Tradition, 2003), pp. 205–15. Especially interesting for my argument is Baert's emphasis in her fifth chapter on the legend of the wood of the cross as a search for what she calls "biological origins." The prehistory of the wood of the cross involves a number of stories of wooden pieces growing and flowering.

128. On Damian, see Introduction, n. 16. On Rupert's vision, see John van Engen, *Rupert of Deutz* (Berkeley: University of California Press, 1983), pp. 51–52. According to Rupert's own account, he tasted inner sweetness upon kissing an actual wooden crucifix; later, he received an open-mouthed kiss in a dream.

129. See Introduction, n. 17.

130. On stigmata, see Giles Constable, *Three Studies in Medieval Religious and Social Thought* (Cambridge: Cambridge University Press, 1998), pp. 199–203 and 212–25. For other bodily signs as well, especially in women, see Bynum, *Holy Feast*, pp. 122–23, 200–204, 210–12, 255–56, 268–69, and 273–75. For holy women found to have the instruments of the Passion in their bodies at autopsy, see Katherine Park, "The Criminal and the Saintly Body: Autopsy and Dissection in Renaissance Italy," *Renaissance Quarterly* 47 (1994): pp. 1–33, and *eadem*, *Secrets of Women: Gender, Generation, and the Origins of Human Dissection* (New York: Zone Books, 2006).

131. Chiara Frugoni, *Francesco e l'invenzione delle stimmate: Una storia per parole e immagini fino a Bonaventura e Giotto* (Turin: G. Einaudi, 1993). And see Hans Belting, "Franziskus: Der Körper als Bild," in Marek, Preisinger, Rimmele, and Kärcher (eds.), *Bild und Körper im Mittelalter*, pp. 21–36.

132. Bonaventure, *Legenda maior S. Francisci Assisiensis et eiusdem legenda minor*, chapter 13, section 5, ed. Collegium S. Bonaventurae (Florence-Quaracchi: Collegium S. Bonaventurae, 1941), p. 109. In a previous section, Bonaventure speaks of an image "impressed" in Francis's flesh: "in carne non minus mirabilem signorum impressit effigiem." *Ibid.*, chapter 13, section 3, p. 108.

133. For discussion circa 1300 of how the imagination can cooperate with God in creating stigmata, see Chapter 4, n. 42.

134. On figure 35, see Frugoni, *Francesco e l'invenzione delle stimmate*, plate 77. For another example, see *ibid.*, plate 22: St. Francis receiving the stigmata, Maestro delle tempere francescane (Pietro Orimina?), about 1336. Panel painting. Private collection.

135. Baert, *A Heritage of Holy Wood*, chapter 5. See n. 127 above.

136. I return to this topic in my next chapter, pp. 126–27 and 149–50. Schmitt, *Le Corps des images*, pp. 273–94, writes thoughtfully about various conflations and differences among these types of holy matter.

137. Annika Elisabeth Fisher, "Cross Altar and Crucifix in Ottonian Cologne: Past Narrative, Present Ritual, Future Resurrection," in Søren Kaspersen and Erik Thunø (eds.), *Decorating the Lord's Table: On the Dynamics between Image and Altar in the Middle Ages* (Copenhagen: Museum Tusculanum Press, 2006), pp. 48–49 and figure 4, and p. 59 nn. 21–23; and Suckale, "An Unrecognized Statuette," p. 107. Both Suckale and Fisher discuss the well-known story that a fissure in the wood of the Gero crucifix was healed by insertion of a host and understand this as an example of inserting relics into statues to enhance their holiness and ward off charges of idolatry. For discussion of a crucifix with cross relics in the head (and a reproduction of both the *corpus* and the relics contained therein), see Harald Meller, Ingo Mundt, and Boje E. Hans Schmuhl (eds.), with photographs by Juraj Lipták, *Der Heilige Schatz im Dom zu Halberstadt* (Regensburg: Schnell and Steiner, 2008), pp. 326–32.

138. Van Os et al., *The Art of Devotion*, p. 99.

139. *Krone und Schleier*, p. 352; and Dagmar Preising, "Bild und Reliquie: Gestalt und Funktion gotischer Reliquientafeln und -altärchen," *Aachener*

Kunstblätter 61 (1995–97): 13–84. I thank Jeffrey F. Hamburger for advice about relics embedded in objects.

140. See Schmiddunser, *Körper der Passionen*.

141. See nn. 106 and 114 above.

142. See above, n. 78.

143. Herbert Kessler and Johanna Zacharias, *Rome 1300: On the Path of the Pilgrim* (New Haven, CT: Yale University Press, 2000), pp. 59–62, and Riccardo Cattani, *St. John Lateran*, trans. Angela Arnone (Rome, 2006), pp. 23–24.

144. It is also extremely important to note that there are elements of what we think of as "art" earlier than Belting wants to admit. Many images from the central to later Middle Ages were not primarily "*Kult*." See n. 106 above.

145. Quoted in Duffy, "Devotion to the Crucifix," p. 32. Duffy contrasts this passage with exactly this image, and I borrow from him here to make an almost opposite point. In another interpretation of image smashing different from (but not incompatible with) my own, Horst Bredekamp argues that iconoclasm was an effort to demonstrate that images were really empty rather than God-filled; cutting them open or decapitating them showed that nothing was inside. See Bredekamp, *Kunst als Medium sozialer Konflikte*, pp. 299–300. My Chapter 4 gives the context for the medieval tendency to see matter as "rotten, not dead."

146. The point I make here is one with which many scholars would, of course, agree. As Jeremy Dimmick, James Simpson, and Nicolette Zeeman put it: "Iconoclasm is always an acknowledgement of the power of the image." See "Introduction" to Dimmick, Simpson, and Zeeman (eds.), *Images, Idolatry, and Iconoclasm in Late Medieval England*, p. 1.

CHAPTER TWO: THE POWER OF OBJECTS

1. See Chapter 1, nn. 99, 100, and 108.

2. Living images were more common in early modern than in medieval Europe. See Chapter 1, n. 106.

3. In connection with this, it is worth noting that documentation of historical provenance for relics mattered, especially in the late Middle Ages. For example, the blood relic of Cismar, discussed in Chapter 3, p. 212, was

questioned because evidence of provenance was lacking. This suggests that proof of actual origin and/or of actual contact with an original relic was important to the authentication of objects, especially for ecclesiastical authorities. On this, see the example of the blood relic of Westminster, analyzed by Nicholas Vincent, *The Holy Blood: Henry III and the Westminster Blood Relic* (Cambridge: Cambridge University Press, 2001), esp. pp. 39, 78–81, 131–34, 187–88, and 197. For the general concern with authentication (especially of sources) in the fourteenth and fifteenth centuries, see Daniel Hobbins, *Authorship and Publicity before Print: Jean Gerson and the Transformation of Late Medieval Learning* (Philadelphia: University of Pennsylvania Press, 2009), pp. 28–31.

4. On the conflation of image and relic, see also the excellent discussion by Gary Vikan, "Sacred Image, Sacred Power," reprinted in Gary Vikan, *Sacred Images and Sacred Power in Byzantium*, Variorum Collected Studies Series (Aldershot, UK: Ashgate, 2003), essay 1, pp. 6–10. For a sophisticated assertion of the differences, which may nonetheless go too far, see Robert H. Sharf, "On the Allure of Buddhist Relics," *Representations* 66 (Spring 1999): 85, reprinted in David Germano and Kevin Trainor (eds.), *Embodying the Dharma: Buddhist Relic Veneration in Asia* (Albany: State University of New York Press, 2004). And see my Conclusion in this volume, nn. 49–50.

5. On *acheiropoieta*, see Chapter 1, p. 120. On depictions of Christ's wound and generally on measures, see pp. 94–99; on the Fritzlar pietà, see p. 62.

6. On this, see Uta Reinhold, "Das Fritzlarer Vesperbild: Ein Meisterwerk mittelalterlicher Schnitz- und Fasskunst," *Denkmale und Kulturgeschichte* 2 (2000): 33–38; and Caroline Walker Bynum, *Wonderful Blood: Theology and Practice in Late Medieval Northern Germany and Beyond* (Philadelphia: University of Pennsylvania Press, 2007), p. 177, p. 327 nn. 23 and 24, and p. 328 n. 27. According to Reinhold, the side wound "certainly" had a relic container attached where we see two holes. It is impossible to tell what such a monstrance would have held. On late medieval and Counter-Reformation Christ figures with Eucharistic monstrances in the chest, see Agathe Schmiddunser, *Körper der Passionen: Die lebensgrosse Liegefigur des toten Christus vom Mittelalter bis zum spanischen Yacente des Frühbarock* (Regensburg: Schnell & Steiner, 2008).

7. See figure 12 and Introduction, n. 35. See fig. 43, p. 152, and n. 81 in this chapter for another kind of visual conflation.

8. See, for example, the Exeter list cited in n. 38 below. But compare the

140 Exeter relics with the 19,000 relics of Frederick the Wise; see nn. 29 and 36 below.

9. See this chapter, pp. 145–48 and n. 70.

10. Robert W. Scribner, "Cosmic Order and Daily Life: Sacred and Secular in Pre-Industrial German Society," in Kaspar von Greyerz (ed.), *Religion and Society in Early Modern Europe, 1500–1800* (London: George Allen and Unwin, 1984), p. 21.

11. See Chapter 1, n. 43, and André Goossens, "Résonances eucharistiques à la fin du moyen âge," in André Haquin (ed.), *Fête-Dieu, 1247–1996*, vol. 1, *Actes du Colloque de Liège, 12–14 Septembre 1996*, Publications de l'Institute d'Études Médiévales 19 (Louvain-la-Neuve: Institute d'Études Médiévales de l'Université Catholique de Louvain, 1999), pp. 173–91. For Gabriel Biel's emphasis on physical reception, see Gabriel Biel, *Canonis misse expositio, lectio* 51, ed. Heiko A. Oberman and William J. Courtenay, 5 vols., Veröffentlichungen des Instituts für europäische Geschichte Mainz 31–34, 79: Abteilung für abendländische Religionsgeschichte (Wiesbaden: Franz Steiner, 1963–76), vol. 2, pp. 287–97, and Peter Browe, "Die scholastische Theorie der eucharistischen Verwandlungswunder," *Theologische Quartalschrift* 110 (1929): 311 n. 2.

12. André Vauchez has argued for the decline of miracles in the conception of sanctity in the later Middle Ages, although his most recent work tends to emphasize this trend less; see *Les Laïcs au moyen âge: Pratiques et expériences religieuses* (Paris: Éditions du Cerf, 1987), pp. 49–92; *idem*, "Formes des merveilleux et pouvoir surnaturel au moyen âge," in *Saints, prophètes et visionnaires: Le Pouvoir surnaturel au moyen âge* (Paris: Albin Michel, 1999), pp. 7–16; and *idem*, "Saints admirables et saints imitables: Les Fonctions de l'hagiographie ont-elles changé aux derniers siècles du moyen âge?" in *Les Fonctions des saints dans le monde occidental (IIIe–XIII siècle)* (Rome: École Française de Rome, 1991), pp. 161–72. See also Michel Balard, "Preface," *Miracles, prodiges et merveilles au moyen âge*, XXVe Congrès de la S.H.M.E.S., Orléans, juin 1994, Société des historiens médiévistes de l'enseignement supérieur publique, série histoire ancienne et médiévale 34 (Paris: Publications de la Sorbonne, 1995), pp. 7–8. I should add here that I am in agreement with the elegant recent article by Steven Justice, "Did the Middle Ages Believe in Their Miracles?" *Representations* 103 (Summer 2008): 1–30, which argues that many medieval people did believe in miracles as recounted, but that belief meant that questioning went hand in

hand with devotion. I suggested the same interpretation in a slight piece titled "The Woman with the Pearl Necklace," *Common Knowledge* 8, no. 2 (Spring 2002): 280–83.

13. See Aron Gurevich, *Medieval Popular Culture: Problems of Belief and Perception*, trans. János M. Bak and Paul A. Hollingsworth (Cambridge: Cambridge University Press, 1988); Jacques Le Goff, *The Medieval Imagination*, trans. Arthur Goldhammer (Chicago: University of Chicago Press, 1988); and Jean-Claude Schmitt, "'Religion populaire' et culture folklorique," *Annales ESC* 31 (1976): 941–53.

14. Peter Brown, *The Cult of the Saints: Its Rise and Function in Latin Christianity* (Chicago: University of Chicago Press, 1981), pp. 13–22. Brown called this the "two-tiered model" and traced it back, in the English tradition, to the 1750s. For an approach in which "popular religion" basically means religious practice, see Rosalind and Christopher N.L. Brooke, *Popular Religion in the Middle Ages: Western Europe 1000–1300* (London: Thames and Hudson, 1984). For early and wise evaluations of the concept, see Natalie Zemon Davis, "From 'Popular Religion' to Religious Cultures," in Steven Ozment (ed.), *Reformation Europe: A Guide to Research* (St. Louis: Center for Reformation Research, 1982), pp. 321–41; and Mary R. O'Neil, "From 'Popular' to 'Local' Religion: Issues in Early Modern European History," *Religious Studies Review* 12 (1986): 222–26. For recent discussion, see Robert N. Swanson, *Religion and Devotion in Europe, c. 1215–c. 1515* (Cambridge: Cambridge University Press, 1995), pp. 184–88, and Carl S. Watkins, *History and the Supernatural in Medieval England* (Cambridge: Cambridge University Press, 2007), pp. 4–12.

15. Even the categories "clergy" and "laity" were problematic and somewhat fluid; see Caroline Walker Bynum, *Docere Verbo et Exemplo: An Aspect of Twelfth-Century Spirituality*, Harvard Theological Studies 31 (Missoula, MT: Scholars Press, 1979), pp. 19–21 and 88–89. Moreover, social status influenced attitude at least as much as ecclesiastical affiliation. Parish priests were usually recruited from local communities and shared values with the people of their parish; prelates of the church, recruited from the aristocracy, often shared aristocratic mores, as the emergence of the military orders makes clear.

16. Caroline Walker Bynum, *Metamorphosis and Identity* (New York: Zone Books, 2001), pp. 53–56, and Watkins, *History and the Supernatural*. Indeed, much of our evidence for so-called "popular" practices (such as amulets,

blessings, and curses) derives from reports by clerics, who may have had their own reasons for stressing, while castigating, the credulity of their flocks.

17. Justice, "Did the Middle Ages Believe in Their Miracles?" To say that there were tensions concerning holy matter at every cultural level is not to espouse the notion of a universal Christianity held by some earlier theorists, such as Raoul Manselli; on this, see O'Neil, "From 'Popular' to 'Local.'"

18. To say this is not to hold that the tracing of folkloric motifs is irrelevant or useless. For a stunningly successful example, see Jean-Claude Schmitt, *The Holy Greyhound: Guinefort, Healer of Children Since the Thirteenth Century*, trans. Martin Thom, Cambridge Studies in Oral and Literate Culture 6 (Cambridge: Cambridge University Press, 1983). For some other examples of practices that absorbed earlier folklore, see Karen Louise Jolly, *Popular Religion in Late Saxon England: Elf Charms in Context* (Chapel Hill: University of North Carolina Press, 1996) and Derek A. Rivard, *Blessing the World: Ritual and Lay Piety in Medieval Religion* (Washington, D.C.: The Catholic University of America Press, 2009), p. 181. For more on this, see Conclusion, n. 8.

19. The recent bibliography on relics is voluminous. For an introduction, see P. Séjourné, s.v. "Reliques," DTC, vol. 13, part 2, cols. 2330–65; Nicole Hermann-Mascard, *Les Reliques des saints: Formation coutumière d'un droit* (Paris: Klincksieck, 1975); Peter Dinzelbacher, "Die 'Realpräsenz' der Heiligen in ihren Reliquiaren und Gräbern nach mittelalterlichen Quellen," in Peter Dinzelbacher and Dieter Bauer (eds.), *Heiligenverehrung in Geschichte und Gegenwart* (Ostfildern: Schwabenverlag, 1990), pp. 115–74; Arnold Angenendt, *Heilige und Reliquien: Die Geschichte ihres Kultes vom frühen Christentum bis zur Gegenwart* (Munich: C.H. Beck, 1994); Anton Legner, *Reliquien in Kunst und Kult zwischen Antike und Aufklärung* (Darmstadt: Wissenschaftliche Buchgesellschaft, 1995); Henk W. van Os, *The Way to Heaven: Relic Veneration in the Middle Ages* (Baarn, the Netherlands: De Prom, 2000); Thomas Head, s.v. "Relics," in Joseph R. Strayer (ed.), *Dictionary of the Middle Ages*, 13 vols. and supplement (New York: Charles Scribner's Sons, 1982–2004), vol. 10, pp. 296–99; and John Crook, *The Architectural Setting of the Cult of Saints in the Early Christian West, c. 300–1200* (Oxford: Oxford University Press, 2000), pp. 5–39. For a lively general account of the development of martyrdom and saint cult, see Aviad Kleinberg, *Flesh Made Word: Saints' Stories and the Western Imagination* (Cambridge, MA: Harvard University Press, 2008), pp. 1–53. See also the works

cited in Introduction, n. 14.

20. The process of canonization—that is, the way in which people were designated as holy (and therefore potential relics) after death—also changed. On changes in canonization procedure, see Patrick Geary, s.v. "Canonization," in Strayer (ed.), *Dictionary of the Middle Ages*, vol. 3, pp. 67–69, and André Vauchez, *Sainthood in the Later Middle Ages*, trans. Jean Birrell (Cambridge: Cambridge University Press, 1997), pp. 48–50 and passim. For other changes, especially in the relation of site to miracle, see my Introduction, n. 9.

21. Cynthia Hahn, "Seeing and Believing: The Construction of Sanctity in Early-Medieval Saints' Shrines," *Speculum* 72, no. 4 (1997): 1104–106. And see Crook, *The Architectural Setting of the Cult of Saints.*

22. On this point, see Jean-Claude Schmitt, *Le Corps des images: Essais sur la culture visuelle au moyen âge*, Le Temps des images (Paris: Gallimard, 2002), pp. 280–83 and plate 43.

23. See Katherine Park, "The Criminal and the Saintly Body: Autopsy and Dissection in Renaissance Italy," *Renaissance Quarterly* 47 (1994): 1–7. The body of Chiara of Montefalco, in the heart of which the *arma Christi* were found, allegedly remained sweet smelling and uncorrupt for the five days before dissection. For a stone marked with the Holy Family, found in the body of another female saint, see below, n. 82.

24. See Lezlie S. Knox, *Creating Clare of Assisi: Female Franciscan Identities in Later Medieval Italy* (Leiden: Brill, 2008), p. 45.

25. Louise Bourdua, "Displaying the Bodily Remains of Antony of Padua," in Kristin Marek, Raphaèle Preisinger, Marius Rimmele, and Katrin Kärcher (eds.), *Bild und Körper im Mittelalter* (Munich: Wilhelm Fink, 2006), pp. 243–55.

26. *Ibid.*, pp. 247 and 250–52.

27. See Claude Carozzi, "Douceline et les autres," *La Religion populaire en Languedoc du XIIIe siècle à la moitié du XIVe siècle*, Cahiers de Fanjeaux 11 (Toulouse: Privat, 1976), pp. 251–67.

28. See Chapter 1, p. 70.

29. Steven Ozment, *The Age of Reform (1250–1550): An Intellectual and Religious History of Late Medieval and Reformation Europe* (New Haven, CT: Yale University Press, 1980), pp. 90 and 250, and John van Engen, "Multiple Options: The World of the Fifteenth-Century Church," *Church History* 77,

no. 2 (2008): 269–70. On *Wunderkammern*, see Oliver Impey and Arthur MacGregor (eds.), *The Origins of Museums: The Cabinet of Curiosities in Sixteenth- and Seventeenth-Century Europe* (Oxford: Oxford University Press, 1985), and Paula Findlen, *Possessing Nature: Museums, Collecting, and Scientific Culture in Early Modern Italy* (Berkeley: University of California Press, 1994). On the similarities and affinities of relics and natural wonders in medieval collections, see Lorraine Daston and Katharine Park, *Wonders and the Order of Nature, 1150–1750* (New York: Zone Books, 1998), pp. 69–88. And on the tendency to collect, see Schmitt, *Le Corps des images*, plate 43.

30. For flowers, herbs, and water as contact relics, see Adolph Franz, *Die kirchlichen Benediktionen im Mittelalter*, 2 vols. (Freiburg: Herder, 1909), vol. 2, pp. 450–56. On the curative effect of water in which the saints, either living persons or their bodies, had been washed, see Hermann-Mascard, *Les Reliques des saints*, p. 274 n. 21.

31. Gregory of Tours, *Glory of the Martyrs*, chapter 27, trans. Raymond van Dam, Translated Texts for Historians, Latin Series 3 (Liverpool: Liverpool University Press, 1988), pp. 45–46. It is worth noting that the text goes on to say: "Many people fashion gold keys for unlocking the railings of this blessed tomb; after they present them for a blessing, the keys cure the afflictions of ill people." The cloths lowered into the tomb seem to absorb sanctity by touch or near touch; the keys absorb their healing power from clerical blessing, but presumably convey it by touch. For an example of an early miracle list that cured by being placed on the body of a sick boy, see Isabel Moreira, *Dreams, Visions, and Spiritual Authority in Merovingian Gaul* (Ithaca, NY: Cornell University Press, 2000), p. 127.

32. Hahn, "Seeing and Believing," p. 1087.

33. Sean L. Field, *Isabelle of France: Capetian Sanctity and Franciscan Identity in the Thirteenth Century* (Notre Dame, IN: University of Notre Dame Press, 2006), pp. 135, 141, 145, and 167. For other cases of mud healing, see Rivard, *Blessing the World*, pp. 188, 200–201; the model is clearly John 9:1–41.

34. Bourdua, "Displaying the Bodily Remains," p. 254. Antony's tumbler not only survived its fall, it also allegedly fragmented the paving stone onto which it fell.

35. For the Schöne Maria in Regensburg, see Michael Baxandall, *The Limewood Sculptors of Renaissance Germany, 1475–1525: Images and Circumstances* (New

Haven, CT: Yale University Press, 1980), pp. 83–84. For the nun who saw an image of the Christ child extend his hand, see Barbara Newman, "The Visionary Texts and Visual Worlds of Religious Women," in Jeffrey F. Hamburger and Susan Marti (eds.), *Crown and Veil: Female Monasticism from the Fifth to the Fifteenth Centuries*, trans. Dietlinde Hamburger (New York: Columbia University Press, 2008), p. 164.

36. Ozment, *Age of Reform*, p. 250. The Exeter relic list from hundreds of years earlier also claims a relic of the burning bush; see n. 38 below.

37. Frederick the Wise's collection had straw from the manger at Bethlehem; see Euan Cameron, *The European Reformation* (Oxford: Oxford University Press, 1991), p. 14. On crib relics, see n. 39 below. For a study of the uses of the relic of the Virgin's shoe at Notre-Dame de Soissons in northern France, see Anne L. Clark, "Guardians of the Sacred: The Nuns of Soissons and the Slipper of the Virgin Mary," *Church History* 76, no. 4 (2007): 724–49.

38. See Vincent, *Holy Blood*, pp. 39–40 and nn. 31 and 32. An interesting list from the mid-eleventh century from Exeter lists 140 relics, most of them relics of saints, although at least 10 are contact relics of Christ. See the appendix in Patrick W. Conner, *Anglo-Saxon Exeter: A Tenth-Century Cultural History* (Woodbridge, Suffolk and Rochester, NY: Boydell Press, 1993), pp. 176–87. I am grateful to Julia M. H. Smith for discussion of this list.

39. For example, the Holy House of Loreto is alleged to have been inhabited by Mary at the time of the Annunciation and to have been miraculously transported to Dalmatia and then to Loreto in Italy near Ancona in the late thirteenth century. The earliest attestation of the legend is from an account of about 1470; see s.v. "Loreto" in F. L. Cross and E. A. Livingstone (eds.), *The Oxford Dictionary of the Christian Church*, 2nd ed., with corrections (Oxford: Oxford University Press, 1983), pp. 836–37, and Thomas Raff, *Die Sprache der Materialien: Anleitung zu einer Ikonologie der Werkstoffe*, Kunstwissenschaftliche Studien 61 (Munich: Deutscher Kunstverlag, 1994), pp. 69–70. The church of Santa Maria Maggiore in Rome has a supposed relic of the crib from Bethlehem. The claim goes back only to the twelfth century; see Patrizia Riccitelli and Giammarco Limardi, *A Visit to the Patriarchal Basilica of Santa Maria Maggiore* (Vatican City, 2005), pp. 30–32; and Peter Keller, *Die Wiege des Christkindes: Ein Haushaltsgerät in Kunst und Kult* (Worms: Werner, 1998).

40. Bynum, *Wonderful Blood*, pp. 64–68 and 57–58, respectively.

41. *Ibid.*, pp. 66–67.

42. On the steps at the Lateran, see Riccardo Cattani, *St. John Lateran*, trans. Angela Arnone (Rome, 2006), p. 23; Raff, *Die Sprache der Materialien*, pp. 70–71. On the Virgin's bloodied veil, see Michal Šroněk, "The Veil of the Virgin Mary: Relics in the Conflict between Roman Catholics and Utraquists in Bohemia in the 14th and 15th Centuries," *Umění* 57 (2009): 118–39.

43. Jacques Toussaert, *Le Sentiment religieux en Flandre à la fin du moyen âge* (Paris: Librairie Plon, 1963), p. 261. Such stories were also told about the Weingarten relic; see Johannes Heuser, "'Heilig-Blut' in Kult und Brauchtum des deutschen Kulturraumes: Ein Beitrag zur religiösen Volkskunde," Dissertation, Bonn, 1948, p. 133. For a supposed liquefaction in Lützel in Alsace, see Karl Kolb, *Vom Heiligen Blut: Eine Bilddokumentation der Wallfahrt und Verehrung* (Würzburg: Echter, 1980), p. 19. And see Chapter 3, n. 16.

44. See Introduction, n. 20.

45. On Mary, see below, Chapter 3, n. 14. On Agnes, see Raymond of Capua, Life of Agnes of Montepulciano, chapter 9, paragraphs 78–81, AASS, April, vol. 2 (Paris, 1865), p. 806, for exuding oil. For rains of manna and the foot that comes alive, see Raymond of Capua, Life of Catherine of Siena, part 2, chapter 12, paragraphs 326–28, AASS, April, vol. 3 (Paris, 1866), pp. 943–44. On myroblytes (oil-exuding saints), see Caroline Walker Bynum, *Holy Feast and Holy Fast: The Religious Significance of Food to Medieval Women* (Berkeley: University of California Press, 1987), pp. 391–92 nn. 85 and 87. Spontaneous multiplication of relics is even more common in Buddhism than in Christianity; see John S. Strong, *Relics of the Buddha* (Princeton, NJ: Princeton University Press, 2004), p. xiv, and see nn. 144 and 145 below.

46. For Jane Mary's cross relic, see Process of Canonization for Jane Mary of Maillé, chapter 3, paragraph 24, AASS, March, vol. 3 (Paris, 1865), p. 749. For Alda's nail, see Life of Alda (or Aldobrandesca) of Siena, AASS, April, vol. 3 (Paris, 1866), chapter 2, paragraph 17, p. 474. For the holy well of St. Winefride in Wales that supposedly flowed with milk rather than water after the expulsion of the French, see Jane Cartwright, *Feminine Sanctity and Spirituality in Medieval Wales* (Cardiff: University of Wales Press, 2008), p. 75. An early example of bleeding relics is found in Gregory of Tours, *Glory of the Martyrs*, chapter 46, trans. van Dam, p. 69.

47. On the Eucharist as a kind of relic, see Godefridus J. C. Snoek, *Medieval*

Piety from Relics to the Eucharist: A Process of Mutual Interaction, Studies in the History of Christian Thought 63 (Leiden: Brill, 1995); and Hubertus Lutterbach, "The Mass and Holy Communion in the Medieval Penitentials (600–1200): Liturgical and Religio-Historical Perspectives," in Charles Caspers, Gerard Lukken, and Gerard Rouwhorst (eds.), *Bread of Heaven: Customs and Practices Surrounding Holy Communion: Essays in the History of Liturgy and Culture* (Kampen, the Netherlands: Kok Pharos, 1995), pp. 61–81. On the competition between Eucharist and relics, see Yrjö Hirn, *The Sacred Shrine: A Study of the Poetry and Art of the Catholic Church* (London: Macmillan, 1912), and Jaroslav Pelikan, *The Growth of Medieval Theology (600–1300)*, vol. 3 of *The Christian Tradition: A History of the Development of Doctrine* (Chicago: University of Chicago Press, 1978), pp. 181–84.

48. See Scribner, "Cosmic Order and Daily Life," p. 23, and Peter Browe, "Die Eucharistie als Zaubermittel im Mittelalter," *Archiv für Kulturgeschichte* 20 (1930): 134–54. For one example, see Thomas of Celano, Life of Clare of Assisi, chapter 13, paragraph 21, in *Legenda sanctae Clarae virginis*, ed. Francesco Pennacchi, Società internazionale di studi Francescani in Assisi (Assisi: Tip. Metastasio, 1910), pp. 30–31, where Clare is described as putting an enemy to flight with the host.

49. In the case of Zehdenick (see below, n. 133), the miracle of bleeding earth allegedly occurred after the alewife who had buried the host heard a sermon that made her feel guilty and led her to reveal to the priest what she had done.

50. These examples come from Bynum, *Holy Feast*, pp. 118 and 144. For other examples, see *ibid.*, pp. 113–49, and Newman, "Visionary Texts," pp. 160–70.

51. Peter of Vaux, Life of Colette of Corbie, trans. Stephen Juliacus, chapter 10, paragraph 84, AASS, March, vol. 1 (Paris, 1865), p. 558. And see *Holy Feast*, p. 67.

52. See *Crown and Veil*, figure 2.14, and, for a fuller description, *Krone und Schleier: Kunst aus mittelalterlichen Frauenklöstern*, exhibition catalogue published by the Kunst- und Ausstellungshalle der Bundesrepublik Deutschland, Bonn, and the Ruhrlandmuseum (Munich: Hirmer, 2005), pp. 509–13. On the question of what visionaries saw, see Chapter 1, nn. 93, 95, and 101–102. For a discussion of how the Gregory Mass motif depicts a vision as animated art,

see Chapter 1, n. 104.

53. Stockholm, Royal Library, MS A 225, fol. 158v; see Jeffrey F. Hamburger, "Bosch's *Conjuror*: An Attack on Magic and Sacramental Heresy," *Simiolus: Netherlands Quarterly for the History of Art* 14, no. 1 (1984): 12–14 and figure 5; Karl-Georg Pfändtner, "Das Gebetbuch des Johann Siebenhirter in Stockholm: Geschichte—Ausstattung—Bedeutung," *Carinthia I: Zeitschrift für geschichtliche Landeskunde von Kärnten* 197 (2007): 124 and plate 27; and Chapter 1, n. 62. The interpretation I give here is Hamburger's and Pfändtner's. There is no text explaining the image in the *Siebenhirter Hours*. Given the order of placement of the figures, it seems likely that reception of a child is a reward, and reception of mere bread an indication of doubt, but it is worth noting that in other medieval visions, as in some I discuss later in this chapter, seeing a child in the wafer is itself a sign that the recipient has doubted, rather than believed.

54. The classic work is still Peter Browe, *Die eucharistischen Wunder des Mittelalters*, Breslauer Studien zur historischen Theologie N.F. 4 (Breslau: Müller & Seiffert, 1938).

55. Paschasius Radbertus, *De corpore et sanguine Domini*, chapters 6, 9, 13 and 14, ed. Beda Paulus, Corpus christianorum: Continuatio mediaevalis 16 (Turnhout: Brepols, 1969), pp. 35, 59–60, 83–84, and 84–91, respectively. On the dating of the various interpolations, see *ibid.*, p. lviii. Miri Rubin, *Gentile Tales: The Narrative Assault on Late Medieval Jews* (Philadelphia: University of Pennsylvania Press, 2004), pp. 9 and 202 n. 11, has misread the rubrics and hence misdated the story of the Jewish boy.

56. Paschasius, *De corpore*, chapter 14, pp. 88–89. This story is a later interpolation but borrowed from an early text. It is sandwiched between the story of Gregory and the finger in the chalice and the story of Plecgils, both of which Paschasius apparently added to his own manuscript.

57. Guitmond of Aversa, *De corporis et sanguinis Domini veritate libri tres*, book 3, PL 149 (Paris, 1882), col. 1479D.

58. Some later stories do stress horror at such appearances; see Chapter 4, pp. 222–23, on Waltmann and Wilsnack, for example. But a number of stories appear that are characterized by a rather matter-of-fact familiarity. For example, Heribert of Clairvaux's twelfth-century miracle collection tells of a priest who sees both host and chalice turn to blood and "is not horrified," but drinks

the blood. The bishop tells him such things should be saved for reverencing, and the miracle obligingly occurs again. Heribert, *De miraculis libri tres*, book 3, chapter 22, PL 195bis (Paris, 1854), cols. 1370–71.

59. As early as the nineteenth century, there were theories that attributed the miracle to the phenomenon of the *Hostienpilz* (or *Micrococcus prodigiosus*), a red fungus that appears on damp bread. See Romuald Bauerreiss, *Pie Jesu: Das Schmerzensmann-Bild und sein Einfluss auf die mittelalterliche Frömmigkeit* (Munich: Karl Widmann, 1931), p. 20; Browe, "Die scholastische Theorie der eucharistischen Verwandlungswunder," p. 332; and K. Löffler, "Mittelalterliche Hostienwunder und Wunderhostien in Westfalen und Niedersachsen," *Auf Roter Erde: Beiträge zur Geschichte des Münsterlandes und der Nachbargebiete* 6 (1931): 9. The fact that fifteenth-century theologians were concerned about avoiding mold and affirmed that changes in the species could be owing to worms or dust suggests that they were aware of possible natural causes. See, for example, "Super dubiis," Wolfenbüttel H.A.B. Cod. Guelf. 152 Helmst., *questio* 1, fols. 160vb–161rb.

60. Guitmond of Aversa refers to a story Lanfranc tells of something that happened in Italy when he was a boy. Guitmond reports that Lanfranc reports that the bishop summoned a council after a host miracle and had the miraculous stuff preserved. Guitmond, *De corporis et sanguinis Domini veritate*, book 2, PL 149, cols. 1449–50. For an account of a similar miracle from around 1200 in which the holy stuff was preserved, see Adam of Eynsham, *Magna vita sancti Hugonis: The Life of St. Hugh of Lincoln*, book 5, chapter 4, ed. Decima L. Douie and Hugh Farmer, 2 vols. (London: Thomas Nelson and Sons, 1961), vol. 2, pp. 92–95, esp. p. 94.

61. Gerald of Wales, *Gemma ecclesiastica*, distinction 1, chapter 11, in *Giraldi Cambrensis opera*, ed. J.S. Brewer, J.F. Dimock, and G.F. Warner, 8 vols., Rerum Britannicarum medii aevi scriptores 21, part 2 (London: Longman & Co., 1862), pp. 40–41, and Heribert, *De miraculis libri tres*, book 3, chapter 21, col. 1370.

62. For background to the 1290 miracle, see my Introduction, n. 19. Although it is regularly claimed that the miracle of Bolsena induced Urban IV to institute the Feast of Corpus Christi in 1264, the story is apocryphal. There is no reflection of the event in art or text before the fourteenth century and none in Urban's bull.

63. Lionel Rothkrug has made the original and convincing argument that differences between northern and southern Europe, both in styles of piety and in the course of religious development, were due in great part to the availability of various kinds of holy matter, relics being more easily obtainable in the Mediterranean areas. See Lionel Rothkrug, "German Holiness and Western Sanctity in Medieval and Modern History," *Historical Reflections/Réflexions historiques* 15, no. 1 (1988): 161–249; *idem*, "Popular Religion and Holy Shrines: Their Influence on the Origins of the German Reformation and Their Role in German Cultural Development," in James Obelkevich (ed.), *Religion and the People, 800–1700* (Chapel Hill: University of North Carolina Press, 1979), pp. 20–86; and *idem*, "Religious Practices and Collective Perceptions: Hidden Homologies in the Renaissance and Reformation," *Historical Reflections/Réflexions historiques* 7, no. 1 (1980): 3–251.

64. Fundamental are Peter Browe, "Die eucharistischen Verwandlungswunder des Mittelalters," *Römische Quartalschrift* 37 (1929): 137–69; *idem*, *Die eucharistischen Wunder*; and *idem*, "Die Hostienschändungen der Juden im Mittelalter," *Römische Quartalschrift* 34, no. 4 (1926): 67–97. For more recent treatments, see Rubin, *Gentile Tales*, and Bynum, *Wonderful Blood*, pp. 75–81 and passim. The bibliography on the Eucharist and Eucharistic theology is enormous. For an introduction, see Hans Jorissen, *Die Entfaltung der Transsubstantiationslehre bis zum Beginn der Hochscholastik* (Münster: Aschendorff, 1965); J. F. McCue, "The Doctrine of Transubstantiation from Berengar through the Council of Trent," *Harvard Theological Review* 61 (1968): 385–430; Miri Rubin, *Corpus Christi: The Eucharist in Late Medieval Culture* (Cambridge: Cambridge University Press, 1991); and Gary Macy, *Treasures from the Storeroom: Medieval Religion and the Eucharist* (Collegeville, MN: Liturgical Press, 1999).

65. Volker Honemann, "Die Sternberger Hostienschändung und ihre Quellen," in Hartmut Boockmann (ed.), *Kirche und Gesellschaft im heiligen Römischen Reich des 15. und 16. Jahrhunderts*, Abhandlungen der Akademie der Wissenschaften in Göttingen, Phil.-Hist. Kl. 3 Folge, Nr. 206 (Göttingen: Vandenhoeck & Ruprecht, 1994), pp. 75–102.

66. Heiko Oberman, *The Roots of Anti-Semitism in the Age of Renaissance and Reformation*, trans. James I. Porter (Philadelphia: Fortress Press, 1984), pp. 97–99 and 147–49; Hans Lichtenstein, "Der Vorwurf der Hostienschändung und das erste Auftreten der Juden in der Mark Brandenburg," *Zeitschrift für die*

Geschichte der Juden in Deutschland 4 (1932): 189–97; and Fritz Backhaus, "Die Hostienschändungsprozesse von Sternberg (1492) und Berlin (1510) und die Ausweisung der Juden aus Mecklenburg und der Mark Brandenburg," *Jahrbuch für Brandenburgische Landesgeschichte* 39 (1988): 7–26. The parallel to objects such as candles and girdles left behind by apparitions is obvious. The material traces of a vision were proof that the vision had occurred. See William Christian Jr., in *Apparitions in Late Medieval and Renaissance Spain* (Princeton, NJ: Princeton University Press, 1981), p. 8.

67. The sacraments in medieval understanding from the twelfth century on were not only signs and rituals but also objects (although see n. 109 below). They were analyzed in the hylomorphic language of form and matter, the physical element being the "matter," and this sensible element was understood to be necessary for three reasons: because human beings know through the sensible, because Christ had a material element through the Incarnation, and because humans are psychosomatic unities (that is, body and soul). See A. Michel, s.v. "Sacrements," DTC, vol. 14, cols. 485–644. It is worth noting that the Lateran Council of 1179, which forbade charging money for the sacraments, included under sacraments some things that would later be seen as sacramentals. See Franz, *Die kirchlichen Benediktionen*, vol. 1, p. 9. On the development of sacramental theology, see Herbert Vorgrimler, *Sacramental Theology*, trans Linda M. Maloney (Collegeville, MN: The Liturgical Press, 1992), pp. 50–55 and 314–18. For the emphasis of theology in the high Middle Ages on the matter of the sacrament (that is, the necessity for an object to convey the grace), see *ibid.*, p. 53.

68. Franz, *Die kirchlichen Benediktionen*, vol. 1, pp. 8–24; Stephen Wilson, *The Magical Universe: Everyday Ritual and Magic in Pre-Modern Europe* (London: Hambledon and London, 2000), pp. 78, 181–82, 301, 366, and 464–65; Swanson, *Religion and Devotion*, pp. 182–84; and Rivard, *Blessing the World*, pp. 38–42. For some twelfth-century examples, see Watkins, *History and the Supernatural*, pp. 110–14. For coins bent or marked to vow them to a saint, see *ibid.*, p. 123. While in the technical sense used by theologians, "sacramentals" had to be blessed by the clergy to have efficacy, it is clear that a number of objects in contact with something numinous, such as a saint's body or tomb, could be used as similarly powerful. Hence, there is no clear division between contact relics and sacramentals. Almost any devotional object could function as a sacramental functioned. Moreover, the understanding of blessing could

also be so broad as to mean any sort of contact. See the cases cited by Augustine Thompson, *Cities of God: The Religion of the Italian Communes, 1125–1325* (University Park: Pennsylvania State University Press, 2005), p. 406, of lay people who grasped and blessed themselves with the bodies of the saints or their relics.

69. Rivard, *Blessing the World*, p. 157.

70. Franz, *Die kirchlichen Benediktionen*, vol. 1, pp. 24–37; Scribner, "Cosmic Order and Daily Life," pp. 21–24; Cameron, *European Reformation*, pp. 9–11; Rivard, *Blessing the World*, p. 278. I cannot tackle in this short book the question of how much of the change we perceive by the fourteenth and fifteenth centuries is owing to the availability of more source material. Our awareness as historians of the increasing complexity of late medieval religion does owe something to our increasing ability to access practices and customs that perhaps had roots in a distant (in some cases even a pre-Christian or non-Christian) past—an access aided in part by the documentation produced by critics and reformers. But the proliferation of sacramentals, like that of other holy objects, was not merely a matter of better reporting. The large-scale survival of such things and of texts about them attests to proliferation.

71. Franz, *Die kirchlichen Benediktionen*, vol. 1, p. 262.

72. *Ibid.*, p. 392. The blessing text comes from Breslau, 1499.

73. Scribner, "Cosmic Order and Daily Life," p. 20; Wilson, *The Magical Universe*, p. 275. And see Walter Stephens, *Demon Lovers: Witchcraft, Sex, and the Crisis of Belief* (Chicago: University of Chicago Press, 2002), pp. 185–90.

74. Franz, *Die kirchlichen Benediktionen*, vol. 1, pp. 264–68.

75. Van Engen, "Multiple Options," p. 280. On the emblem "IHS" as popularized by Bernardino of Siena, see Daniel Arasse, "Entre dévotion et hérésie: La Tablette de saint Bernardin ou le secret d'un prédicateur," *Res* 28 (1995): 118–39. On prayers to the Holy Name ("IHS" or "IHC") in England, see Catherine A. Carsley, "Devotion to the Holy Name: Late Medieval Piety in England," *Princeton University Library Chronicle* 53 (1991–92): 156–72, and Denis Renevey, "*The Name Poured Out*: Margins, Illuminations and Miniatures as Evidence for the Practice of Devotions to the Name of Jesus in Late Medieval England," in James Hogg (ed.), *The Mystical Tradition and the Carthusians*, vol. 9, *Analecta Cartusiana* 130 (Salzburg: Institut für Anglistik und Amerikanistik, 1996): 127–47. On Suso, see Chapter 1, n. 80.

76. On Bernardino's creation of the Holy Name tablet and the attack on

him by Bartholomew of Florence, see Arasse, "Entre dévotion et hérésie," pp. 120–25.

77. Nile Green, "Ostrich Eggs and Peacock Feathers: Sacred Objects as Cultural Exchange between Christianity and Islam," *Al-Masāq* 18, no. 1 (2006): 27–66, esp. pp. 40–42, and Avinoam Shalem, *Islam Christianized: Islamic Portable Objects in the Medieval Church Treasuries of the Latin West* (Frankfurt am Main: Peter Lang, 1996).

78. Katharina Pilaski Kaliardos, "Prodigious Relics: Confessional Argument and the Sacralization of the Territory in the Munich *Kunstkammer* of Albrecht V," *Archiv für Reformationsgeschichte* 101 (2011), forthcoming. And on prodigies and portents generally, see Lorraine Daston, "Marvelous Facts and Miraculous Evidence in Early Modern Europe," *Critical Inquiry* 18 (1991): 101–108. I am grateful to Dr. Kaliardos for sharing her unpublished work.

79. See Caroline Walker Bynum, "The Presence of Objects: Medieval Anti-Judaism in Modern Germany," *Common Knowledge* 10, no. 1 (2004): 1–7. On objects received by Spanish visionaries, see Chapter 1 above at nn. 111 and 120. On the complexity of the idea of prodigies and portents as "proof," see Daston, "Marvelous Facts."

80. See Watkins, *History and the Supernatural*, pp. 122–23. On votive objects generally, see David Freedberg, *The Power of Images: Studies in the History and Theory of Response* (Chicago: University of Chicago Press, 1991), pp. 136–60, esp. pp. 157–59.

81. Susan Marti, Till-Holger Borchert, and Gabriele Keck (eds.), *Karl der Kühne (1433–1477): Kunst, Krieg und Hofkultur*, exhibition catalogue, Historisches Museum, Bern, Bruggemuseum & Groeningemuseum, Bruges (Brussels: Mercatorfonds, 2008), Kat. N. 101, p. 283.

82. Life of Margaret, chapter 8, in *Analecta Bollandiana* 19 (1900): 27–28; see also M.-H. Laurent, "La Plus Ancienne Légende de la B. Marguerite de Città di Castello," *Archivum Fratrum Praedicatorum* 10 (1940): 127–28, and Katherine Park, "Impressed Images: Reproducing Wonders," in Caroline A. Jones and Peter Galison (eds.), *Picturing Science, Producing Art* (New York: Routledge, 1998), pp. 254–71.

83. See Chapter 1, n. 110.

84. A clear definition of the difference was given by theologians Bellarmine and Suarez only in the seventeenth century. See Franz, *Die kirchlichen*

Benediktionen, vol. 1, pp. 21–37.

85. Compare the radish prayer in n. 72 above with the story from Caesarius of Heisterbach cited in n. 129 below.

86. Franz, *Die kirchlichen Benediktionen*, vol. 2, pp. 456–65.

87. Kaliardos, "Prodigious Relics."

88. See the passage from Geiler von Kaisersberg, cited in n. 113 below.

89. Thomas Aquinas, *Summa theologiae*, part 4 [part 3], question 25, article 6, in *S. Thomae Aquinatis opera omnia*, ed. Roberto Busa, 7 vols. (Stuttgart–Bad Cannstatt: Frommann-Holzboog, 1980), vol. 2, pp. 808–9. See also *ibid.*, part 4 [part 3], question 15, article 10, objection 3, vol. 2, p. 794.

90. Mark Daniel Holtz, "Cults of the Precious Blood in the Medieval Latin West," Ph.D. dissertation, University of Notre Dame, 1997, pp. 229–30, rightly points to the difference between this formulation, which says all blood that flowed at the Passion rises *because* it belongs to the *veritas humanae naturae*, and *Quodlibet* 5, which simply says the blood that belongs to the *veritas humanae naturae* rises.

91. Thomas Aquinas, *Summa theologiae*, part 3 [part 2 of part 2], question 54, article 3, *ra* 3, in Busa (ed.), *Opera omnia*, vol. 2, p. 854; *Summa theologica*, trans. the Fathers of the English Dominican Province (New York: Benziger, 1948; Westminster, Maryland, 1981), vol. 4, p. 2310. And see Caroline Walker Bynum, *The Resurrection of the Body in Western Christianity, 200–1336* (New York: Columbia University Press, 1995), pp. 263–64, esp. nn. 137–39.

92. Thomas Aquinas, *Questiones quodlibetales* 5, question 3, article 1, in Busa (ed.), *Opera omnia* vol. 3, p. 466, col. 2. The principle of *quod assumpsit* ("what is assumed is never laid down") was widely used in thirteenth-century debates over Christology and soteriology. The idea was often attributed to John Damascene (d. between 754 and 787), *De fide orthodoxa*, book 3, chapter 27, PG 94, cols. 1096–97.

93. Browe, *Die eucharistischen Wunder*; Caroline Walker Bynum, "Women Mystics and Eucharistic Devotion in the Thirteenth Century," *Women's Studies* 11 (1984): 179–214.

94. See Bynum, *Holy Feast*, pp. 376–77 n. 135. Rival foreskin relics were attributed by legend to Antwerp, Reading Abbey in England, and Niedermünster in Alsace. On foreskin relics generally, see Vincent, *Holy Blood*, pp. 62 n. 107, pp. 86–87 nn. 19–20, p. 141 n. 14, and p. 170 n. 44.

95. Innocent III mentions the foreskin relic at the Lateran and the one at Charroux (which supposedly went back to Charlemagne) in his *De sacro altaris mysterio*, book 4, chapter 30, PL 217, cols. 876D–877B.

96. See Browe, "Die scholastische Theorie der eucharistischen Verwandlungswunder," and Bynum, *Wonderful Blood*, pp. 86–98.

97. On such attitudes in the Carolingian period, see Celia Chazelle, "Matter, Spirit and Image in the *Libri Carolini*," *Recherches Augustiniennes* 21 (1986): 163–84.

98. Cited in Snoek, *Medieval Piety from Relics to the Eucharist*, pp. 372–73 and n. 67.

99. Cited in Newman, "Visionary Texts," p. 170. On the veiling of presence, see Marsha Dutton, "Eat, Drink and Be Merry: the Eucharistic Spirituality of the Cistercian Fathers," in John R. Sommerfeldt (ed.), *Erudition at God's Service*, Studies in Medieval Cistercian History 11 (Kalamazoo, MI: Cistercian Publications, 1987), pp. 9–10.

100. There was a long theological tradition that God veiled Christ's presence in bread and wine exactly because the appearance of flesh and blood, eaten by Christians, would be unbearable. For two examples of such discussion, see Alger of Liège, *De sacramentis*, book 2, chapter 3, PL 180, col. 815, and Roger Bacon, *Opus majus*, part 4 of part 7, in *The Opus Majus of Roger Bacon*, 2 vols., trans. R. B. Burke (Philadelphia: University of Pennsylvania Press, 1928), vol. 2, p. 822.

101. On Christian doubt about Eucharistic presence, see Gavin Langmuir, "The Tortures of the Body of Christ," in Scott Waugh and Peter Diehl (eds.), *Christendom and Its Discontents: Exclusion, Persecution, and Rebellion, 1000–1500* (Cambridge: Cambridge University Press, 1996), pp. 287–309. Vauchez, "Les Images saints," in *Saints, prophètes et visionnaires*, pp. 79–91, argues for a "skeptical ambiance" among Christians, especially about the Eucharist. For the theologian Giles of Rome on doubts about the Eucharist, see Chapter 4, n. 25. For doubts about the Wilsnack hosts and their attendant miracles, see Chapter 4 at nn. 19, 75, and 92. And see Chapter 4, nn. 18, 19, 23, and 24 for other evidence of doubt.

102. For just two examples of such exegesis, see Rupert of Deutz, *Commentaria in Joannem*, book 6, section 206, PL 169, cols. 468–69 and 483D–484A; and Gabriel Biel, *Canonis misse expositio, lectio* 52, vol. 2, p. 304.

103. Nancy Caciola, *Discerning Spirits: Divine and Demonic Possession in the Middle Ages* (Ithaca, NY: Cornell University Press, 2003); Dyan Elliott, *Proving Women: Female Spirituality and Inquisitional Culture in the Later Middle Ages* (Princeton, NJ: Princeton University Press, 2004).

104. For the host at Klosterneuburg in 1298, generally agreed to have been a fraud, see Browe, "Die eucharistischen Verwandlungswunder des Mittelalters," p. 162. For the alleged fraud at Wartenburg bei Wittenberg in 1429, see Tocke, "Synodalrede," trans. Ernst Breest in "Synodalrede des Domherrn Dr. Heinrich Tocke von Magdeburg... Nach einem Manuscripte der herzoglichen Behörden-Bibliothek zu Dessau," *Blätter für Handel, Gewerbe und sociales Leben (Beiblatt zur Magdeburgischen Zeitung)* 23 (Monday, June 5, 1882): 175–76.

105. Gerhoh of Reichersberg, *Commentarium in Psalmos*, part 2, Psalm 22, PL 193, cols. 150C–151A.

106. For Edmund Rich, see Louis Gougaud, *Dévotions et pratiques ascétiques du moyen âge* (Paris: Desclée de Brouwer, 1925), pp. 77–78; on Weingarten, see Rainer Jensch, "Die Weingartener Heilig-Blut- und Stiftertradition: Ein Bilderkreis klösterlicher Selbstdarstellung," Dissertation, Tübingen, 1996, pp. 23–24, and Adalbert Nagel, "Das Heilige Blut Christi," in Gebhard Spahr (ed.), *Festschrift zur 900-Jahr-Feier des Klosters: 1056–1956* (Weingarten: Weingarten Abtei, 1956), pp. 201–203.

107. Cesare Baronio/Ordericus Raynaldus, *Annales ecclesiastici 1198–1534*, 21 vols. (Antwerp: Platiniana, 1611–77), vol. 19, no. 23 for 1487 [no pagination]: "subito in dicto calice miraculose verus sanguis oculis corporeis visibilis apparuit, eiusque pars ex dicto calice in corporalibus super altare existentibus effusus est, atque item sanguis ita visiblis mansit, et hodie pro reliquijs reseruatus conspicitur, vt sanguis hominis vel hoedi recenter effusus, coagulatus tamen videatur." It is important that the letter describes the miracle as "olim quampluribus annis effluxis." See Browe, "Die eucharistischen Verwandlungswunder des Mittelalters," p. 147 n. 20, and *idem*, "Die scholastische Theorie der eucharistischen Verwandlungswunder," p. 317 n. 2.

108. Johannes von Paltz, *Supplementum Coelifodinae*, ed. Berndt Hamm, with Christoph Burger and Venicio Marcolino, in Johannes von Paltz, *Werke*, vol. 2, Spätmittelalter und Reformation Texte und Untersuchungen 3 (Berlin: Walter de Gruyter, 1983), pp. 405–407.

109. See nn. 67–74 above. There was even ambiguity about the power of

the material element of the sacraments. Bonaventure, for example, held that the water of baptism did not gain through consecration any power it lacked earlier. Christ had established baptism, he said, not in the water, but in the water and the blessing formula together. See Franz, *Die kirchlichen Benediktionen*, vol. 1, pp. 24–26.

110. For example, the fifteenth-century theologian Johannes Torquemada (not to be confused with his nephew, the Grand Inquisitor) argued that holy water purifies the mind from phantasms and prepares it for prayer, but it also removes the sterility of cows and women, increases the fertility of fields, and protects against disease. Its effects are not automatic, but dependent on the faith and intention not only of the petitioner but also of the universal church, yet to deny its efficacy, as heretics do, is to deny that the church is led by the Holy Spirit. See Franz, *Die kirchlichen Benediktionen*, vol. 1, pp. 117–21.

111. William of Auvergne, *De legibus*, chapter 27, in *Guilielmi Alverni episcopi Parisiensis, mathematici . . . opera omnia*, 2 vols. (Paris: A. Pralard, 1674), vol. 1, pp. 86D–87D; and see Franz, *Die kirchlichen Benediktionen*, vol. 1, pp. 26–27. For discussion of whether consecration was necessary to make Christian objects "work," see Freedberg, *The Power of Images*, pp. 82–91.

112. Geiler von Kaisersberg, *Zur Geschichte des Volks-Aberglaubens im Anfange des XVI. Jahrhunderts: Aus der Emeis von Dr. Joh. Geiler von Kaisersberg*, ed. August Stöber, 2nd ed. (Basel: Schweighauserische Verlagsbuchhandlung [Hugo Richter], 1875), pp. 52–55, and see Scribner, "Cosmic Order and Daily Life," p. 24.

113. Geiler von Kaisersberg, *Zur Geschichte*, ed. Stöber, pp. 53–54.

114. On this, see Swanson, *Religion and Devotion*, pp. 182–84.

115. On reading antiheretical propaganda as construction of heresy, see Uwe Brunn, *Des Contestataires aux "Cathares": Discours de réforme et propagande anti-hérétique dans les pays du Rhin et de la Meuse avant l'Inquisition*, Collection des Études Augustiniennes: Série moyen âge et temps modernes 41 (Paris: Institut d'Études Augustiniennes, 2006), and Mark Pegg, *A Most Holy War: The Albigensian Crusade and the Battle for Christendom* (Oxford: Oxford University Press, 2008). On the ways in which later reports seriously distorted the beliefs of Waldensians, see Euan Cameron, *The Reformation of the Heretics: The Waldenses of the Alps, 1480–1580* (Oxford: Oxford University Press, 1984).

116. Cited in Heinrich Fichtenau, *Heretics and Scholars in the High Middle Ages, 1000–1200*, trans. Denise A. Kaiser (University Park: Pennsylvania State

University Press, 1998), p. 24. As Fichtenau points out, there is no evidence the heretics actually put things quite this way; it is Gerard who goes on at some length defending the use of "material water" in baptism. And see Walter L. Wakefield and Austin P. Evans (eds. and trans.), *Heresies of the High Middle Ages: Selected Sources Translated and Annotated* (New York: Columbia University Press, 1969), pp. 82–85. For more on this, see Chapter 3 at nn. 31–34.

117. See Horst Bredekamp, *Kunst als Medium sozialer Konflikte: Bilderkämpfe von der Spätantike bis zur Hussitenrevolution* (Frankfurt am Main: Suhrkamp, 1975), p. 300.

118. See Chapter 1 n. 25.

119. See Margaret Aston, *England's Iconoclasts*, vol. 1, *Laws against Images* (Oxford: Oxford University Press, 1988), p. 117.

120. See *ibid.* and my Chapter 1, n. 24, for "Die Hymelstrasse." For Biel on Eucharistic reception, see n. 11 above.

121. See the works cited in Chapter 1, n. 76, and Browe, "Die scholastische Theorie der eucharistischen Verwandlungswunder."

122. Kaliardos, "Prodigious Relics," and Irene Ewinkel, *De monstris: Deutung und Funktion von Wundergeburten auf Flugblättern im Deutschland des 16. Jahrhunderts*, Frühe Neuzeit 23 (Tübingen: Niemeyer, 1995), pp. 15–34.

123. As is well known, politics often accounted for which positions were condemned and which accepted. Van Engen, "Multiple Options," pp. 263–64, makes this point by contrasting the hostility of English bishops and the crown to Lollardy with the acceptance of the similar *devotio moderna* movement by Münster and Cologne.

124. Note that Bremer says "*are* of the humanity" and "*were* joined." He would seem to be arguing here the traditional Franciscan position that the blood of Christ's body had been assumed by the Logos in the womb, but that shed blood was not united with the Logos during the *triduum* (the three days between Good Friday and Easter Sunday); hence, a bit of it could remain behind.

125. Ludger Meier, "Der Erfurter Franziskanertheologe Johannes Bremer und der Streit um das Wilsnacker Wunderblut," in Albert Lang et al. (eds.), *Aus der Geisteswelt des Mittelalters (Festschrift Grabmann)*, Beiträge zur Geschichte der Philosophie und Theologie des Mittelalters: Texte und Untersuchungen, Supplementband 3 (Münster: Aschendorff, 1935), p. 1262, transcribed from

Braunschweig Stadtbibliothek MS 48, fol. 209d. And see Bynum, *Wonderful Blood*, pp. 40–41, on the *questio magistralis*; pp. 222–23 on Bremer's sermons.

126. See Bynum, *Wonderful Blood*, pp. 26–27, 33, and 92. The same argument can be made about the concern both authorities and the faithful felt about false relics. See *ibid.*, p. 66, for an example.

127. For an example, see Eugene IV's support of miracle hosts. Rubin, *Gentile Tales*, pp. 163 and 187; Vincent, *Holy Blood*, p. 122 n. 16 and p. 138 n. 5.

128. On the controversy over the miracle host at La Rochelle in 1448, where many of these issues came into play, see Michelle E. Garceau, "Fear of a 'Public Sphere': The Trial Records of Francis Baiuli in MS Add. 22795," M.A. thesis, University of London, 2003. For Eugene IV's and Nicholas V's requirement that a consecrated host be laid over a host miracle, see Chapter 3, n. 86.

129. A number of the stories in Caesarius of Heisterbach's "Dialogue on Miracles" are clearly *exempla* for the instruction of novices in Eucharistic doctrine. See Caesarius, *Dialogus miraculorum*, distinction 9, chapters 8 and 9, ed. Joseph Strange, 2 vols. (Cologne: Heberle, 1851), vol. 2, pp. 172–74, which tell of bees reverencing a stolen host placed in their hive and of a woman who sprinkled ground-up host on her cabbages. The stories suggest that people practiced such things and that the clergy disapproved.

130. On all this, see Bynum, *Wonderful Blood*, pp. 25–81 and 239–58, and Browe, *Die eucharistischen Wunder*.

131. See above, n. 113.

132. It was alleged, for example, that when the bishop of Havelberg tried to reconsecrate the Wilsnack miracle hosts, the wafers themselves protested. And note the opposition of the bishop and clergy of Bohemia to the Wilsnack pilgrimage. For both examples, see Bynum, *Wonderful Blood*, p. 26. And see the case of the Halberstadt-Wasserleben miracle discussed in n. 133 below. There was also a subset of Eucharistic miracles that supposedly occurred to priests who violated liturgical prescriptions by such acts as not cleaning the chalice, misspeaking liturgical formulae, and so on. These miracles also in a sense reinforced ecclesiastical control and supervision.

133. The miracle at Zehdenick supposedly occurred in 1247; the account is from the sixteenth-century. There was an active blood pilgrimage circa 1500. See Bynum, *Wonderful Blood*, pp. 58–59. The Halberstadt-Wasserleben miracle, for which the evidence is extremely complicated, supposedly occurred in 1231.

There seem to have been pilgrims to Wasserleben circa 1300, and there are fifteenth- and sixteenth-century accounts of the miracle and of the competition of Halberstadt and Wasserleben for the relics. See *ibid.*, pp. 53–54. On such accounts generally, see Browe, *Die eucharistischen Wunder*, and Heuser, "'Heilig-Blut.'" A number of recent historians emphasize that narratives of miracles cannot simply be mined for social or political history. See, for example, Rubin, *Gentile Tales*.

134. See Bynum, *Wonderful Blood*, pp. 33 and 252.

135. On the parallels between host desecration and ritual murder charges, see Elsa Marmursztejn, "Du Récit exemplaire au *casus* universitaire: Une Variation théologique sur le thème de la profanation d'hosties par les juifs (1290)," in *La Rouelle et la croix destins des juifs d'Occident*, coordinated by Domenique Iogna-Prat and Danièle Sansy, *Médiévales* 41 (Autumn 2001): 39; and Gilbert Dahan, *Les Intellectuels chrétiens et les juifs au moyen âge* (Paris: Éditions du Cerf, 1990).

136. At Iphofen and Deggendorf, pogroms can be demonstrated to have predated host-desecration charges by decades. See Harald Swillus, "Hostienfrevellegende und Judenverfolgung in Iphofen: Ein Beitrag zur Entstehungsgeschichte der Kirche zum hl. Blut im Gräbenviertel," *Würzburger Diözesan-Geschichtsblätter* 58 (1996): 87–107, and Manfred Eder, *"Die Deggendorfer Gnad": Entstehung und Entwicklung einer Hostienwallfahrt im Kontext von Theologie und Geschichte*, Deggendorf Archäologie und Stadtgeschichte 3 (Deggendorf/Passau: Passavia-Univ.-Verlag, 1992). On the change from lynching to legal process, see Oberman, *Roots of Anti-Semitism*.

137. In *Wonderful Blood*, pp. 229–48 and passim, I have given as well a more complex argument about the roots of such anti-Jewish persecution in the theology of sacrifice that dominated late medieval understandings of the death of Christ. This argument, which I do not repeat here, locates anti-Semitism at the very heart of late medieval theology and goes beyond the tendency of some recent scholarship to reduce persecution simply to vague fears of "the other" or to economic greed.

138. The most influential and elegant of the interpretations of such phenomena that stress social control has been Charles Zika, "Hosts, Processions and Pilgrimages: Controlling the Sacred in Fifteenth-Century Germany," *Past and Present* 118 (1988): 25–64. For perceptive political interpretations, see

Bruno Hennig, "Kurfürst Friedrich II. und das Wunderblut zu Wilsnack," *Forschungen zur brandenburgischen und preussischen Geschichte* 19 (1906): 73–104; Honemann, "Die Sternberger Hostienschändung und ihre Quellen," pp. 75–102; and Hartmut Boockmann, "Der Streit um das Wilsnacker Blut: zur Situation des deutschen Klerus in der Mitte des 15. Jahrhunderts," *Zeitschrift für historische Forschung* 9 (1982): 385–408.

139. Such accusations were tied to folk assumptions as varied as the notion that corpses bleed to accuse murderers or the idea that red objects both stimulate and control bleeding. On the assumption that like controls like, see Chapter 1, n. 48. On corpses bleeding to accuse murderers, see Alain Boureau, *Théologie, science et censure au XIIIe siècle: Le Cas de Jean Peckham* (Paris: Belles Lettres, 1999), pp. 227–28 and 244–91.

140. Bynum, *Wonderful Blood*, pp. 26–45. And see Felix Escher and Hartmut Kühne (eds.), *Die Wilsnackerfahrt: Ein Wallfahrts- und Kommunikationszentrum Nord- und Mitteleuropas im Spätmittelalter*, Europäische Wallfahrtsstudien (Frankfurt am Main: Peter Lang, 2006), which appeared after *Wonderful Blood* went to press. For complicated questions concerning the badges from Wilsnack, see *Wonderful Blood*, pp. 31, 32, 43, 278 n. 48, and 286 n. 7. For the various theological positions taken in the controversy, see Chapter 4, pp. 221–22, 240, 243–46.

141. Matthias Döring, in his "Determinatio de sanguine Christi contra Johannem Hus," also known as the "Quoniam/Cum olim," the first major answer to Heinrich Tocke's anti-Wilsnack polemic, argued that the Wilsnack pilgrimage had had a healthy effect on the region; see Döring, "Determinatio," Wolfenbüttel H. A. B. Cod. Guelf. 152 Helmst., fols. 164va–170vb, at fol. 170rb. James of Jüterbog, in his "Tractatus de concertatione super cruore in Welsenaco," Wolfenbüttel H. A. B. Cod. Guelf. 152 Helmst., fol. 186va, saw the poverty of the village of Wilsnack and the devastation of the original fire as reasons behind the need for and success of the pilgrimage. Johannes von Paltz, *Supplementum Coelifodinae*, pp. 390–96, charged that pilgrimages to Wilsnack and elsewhere induced in their participants lying, blasphemy, and ribaldry.

142. Paltz, *Supplementum Coelifodinae*, p. 407; Paltz is here following Johannes von Dorsten, who wrote in the 1470s.

143. Paltz, *Supplementum Coelifodinae*, p. 405.

144. For received opinion about the differences in this regard of

Christianity, Judaism, and Islam, see Daniel Miller, "Materiality: An Introduction," in Daniel Miller (ed.), *Materiality* (Durham, NC: Duke University Press, 2005), pp. 1–50, esp. pp. 16–33. Interestingly enough, the closest parallels to Christian practice are found in Buddhism, where, as John Strong remarks, "though the meanings of the various terms [i.e. in Christian and Buddhist theology] may differ, the treatment of relics in both Christian and Buddhist traditions—what is done for them or to them, what is said about them, and what they themselves do—is very often similar." See John S. Strong, *Relics of the Buddha* (Princeton, NJ: Princeton University Press, 2004), p. xvi; and my Chapter 1, n. 59, and Conclusion, n. 16. In "Buddhist Relics in Comparative Perspective: Beyond the Parallels," in Germano and Trainor (eds.), *Embodying the Dharma*, pp. 27–49, Strong argues for a number of differences in both practice and theology. An excellent description of what Buddhist relics are can be found in David Germano, "Living Relics of the Buddha(s) in Tibet," in Germano and Trainor (eds.), *Embodying the Dharma*, pp. 52–53.

145. Proliferation of relics also multiplies presence in Buddhism. As John Strong puts it, Buddhist relics "arise from multiplication rather than subtraction." While he contrasts this with Christian understanding, arguing from the Latin work *reliquere*, the Buddhist and Christian understandings may actually be quite similar. The Sanskrit word *dhātu* (translated "relic") means "constituent element of an essential ingredient." This is not quite the concept of *pars pro toto*, but it does express the sense that a piece or part carries the full essence of the body. See Strong, *Relics of the Buddha*, pp. xiv, xvi, and 5; *idem*, "Buddhist Relics in Comparative Perspective," p. 40; and John Kieschnick, *The Impact of Buddhism on Chinese Material Culture* (Princeton, NJ: Princeton University Press, 2003), pp. 29–44.

CHAPTER THREE: HOLY PIECES

1. On incorrupt bodies, see nn. 12, 13, and 24 below. On polemics about eating and excreting the Eucharist, see n. 77 below. The question of incorruption is more complicated than I can deal with here. The bodies of both the very holy and the very wicked were thought to resist corruption. See Caroline Walker Bynum, *The Resurrection of the Body in Western Christianity, 200–1336* (New York: Columbia University Press, 1995), pp. 206–208 and 221–25, esp.

p. 206 n. 20.

2. Jerome, *Contra Vigilantium*, PL 23, cols. 358–60. Some of what follows in the next two pages reuses material I discussed from a different perspective in *The Resurrection of the Body*, pp. 86–94, 106–108, 176–80, and 210–11.

3. Jerome, Letter 109, chapters 1–2, in *Saint Jerome: Lettres*, ed. and trans. Jerome Labourt, 8 vols. (Paris: Belles Lettres, 1949–63), vol. 5, pp. 202–205; also in PL 22, cols. 906–908.

4. Victricius of Rouen, *De laude sanctorum*, chapters 10–12, ed. Jacob Mulders and R. Demeulenaere, Corpus christianorum: Series latina 64 (Turnhout: Brepols, 1985), pp. 83–90; trans. (with different chapter divisions) by J. N. Hillgarth in *The Conversion of Western Europe, 350–750* (Englewood Cliffs: Prentice-Hall, 1969), pp. 22–27.

5. See this Chapter at n. 40.

6. Peter the Venerable, "Sermo cuius supra in honore sancti illius cuius reliquiae sunt in presenti," ed. Giles Constable, in "Petri Venerabilis sermones tres," *Revue bénédictine* 64 (1954): 265–70. For more discussion of this text, see Chapter 4, pp. 220–21.

7. Walter Daniel, *The Life of Ailred of Rievaulx*, trans. F. M. Powicke (London: Thomas Nelson and Sons, 1950), pp. 62–63; cited in Ellert Dahl, "Heavenly Images: The Statue of St. Foy of Conques and the Signification of the Medieval Cult-Image in the West," *Acta ad archaeologiam et Artium historiam pertinentia* 8 (1979): 184.

8. Peter Damian, Life of St. Romuald, chapter 69, PL 144 (Paris, 1853), col. 1006c, cited in Dahl, "Heavenly Images," p. 184.

9. James of Vitry, Life of Mary of Oignies, book 2, chapter 12, paragraph 109, AASS, June, vol. 5 (Paris, 1867), p. 572.

10. Mechtild, *Das fliessende Licht*, book 2, chapter 3, in *Mechtild of Magdeburg: "Das fliessende Licht der Gottheit" nach der Einsiedler Handschrift in kritischem Vergleich mit der gesamten Überlieferung*, ed. Hans Neumann (Munich: Artemis, 1990), pp. 39–41.

11. On stones as alive, see J. C. Plumpe, "Vivum saxum, vivi lapides: The Concept of 'Living Stone' in Classical and Christian Antiquity," *Traditio* 1 (1943): 1–14; and Jacqueline Jung, "Crystalline Wombs and Pregnant Hearts," in Rachel Fulton and Bruce Holsinger (eds.), *History in the Comic Mode: Medieval Communities and the Matter of Person* (New York: Columbia University Press,

2007), pp. 223–37, esp. n. 13. Albert the Great argues, in a more complex and Aristotelian move, that stones are not alive, because they do not have souls. But they do have forms, which are more than simply shape or structure. Because of these forms, they have certain powers, such as magnetism, that enable them to act. See Albertus Magnus, *Book of Minerals*, book 2, tractate 1, chapters 1–4, trans. Dorothy Wyckoff (Oxford: Oxford University Press, 1967), pp. 55–62, and see also Wyckoff, "Introduction," pp. xxxiii–xxxv. One of the basic assumptions of alchemical theory as it developed in the later Middle Ages was that metals grow in the earth. See Chapter 4 at nn. 55–57, 68, 105, and 113.

12. See Louise Bourdua, "Displaying the Bodily Remains of Antony of Padua," in Kristin Marek, Raphaèle Preisinger, Marius Rimmele, and Katrin Kärcher (eds.), *Bild und Körper im Mittelalter* (Munich: Wilhelm Fink, 2006), pp. 243–55, and Ellen M. Shortell, "Dismembering St. Quentin: Gothic Architecture and the Display of Relics," in special issue, *Body-Part Reliquaries and Body Parts in the Middle Ages*, ed. Caroline Walker Bynum and Paula Gerson, *Gesta* 36 (1997): 32–47; see figure 7, p. 38, for the hand.

13. See Caroline Walker Bynum, *Fragmentation and Redemption: Essays on Gender and the Human Body in Medieval Religion* (New York: Zone Books, 1991), p. 372 n. 32; see also *ibid.*, p. 413 n. 120.

14. Thomas of Cantimpré, *Supplementum* [to the Life of Mary of Oignies], chapter 1, paragraphs 6–7 and 14, AASS, June, vol. 5 (Paris, 1867), pp. 574–75 and 577. For a miracle worked by Mary's finger, see *ibid.*, chapter 3, paragraphs 15–17, pp. 577–78.

15. See Chapter 2, n. 46 above.

16. Jean-Paul Roux, *Le Sang: Mythes, symboles et réalités* (Paris: Fayard, 1988), pp. 202–203. For other Italian claims to liquefied blood, see Benjamin B. Warfield, *Counterfeit Miracles* (New York: Charles Scribner's Sons, 1918), pp. 96–97.

17. Michele Bacci, "Relics of the Pharos Chapel: A View from the Latin West," in Alekseĭ Lidov (ed.), *Eastern Christian Relics* (Moscow: Progress-Tradition, 2003), pp. 234–48.

18. On the Halberstadt-Wasserleben miracle, see Chapter 2, n. 133; on the Spandau host, see this chapter at n. 44; on the miracle of the Gero crucifix, see Chapter 1, n. 137.

19. For more on reliquaries, see Chapter 1, p. 70.

20. Mechtild, *Das fliessende Licht*, book 7, chapter 1, pp. 254–58. For Mechtild's view of the resurrection body, which is more complicated than I indicate here, see Bynum, *The Resurrection of the Body*, pp. 337–41.

21. See the description in *Krone und Schleier: Kunst aus mittelalterlichen Frauenklöstern*, exhibition catalogue published by the Kunst- und Ausstellungshalle der Bundesrepublik Deutschland, Bonn, and the Ruhrlandmuseum, Essen (Munich: Hirmer, 2005), p. 270.

22. In the second half of the fourteenth century, the relic seems to have been used to bless the faithful on the feast day of the saint. See *ibid.*, p. 268.

23. Cynthia Hahn, "The Voices of the Saints: Speaking Reliquaries," *Gesta* 36, no. 1 (1997): 20–31, and see Chapter 1 at n. 65.

24. Herbert Thurston, *The Physical Phenomena of Mysticism* (Chicago: Henry Regnery, 1952), pp. 233–82, esp. pp. 246–52, and Michel Bouvier, "De l'incorruptibilité des corps saints," in *Les Miracles, miroirs des corps*, ed. Jacques Gélis and Odile Redon (Paris: Presses et Publications de l'Université de Paris-VIII, 1983), pp. 193–221. The Catholic Church has never accepted incorruption of body as proof per se of sanctity.

25. On the popularity of vernacular martyr accounts and the reasons for it, see Brigitte Cazelles, *Le Corps de sainteté d'après Jehan Bouche d'Or, Jehan Paulus, et quelques vies des XIIe et XIIIe siècles* (Geneva: Droz, 1982). On Catherine of Genoa, see Umile Bonzi da Genova, *S. Caterina Fieschi Adorno*, 2 vols. (Turin: Marietti, 1961–62).

26. Saul N. Brody, *The Disease of the Soul: Leprosy in Medieval Literature* (Ithaca, NY: Cornell University Press, 1974), esp. pp. 64–66, 79, and 85–86; and R.I. Moore, *The Formation of a Persecuting Society: Power and Deviance in Western Europe, 950–1250* (Oxford: Basil Blackwell, 1987), pp. 58–63.

27. On burial practices cross-culturally as efforts to cope with putrefaction, see Louis-Vincent Thomas, *Le Cadavre: De la biologie à l'anthropologie* (Brussels: Éditions Complexe, 1980), and Daniel Miller (ed.), *Materiality* (Durham, NC: Duke University Press, 2005), especially the essay by Lynn Meskill, "Objects in the Mirror Appear Closer Than They Are," *ibid.*, pp. 51–71. On fear of decay in Western medieval culture generally, see Piero Camporesi, *The Incorruptible Flesh: Bodily Mutation and Mortification in Religion and Folklore*, trans. Tania Croft-Murray and Helen Elsom (Cambridge: Cambridge University Press, 1988).

28. See Chapter 2, p. 132.

29. Thiofrid of Echternach, *Flores epytaphii sanctorum*, book 1, chapter 3, and book 2, chapter 1, ed. Michele Camillo Ferrari, Corpus christianorum: Continuatio mediaevalis 133 (Turnhout: Brepols, 1996), pp. 16–17 and 31–33, quoted passage on p. 16.

30. Guibert of Nogent, *De pigneribus*, book 3, ed. R.B.C. Huygens, in Guibert of Nogent, *Quo ordine sermo fieri debeat; De bucella iudae data et de veritate dominici corporis; De sanctis et eorum pigneribus*, Corpus christianorum: Continuatio mediaevalis 127 (Turnhout: Brepols, 1993), p. 143. On Guibert, see Klaus Guth, *Guibert von Nogent und die hochmittelalterliche Kritik an der Reliquienverehrung*, Studien und Mitteilungen zur Geschichte des Benediktiner-Ordens und seiner Zweige, Supplement 21 (Augsburg: Winfried, 1970); John F. Benton, "Introduction," in Guibert of Nogent, *Self and Society in Medieval France: The Memoirs of Abbot Guibert of Nogent*, eds. J.F. Benton and trans. C.C.S. Bland (New York: Harper & Row, 1970), pp. 7–33; and Jay Rubenstein, *Guibert of Nogent: Portrait of a Medieval Mind* (New York: Routledge, 2002), pp. 124–30 and 138–43.

31. For a fifteenth-century example, see John of Capistrano, *Tractatus de Christi sanguine pretioso*, article 4, section C, ed. in Natale da Terrinca, *La devozione al Preziosissimo Sangue di nostro Signore Gesú Cristo: Studio storico teologico a proposito di un trattato inedito di S. Giovanni da Capestrano* (Rome: Pia Unione del Preziosissimo Sangue, 1969), pp. 5*–6* and in Natale Cocci, "Il sangue di Cristo in San Giovanni da Capestrano," in *Sangue e antropologia nella teologia. Atti della VII settimana, Roma 27 novembre – 2 dicembre 1989*, ed. Francesco Vattioni, vol. 3 (Rome: Pia Unione del Preziosissimo Sangue, 1991), pp. 1349–50.

32. James Capelli, *Summa contra haereticos*; trans. in Walter L. Wakefield and Austin P. Evans (eds. and trans.), *Heresies of the High Middle Ages: Selected Sources Translated and Annotated* (New York: Columbia University Press, 1969), pp. 304–305.

33. Rainerius, *Summa de Catharis*, chapter 25; trans. in Wakefield and Evans (eds. and trans.), *Heresies*, p. 344.

34. M.D. Lambert argues that the heretical sense of the body expressed disgust at organic processes. M.D. Lambert, "The Motives of the Cathars: Some Reflections...," in Derek Baker (ed.), *Religious Motivation: Biographical*

and Sociological Problems for the Church Historian, Studies in Church History 15 (Oxford: Basil Blackwell for the Ecclesiastical History Society, 1978), pp. 49–59. For recent debate about what Cathars held, see Chapter 1, n. 22.

35. Henry of Ghent, *Quodlibet* 10, question 6, in *Henrici de Gandavo Quodlibet X*, ed. R. Macken, *Henrici de Gandavo opera omnia* 14 (Leuven and Leiden: University Press and Brill, 1981), p. 132: "quoniam si sit adorandum, hoc est quia id quod erat in vivo, manet in mortuo. Aliud enim non est in mortuo propter quod est adorandum. Hoc autem falsum est, quia in verme generato de corpore sancti mortuo manet saltem materia. Qui tamen non propter hoc est adorandus. Ergo etc."

36. *Ibid.*, pp. 132–45. Discussed in a different edition and for a different point in Jean Wirth, "La Critique scolastique de la théorie thomiste de l'image," in Olivier Christin and Dario Gamboni (eds.), *Krisen religiöser Kunst: Vom 2. Niceanum bis zum 2. Vatikanischen Konzil/Crises de l'image religieuse: De Nicée à Vatican II* (Paris: Éditions de la Maison des Sciences de l'Homme, 1999), pp. 102–103.

37. Henry of Ghent, *Quodlibet* 10, question 6, pp. 141 and 143.

38. *Ibid.*, p. 142.

39. There are thus connections between what Henry argues here and the theology of bodily resurrection being discussed at the same period; see Bynum, *The Resurrection of the Body*, esp. pp. 229–78 (and on Henry, pp. 243, 261, 270–71, and 275). Although scholastic theologians of the twelfth to the fifteenth centuries tended to locate personal identity (in the sense of continuity over time) in soul or form, all held that except in extraordinary circumstances, God would reassemble the physical particles of a person's body at the end of time, no matter how widely dispersed they had been. Bits thus remained in a sense part of—or tagged for—the original body, which would be reformed *as body* by its soul at resurrection, although this was, of course, a miracle, not a natural process. By the later Middle Ages, those in the Thomist tradition, who held that particularity is carried by the soul as the single form of the body, had less trouble explaining how any bits of matter might be shaped by soul into its body if sufficient stuff were lacking. Those in the Franciscan tradition, such as Henry, argued that there is a form for the body (the *forma corporeitatis*) that holds the material of a cadaver together *as body*, even after death. Nonetheless, even Thomists maintained that there would be some sort of material continuity

in resurrection. This assumption of material continuity undergirds both Henry of Ghent's theorizing that pieces of the saints that survive in worms can be revered and Thomas Aquinas's argument that the relic *is* the saint, at least insofar as it will be raised and reconstructed into the saint's body at the end of time.

40. See, among others, Victor Saxer, *Morts, martyrs, reliques en Afrique chrétienne aux premiers siècles: Les Témoignages de Tertullien, Cyprien, et Augustin à la lumière de l'archéologie africaine* (Paris: Édition Beauchesne, 1980); Henri Leclercq, s.v. "Martyr," in Fernand Cabrol and Henri Leclercq (eds.), *Dictionnaire d'archéologie chrétienne et de liturgie*, vol. 10 (Paris: Letouzey et Ané, 1932), cols. 2435–57; Philippe Ariès, *The Hour of Our Death*, trans. Helen Weaver (Oxford: Oxford University Press, 1981), pp. 29–33 and passim; and Thomas Head, s.v. "Relics," in Joseph R. Strayer (ed.), *Dictionary of the Middle Ages*, 13 vols. and Supplement (New York: Charles Scribner's Sons, 1982–2004), vol. 10, pp. 296–99. And for ambivalence about (but not necessarily opposition to) relic division in the Eastern church, see Sergey A. Ivanov, "Pious Dismemberment: The Paradox of Relics in Byzantine Hagiography," in Lidov (ed.), *Eastern Christian Relics*, pp. 121–31.

41. James of Vitry and Thomas of Cantimpré, the biographers of Mary of Oignies (d. 1213), clearly hoped to gain a piece of her body as a result of pressing for her holy reputation; see above, nn. 9 and 14. For the finger reliquary, see Sharon Farmer, "Low Country Ascetics and Oriental Luxury: Jacques de Vitry, Marie of Oignies, and the Treasures of Oignies," in Fulton and Holsinger (eds.), *History in the Comic Mode*, pp. 205–22. There is some evidence that the body of Thomas Aquinas was boiled about thirty years after his death; see Elizabeth A. R. Brown, "Death and the Human Body in the Later Middle Ages: The Legislation of Boniface VIII on the Division of the Corpse," *Viator* 12 (1981): 234 n. 48. The sisters of Chiara of Montefalco (d. 1308) autopsied her body soon after death and found physical signs of Christ's Passion in her heart; see Chapter 2, nn. 23 and 82.

42. Weingarten, near Lake Constance, provides an example of a medieval procession in which a relic goes out to mark off boundaries. The procession continues to the present day. See Norbert Kruse and Hans Ulrich Rudolf (eds.), *900 Jahre Heilig-Blut-Verehrung in Weingarten 1094–1994: Festschrift zum Heilig-Blut-Jubiläum am 12. März 1994*, 3 vols. (Sigmaringen: J. Thorbecke, 1994). On division and distribution of the stuff of sacramentals, see Stephen Wilson, *The*

Magical Universe: Everyday Ritual and Magic in Pre-Modern Europe (London: Hambledon and London, 2000), p. 366.

43. Brown, "Death and the Human Body," pp. 221–70.

44. Hans Lichtenstein, "Der Vorwurf der Hostienschändung und das erste Auftreten der Juden in der Mark Brandenburg," *Zeitschrift für die Geschichte der Juden in Deutschland* 4 (1932): 189-97; Heiko Oberman, *The Roots of Anti-Semitism in the Age of Renaissance and Reformation*, trans. James I. Porter (Philadelphia: Fortress Press, 1984), esp. pp. 97–99; Fritz Backhaus, "Die Hostienschändungsprozesse von Sternberg (1492) und Berlin (1510) und die Ausweisung der Juden aus Mecklenburg und der Mark Brandenburg," *Jahrbuch für Brandenburgische Landesgeschichte* 39 (1988): 7–26.

45. Robert L. Cohn, "Sainthood on the Periphery: The Case of Judaism," in Richard Kieckhefer and George D. Bond (eds.), *Sainthood: Its Manifestations in World Religions* (Berkeley: University of California Press, 1988), p. 44.

46. Josef W. Meri, *The Cult of Saints among Muslims and Jews in Medieval Syria* (Oxford: Oxford University Press, 2002), pp. 1–10, 25–26, 60–66, 101–7, 195–205, 214–50, 276, and 282. Meri recounts (p. 19) the case of a fifteenth-century rabbi of Málaga who saw a red stone fixed in the wall of the synagogue that had allegedly been one of the stones of the Temple brought thither by Ezra. And Cohn, "Sainthood on the Periphery," p. 51, reports the use of soil from a holy grave to bring down fever.

47. Cohn, "Sainthood on the Periphery," pp. 44–46 and 53. Meri says: "Evidence for Jewish veneration of saints is significantly less than Islamic." *Cult of Saints*, p. 6.

48. Cohn, "Sainthood on the Periphery," p. 51.

49. Ephraim Shoham-Steiner, "'For a Prayer in That Place Would be Most Welcome': Jews, Holy Shrines, and Miracles—a New Approach," *Viator* 37 (2006): 369–95. The rabbis argued that God permits miracles at Christian tombs in order to mislead Christians. See also Lucia Raspe, *Jüdische Hagiographie im mittelalterlichen Aschkenas*, Texts and Studies in Medieval and Early Modern Judaism 19 (Tübingen: Mohr Siebeck, 2006), esp. pp. 26–33 and 177–98; Susan L. Einbinder, *Beautiful Death: Jewish Poetry and Martyrdom in Medieval France* (Princeton, NJ: Princeton University Press, 2002), p. 171; and Israel Yuval, "Vengeance and Curse, Blood and Libel: From Saints' Stories to Blood Libel" (in Hebrew), *Zion* 58 (1993): 34–45, cited in Einbinder, *Beautiful*

Death. David Biale, *Blood and Belief: The Circulation of a Symbol Between Jews and Christians* (Berkeley: University of California Press, 2007), p. 116, tells a story of eighteenth-century Jews prizing the ashes and blood of an executed convert to Judaism, but this legend, of course, comes from long after the Middle Ages. J. M. Minty, "Judengasse to Christian Quarter: The Phenomenon of the Converted Synagogue in the Late Medieval and Early Modern Holy Roman Empire," in Robert W. Scribner and Trevor Johnson (eds.), *Popular Religion in Germany and Central Europe, 1400–1800* (New York: St. Martin's Press, 1996), p. 79, cites cases of Jewish relics. These Jewish relics are not bodies or body parts but rather contact relics.

50. For the stress on quantification and accumulation in late medieval piety, see Andrew Breeze, "The Number of Christ's Wounds," *The Bulletin of the Board of Celtic Studies* 32 (1985): 84–91; Thomas Lentes, "Gezählte Frömmigkeit im späten Mittelalter," *Frühmittelalterliche Studien* 20 (1995): 40–71; and David Areford, "The Passion Measured: A Late-Medieval Diagram of the Body of Christ," in A. A. MacDonald, H. N. B. Ridderbos, and R. M. Schlusemann (eds.), *The Broken Body: Passion Devotion in Late-Medieval Culture* (Groningen: Egbert Forsten, 1998), pp. 211–38. On understanding grace as available in units, see Euan Cameron, "The Power of the Word: Renaissance and Reformation," in Euan Cameron (ed.), *Early Modern Europe: An Oxford History* (Oxford: Oxford University Press, 1999), p. 83. For an especially arresting example, see plate 32 in Caroline Walker Bynum, *Wonderful Blood: Theology and Practice in Late Medieval Northern Germany and Beyond* (Philadelphia: University of Pennsylvania Press, 2007).

51. On framing, see Chapter 1, pp. 93–94.

52. For more on this, see Chapter 2, n. 142 above and Chapter 4, p. 222.

53. "O Man Unkynde" and wounded heart of Christ, in Brit. Lib. Add. MS 37049, fol. 20r; in James Hogg (ed.), *An Illustrated Yorkshire Carthusian Religious Miscellany: British Library London Additional MS. 37049*, vol. 3 (1981), *Analecta Cartusiana* 95, p. 22.

54. Flora Lewis, "The Wound in Christ's Side and the Instruments of the Passion: Gendered Experience and Response," in Lesley Smith and Jane H. M. Taylor (eds.), *Women and the Book: Assessing the Visual Experience* (London: The British Library, 1996), pp. 204–29, esp. pp. 212–17; Karma Lochrie, "Mystical Acts, Queer Tendencies," in Karma Lochrie, Peggy McCracken, and James

A. Schultz (eds.), *Constructing Medieval Sexuality* (Minneapolis: University of Minnesota Press, 1997), pp. 180–200; and Caroline Walker Bynum, "Violence Occluded: The Wound in Christ's Side in Late Medieval Devotion," in Tracey Billado and Belle Tuten (eds.), *Feud, Violence and Practice: Essays in Medieval Studies in Honor of Stephen D. White* (Aldershot, UK: Ashgate, 2010), pp. 95–116. See also Martha Easton, "The Wound of Christ, the Mouth of Hell: Appropriations and Inversions of Female Anatomy in the Later Middle Ages," in Susan L'Engle and Gerald B. Guest (eds.), *Tributes to Jonathan J. G. Alexander: The Making and Meaning of Illuminated Medieval and Renaissance Manuscripts, Art and Architecture* (London/Turnhout: Harvey Miller, 2006), pp. 395–414; Silke Tammen, "Blick und Wunde—Blick und Form: Zur Deutungsproblematik der Seitenwunde Christi in der spätmittelalterlichen Buchmalerei," in Marek, Preisinger, Rimmele, and Kärcher (eds.), *Bild und Körper im Mittelalter*, pp. 85–114; and Amy Hollywood, "'That Glorious Slit': Irigaray and the Medieval Devotion to Christ's Side Wound," in Theresa Krier and Elizabeth D. Harvey (eds.), *Luce Irigaray and Premodern Culture*, Routledge Studies in Renaissance Literature and Culture 4 (London: Routledge, 2004), pp. 105–25. Tammen, in "Blick und Wunde—Blick und Form" (p. 90), makes the telling point that interpretations of the side wound as vagina/vulva tend to neglect the importance of the mandorla shape in devotion. I find the interpretations of Lochrie and Hollywood quite possible readings and would indeed argue that they depend more on the fluidity of symbols I pointed out in the 1980s than these authors quite admit. Nevertheless, I think one must separate more than they do the multiple valences and interpretations suggested by the medieval texts themselves (which implications extend, as Tammen convincingly argues, to exploration of the nature of sight as penetration) from modern psychoanalytic readings, however powerful.

55. The bibliography on Julian is voluminous. I have given my interpretation in *Wonderful Blood*, pp. 204–208. Especially good are Frederick C. Bauerschmidt, *Julian of Norwich and the Mystical Body Politic of Christ*, Studies in Spirituality and Theology 5 (Notre Dame: University of Notre Dame, 1999) and Barbara Newman, *God and the Goddesses: Vision, Poetry and Belief in the Middle Ages* (Philadelphia: University of Pennsylvania Press, 2003), pp. 222–34 and 301–302.

56. On the wound as birthing talisman, see F. Lewis, "The Wound in

Christ's Side," p. 217; W. Sparrow Simpson, "On the Measure of the Wound in the Side of the Redeemer, Worn Anciently as a Charm, and on the Five Wounds as Represented in Art," *Journal of the British Archaeological Association* 30 (1874): 358; and Mary Morse, "Seeing and Hearing: Margery Kempe and the mise-en-page," *Studia Mystica* 20 (1999): 15–42. Wellcome MS 632, details of which are shown in figure 46, is such a girdle, quite worn from use. A narrow (10-cm) scroll sewn from four pieces of vellum, it features the *arma Christi*, including a large cross, and an image of the five wounds. The large and diamond-shaped side wound, which contains an IHS monogram, sheds clearly articulated blood drops. See Morse, "Seeing and Hearing," esp. figures 2 and 3. I am grateful to Mary and Stephen Morse for help with the image. On the *similia similibus* principle, see Chapter 1, n. 48.

57. It is worth noting here that not only measures of the side wound but also measures of the height of Christ were considered powerful in allaying the pains of childbirth; see Adolf Jacoby, "Heilige Längenmasse: Eine Untersuchung zur Geschichte der Amulette," *Schweizerisches Archiv für Volkskunde* 29, no. 1 (1929): 1–17, and no. 4 (1929): 181–216. This deserves more consideration than I can give it here.

58. For other examples of images abraded by fondling, see Chapter 1, nn. 57 and 58. And note that the tips of the fingers in the reliquary shown in figure 20 are quite worn from use.

59. Opposition to the *Vierge ouvrante* was to its supposedly aberrant Trinitarian theology, but it may also have reflected a worry about interest in the female body. And there were moralists and reformers in the fifteenth century who were concerned about the erotic overtones of medieval images. See Chapter 1, nn. 73, 74, and 77. For examples of the interest of theologians in the workings of female reproduction and birthing, see Maaike van der Lugt, *Le Ver, le démon et la vierge: Les Théories médiévales de la génération extraordinaire* (Paris: Les Belles Lettres, 2004), pp. 365–473; Donald Mowbray, *Pain and Suffering in Medieval Theology: Academic Debates at the University of Paris in the Thirteenth Century* (Woodbridge, UK: Boydell & Brewer, 2009), pp. 52–53; and the works cited in Chapter 4, n. 95.

60. See Jos Koldeweij, "'Shameless and Naked Images': Obscene Badges as Parodies of Popular Devotion," in Sarah Blick and Rita Tekippe (eds.), *Art and Architecture of Late Medieval Pilgrimage in Northern Europe and the British Isles*,

2 vols. (Leiden: Brill, 2005), vol. 1, pp. 493–519, and vol. 2, figures 237–56; Malcolm Jones, *The Secret Middle Ages: Discovering the Real Medieval World* (Phoenix Mill, UK: Sutton Publishing Ltd., 2002), pp. 248–73; and Ann Marie Rasmussen, *Wandering Genitalia: Sexuality and the Body in German Culture between the Late Middle Ages and Early Modernity*, King's College London Centre for Antique and Medieval Studies Occasional Publications 2 (London: King's College London Centre for Antique and Medieval Studies, 2009). Koldeweij asserts (vol. 1, p. 499) that such obscene badges "turn up in an archeological context with astonishing frequency and in mind-boggling variety," although he cites no numbers. Jones stresses (p. 249) that the badges were "mass-produced in the cheapest of materials." Most have been found in the drowned villages of the Schelde estuary.

61. Élisabeth Taburet-Delahaye et al. (eds.), *Termes et Hotel de Cluny Musée du Moyen Âge: Oeuvres nouvelles 1995–2005* (Paris: Réunion des Musées Nationaux, 2006), p. 58, figure 28. See also Madeline H. Caviness, "A Son's Gaze on Noah: Case or Cause of Viriliphobia?" in *Comportamenti e immaginario della sessualità nell'alto medioevo*, Settimane di studio della Fondazione Centro Italiano di Studi sul'Alto Medioevo 53, March 31–April 5, 2005 (Spoleto: Presso la Sede della Fondazione, 2006), pp. 981–1026, esp. figure 20. The Rotterdam badge is reproduced in Joseph Leo Koerner, "Bosch's Equipment," in Lorraine Daston (ed.), *Things That Talk: Object Lessons from Art and Science* (New York: Zone Books, 2004), figure 1.5, p. 35; in Koldeweij, "'Shameless and Naked Images'"; in Jones, *Secret Middle Ages*, p. 255, figure 12.2; and in Rasmussen, *Wandering Genitalia*, figure 10.

62. Koldeweij, "'Shameless and Naked Images,'" vol. 1, p. 504. Koldeweij has no hesitations about calling such badges "parodies," but seems to consider them as parodies of pilgrims.

63. See Rasmussen, *Wandering Genitalia*, p. 4 n. 10 for further bibliography and three Web sites devoted to badges.

64. Jones, *The Secret Middle Ages*, pp. 248–51. Jones suggests that the female exhibitionist carvings called *sheelagh-na-gigs* are the most convincing examples of genital images as apotropaic.

65. Koldeweij, "'Shameless and Naked Images,'" vol. 2, figures 253–55; also Rasmussen, *Wandering Genitalia*, figures 8, 9, and 12. On badges and medals as devotional objects, see Eli Heldaas Seland, "Nineteenth Century Devotional

Medals," in Henning Laugerud and Laura Katrine Skinnebach (eds.), *Instruments of Devotion: The Practices and Objects of Religious Piety from the Late Middle Ages to the 20th Century* (Aarhus, Denmark: Aarhus University Press, 2007), which deals with medieval badges on pp. 162–63.

66. R. Howard Bloch, *The Scandal of the Fabliaux* (Chicago: University of Chicago Press, 1986), p. 61.

67. Rasmussen, *Wandering Genitalia*.

68. *Ibid.*, p. 9.

69. The poem is "Rhythmica oratio ad unum quodlibet membrorum Christi patientis et a cruce pendentis," PL 184, cols. 1319–24; a Belgian manuscript that contains it is discussed in Areford, "Passion Measured," p. 215. See also F. Lewis, "The Wound in Christ's Side," p. 210. On the Lentulus letter, see Kurt Ruh, s.v. "Der sog. 'Lentulus Brief über Christi Gestalt,'" in Kurt Ruh et al. (eds.), *Die deutsche Literatur des Mittelalters. Verfasserlexikon*, vol. 5 (Berlin: de Gruyter, 1985), cols. 705–709.

70. See, for example, Sylvie Barnay, "Le Coeur de la Vierge Marie et l'épiphanie du sang de Dieu: Visions et apparitions mariales à coeur et à corps du Christ (XIIIe siècle)," in Marcel Faure (ed.), *Le Sang au moyen âge: Actes du quatrième colloque international de Montpellier, Université de Paul Valéry (27–29 novembre 1997)*, Les Cahiers du C.R.I.S.I.M.A. 4 (Montpellier: Université Paul Valéry, 1999), pp. 361–75. For a Welsh example, see Jane Cartwright, *Feminine Sanctity and Spirituality in Medieval Wales* (Cardiff: University of Wales Press, 2008), p. 44. It is worth noting the same trope in a Jewish poet, Solomon Simhah, talking about martyrs; see Susan Einbinder, "On the Borders of Exile: The Poetry of Solomon Simhah of Troyes," in Teodolinda Barolini (ed.), *Medieval Constructions in Gender and Identity: Essays in Honor of Joan M. Ferrante* (Tempe: Arizona Center for Medieval and Renaissance Studies, 2005), pp. 69–85.

71. Rasmussen, *Wandering Genitalia*, pp. 8–9.

72. See Einbinder, "On the Borders," p. 74. Bloch, *The Scandal of the Fabliaux*, pp. 59–64, discusses cases of "detached sexual organs circulating freely" in the fabliaux.

73. Michael Camille, *The Gothic Idol: Ideology and Image-Making in Medieval Art* (Cambridge: Cambridge University Press, 1989), pp. 322–24 and figure 173. For a rape poem that uses religious imagery, see Cartwright, *Feminine Sanctity and Spirituality*, p. 193, although it would be hard to argue that this is irony,

rather than sheer sadism and male rape fantasy. For a stunning visual parallel to fifteenth-century treatments of the wounded heart of Jesus, see the 1485 woodcut of Frau Venus wounding the hearts of her lovers in Henrik von Achen, "Piety, Practise and Process," in Laugerud and Skinnebach (eds.), *Instruments of Devotion*, p. 33, figure 3.

74. Here I agree with Rasmussen's interpretation in *Wandering Genitalia*, pp. 13 and 15–17.

75. In a brilliant analysis, Silke Tammen argues that the side wound is less a body part than a threshold or way in, analogous to a slit in Christ's garment that covers as much as it reveals, and interprets the earliest depictions of it as a mandorla shape that links Christ's humanity with his divinity; see Tammen, "Blick und Wunde—Blick und Form," p. 101. She sees the wounded heart, however, as a part standing for whole; *ibid.*, p. 112.

76. James J. Megivern, *Concomitance and Communion: A Study in Eucharistic Doctrine and Practice*, Studia Friburgensia n.s. 33 (Fribourg, Switzerland: University Press, and New York: Herder, 1963).

77. See A. Gaudel, s.v. "Stercoranisme," in DTC, vol. 14, cols. 2590–2612, and Gary Macy, *The Theologies of the Eucharist in the Early Scholastic Period: A Study of the Salvific Function of the Sacrament According to the Theologians, c. 1080 – c. 1220* (Oxford: Oxford University Press, 1984), pp. 31–35. It is difficult to find anyone who thought Christ could be literally chewed or excreted, but it is significant that charging an opponent with thinking so was an effective polemical tool.

78. Adam of Eynsham, *Magna vita sancti Hugonis: The Life of St. Hugh of Lincoln*, book 5, chapter 4, ed. Decima L. Douie and Hugh Farmer, 2 vols. (London: Thomas Nelson and Sons, 1961), vol. 2, p. 95. And see Benedicta Ward, *Miracles and the Medieval Mind: Theory, Record, and Event, 1000–1215* (Philadelphia: University of Pennsylvania Press, 1982), p. 17 n. 82.

79. Johannes von Paltz, *Supplementum Coelifodinae*, ed. Berndt Hamm, with Christoph Burger and Venicio Marcolino, in Johannes von Paltz, *Werke*, vol. 2, Spätmittelalter und Reformation Texte und Untersuchungen 3 (Berlin: Walter de Gruyter, 1983), pp. 405–407, quoting Johannes von Dorsten. For examples of bleeding-host miracles used by Bonaventure and William of Melitona to prove concomitance, see Megivern, *Concomitance*, pp. 195 and 213.

80. Gerhard of Cologne. *Tractatus de sacratissimo sanguine domini*, ed. Klaus

Berg, in "Der Traktat des Gerhard von Köln," in Kruse and Rudolf (eds.), *900 Jahre Heilig-Blut-Verehrung*, vol. 1, p. 467.

81. Thomas's treatise (from ca. 1210) is cited in Nicholas Vincent, *The Holy Blood: King Henry III and the Westminster Blood Relic* (Cambridge: Cambridge University Press, 2001), p. 85. It is worth noting that Eberhard Waltmann, the opponent of the Wilsnack miracle, argued against foreskin relics exactly because there were several of them. It is ridiculous, says Waltmann, to think God would have multiplied them; "De adoratione et contra cruorem," Wolfenbüttel H. A. B. Cod. Guelf. 630b Helmst. fol. 14r–v.

82. For the text, see Oberman, *Roots*, pp. 147–49 (the quoted passage is on p. 148) and on the event generally, see above, n. 44.

83. *Die Legende vom Ursprunge des Klosters Heiligengrabe in der Prignitz: Nach dem Drucke von 1521 neu herausgegeben und erläutert*, ed. Johannes Simon (Heiligengrabe: Museumsverein Heiligengrabe, 1928), p. [10] of facsimile; p. 23 of transcription. On Heiligengrabe, see Gerlinde Strohmaier-Wiederanders, *Geschichte vom Kloster Stift Heiligengrabe* (Berlin: Nicolai, 1995).

84. H. Finke, "Zur Geschichte der holsteinischen Klöster im 15. und 16. Jahrhundert," *Zeitschrift der Gesellschaft für Schleswig-Holstein-Lauenburgische Geschichte* 13 (1883): 169; Donald L. Ehresmann, "The Iconography of the Cismar Altarpiece and the Role of Relics in an Early Winged Altarpiece," *Zeitschrift für Kunstgeschichte* 64 (2001): 29–30.

85. Manfred Eder, *"Die Deggendorfer Gnad": Entstehung und Entwicklung einer Hostienwallfahrt im Kontext von Theologie und Geschichte*, Deggendorf Archäologie und Stadtgeschichte 3 (Deggendorf/Passau: Passavia-Univ.-Verlag, 1992).

86. For the decrees of Eugene IV and Nicholas V, see Adolph Friedrich Riedel (ed.), *Codex diplomaticus Brandenburgensis: Sammlung der Urkunden, Chroniken und sonstigen Quellenschriften für die Geschichte der Mark Brandenburg und ihrer Regenten*, 41 vols. in 32 (Berlin: Morin, 1838–69), A2, docs. 13–15, pp. 149–52.

87. Modern students of magic and folk practices, such as James George Frazer and Michel Mauss, see the tendency to treat part as standing for whole as a basic principle of the magical way of viewing the universe. For a discussion of this, see Wilson, *The Magical Universe*, pp. xxiv–xxix. Such quasi-universal tendencies may stand behind some of what interests me in this book, but I am more concerned with the specific attitudes and practices of the later Middle

Ages. For cross-cultural comparisons, see Chapter 1, n. 59; Chapter 2, nn. 144 and 145; and Conclusion, n. 16, all of which make it clear that there are profound differences as well as parallels, not only in theory but also in practice, between religions that have a sense of self- multiplying and presence-carrying holy matter.

In ways too complex to explain fully here, concomitance or synecdoche was also the typical medieval Christian way of understanding redemption. The death of one man on the cross and his subsequent resurrection atoned to God for the debt of all sinners and assimilated humankind to that return to life, because all *humanitas* was subsumed first in Adam, who fell, and then in Christ, who, sinless, died and rose again. Unless one can be all, part can be whole, and instances can be subsumed in exemplar, it is hard to explain the idea of the Atonement of all through one, even if the one is also God. See Stephen T. Davis, Daniel Kendall, and Gerald O'Collins (eds.), *The Redemption: An Interdisciplinary Symposium on Christ as Redeemer* (Oxford: Oxford University Press, 2004) and much relevant discussion in Bauerschmidt, *Julian of Norwich*.

88. For an example of a material miracle that not only stills decay but also generates new matter, see the case of the manna at Agnes of Montepulciano's tomb, Chapter 2, n. 45. It seems entirely appropriate therefore that among the earliest miracles performed by the Wilsnack hosts (themselves manifestations of life in consecrated bread) were several resurrections of the dead. Resurrections are not just healing miracles of a particularly intense kind; they are a kind of regeneration. See Bynum, *Wonderful Blood*, pp. 26 and 137.

89. Over the centuries, the Catholic Church has dealt with this problem by replacing supposedly miraculous hosts with newly consecrated ones. The action is theologically acceptable because, according to the doctrine of transubstantiation, Christ is present in any consecrated host. Nonetheless, the faithful sometimes thought they were revering the original miraculous host even after new ones had been repeatedly substituted. For an exploration of the problems this has raised, see the fine study of the Deggendorf pilgrimage, Eder, *"Die Deggendorfer Gnad."*

90. See Carlin Barton, writing about a different period: "An Emotional Economy of Sacrifice and Execution in Ancient Rome," *Historical Reflections/Reflexions historiques* 29, no. 2 (2003): 341–60.

CHAPTER FOUR: MATTER AND MIRACLES

1. Here I agree with Edward Grant, *God and Reason in the Middle Ages* (Cambridge: Cambridge University Press, 2001). For debate about how far the study of nature was simply analogous to the "science" of today and how far it was a consequence of theological exploration, see Joseph Ziegler, "Faith and the Intellectuals: I," in Miri Rubin and Walter Simons (eds.), *The Cambridge History of Christianity*, vol. 4, *Christianity in Western Europe c. 1100 – c. 1500* (Cambridge: Cambridge University Press, 2009), pp. 376–77. For discussion of how far thinkers in this period were free to engage in speculation—a question I do not directly engage—see J. M. M. H. Thijssen, *Censure and Heresy at the University of Paris 1200–1400* (Philadelphia: University of Pennsylvania Press, 1998), and Luca Bianchi, *Censure et liberté intellectuelle à l'université de Paris (XIIIe–XIVe siècles)* (Paris: Les Belles Lettres, 1999).

2. Events that could fairly easily have been naturalistically explained (such as a fire or cloud formations) were sometimes taken as omens or prodigies—especially in historical writing. Thus, under certain genre, or narrative, or life circumstances, a supernatural gloss was preferred. Such glosses sometimes coexisted with natural explanations.

3. In the early thirteenth century, some writers drew a technical distinction between marvels and magic on the one hand, and miracles, on the other; only miracles were per se beyond natural explanation. By the middle of the same century, theologians added the category of "*praeter*-natural" events, which may have natural explanations but are still a cause of wonder. See Ziegler, "Faith and the Intellectuals," p. 381, and this Chapter, p. 230 and nn. 30 and 47.

4. See Chapter 3, n. 6, for reference to the full citation.

5. In *The Resurrection of the Body in Western Christianity, 200–1336* (New York: Columbia University Press, 1995), what I stressed about this passage was the understanding of person displayed here. To Peter, the saint is neither soul nor body alone but rather both. Person is a psychosomatic unity. What I stress here is the consequence of this for the conceptualization of matter, which rests in the grave or the reliquary yet is in some sense already alive in anticipation of future glory. Compare *The Resurrection of the Body*, pp. 176–80. For a similar slippage between living saint and saintly bones, see the passage from Thiofrid of Echternach quoted in Chapter 3 at n. 29.

6. By the time full-fledged Renaissance Neoplatonism developed, many

philosophers saw the entire universe as alive. Not only did the cosmos have an *anima mundi*, but each region and celestial body had its attendant soul as well. Opponents of such views often saw them as conducive to demonology. See Brian Copenhaver, *Symphorien Champier and the Reception of the Occultist Tradition in Renaissance France* (The Hague: Mouton, 1978), p. 176, and this Chapter at n. 68 for Ficino.

7. Nicole Oresme, *Le Livre du ciel et du monde*, book 2, chapter 5, ed. Albert D. Menut and Alexander J. Denomy, trans. Albert D. Menut (Madison: University of Wisconsin Press, 1968), p. 319.

8. *Ibid.*, book 1, chapter 6, p. 83.

9. Zoe Bosemberg, "Nicole Oresme et Robert Grosseteste: La Conception dynamique de la matière," in Stefano Caroti and Jean Celeyrette (eds.), *Quia inter doctores est magna dissensio: Les Débats de philosophie naturelle à Paris au* XIVe *siècle* (Florence: Leo S. Olschki, 2004), pp. 119–33.

10. Nicole Oresme, *Nicole Oresme and the Medieval Geometry of Qualities and Motions: A Treatise on the Uniformity and Difformity of Intensities Known as Tractatus de configurationibus qualitatum et motuum*, book 1, chapter 25, and book 2, chapter 32, ed. and trans. Marshall Clagett (Madison: University of Wisconsin Press, 1968), pp. 236–38 and 361, respectively.

11. Eberhard Waltmann, "De adoratione et contra cruorem," Wolfenbüttel H. A. B. Cod. Guelf. 630b Helmst., fols. 14r–23v; also in Wolfenbüttel H. A. B. Cod. Guelf. 153 Helmst., fols. 280r–286r.

12. Waltmann, "De adoratione et contra cruorem," Wolfenbüttel H. A. B. Cod. Guelf. 630b Helmst., fols. 14v–17v and 19r.

13. It was an alternative version of Gregory's vision that was depicted on the Ihlower/Aurich altarpiece I discussed in Chapter 1, and it is important to note that the iconographical motif of the Gregory Mass (in the alternative version) was extraordinarily widespread in the art of the fifteenth-century North. See Chapter 1, nn. 60–62. And see Chapter 2, n. 57, for Guitmond of Aversa's similar stress on the reconversion of the miraculous stuff.

14. See Denise Bouthillier and Jean-Pierre Torrell, "'Miraculum': Une Catégorie fondamentale chez Pierre le Vénérable," *Revue thomiste: Revue doctrinale de théologie et de philosophie* 80 (1980): 357–86, and Dominique Iogna-Prat, *Order and Exclusion: Cluny and Christendom Face Heresy, Judaism and Islam (1000–1150)*, trans. Graham Robert Edward (Ithaca, NY: Cornell University

Press, 2002), pp. 102–104 and 207–208.

15. See n. 91 below. Oresme's position is somewhat inconsistent from work to work, and modern historians have differed on how far he moves toward entirely naturalistic explanation. See Lynn Thorndike, *A History of Magic and Experimental Science*, History of Science Society Publications, new series 4, vol. 3 (New York: Columbia University Press, 1934), chapters 25–27, pp. 398–471; Clagett, "Introduction," in *Nicole Oresme and the Medieval Geometry of Qualities*, pp. 40–44 and passim; and Bert Hansen, "Introduction," in Bert Hansen (ed.), *Nicole Oresme and the Marvels of Nature: A Study of His De causis mirabilium* (Toronto: The Pontifical Institute of Mediaeval Studies, 1985), pp. 50–73. Oresme (like William of Auvergne and the author of the pseudo-Albertine *Liber de mirabilibus mundi*) did think most events have natural causes; see Nicole Oresme, *De causis*, chapter 1, in Hansen (ed.), *Nicole Oresme and the Marvels of Nature*, pp. 160–63, 51 n. 3, and 61 n. 36.

16. Oresme, *Le Livre du ciel*, book 1, chapter 7, p. 86; book 2, chapter 8, pp. 363–73; book 2, chapter 25, pp. 521–37. Oresme says God stopped the sun for Joshua and allowed it to return under Hezekiah (Isa. 38:8). He also performed a miraculous eclipse at the time of Christ's crucifixion (Luke 28:45). It is important to note that Oresme felt constrained to reject the more philosophically acceptable explanation of the Joshua miracle because the Bible says otherwise.

17. John of Sacrobosco (d. 1256) also argued that the eclipse at the time of the Passion had to be miraculous. As proof, he gives the naturalistic argument that it is "contrary to nature" to have a solar eclipse at the full moon and reports that Dionysius the Areopagite said at the time: "Either the God of nature suffers or the mechanism of the universe is dissolved." The implication of the latter remark is clearly that the universe has rules, established by its God—rules that would be broken only in the truly exceptional case where that God himself suffers. On John, see Edward Grant (ed.), *A Source Book in Medieval Science* (Cambridge, MA: Harvard University Press, 1974), pp. 451–52.

18. Several scholars have recently been interested in medieval skepticism and doubt—a topic that was earlier more or less ignored. See Gavin Langmuir, "The Tortures of the Body of Christ," in Scott Waugh and Peter Diehl (eds.), *Christendom and Its Discontents: Exclusion, Persecution, and Rebellion, 1000–1500* (Cambridge: Cambridge University Press, 1996), pp. 287–309; and André Vauchez, "Les Images saints," in *Saints, prophètes et visionnaires: Le Pouvoir*

surnaturel au moyen âge (Paris: Albin Michel, 1999), pp. 79–91. Martha Newman of the University of Texas, Karl Shoemaker of the University of Wisconsin, and Kevin Madigan of the Harvard Divinity School are all at work on aspects of the topic of religious doubt. On unbelief generally, see the important new study by Peter Dinzelbacher, *Unglaube im "Zeitalter des Glaubens": Atheismus und Skeptizismus im Mittelalter* (Badenweiler: Bachmann, 2009). Given the nature of the surviving evidence, it is not possible to say how many questioned or felt anger, repugnance, or anxiety over holy objects and material miracles. On this point, see Robert N. Swanson, *Religion and Devotion in Europe, c. 1215–c. 1515* (Cambridge: Cambridge University Press, 1995), pp. 329–40.

19. See, for example, the story of the dying student who wants to be persuaded of personal resurrection by rational argument: Alexander Neckam, *De naturis rerum*, book 2, chapter 73, Rerum Britannicarum medii aevi scriptores 34 (London: Longman, Green, 1863), p. 297. For Walter Map's spoof of resurrection claims, see Walter Map, *De nugis curialium: Courtier's Trifles*, distinction 1, chapter 24, ed. and trans. M. R. James, revised by C. N. L. Brooke and R. A. B. Mynors (Oxford: Oxford University Press, 1983), p. 80. For doubts about the Wilsnack miracles, see Ernst Breest, *Das Wilsnacker Wunderblut*, Für die Feste und Freunde des Gustav-Adolf-Vereins 77 (Barmen: Hugo Klein, 1888), pp. 3–27. For an attack on the credibility of claims for the Wilsnack hosts themselves, see Heinrich Tocke, "Synodalrede," trans. Ernst Breest, in "Synodalrede des Domherrn Dr. Heinrich Tocke von Magdeburg... Nach einem Manuscripte der herzoglichen Behörden-Bibliothek zu Dessau," *Blätter für Handel, Gewerbe und sociales Leben (Beiblatt zur Magdeburgischen Zeitung)* 23 (Monday, June 5, 1882): 167–68, 174–76, 177–80.

20. See Chapter 1, n. 96.

21. Steven Justice, "Did the Middle Ages Believe in Their Miracles?" *Representations* 103 (Summer 2008): 1–30.

22. *Ibid.*, p. 7.

23. See Robert Bartlett, *England Under the Norman and Angevin Kings, 1075–1225* (Oxford: Oxford University Press, 2000), p. 478. For a similar description of doubters given by Gervase of Tilbury, see Carl S. Watkins, *History and the Supernatural in Medieval England* (Cambridge: Cambridge University Press, 2007), p. 219. For further examples of canonization and inquisition documents and confessors' manuals that contain much evidence of doubts about miracles,

see Justice, "Did the Middle Ages Believe in Their Miracles ?", pp. 29–30 and n. 70.

24. Walter Stephens, *Demon Lovers: Witchcraft, Sex, and the Crisis of Belief* (Chicago: University of Chicago Press, 2002), pp. 27, 84–88, 100–101, 366, and passim.

25. Giles of Rome, "Theoremata de corpore Christi," *Opera exegetica: Opuscula I* (1554–55; reprint, Frankfurt: Minerva, 1968), proposition 23, fol. 14v.

26. Peter Dronke, *Women Writers of the Middle Ages: A Critical Study of Texts from Perpetua (+203) to Marguerite Porete (+1310)* (Cambridge: Cambridge University Press, 1984), p. 214. Aude's obsession with the host as a woman's placenta arose in the context of a spirituality that laid graphic emphasis on the consecrated wafer as a product of—an exuding of—the female womb.

27. On Johannes Bremer, see Chapter 2, pp. 165–67. Examples of cases in which popular ideas and practices seem to have influenced or constrained ideas include Thomas Aquinas's insistence that relics were still the bodies of the saints once the soul had departed (see Bynum, *The Resurrection of the Body*, pp. 270–71); Henry of Ghent's discussion of the Paris host-desecration miracle of 1290 (see Elsa Marmursztejn, "Du Récit exemplaire au *casus* universitaire: Une Variation théologique sur le thème de la profanation d'hosties par les juifs [1290]," in *La Rouelle et la croix destins des juifs d'Occident*, coordinated by Dominique Iogna-Prat and Danièle Sansy, *Médiévales* 41 [Autumn 2001]: 37–38); and quodlibetal discussions of the bleeding of cadavers and of relics from circa 1300 (see Alain Boureau, *Théologie, science et censure au XIIIe siècle: Le Cas de Jean Peckham* [Paris: Belles Lettres, 1999], pp. 5, 110–11 and 245–87). For examples of cases where theologians censured their ideas about physiological processes for reasons of theology or even of taste, see Maaike van der Lugt on Bonaventure's discussion of the conception of Christ by Mary and Mark Jordan on Albert the Great's discussion of sodomy: Maaike Van der Lugt, *Le Ver, le démon et la vierge: Les Théories médiévales de la génération extraordinaire* (Paris: Les Belles Lettres, 2004), pp. 421–23; Mark Jordan, *The Invention of Sodomy in Christian Theology* (Chicago: University of Chicago Press, 1998), pp. 114–35. See also Ziegler, "Faith and the Intellectuals," p. 382.

28. Nile Green, "Ostrich Eggs and Peacock Feathers: Sacred Objects as Cultural Exchange between Christianity and Islam," *Al-Masāq* 18, no. 1 (2006): 65–66.

29. It should thus be clear that I am not arguing that the ideas of intellectuals are the interpretive lens through which we should view a period—an approach that sometimes leads its practitioners merely to paraphrase their sources. For better or worse, my approach here, as in everything I write, is to probe behind articulated arguments for assumptions of which their authors were not aware and that they did not make overt. My success (if any) in finding such assumptions is inevitably influenced and facilitated by reading contemporary theoretical discussions, such as those of materiality and agency that I discuss in the Introduction and Chapter 1 above. But I have not adopted explicitly any theory currently available, in large part because no current theory fully accounts for the role of holy objects in medieval Christianity—from animated statues and relics, to scientized theories of miracle, to the insistent materiality of devotional objects.

30. On miracles generally, see Benedicta Ward, *Miracles and the Medieval Mind: Theory, Record, and Event, 1000–1215* (Philadelphia: University of Pennsylvania Press, 1982); John Hardon, "The Concept of Miracle from St. Augustine to Modern Apologetics," *Theological Studies* 15 (1954): 229–57; Bernhard Bron, *Das Wunder: Das theologische Wunderverständnis im Horizont des neuzeitlichen Natur- und Geschichtsbegriffs* (Göttingen: Vandenhoeck & Ruprecht, 1975); Lorraine Daston, "Marvelous Facts and Miraculous Evidence in Early Modern Europe," *Critical Inquiry* 18 (1991): 93–124; and Robert Bartlett, *The Natural and the Supernatural in the Middle Ages: The Wiles Lectures Given at the Queen's University of Belfast, 2006* (Cambridge: Cambridge University Press, 2008), esp. chapter 1. Writing in the early thirteenth century, Caesarius of Heisterbach gave the classic definition of "miracle" in his *Dialogus miraculorum*, distinction 10, chapter 1, ed. Joseph Strange, 2 vols. (Cologne: Heberle, 1851), vol. 2, p. 217: "We call a miracle whatever is done contrary to the usual course of nature [*contra solitum cursum naturae*]." The categorization of miracles used in the later Middle Ages went back to Thomas Aquinas (d. 1274), who distinguished miracles *supra*, *contra*, and *praeter naturam*; those *supra* cannot be produced by nature (for example, the resurrection or glorification of the body); those *contra* are opposed to a disposition of nature (for example, fire not burning); those *praeter* can be produced by nature, but God does them in a way nature does not (for example, the multiplication of bread or the instantaneous healing of the sick). Aquinas, *De potentia Dei*, question 6, article 2, *ra* 3, in *S. Thomae Aquinatis*

opera omnia, ed. Roberto Busa, 7 vols. (Stuttgart–Bad Cannstatt: Frommann-Holzboog, 1980), vol. 3, p. 232 col. 1. The distinction occurs again, stated slightly differently, in *idem*, *Summa contra Gentiles*, book 3, part 2, chapters 101–102, in Busa (ed.), *Opera omnia*, vol. 2, p. 94. Although Aquinas stresses that a miracle is a matter of response, pointing out that the word "miracle" comes from "what is of itself filled with admirable wonder," it is important to note that for him, all three categories of miraculous events are done by God "without the operation of the principles of nature."

31. Ward, *Miracles and the Medieval Mind*, chapter 3, pp. 33–66. For discussion of the incidence of miracles in later medieval hagiographical accounts and canonization processes, see Chapter 2, n. 12 above.

32. Sean L. Field, *Isabelle of France: Capetian Sanctity and Franciscan Identity in the Thirteenth Century* (Notre Dame, IN: University of Notre Dame Press, 2006), p. 135.

33. See Chapter 3, nn. 1 and 24.

34. See Caroline Walker Bynum, *Metamorphosis and Identity* (New York: Zone Books, 2001), pp. 89–92.

35. There was much scholastic discussion of whether demons can use or change bodies. For examples from Caesarius of Heisterbach and Thomas Aquinas, see Bynum, *Metamorphosis and Identity*, pp. 102–104. On Aquinas's treatment in the *De malo* of whether demons can change substantial forms or move material objects, see Alain Boureau, "Demons and the Christian Community," in Rubin and Simons (eds.), *The Cambridge History of Christianity*, j385vol. 4, pp. 425–26.

36. Peter the Venerable, *Adversos Iudeorum inveteratam duritiem*, chapter 4, ed. Yvonne Friedman, Corpus christianorum: Continuatio mediaevalis 58 (Turnhout: Brepols, 1985), pp. 106–18; *idem*, *Contra Petrobrusianos haereticos*, PL 189, cols. 802–803; and Bouthillier and Torrell, "'Miraculum,'" pp. 363–65. Thomas Aquinas argued, a century later, that Pharaoh's magicians did magic, but Aaron effected the same transformation by miracle. Thomas Aquinas, *Summa theologiae*, part 1, question 114, article 4, in Busa (ed.), *Opera omnia*, vol. 2, pp. 347–48; *ibid.*, part 3 [part 2 of part 2], question 178, articles 1 and 2, in vol. 2, pp. 741–42; *Summa contra Gentiles*, book 3, chapter 104, in Busa (ed.), *Opera omnia*, vol. 2, p. 95; *De potentia Dei*, question 6, article 5, *ra* 8, in Busa (ed.), *Opera omnia*, vol. 3, pp. 234–35.

37. Albertus Magnus, *Summa theologiae*, part 2, tractate 8, question 32, *membrum* 2, in S.C.A. Borgnet (ed.), *Opera omnia*, vols. 31–33 (Paris: Vives, 1895), vol. 32, p. 360.

38. Thomas Aquinas, *Summa theologiae*, part 1, question 114, article 4, objection 2, in Busa (ed.), *Opera omnia*, vol. 2, p. 347. Lorraine Daston points out that "within Christianity, miracles were almost always worked in things." Lorraine Daston, "Introduction: Speechless," in Lorraine Daston (ed.), *Things That Talk: Object Lessons from Art and Science* (New York: Zone Books, 2004), p. 13.

39. Nicholas of Autrecourt, *The Universal Treatise of Nicholas of Autrecourt*, trans. Leonard A. Kennedy et al. (Milwaukee: Marquette University Press, 1971), p. 141. Autrecourt explains elsewhere (pp. 101–102) that "I" might be understood to exist eternally in the sense that my atoms perdure, sometimes dispersed and sometimes recombined; this is hardly the Christian idea of resurrection.

40. Theologians held resurrection to be a miracle, arguing that if God can create, he can certainly recreate. See Bynum, *The Resurrection of the Body*, pp. 43, 133–35, 233–35, 246, 248, and passim. There were, however, approaches to resurrection that almost made it naturalistic; see, for example, Roger Bacon, *Opus majus*, part 6, and part 1 of part 7, in *The Opus Majus of Roger Bacon*, trans. R.B. Burke, 2 vols. (Philadelphia: University of Pennsylvania Press, 1928), vol. 2, pp. 617–25, and vol. 2, p. 651, respectively.

41. Nicole Oresme, *Nicole Oresme and the Medieval Geometry of Qualities... Tractatus de configurationibus*, book 2, chapter 38, ed. Clagett, pp. 381–85.

42. Alain Boureau, "Miracle, volonté et imagination: La Mutation scolastique (1270–1320)," in *Miracles, prodiges et merveilles au moyen âge*, XXVe Congrès de la S.H.M.E.S., Orléans, juin 1994, Société des historiens médiévistes de l'enseignement supérieur publique, série histoire ancienne et médiévale 34 (Paris: Publications de la Sorbonne, 1995), pp. 159–72.

43. See above, Chapter 2, pp. 147–48 and pp. 160–62.

44. See Alan C. Kors and Edward Peters (eds.), *Witchcraft in Europe, 400–1700: A Documentary History*, 2nd ed. (Philadelphia: University of Pennsylvania Press, 2001); Steven P. Marrone, "Magic, Bodies, University Masters, and the Invention of the Late Medieval Witch," in Rachel Fulton and Bruce Holsinger (eds.), *History in the Comic Mode: Medieval Communities and the Matter*

of Person (New York: Columbia University Press, 2007), pp. 262–78; Bartlett, *Natural and Supernatural*, pp. 79–91; and Stephens, *Demon Lovers*, esp. pp. 125 and 134–37. For similar ideas about demons, see Boureau, "Demons and the Christian Community."

45. Jean Gerson, "On Distinguishing True From False Revelations," in *Jean Gerson: Early Works*, trans. Brian Patrick McGuire (New York: Paulist Press, 1998), p. 350. McGuire notes that there does not seem to be any such claim in the Life of Bernard; see *ibid.*, p. 458 n. 38. Gerson worried obsessively about the possibility that the vulnerable, especially women, might mistake delusions for revelations; see Dyan Elliott, "Seeing Double: John Gerson, the Discernment of Spirits and Joan of Arc," *American Historical Review* 197, no. 1 (2002): 26–54.

46. On vision theory, see Suzannah Biernoff, *Sight and Embodiment in the Middle Ages* (New York: Palgrave Macmillan, 2002), pp. 63–107, and Robert W. Scribner, "Popular Piety and Modes of Visual Perception in Late-Medieval and Reformation Germany," *The Journal of Religious History* 15 (1989): 463–65.

47. See Ward, *Miracles and the Medieval Mind*, pp. 4–10; Jacques Le Goff, "Preface," in Gervase of Tilbury, *Le Livre des merveilles: Divertissement pour un empereur (troisième partie)*, trans. Annie Duchesne (Paris: Les Belles Lettres, 1992), pp. ix–xvi; Bynum, *Metamorphosis and Identity*, pp. 53–68; Vauchez, "Les Images saints," in *Saints, prophètes et visionnaires*; Joel Kaye, "Law, Magic, and Science: Constructing a Border between Licit and Illicit Knowledge in the Writings of Nicole Oresme," in Ruth Mazzo Karras, Joel Kaye, and E. Ann Matter (eds.), *Law and the Illicit in Medieval Europe* (Philadelphia: University of Pennsylvania Press, 2008), pp. 225–37; Ziegler, "Faith and the Intellectuals"; and see nn. 3 and 30 above.

48. Ernan McMullin (ed.), *The Concept of Matter in Greek and Medieval Philosophy* (Notre Dame: University of Notre Dame Press, 1963); *idem*, "Introduction," in Ernan McMullin (ed.), *The Concept of Matter in Modern Philosophy*, 2nd ed. (Notre Dame: University of Notre Dame Press, 1978), pp. 1–55; and *idem*, s.v. "Matter, Philosophy of," *New Catholic Encyclopedia*, 2nd ed., vol. 9 (Washington, D.C.: Thomson-Gale and Catholic University of America, 2003), pp. 339–44. See also Max Jammer and Christian Schwarke, s.v. "Materie," in Hans Dieter Betz et al. (eds.), *Religion in Geschichte und Gegenwart*, 4th ed., vol. 5 (Tübingen: Mohr Siebeck, 2002), col. 907–11; M. Moser and H. Dolch, s.v. "Materie," *Lexikon für Theologie und Kirche*, vol. 7 (Freiburg: Herder, 1962),

cols. 163–65; s.v. "Matière," in Christian Godin, *Dictionnaire de philosophie* (Paris: Fayard, 2004), pp. 772–74, and Jean-Marc Lévy-Leblond, s.v. "Matière," in Dominique Lecourt (ed.), *Dictionnaire d'histoire et philosophie des sciences* (Paris: Presses universitaires de France, 1999), pp. 619–23. Most of the encyclopedia articles make a clear division between "matter" as a scientific category and "matter" as a philosophical concept.

49. Even the Thomists, for whom prime matter is pure potency, have an understanding of the secondary matter of objects as carrying characteristics.

50. McMullin, "Introduction," in McMullin (ed.), *The Concept of Matter in Modern Philosophy*; Stephen Toulmin and June Goodfield, *The Architecture of Matter*, The Ancestry of Science 2 (London: Hutchinson, 1962); Bernhard Pabst, *Atomtheorien des lateinischen Mittelalters* (Darmstadt: Wissenschaftliche Buchgesellschaft, 1994); Andrew Pyle, *Atomism and Its Critics: Problem Areas Associated with the Development of the Atomic Theory of Matter from Democritus to Newton* (Bristol: Thoemmes Press, 1995). A recent and very welcome new direction is the project "Structure de la matière animée face au monde inanimé: Histoire d'un savior scientifique et de ses enjeux intellectuals et sociaux Occident, XIIe–XVe siècles" under the direction of Nicolas Weill-Parot at CNRS, Paris, for which see Karine Chemla (ed.), with the help of Mireille Delbraccio, "Action Concertée 'Histoire des savoirs' 2003–2007: Recueil de synthèses, 2007," available on-line at: http://www.cnrs.fr/prg/PIR/programmes-termines/histsavoirs/synth2003-2007Histoiredessavoirs.pdf (CNRS, 2007), last accessed April 20, 2010. This material came to my attention only in the last stages of writing this book.

51. Pyle's discussion of Aristotle makes this clear: see Pyle, *Atomism and Its Critics*, pp. 110–19. And see the passage from Niccolò Tignosi da Foligno discussed in this Chapter at nn. 71–72.

52. Isidore of Seville, *Isidori Hispalensis episcopi Etymologiarvm sive originvm libri xx*, book 19, section 19.3–5, ed. W.M. Lindsay, 2 vols. (Oxford: Oxford University Press, 1911), vol. 2 [pp. 321–22]. And for background, see Robert Maltby, *A Lexicon of Ancient Latin Etymologies* (Leeds: Francis Cairns, 1991), p. 371. On medieval etymology, see Roswitha Klinck, *Die lateinische Etymologie des Mittelalters* (Munich: Wilhelm Fink, 1970). It is important to note that such etymological analysis is not based on arguments concerning the historical or philological derivation of words, but rather on the assumption that to unpack

their components (even down to the individual letters) is to unpack the nature of that to which they refer.

53. For "materia quasi mater dicit," see Isidore, *Etymologiarvm . . . libri*, book 19, section 19.5, vol. 2 [p. 321]; for *corpus* and *caro*, see *ibid*., book 11, section 1.14–18, vol. 2 [p. 3].

54. Many recent books speak of "bodies" as desiring, or gendered, or disabled, where medieval thinkers would speak of "persons." See my Introduction, nn. 46–48. In medieval discussions, "body" tends to mean "thing."

55. Giles of Rome, *B. Aegidii Columnae Romani . . . Quodlibeta revisa, correcta, et varie illustrata, studio M. F. Petri de Coninck* (Louvain, 1646), pp. 147–49, cited in William R. Newman, "Introduction: Alchemical Debate in the Thirteenth Century: The Defense of Art," in William R. Newman (ed.), *The Summa perfectionis of Pseudo-Geber: A Critical Edition, Translation and Study*, Collection de travaux de l'Académie Internationale d'Histoire des Science 35 (Leiden: Brill, 1991), pp. 32–34.

56. It is important to note that alchemists referred to such things as "bodies." For an example, see the opening pages of Constantine of Pisa's "Book of the Secrets of Alchemy" in Barbara Obrist (ed.), *Constantine of Pisa: The Book of the Secrets of Alchemy: Introduction, Critical Edition, Translation and Commentary*, Collection de travaux de l'Académie Internationale d'Histoire des Sciences 34 (Leiden: Brill, 1990), pp. 65–71. Oresme called the impact of a woman's glance on a mirror the impact of body on body; see n. 41 above.

57. Report, "Corps célestes et corps humain: L'Exemple de Pietro d'Abano," in Weill-Parot, director, "Structure de la matière animée," in Chemla (ed.), "Action Concertée 'Histoire des Savoirs' 2003–2007," p. 23, reporting on the work especially of Chiara Crisciani. And see Chiara Crisciani, *Il Papa e l'alchimia: Felice V, Guglielmo Fabri e l'elixir* (Rome: Viella, 2002). On changing attitudes toward alchemy between the twelfth and fourteenth centuries, see p. 251 and n. 105 in this chapter.

58. Ovid, *Metamorphoses*, 2 vols., 3rd ed., trans. F. J. Miller, revised by G. P. Goold, Loeb Classical Library 42–43 (Cambridge, MA: Harvard University Press, 1977). See esp. books 1 and 15; quoted lines 1–2 from book 1, p. 3. Aristotle, *On Sophistical Refutations; On Coming-To-Be and Passing Away; On the Cosmos*, trans. E. S. Forster and D. J. Furley, Loeb Classical Library 400 (Cambridge, MA: Harvard University Press, 1978). Although as Stefano Caroti

points out, the *On Generation and Corruption* did not have as great a success in the West as Aristotle's *Physics* and *De caelo*, it was nonetheless important, and in the second quarter of the fourteenth century, it received significant new attention. See Nicole Oresme, *Quaestiones super De generatione et corruptione*, ed. Stefano Caroti, Bayerische Akademie der Wissenschaften: Veröffentlichungen der Kommission für die Herausgabe ungedruckter Texte aus der mittelalterlichen Geisteswelt 20 (Munich: Beck, 1996), pp. 58*–59*.

59. Bernard Sylvestris, *The "Cosmographia" of Bernardus Sylvestris: A Translation with Introduction and Notes*, trans. Winthrop Wetherbee (New York: Columbia University Press, 1973). See also Brian Stock, *Myth and Science in the Twelfth Century: A Study of Bernard Silvester* (Princeton, NJ: Princeton University Press, 1972), pp. 14, 78–161, 187–92, 231–34.

60. Bernard Sylvestris, *The "Cosmographia,"* book 2, chapters 8 and 14, trans. Wetherbee, pp. 109–10 and 126.

61. See Simone Viarre, *La Survie d'Ovide dans la littérature scientifique des XIIe et XIIIe siècles* (Poitiers: Centre d'Études Supérieures de Civilisation Médiévale, 1966), and, on the Ovid revival generally, see Marilynn R. Desmond (ed.), *Mediaevalia: A Journal of Medieval Studies* 13 (1989, for 1987): *Ovid in Medieval Culture: A Special Issue.*

62. For examples of this reading of Ovid by commentators, see Bynum, *Metamorphosis and Identity*, pp. 228–29 n. 43.

63. This is why eternity is so hard for us to grasp, says Oresme. *Le Livre du ciel*, book 1, chapter 24, p. 177.

64. Oresme, *Quaestiones super De generatione et corruptione*, book 2, chapter 15, ed. Caroti, p. 295.

65. Bosemberg, "Nicole Oresme et Robert Grosseteste."

66. Report, "Synthèse: Matière animée/matière inanimée au moyen âge," in Weill-Parot, director, "Structure de la matière animée," in Chemla (ed.), "Action Concertée 'Histoire des Savoirs' 2003–2007," summarizing the analysis of Christof Lüthy.

67. *Ibid.*, p. 24, reporting on the work especially of Anna Rodolfi. On the desire of matter/body in Bonaventure, see Bynum, *The Resurrection of the Body*, pp. 247–55.

68. Report, "Synthèse: Matière animée/matière inanimée au moyen âge," in Weill-Parot, director, "Structure de la matière animée," in Chemla (ed.),

"Action Concertée 'Histoire des Savoirs' 2003–2007," p. 24, summarizing the work of Jean-Marc Mandosio. And see n. 105 below on the change in alchemical thinking from twelfth-century disbelief in the possibility of transmutation to later acceptance.

69. On the fusing of astrology and natural philosophical speculation about the world in the late fourteenth- and early fifteenth-century thinker Pierre d'Ailly, see Laura Ackerman Smoller, *History, Prophecy, and the Stars: The Christian Astrology of Pierre d'Ailly, 1350–1420* (Princeton, NJ: Princeton University Press, 1994). D'Ailly understood astrology as the search for general patterns in earthly events. We see something of the same fusion of the religious, prophetic, and alchemical in John of Rupiscissa. See Leah Devun, *Prophecy, Alchemy, and the End of Time: John of Rupescissa in the Late Middle Ages* (New York: Columbia University Press, 2009). On natural-philosophical thought in the area of astrology generally, see Nicolas Weill-Parot, *Les 'Images astrologiques' au moyen âge et à la renaissance: Spéculations intellectuelles et pratiques magiques (XIIe–XVe siècle)* (Paris: Honoré Champion, 2002).

70. Lynn Thorndike, *Science and Thought in the Fifteenth Century: Studies in the History of Medicine and Surgery, Natural and Mathematical Science, Philosophy, and Politics* (New York: Columbia University Press, 1929), pp. 175–76. According to Thorndike, it is not certain that both treatises are by Niccolò. What recent scholarship there is concerning him is devoted mostly to his commentary on Aristotle's *Nicomachean Ethics*. For general bibliography, see James Hankins, *Plato in the Renaissance*, 2 vols. (Leiden: Brill, 1990), p. 271 n. 14, and David A. Lines, *Aristotle's Ethics in the Italian Renaissance (ca. 1300–1650): The Universities and the Problem of Moral Education* (Leiden: Brill, 2002), pp. 490–91. According to Arthur Field, in *The Origins of the Platonic Academy of Florence* (Princeton, NJ: Princeton University Press, 1988), p. 141 n. 48, the treatise on Platonic Ideas is from about 1470. Field seems to accept Thorndike's attribution, as do Mario Sensi and Lines; see Mario Sensi, "Niccolò da Foligno: L'opere e il pensiero," *Annali della Facoltà di Lettere e Filosofia, Università degli studi di Perugia* 9 (1971–72 [1973]): 404 and passim, and David Lines, "'Faciliter edoceri': Niccolò Tignosi and the Audience of Aristotle's 'Ethics' in Fifteenth-Century Florence," *Studi Medievali* 40, no. 1 (1999): 163 n. 79. It used to be claimed that Tignosi was Ficino's teacher, but Lines doubts this; see Lines, "'Faciliter edoceri,'" p. 143 n. 13, and *idem*, *Aristotle's Ethics*, p. 192. I am

grateful to James Hankins for helping me locate information about Tignosi.

71. Most modern discussion of Tignosi has concerned the extent of his Platonism and his "humanism"; see Lines, "'Faciliter edoceri,'" pp. 161–66.

72. Thorndike, *Science and Thought*, appendix 18, p. 330. The treatises are edited by Thorndike in appendices 18–19, on pp. 308–31 and 33–63, respectively; see also *ibid.*, pp. 161–79 and 364–65.

73. For medieval etymological analysis as disclosing the nature of things rather than the semantic roots of words, see above, n. 52.

74. Hence, we find theologians from Guibert of Nogent in the early twelfth century to John of Capistrano in the fifteenth repeating obsessively the verse from Psalm 15:10: "He will not give his holy one to see corruption." Often conjoined to this were Psalm 29:9: "What profit is there in my blood if I descend into the pit [*corruptionem*]?" applied to Christ, and Luke 21:18 "But a hair of your head shall not perish," applied to God's promise of bodily resurrection to the individual Christian. On Guibert, see Chapter 3, n. 30; on Capistrano, see Chapter 3, n. 31.

75. James of Klusa (or Jüterbog), "Tractatus de concertatione super cruore in Welsenaco," Wolfenbüttel H. A. B. Cod. Guelf. 152 Helmst., fol. 186vb.

76. Margaret Aston, *England's Iconoclasts*, vol. 1, *Laws against Images* (Oxford: Oxford University Press, 1988), pp. 133–37.

77. See Ziegler, in "Faith and the Intellectuals," p. 375, who comments that the growing emphasis on the *potentia absoluta Dei* "encouraged thinkers to introduce into their philosophical debates subtle, daring and imaginative questions which generated new . . . replies and substantially broadened the scope of scientific thought."

78. See Chapter 2, p. 157.

79. See, for example, William of Auvergne, *De universo*, part 3 of part 2, chapter 13, in *Guilielmi Alverni episcopi Parisiensis, mathematici . . . opera omnia*, 2 vols. (Paris: A. Pralard, 1674), vol. 1, pp. 1040–44, esp. p. 1043; William of Malmesbury, *De gestis rerum Anglorum*, book 2, paragraph 171, ed. William Stubbs, 2 vols., Rerum Britannicarum medii aevi scriptores 90 (1889; reprint, Wiesbaden: Kraus, 1964), vol. 1, pp. 201–2; and [pseudo-Augustine], *De spiritu et anima*, chapter 26, PL 40, col. 798. By the sixteenth century, there was some tendency to treat such changes as actual; see my discussion of werewolves in *Metamorphosis and Identity*, pp. 92–98 and 105–109.

80. Heinrich Kramer, *Malleus maleficarum*, trans. Montague Summers, in Kors and Peters (eds.), *Witchcraft*, p. 201.

81. *Ibid.*, p. 202. On the ambiguity of such arguments and their background, see Bartlett, *Natural and Supernatural*, pp. 79–91, and Boureau, "Demons and the Christian Community."

82. Caesarius of Heisterbach, *Dialogus miraculorum*, distinction 5, chapter 15, ed. Strange, vol. 1, pp. 293–94.

83. Oresme, *Le Livre du ciel*, book 2, chapter 2, pp. 289–90. For Aquinas's discussions of demons, see n. 35 above.

84. For more on the twelfth-century sense of nature as Ovidian, see Bynum, *Metamorphosis and Identity*, pp. 86–89.

85. Peter Lombard, *Sententiae in IV libris distinctae*, book 2, distinction 7, chapters 6–8, ed. Collegium S. Bonaventurae, 2 vols. (Grottaferrata: Collegium S. Bonaventurae ad Claras Aquas, 1971–81), vol. 1, pp. 362–64; John of Salisbury, *Policraticus*, book 2, chapter 12, ed. K. S. B. Keats-Rohan, Corpus christianorum: Continuatio mediaevalis 118 (Turnhout: Brepols, 1993), pp. 91–92; Rupert of Deutz, *Commentaria in evangelium S. Joannis*, book 2, PL 169, col. 276–77; Peter the Venerable, *Contra Petrobrusianos*, cols. 803–804. Peter the Venerable indeed went further in his use of natural analogies, arguing as well that transubstantiation (which he understands here as change of substance without change of form) is possible because water undergoes it—that is, water changes from liquid to ice or crystal without losing its form, which is transparency. See Iogna-Pratt, *Order and Exclusion*, p. 195. For Aquinas, see above, n. 38. Guitmond of Aversa made a similar argument; see *De corporis et sanguinis Domini veritate libri tres*, book 1, PL 149 (Paris, 1882), col. 1431.

86. On the survival of the idea of seminal reasons, see Allan B. Wolter, "The Ockhamist Critique," in McMullin (ed.), *The Concept of Matter in Greek and Medieval Philosophy*, p. 142. On seminal reasons in Henry of Langenstein, see Nicholas H. Steneck, *Science and Creation in the Middle Ages: Henry of Langenstein (d. 1397) on Genesis* (Notre Dame, IN: University of Notre Dame Press, 1976), pp. 34–35.

87. Pabst, *Atomtheorien*, pp. 145–50, and, on Autrecourt, see above, n. 39.

88. Albertus Magnus, *Summa theologiae*, part 2, tractate 8, question 31, *membrum* 1, article 4, in Borgnet (ed.), *Opera omnia*, vol. 32, pp. 336–37.

89. Bacon, *Opus majus*, part 1 of part 7, trans. Burke, vol. 2, p. 651.

90. Oresme, *Quaestiones super De generatione et corruptione*, book 2, chapter 9, ed. Caroti, p. 274.

91. Oresme, *Nicole Oresme and the Medieval Geometry of Qualities . . . Tractatus de configurationibus*, book 2, chapter 35, ed. Clagett, pp. 374–75. In *ibid.*, p. 487, Clagett refers to a quodlibet in which Oresme argues that "all things can be saved naturally," although even here Oresme says that demons, whose existence cannot be proved naturally, should be held by faith to exist. On Henry of Hesse (or Langenstein), who followed Oresme in such naturalizing tendencies, see Thorndike, *History of Magic*, vol. 3, pp. 472–510.

92. Jan Hus, "Questio de sangwine Christi," and "Tractatus," in *Opera omnia: Nach neuentdeckten Handschriften*, ed. Wenzel Flajšhans, vol. 1, fasc. 3 (Prague: Vilímek, 1903).

93. Hus, "Tractatus," pp. 16–17. Hus's emphasis on the resurrection of the body makes it clear that the issue to him is primarily soteriological, not merely devotional.

94. What Hus is doing, as a good Thomist, is arguing that the form accounts for the nature of the person reconstituted. How the person is the same person in his or her nature is explained by metaphysical analysis. It is, however, miraculous that the entity—the person—is *numerically* the same person, because, philosophically speaking, an entity that exists and then ceases to exist *as that entity* and then is reconstituted is not numerically speaking "the same thing." Moreover the reconstituting of the person by the action of form on matter at the end of time is, of course, the greatest miracle done by God (after the miracle of creation itself).

95. For the area known as "divine embryology," which involved theologians in long and complex discussions of the role of Mary's blood and vaginal lining in the generation of Christ's fetus as well as of the role of the Holy Spirit as substitute for male semen, see van der Lugt, *Le Ver, le démon et la vierge*, pp. 365–473. And see also Ziegler, "Faith and the Intellectuals," pp. 378–81. Among older discussions, see Charles T. Wood, "The Doctors' Dilemma: Sin, Salvation and the Menstrual Cycle in Medieval Thought," *Speculum* 56, no. 4 (1981): 701–27; and Paulette L'Hermite-Leclercq, "Le Lait et le sang de la Vierge," in Marcel Faure (ed.), *Le Sang au moyen âge: Actes du quatrième colloque international de Montpellier, Université de Paul Valéry (27–29 novembre 1997)*, Cahiers du C.R.I.S.M.A. 4 (Montpellier: Université Paul Valéry, 1999), pp.

145–62. As Walter Stephens underlines, the same period saw increasing concern with the physiology of demons; see Stephens, *Demon Lovers*, pp. 87–124.

96. Boureau, *Théologie, science et censure au XIIIe siècle*, pp. 242–44; Boureau, "Miracle, volonté et imagination"; and Joseph Ziegler, "Medicine and Immortality in Terrestrial Paradise," in Peter Biller and Joseph Ziegler (eds.), *Religion and Medicine in the Middle Ages*, York Studies in Medieval Theology 3 (York and Woodbridge, UK: York Medieval Press, 2001), pp. 237–38. See also Joseph Ziegler, "*Ut dicunt medici*: Medical Knowledge and Theological Debates in the Second Half of the Thirteenth Century," *Bulletin of the History of Medicine* 73 (1999): 208–37. And for physiological explanations of Christ's sweating blood in the Garden given by both Marquard von Lindau (d. 1392) and Ubertino da Casale (d. 1329), see Stephen Mossman, *Marquard von Lindau and the Challenges of Religious Life in Late Medieval Germany: The Passion, the Eucharist, the Virgin Mary*, Oxford Modern Languages and Literature Monographs (Oxford: Oxford University Press, 2010), pp. 58–67 and 82–88.

97. See Robert Grosseteste, *De cessatione legalium*, part 3, section 6, paragraphs 8-9, ed. Richard C. Dales and Edward B. King (London: Oxford University Press, 1986), pp. 150–51. For Marquard von Lindau's emphasis on Christ's choice of bleeding, see Mossman, *Marquard von Lindau and the Challenges of Religious Life*, pp. 62–67.

98. See Caroline Walker Bynum, *Wonderful Blood: Theology and Practice in Late Medieval Northern Germany and Beyond* (Philadelphia: University of Pennsylvania Press, 2007), pp. 96–131, and on the concept of *veritas humanae naturae*, see Philip Lyndon Reynolds, *Food and the Body: Some Peculiar Questions in High Medieval Theology* (Leiden: Brill, 1999).

99. See above, Chapter 2, pp. 156–57.

100. Franz Pfeiffer, *Deutsche Mystiker des vierzehnten Jahrhunderts*, 2 vols. (1845–57; reprint, Göttingen: Vandenhoeck & Ruprecht, 1906–1907), vol. 1, p. 378. On this passage, see also Karl Richstätter, *Die Herz-Jesu-Verehrung des deutschen Mittelalters*, 2nd ed. (Munich and Regensburg: Kösel & Pustet, 1924), p. 56.

101. "Expositio passionis," article 25, in *Doctoris ecstatici D. Dionysii carthusiani opera omnia in unum corpus digesta*, 42 vols. in 44 (Montreuil-Tournai: Typis Cartusiae S. Mariae de Pratis, 1896–1935), vol. 42, pp. 545–46.

102. Later in the passage, this projection becomes anti-Judaism. Dionysius

says: "Thus they saw him who was pierced [Zach. 12:10] and the Jews will see this in a future judgment, for the scars of Christ's five wounds are preserved... also to convict at the Last Judgment those guilty of the sin of his death."

103. Copenhaver, *Symphorien Champier*, pp. 188–89.

104. Bacon, *Opus majus*, part 4, distinction 4, trans. Burke, vol. 1, p. 411, cited in Bartlett, *Natural and Supernatural*,. p. 144.

105. Although modern popularizers continue to assert that medieval thinkers held species inviolability, there is a good deal of evidence that this is not so; see Barbara Obrist, "Die Alchemie in der mittelalterlichen Gesellschaft," in Christoph Meinel (ed.), *Die Alchemie in der europäischen Kultur- und Wissenschaftsgeschichte*, Wolfenbütteler Forschungen 32 (Wiesbaden: Harrassowitz, 1986), pp. 43–45; *eadem*, introduction to *Constantine of Pisa*, pp. 3–43; and Newman, introduction to *The Summa perfectionis of Pseudo-Geber*, pp. 1–38. Early alchemical writing in the West drew on Avicenna's *De congelatione et conglutinatione*, which stated explicitly: "Let alchemists know that they cannot transmute the species of things"; the Latin translations added the phrase "unless [that species] be resolved to prime matter." Roger Bacon changed his mind several times about species inviolability. Albert the Great argued that alchemists could in theory change metal. Paul of Taranto (writing after 1250) simply used the *De congelatione* to support species change. Theorists sometimes got around the problem by quibbling over the definition of "species." See n. 113 below. It is important to note that in the course of the fourteenth century, the church became more suspicious of alchemy, but there was no concerted effort to curb alchemical thinking. See Ziegler, "Faith and the Intellectuals," p. 385.

106. See Bynum, *Metamorphosis and Identity*, pp. 92–97 and 105–109; Gaël Milin, *Les Chiens de Dieu: La Représentation du loup-garou en Occident (XIe–XXe siècles)* (Brest: Centre de Recherches Bretonne et Celtique, 1993); and Charlotte F. Otten (ed.), *A Lycanthropy Reader* (Syracuse, NY: Syracuse University Press, 1986). On the growing tendency to accept witches, fairies, and so forth, see Watkins, *History and the Supernatural*, pp. 222–23. On increasing fears of pacts between humans and demons, see Boureau, "Demons and the Christian Community."

107. Nicolas Weill-Parot, in "Synthèse: Matière animée/matière inanimée au moyen âge," in Weill-Parot, director, "Structure de la matière animée," in

Chemla (ed.), "Action Concertée 'Histoire des Savoirs' 2003–2007," pp. 24–25. And see William Gilbert, *De magnete*, book 5, chapter 12, trans. P. Fleury Mottelay (1893; reprint, New York: Dover Publications, 1958), p. 312. Elsewhere, Gilbert expresses more reservations about the loadstone as animate. See, for example, book 2, chapter 3, p. 101. He, however, generally uses images of generation and reproduction for metals. See, for example, book 1, chapter 7, p. 35: "When, therefore, this concreted matter [that is, the condensed exhalation that makes metals] has settled in more temperate cavities, in these moderately warm spaces it takes shape, just as in the warm uterus the seed or embryo grows."

108. Gilbert, *De magnete*, book 5, chapter 12, pp. 308–10.

109. Copenhaver, *Symphorien Champier*, pp. 189–90; see also *ibid.*, pp 176–88.

110. Caesarius of Heisterbach, *Dialogus miraculorum*, distinction 7, chapter 45, ed. Strange, vol. 2, p. 64. Also discussed in David Freedberg, *The Power of Images: Studies in the History and Theory of Response* (Chicago: The University of Chicago Press, 1989), p. 285.

111. Oresme, *Quaestiones super De generatione et corruptione*, book 2, chapter 15, ed. Caroti, pp. 294–95. Toulmin and Goodfield, in *The Architecture of Matter*; McMullin, in "Introduction," in McMullin (ed.), *The Concept of Matter in Modern Philosophy*; and Pyle, in *Atomism and Its Critics*, all see the Aristotelian paradigm for change as biological, organic, and animate.

112. Quoted in Arthur Field, *Origins of the Platonic Academy*, p. 151.

113. For Petrus Bonus assuming such parallels, see Petrus Bonus, selection from his "New Pearl of Great Price," trans. in Edward Grant (ed.), *A Source Book in Medieval Science* (Cambridge, MA: Harvard University Press, 1974), p. 581, which draws an analogy between hatching eggs and metals and the spontaneous generation of worms. Bonus does not argue that such changes are all exactly the same; see *ibid.*, p. 585. But the crucial difference to him is not that between animate and inanimate. He uses "digestion," for example, to refer to all such changes. (The crucial issue to him is what constitutes a "species.") Nonetheless, to Bonus, the analogy is still an analogy. By the fifteenth century, alchemists seem to have assumed the animation of all matter. On this, see Jean-Marc Mandosio, reported in "Synthèse: Matière animée/matière inanimée au moyen âge," in Weill-Parot, director, "Structure de la matière animée," in Chemla (ed.), "Action Concertée: Histoire des Savoirs, 2003–2007," p. 24.

And see this Chapter at nn. 55 and 57 on Giles of Rome and Pietro d'Abano.

114. Karl Kolb, *Vom Heiligen Blut: Eine Bilddokumentation der Wallfahrt und Verehrung* (Würzburg: Echter, 1980), pp. 79–80. See above, Chapter 1, n. 113.

115. Cited in J. T. Rhodes, "The Body of Christ in English Eucharistic Devotion, c. 1500–c. 1620," in Richard Beadle and A. J. Piper (eds.), *New Science Out of Old Books: Studies in Manuscripts and Early Printed Books in Honour of A. I. Doyle* (Aldershot, UK: Scolar Press, 1995), p. 393, from Durham Univ., Cosin MS V.III.8, fol. 23v.

116. See Christopher Ocker, "Ritual Murder and the Subjectivity of Christ: A Choice in Medieval Christianity," *Harvard Theological Review* 91 (1998): 159–60; Jonathan Elukin, *Living Together, Living Apart: Rethinking Jewish-Christian Relations in the Middle Ages* (Princeton, NJ: Princeton University Press, 2007), pp. 104–105; Miri Rubin, *Gentile Tales: The Narrative Assault on Late Medieval Jews* (Philadelphia: University of Pennsylvania Press, 2004), p. 108; Solomon Grayzel, *The Church and the Jews in the XIIIth Century: A Study of Their Relations during the Years 1198–1254, Based on the Papal Letters and the Conciliar Decrees of the Period*, rev. ed. (New York: Hermon Press, 1966), pp. 274–81; and Kenneth Stow, "The Church and the Jews: St. Paul to Pius IX," in *Popes, Church and Jews in the Middle Ages: Confrontation and Response*, Variorum Collected Studies Series (Aldershot, UK: Ashgate, 2007), pp. 1–70, esp. pp. 38–45. On Christians and Jews, see also the excellent article by Ora Limor, "Christians and Jews," in Rubin and Simons (eds.), *The Cambridge History of Christianity*, vol. 4, pp. 135–48.

117. Heiko Oberman, *The Roots of Anti-Semitism in the Age of Renaissance and Reformation*, trans. James I. Porter (Philadelphia: Fortress Press, 1984), pp. xi, 66–67, 81, 94–102.

118. Simone Weil, *The Notebooks of Simone Weil*, 2 vols., trans. Arthur Wills (1956; reprint, London: Routledge and Kegan Paul, 1976), vol. 2, p. 472. The point is made in a different way in Daniel Miller, "Materiality: An Introduction," in Daniel Miller (ed.), *Materiality* (Durham, NC: Duke University Press, 2005), pp. 1–50, esp. p. 28, where he argues that whether we speak of philosophy, religion, or finance, the paradox is the same: immateriality can be expressed only through materiality.

119. See Introduction, nn. 49, 50, and 53.

120. Examples of medieval commentaries on the six days of creation include

works by Abelard, Honorius Augustodunensis, Rupert of Deutz, Bernard Silvestris, Thierry of Chartres, William of Conches, Grosseteste, Bonaventure, Peter Comestor, Vincent of Beauvais, Hugh of St.-Cher, Henry of Langenstein, Nicholas of Lyra, and Dionysius the Carthusian. See Frank Egleston Robbins, *The Hexaemeral Literature: A Survey of the Greek and Latin Commentaries on Genesis* (Chicago: University of Chicago Press, 1912), pp. 73–104, and E. Mangenot, s.v. "Genèse," DTC, vol. 6, cols. 1206–1208. On Henry's commentary, which is full of scientific speculation, see Steneck, *Science and Creation in the Middle Ages: Henry of Langenstein*.

121. See, for example, Guitmond of Aversa, *De corporis et sanguinis Domini veritate*, book 3, PL 149, col. 1481, and the blessing of the radish quoted in Chapter 2 at n. 72. And see Derek A. Rivard, *Blessing the World: Ritual and Lay Piety in Medieval Religion* (Washington, D.C.: The Catholic University of America Press, 2009), pp. 271–72. For the theme in patristic writers, see Kevin J. Madigan and Jon D. Levenson, *Resurrection: The Power of God for Christians and Jews* (New Haven, CT: Yale University Press, 2008), pp. 221–34.

122. For example, Adam of Eynsham, *Magna vita sancti Hugonis: The Life of St. Hugh of Lincoln*, book 3, prologue, ed. Decima L. Douie and Hugh Farmer, 2 vols. (London: Thomas Nelson and Sons, 1961), vol. 1, pp. 90–91. And see the works cited in n. 30 above. See also Peter Harrison, "Miracles, Early Modern Science, and Rational Religion," *Church History* 75, no. 3 (2006): 493–510, and Bartlett, *Natural and Supernatural*, pp. 62–70, on eclipses as signs.

123. *The Book of Margery Kempe: The Text from the Unique MS. Owned by Colonel W. Butler-Bowdon*, ed. S.B. Meech and Hope Emily Allen, EETS 212 (London: Oxford University Press, 1940), p. 69; and Life of Gherardesca of Pisa, chapter 7, paragraph 69, AASS, May, vol. 7 (Paris, 1866), pp. 175–76. For Bonaventure, see above, Chapter 1, n. 32. Relevant also is the sense, found in medieval Biblical exegesis, that not only the words of Scripture but also the things referred to there have significance; see Friedrich Ohly, "On the Spiritual Sense of the Word in the Middle Ages," (1958) in Friedrich Ohly, *Sensus Spiritualis: Studies in Medieval Significs and the Philology of Culture*, ed. Samuel P. Jaffe, trans. Kenneth J. Northcott (Chicago: University of Chicago Press, 2005), pp. 1–30, and *idem*, *Zur Signaturenlehre der Frühen Neuzeit: Bemerkungen zur mittelalterlichen Vorgeschichte und zur Eigenart einer epochalen Denkform in Wissenschaft, Literatur und Kunst*, ed. Uwe Ruberg and Dietmar Peil (Stuttgart/

Leipzig: Hirzel, 1999).

124. Mechtild of Hackeborn, *Sanctae Mechtildis virginis ordinis sancti Benedicti Liber specialis gratiae*, book 4, chapter 3, in *Revelationes Gertrudianae ac Mechtildianae*, ed. the monks of Solesmes, vol. 2 (Paris: Oudin, 1877), p. 260. For an interpretation of Marian devotion that rightly emphasizes the devotional and theological importance in the late Middle Ages of concern with creation as well as incarnation, see Rachel Fulton, "Mary," in Rubin and Simons (eds.), *The Cambridge History of Christianity*, vol. 4, pp. 283–96, esp. p. 285.

125. Margaret of Oingt, *Speculum*, in *Les Oeuvres de Marguerite d'Oingt*, ed. and trans. Antonin Duraffour, Pierre Gardette, and Paulette Durdilly, Publications de l'Institut de Linguistique Romane de Lyon 21 (Paris: Belles Lettres, 1965), p. 101.

126. Jeanne Ancelet-Hustache (ed.), "Les 'Vitae Sororum' d'Unterlinden: Edition critique du Manuscrit 508 de la Bibliothèque de Colmar," *Archives d'histoire doctrinale et littéraire du moyen âge* 5 (1930): 352.

127. H. Lawrence Bond, "Introduction," in *Nicholas of Cusa: Selected Spiritual Writings*, trans. and ed. H. Lawrence Bond (New York and Mahwah, NJ: Paulist Press, 1997), p. 19; see also pp. 36 and 47. For earlier theorists of *manductio*, see Jeffrey F. Hamburger, "Speculations on Speculation: Vision and Perception in the Theory and Practice of Mystical Devotion," in Walter Haug and Wolfram Schneider-Lastin (eds.), *Deutsche Mystik im abendländischen Zusammenhang: Neu erschlossene Texte, neue methodische Ansätze, neue theoretische Konzepte, Kolloquium Kloster Fischingen 1998* (Tübingen: Niemeyer, 2000), pp. 368–79.

128. Nicholas of Cusa, *De visione Dei*, chapter 7, paragraph 25, trans. Bond, in *Nicholas of Cusa*, pp. 246–47 and quoted in "Introduction," p. 18.

129. See nn. 120–22 above.

CONCLUSION

1. Anthropologist J. C. Heesterman has said of life and death that they are "intimately linked and at the same time each other's absolute denial." Thus, the riddle of their simultaneous presence "cannot be resolved, it can only be reenacted." I think this is true of all paradoxes. J. C. Heesterman, *The Broken World of Sacrifice: An Essay in Ancient Indian Ritual* (Chicago: University of

Chicago Press, 1993), p. 2. On Nicholas of Cusa, see Chapter 4, p. 261, above.

2. For an eloquent plea that scholars do just this, see John van Engen, "Multiple Options: The World of the Fifteenth-Century Church," *Church History* 77, no. 2 (2008): 257–84.

3. Daniel Arasse, "Entre dévotion et hérésie: La Tablette de saint Bernardin ou le secret d'un prédicateur," *Res* 28 (1995): 118–39.

4. On the growth of interiority, see Thomas Lentes, "'Andacht' und 'Gebärde': Das religiöse Ausdrucksverhalten," in Bernhard Jussen and Craig Koslofsky (eds.), *Kulturelle Reformation: Sinnformationen im Umbruch, 1400–1600* (Göttingen: Vandenhoeck & Ruprecht, 1999), pp. 26–67. On mystical theology, see the many works by Bernard McGinn, esp. *The Harvest of Mysticism in Medieval Germany (1300–1500)* (New York: Crossroad, 2005), and Amy Hollywood, "Mysticism and Transcendence," in Miri Rubin and Walter Simons (eds.), *The Cambridge History of Christianity, vol. 4, Christianity in Western Europe c. 1100–c. 1500* (Cambridge: Cambridge University Press, 2009), pp. 297–307. On voluntarism and the late medieval sense of the absolute power of God, nothing, in my opinion, surpasses the older work of Heiko Oberman. See, for example, Heiko Oberman, "Some Notes on the Theology of Nominalism: With Attention to Its Relation to the Renaissance," *Harvard Theological Review* 53, no. 1 (1960): 47–76, and *idem*, *The Dawn of the Reformation: Essays in Late Medieval and Early Reformation Thought* (Grand Rapids, MI: William B. Eerdmans, 1992). And see Chapter 4, n. 77.

5. Carl S. Watkins, *History and the Supernatural in Medieval England* (Cambridge: Cambridge University Press, 2007), p. 169, suggests that a similar dynamic was at work already in the thirteenth century.

6. It is for this reason that I rejected in my earlier work the conventional explanation of late medieval Eucharistic miracles that attributes them to the definition of transubstantiation at the Fourth Lateran Council of 1215. It seems clear that the definition followed a period in which literal Eucharistic miracles were beginning to emerge and therefore expressed this trend rather than creating it.

7. See Chapter 4, nn. 27–28.

8. As I explained in Chapter 2, pp. 129–30, to say this is not to espouse the sense of an enduring "folk" or "popular" culture of the kind for which Aron Gurevich and Jacques Le Goff have in some ways argued. Nor is it to argue

for the tension between elite and popular culture that Le Goff has sometimes assumed. I agree with the many critiques of these points of view that have been penned ever since Peter Brown's *Cult of the Saints: Its Rise and Function in Latin Christianity* (Chicago: University of Chicago Press, 1981), and I consider the issue to be one we have gotten beyond for reasons that are nicely summarized in Watkins, *History and the Supernatural*, pp. 1–18. On Peter Brown's argument, see the essays in James Howard-Johnston and Paul Antony Hayward (eds.), *The Cult of Saints in Late Antiquity and the Middle Ages: Essays on the Contribution of Peter Brown* (Oxford: Oxford University Press, 1999).

9. See, for example, the disappearance of the widespread motif of the Mass of St. Gregory in the late sixteenth century. Caroline Walker Bynum, "Seeing and Seeing Beyond: The Mass of St. Gregory in the Fifteenth Century," in Jeffrey F. Hamburger and Anne-Marie Bouché (eds.), *The Mind's Eye: Art and Theological Argument in the Middle Ages* (Princeton, NJ: Department of Art and Archaeology in cooperation with Princeton University Press, 2006), p. 208 and p. 239 n. 85.

10. Eamon Duffy, *The Stripping of the Altars: Traditional Religion in England, c. 1400–c. 1580* (New Haven, CT: Yale University Press, 1992); *idem*, *Marking the Hours: English People and Their Prayers, 1240–1570* (New Haven, CT: Yale University Press, 2006); John Bossy, *Christianity in the West, 1400–1700* (Oxford: Oxford University Press, 1985); David Aers, "A Whisper in the Ear of Early Modernists, or Reflections on Literary Critics Writing the 'History of the Subject,'" in David Aers (ed.), *Culture and History 1350–1600: Essays on English Communities, Identities, and Writing* (New York: Harvester Wheatsheaf, 1992), pp. 177–202. James Simpson, in "The Rule of Medieval Imagination," in Jeremy Dimmick, James Simpson, and Nicolette Zeeman (eds.), *Images, Idolatry, and Iconoclasm in Late Medieval England: Textuality and the Visual Image* (Oxford: Oxford University Press, 2002), p. 24, says: "Medievalists, no less than their Reformation and Renaissance colleagues, do remain locked within their own synchronies, generating narratives, often unconsciously, around the magnetic rupture of the Reformation. It may well be that there can be no escape from the repulsive-attractive magnet of medieval versus Reformation." Sarah Stanbury, in *The Visual Object of Desire in Late Medieval England* (Philadelphia: University of Pennsylvania Press, 2008), argues against any strict medieval/early modern break, showing the fourteenth- and fifteenth-century

roots of many supposed sixteenth-century concerns.

11. Van Engen, "Multiple Options." For a similar plea to take the fourteenth and fifteenth centuries as "a distinct cultural period," see Daniel Hobbins, *Authorship and Publicity before Print: Jean Gerson and the Transformation of Late Medieval Learning* (Philadelphia: University of Pennsylvania Press, 2009), p. 12. For Fasolt's different approach, see Constantin Fasolt, "Hegel's Ghost: Europe, the Reformation, and the Middle Ages," *Viator* 39 (2008): 345–86.

12. For more on these debates, see Bernhard Jussen, "Der Blick auf die Sinnformationen," and Craig Koslofsky, "'Kulturelle Reformation' und reformationsgeschichtliche Forschung," both in Jussen and Koslofsky (eds.), *Kulturelle Reformation*, pp. 13–17 and 18–22, respectively, and Fasolt, "Hegel's Ghost." For a recent, lively, but surprisingly traditional survey—one that unfortunately limits itself to Protestantism—see Ulinka Rublack, *Reformation Europe* (Cambridge: Cambridge University Press, 2005).

13. See, for example, Paul E. Walker, "Purloined Symbols of the Past: The Theft of Souvenirs and Sacred Relics in the Rivalry between the Abbasids and Fatimids," in Wilferd Madelung, Farhad Daftary, and Josef W. Meri (eds.), *Culture and Memory in Medieval Islam: Essays in Honour of Wilferd Madelung* (London: I. B. Tauris and the Institute of Ismaili Studies, 2003), pp. 364–87.

14. Nile Green, "Ostrich Eggs and Peacock Feathers: Sacred Objects as Cultural Exchange between Christianity and Islam," *Al-Masāq* 18, no. 1 (2006): 27–66.

15. Green points out that in medieval Cairo, a Muslim theologian denounced painted eggs as Christian, and in the tradition of the Ethiopian St. George, they were condemned as Muslim imports, yet eggs continued to be popular in both cultures. *Ibid.*, p. 65.

16. The closest parallels are in fact found in Buddhism. Although the theological understanding of death among Buddhists is very different, Buddhist relic practice is in important ways similar to Western medieval practice. See John S. Strong, *Relics of the Buddha* (Princeton, NJ: Princeton University Press, 2004), p. xvi. Survival is not linked to body in Buddhism, but Buddhist sources make it clear that relics are alive. Destroying a *stūpa* (a monumental reliquary) is a crime similar to murder. The power of the saint can be spread by dust or even by the shadow cast by the *stūpa*.

Given the practice of cremation, bodily relics are usually bones or teeth.

There is a very important cult of the Buddha's tooth in Kandy in Sri Lanka, and several ancient bone fragments are preserved in Myanmar. Jewels (*sheli* or *śarīra*) are sometimes found among the ashes after the cremation of a holy person, and these are revered. Moreover, Buddhist relics carry the essence of the body with them in something like a notion of concomitance. (See above, Chapter 2, n. 145.) There is a sense in which cremation creates many bodies, and *sheli* are sometimes said to multiply by themselves. There are also, in Buddhist practice, what I have called "effluvial relics," such as hair or nails, and contact relics, such as begging bowls. See Strong, *Relics of the Buddha*; John S. Strong, s.v. "Relics," in Lindsay Jones (ed.), *Encyclopedia of Religion*, 2nd ed., vol. 11 (Detroit–New York: Thomson-Gale, 2005), pp. 7690–91; Gregory Schopen, s.v. "Relic," in Mark C. Taylor (ed.), *Critical Terms for Religious Studies* (Chicago: University of Chicago Press, 1998), pp. 258–66; John Kieschnick, *The Impact of Buddhism on Chinese Material Culture* (Princeton, NJ: Princeton University Press, 2003), pp. 24–52; and the essays in David Germano and Kevin Trainor (eds.), *Embodying the Dharma: Buddhist Relic Veneration in Asia* (Albany: State University of New York Press, 2004), esp. David Germano, "Living Relics of the Buddha(s) in Tibet," pp. 51–91.

17. Josef W. Meri, *The Cult of Saints among Muslims and Jews in Medieval Syria* (Oxford: Oxford University Press, 2002); Brannon Wheeler, *Mecca and Eden: Ritual, Relics, and Territory in Islam* (Chicago: University of Chicago Press, 2006); Denise Aigle, "Sainteté et miracles en Islam médiévale: L'Exemple de deux saints fondateurs iraniens," in *Miracles, prodiges et merveilles au moyen âge*, XXVe Congrès de la S.H.M.E.S., Orléans, juin 1994, Société des historiens médiévistes de l'enseignement supérieur publique, série histoire ancienne et médiévale 34 (Paris: Publications de la Sorbonne, 1995), pp. 47–73; and Robert L. Cohn, "Sainthood on the Periphery: The Case of Judaism," in Richard Kieckhefer and George D. Bond (eds.), *Sainthood: Its Manifestations in World Religions* (Berkeley: University of California Press, 1988), pp. 43–68.

18. David S. Margoliouth, "The Relics of the Prophet Mohammed," *Moslem World* 27 (1937): 20–27; Meri, *Cult of Saints*, and Wheeler, *Mecca and Eden*. For Muslim revering of Hebrew relics, see Wheeler, *Mecca and Eden*, pp. 81–82.

19. Wheeler, *Mecca and Eden*, p. 73.

20. Meri, *Cult of Saints*, pp. 191 and 255.

21. Wheeler, *Mecca and Eden*, pp. 75–76.

22. See Chapter 3 at nn. 45–49.

23. See Chapter 3 at n. 72.

24. Meri, *Cult of Saints*, pp. 130–31.

25. The question of whether the will and power of God underlay everything to the point of mitigating natural causation was, of course, a problem of enormous importance in medieval Islamic theology. See Michael E. Marmura, s.v. "Causation in Islamic Thought," in Philip P. Weiner (ed.), *The Dictionary of the History of Ideas: Studies of Selected Pivotal Ideas*, 5 vols. (New York: Scribner, 1973–74), vol. 1, pp. 287–89, available online at Electronic Text Center, University of Virginia: http://xtf.lib.virginia.edu/xtf/view?docId+DicHist/uvaBook/tei/DicHisti.xml, last accessed June 28, 2010.

26. For this as received opinion, see Helmut Ringgren, s.v. "Resurrection," in Mircea Eliade (ed.), *The Encyclopedia of Religion* (New York: Macmillan, 1987), vol. 12, pp. 344–50, and Daniel Miller, "Materiality: An Introduction," in Daniel Miller (ed.), *Materiality* (Durham, NC: Duke University Press, 2005), pp. 1–50, esp. pp. 16–33.

27. Meri, *Cult of Saints*, p. 12. See also pp. 13 and 17. And see Wheeler, *Mecca and Eden*, p. 88.

28. See Cohn, "Sainthood on the Periphery," and Meri, *Cult of Saints*, pp. 62–65 and 214–20.

29. As I note above at n. 22, when a Jewish cult of graves did emerge, northern European rabbis were careful to stress that it was *not* because of bodies or objects located there.

30. The black stone in the Kaaba at Mecca was an inheritance from pre-Islamic Arabian religion.

31. Wheeler, *Mecca and Eden*, p. 88.

32. See Strong, s.v. "Relics," *Encyclopedia of Religion*, vol. 11, p. 7687; and Aigle, "Sainteté et miracles en Islam."

33. Wheeler, *Mecca and Eden*, p. 78. The whisker of Mohammed venerated in Hazratbal in Kashmir, which was stolen in 1963 and supposedly returned in 1964, has been at the center of intense religious and nationalist controversy.

34. See my Introduction at n. 26 for the example of Guadalupe. And see Chapter 1 at n. 120 for Spanish cases analyzed by William Christian.

35. Most important, of course, were the footprints of Christ allegedly left on the rock of the Ascension. The earlier claim was actually that the footprints

were left in earth, which pilgrims collected. See Andrea Worm, "Steine und Fußspuren Christi auf dem Ölberg: Zu zwei ungewöhnlichen Motiven bei Darstellung der Himmelfahrt Christi," *Zeitschrift für Kunstgeschichte* 66, no. 3 (2003): 297–320, esp. 307–14. *Ibid.*, p. 312 n. 48, mentions other places (for example, Rome) that claimed Christ's footprints. As I pointed out above, footprints were important in Islam as well as in Christianity, although in Islam, they are found mostly on the borders of the Islamic world. For footprints in Buddhism, see Strong, *Relics of the Buddha*, pp. 85–97. Stories of miraculous footprints are found in many cultures. On the anti-Jewish relic of the footprints at Sternberg, see Chapter 2 at n. 79. On footprints left behind by visions, see William Christian, Jr., *Apparitions in Late Medieval and Renaissance Spain* (Princeton, NJ: Princeton University Press, 1981), pp. 24–25, 70, 75–76, 80, and 100–102.

36. On Jerusalem, see Maria Evangelatou, "The Holy Sepulchre and Iconophile Arguments on Relics in the Ninth-Century Byzantine Psalters," and Gerhard Wolf, "The Holy Face and the Holy Feet: Preliminary Reflections Before the Novgorod Mandylion," in Alekseĭ Lidov (ed.), *Eastern Christian Relics* (Moscow: Progress-Tradition, 2003), pp. 181–204 and 281–87, respectively.

37. Evangelatou, "The Holy Sepulchre," esp. pp. 181–82.

38. Alekseĭ Lidov, "The Flying *Hodegetria*: The Miraculous Icon as Bearer of Sacred Space," in Erik Thunø and Gerhard Wolf (eds.), *The Miraculous Image in the Late Middle Ages and Renaissance*, Analecta Romana Supplement 35 (Rome: "L'erma" di Bretschneider, 2004), pp. 273–304. Lidov has introduced into scholarly discussion the concept of *hierotropy* and has thus encouraged the study of how objects create the sacrality of space. On the unveiling and processing of icons in the West, see Nino Zchomelidse, "The Aura of the Numinous and Its Reproduction: Medieval Paintings of the Savior in Rome and Latium," *Memoirs of the American Academy in Rome* 55 (2010): forthcoming.

39. On Weingarten, see Norbert Kruse and Hans Ulrich Rudolf (eds.), *900 Jahre Heilig-Blut-Verehrung in Weingarten 1094–1994: Festschrift zum Heilig-Blut-Jubiläum am 12. März 1994*, 3 vols. (Sigmaringen: J. Thorbecke, 1994), and Gebhard Spahr (ed.), *Festschrift zur 900-Jahr-Feier des Klosters: 1056–1956* (Weingarten: Weingarten Abtei, 1956).

40. On Antony, see Chapter 2 at nn. 25–26; on anti-Jewish libels see Chapter 3 at n. 44.

41. J. M. Minty, "Judengasse to Christian Quarter: The Phenomenon of the Converted Synagogue in the Late Medieval and Early Modern Holy Roman Empire," in Robert W. Scribner and Trevor Johnson (eds.), *Popular Religion in Germany and Central Europe, 1400–1800* (New York: St. Martin's Press, 1996), pp. 56–86.

42. Lorraine Daston (ed.), *Things That Talk: Object Lessons from Art and Science* (New York: Zone Books, 2004). See my Introduction above, n. 32.

43. Randolph Starn, "A Historian's Brief Guide to New Museum Studies," *American Historical Review* 110, no. 1 (2005): 84. Starn is characterizing museum studies, but his remark is relevant to the broader trend in historical writing. See also Leora Auslander, "Beyond Words," *American Historical Review* 110, no. 4 (2005): pp. 1015–45; Kieschnick, *The Impact of Buddhism*, pp. 15–23; and Caroline Walker Bynum, "Perspectives, Connections, and Objects: What's Happening in History Now?" *Daedalus* (Winter 2009): 78–80.

44. Barbara Johnson, *Persons and Things* (Cambridge, MA: Harvard University Press, 2008). On Bandmann, see above, Chapter 1, n. 63. His "iconology of the material" is much less universalizing than Freedberg's approach. Freedberg makes the crucial point that behaving as if something is alive and saying it is alive are different; he also pays attention to the aniconic, as well as the iconic, and understands that response is a more complex matter than whether or not the object is "like a human being." See, for example, David Freedberg, *The Power of Images: Studies in the History and Theory of Response* (Chicago: University of Chicago Press, 1989), pp. xxii, 73, 76, and 132. But his basic assumption is that response has something to do with likeness to the human.

45. For an effort to put medieval devotional objects—especially, of course, what we call "images"—in the context of medieval theorizing, see Hamburger and Bouché, *The Mind's Eye*.

46. Daston recognizes something like this when she talks about the "bony materiality" of even malleable things. Lorraine Daston, "Introduction: Speechless," in Daston (ed.), *Things That Talk*, p. 18.

47. Nile Green asserts that "in complex trading regions, objects move almost irresistibly, bringing with them their associated practices as part of a package against which theology or other forms of ideology can only resist so far or else accommodate." Green, "Ostrich Eggs," p. 66. Barbara Johnson, *Persons and Things*, p. 231, drawing on Lacan, asserts that only things can achieve stasis

and hence perfection.

48. Daston, "Introduction: Speechless," pp. 17 and 22.

49. For this, see Freedberg, *The Power of Images*. Even Kieschnick, who offers thoughtful criticism of the tendency to think relics cross the line between life and death, gives a very Freedbergian theory of animated images; see Kieschnick, *The Impact of Buddhism*, pp. 48–49 and 59–69. If this theory were right, the *Mona Lisa* would be more apt to animate than the wall painting at Prato.

I do not, however, discount modern studies of the tendency for people to respond differently to humanoid or humanlike figures, on the one hand, and machines or clearly (in our terms) inanimate objects, on the other. See Jerome Groopman, "Medical Dispatch: Robots That Care," *The New Yorker*, November 2, 2009, pp. 66–77, esp. p. 72, on the "uncanny valley" effect. Moreover, I am aware of the relevance to this discussion of South Asian rituals in which the incising or painting in of eyes is the final stage in bringing an image of a god or goddess to life. But "animation" in the Indian cases does not mean quite the same thing as in the case of Western images. The issue of the relationship between human form and animation is too complicated to go into further here.

50. Robert H. Sharf, "On the Allure of Buddhist Relics," *Representations* 66 (Spring 1999): 75-99. Sharf's essay has been reprinted in Germano and Trainor (eds.), *Embodying the Dharma*, pp. 163–91.

51. See, for example, George Rice, "Are Viruses Alive?" available online at http://serc.carleton.edu/microbelife/yellowstone/viruslive.html, last accessed April 22, 2010; and Carl Zimmer, "The Meaning of Life," *Seed*, September 5, 2007, available online at http://seedmagazine.com/news/2007/09/the_meaning_of_life.php, last accessed April 22, 2010, which argues that there is no agreed-upon definition of life in scientific literature today.

Index

Zone Books series design by Bruce Mau
Typesetting by Meighan Gale
Image placement and production by Julie Fry
Printed and bound by Thomson-Shore